HENRY STEDMAN wrote the first edition of this book and updated many of the editions that followed it. He's been writing guidebooks for over a quarter of a century and is also the author of *Kilimanjaro, Hadrian's Wall Path, Dales Way, Cleveland Way, London LOOP* and co-author, with Joel, of all three books in the *South-West Coast Path* series. Usually accompanied by his (mostly) faithful dog, Daisy, he's also updated *Offa's Dyke Path, Pembrokeshire Coast Path, North Downs Way, South Downs Way* and *The Ridgeway*.

JOEL NEWTON updated this **tenth** edition. He has been walking long-distance footpaths for fifteen years and contributing to Trailblazer guides for ten. The first books he co-authored were Trailblazer's three-part series to the South-West Coast Path. Since then he has written the first edition of *Thames Path* and researched and updated

West Highland Way and *Offa's Dyke Path*, among others. When not working for Trailblazer he lives and works in Hastings.

Authors

Coast to Coast Path First edition: 2004; **this 10th edition: 2023**

Publisher Trailblazer Publications
The Old Manse, Tower Rd, Hindhead, Surrey, GU26 6SU, UK
info@trailblazer-guides.com, trailblazer-guides.com

British Library Cataloguing in Publication Data
A catalogue record for this book is available from the British Library

ISBN 978-1-912716-25-8

© **Trailblazer** 2004, 2006, 2008, 2010, 2012, 2014, 2016, 2018, 2020, 2023: Text and maps

Series Editor: Anna Jacomb-Hood
Editing & layout: Anna Jacomb-Hood **Proof-reading**: Jane Thomas & Bryn Thomas
Illustrations: © Nick Hill (pp63-4) **Photographs (flora)**: © Bryn Thomas
All other photographs: © Joel Newton (unless otherwise indicated)
Cartography: Nick Hill **Index**: Anna Jacomb-Hood

The maps in this guide were prepared from out-of-Crown-
copyright Ordnance Survey maps amended and updated by Trailblazer.

Acknowledgements

From Joel: Thank you to Michela Prescott for helping me with the research in the Lake
District, and for joining me in the long hike up to St Sunday Crag to take photos. Thanks
to Paul and Jane Newton for the company in Kirkby Stephen, and for allowing my shoul-
ders a day's respite by transporting my camping gear to Keld. Thank you, too, to all those
I met along the path; there's a sense of being part of a community among those who hike
the Coast to Coast, more so than on any other trail I've walked. Thanks to Henry Stedman
for writing the first edition of this book; and, as ever, thank you to Bryn Thomas, Anna
Jacomb-Hood, Nick Hill and Jane Thomas at Trailblazer for the dedication and hard work
that has gone into this and the previous editions of this guide, and making this one such a
pleasure to work on.
 Thanks also to all the Trailblazer readers who emailed us with fantastic tips and recommendations – see p6 for their names.

A request

The author and publisher have tried to ensure that this guide is as accurate and up to date
as possible. Nevertheless, things change. If you notice any changes or omissions, please
write to Trailblazer (address above) or email us at ✉ info@trailblazer-guides.com. A free
copy of the next edition will be sent to persons making a significant contribution.

Warning: hill walking can be dangerous

Please read the notes on when to go (pp14-16) and safety (pp80-4 & pp90-2). Every effort
has been made by the author and publisher to ensure that the information contained herein
is as accurate and up to date as possible. However, they are unable to accept responsibility
for any inconvenience, loss or injury sustained by anyone as a result of the advice and information given in this guide.

PHOTOS – Front cover and this page: Descending the St Sunday Crag route to
Patterdale, the view over Ullswater (Map 24) makes the steep hike up and over from
Grasmere worth every step. **Previous page**: En route to Grisedale Tarn (Map 19),
Overleaf: Surveying the moors from Lion Inn (Map 81).

Updated information will be available on: 🖥 **trailblazer-guides.com**

Printed in China; print production by D'Print (☎ +65-6581 3832), Singapore

★ trailblazer

Coast to Coast
PATH

109 large-scale maps & guides to 33 towns and villages
PLANNING – PLACES TO STAY – PLACES TO EAT
ST BEES TO ROBIN HOOD'S BAY

HENRY STEDMAN &
JOËL NEWTON

TRAILBLAZER PUBLICATIONS

INTRODUCTION

About the Coast to Coast path

PART 1: PLANNING YOUR WALK

Practical information for the walker

Budgeting 32

Itineraries

What to take

Getting to and from the Coast to Coast path

PART 2: THE ENVIRONMENT & NATURE

Conserving the Coast to Coast path

Flora and fauna

PART 3: MINIMUM IMPACT WALKING & OUTDOOR SAFETY

Minimum impact walking

Outdoor safety

Contents

PART 4: ROUTE GUIDE & MAPS

Contents

ABOUT THIS BOOK

This guidebook contains all the information you need. The hard work has been done for you so you can plan your trip without having to consult numerous websites and other books and maps. When you're ready to go, there's comprehensive public transport information to get you to and from the trail and detailed maps (1:20,000) to help you find your way along it.

● All standards of accommodation with reviews of campsites, bunkhouses, hostels, B&Bs, guesthouses and hotels
● Walking companies if you want an organised tour and baggage-transfer services if you just want your luggage carried
● Itineraries for all levels of walkers
● Answers to all your questions: when to go, degree of difficulty, what to pack, and how much the whole walking holiday will cost
● Walking times and GPS waypoints with what3words refs
● Cafés, pubs, tearooms, takeaways, restaurants and food shops
● Rail, bus and taxi information for all places along the path
● Street plans of the main towns both on and off the path
● Historical, cultural and geographical background information

THANKS

In addition to everyone listed on p2, thanks to Roderick Leslie for bird text checking, to Bradley Mayhew for last-minute route checks and to all those readers who contacted us with suggestions – in particular:

Tim and Susana, Tony Barry, Karina Bowes, Olaf Brock, Bruce G. Burton, Sue and Andrew Cooper, John Crowther, Stephen Cunliffe, John Cunningham, Christopher Day, Roger Denson, John Dunn, Robert Eames, Mary Edwards, Matt Falvey, Mark Faust and Sara Fischer, Nick Funnell, Mark Goodbody, Annie Green, Volker Gringmuth, Peter Hart, John Hedrick, Mick Hellewell, Keith Hills, Karen Johnson, Charlie Knight, Chis Linke, Mark and Jan Moore, Jan Newton, Tony Oldershaw, Bill Paine, Andy Parrett, David Perry, Edith Peters, Arie Pieter, John Potter, Ken Potter, Lee Richardson, Malcolm Rose, Eli Schuenemann, Philip Scriver, Steve Sharpe, Robert Shield, Alexandra Sirugue-Macleod, Stephen Slater, Ken and Alison Smedley, Philip Spahr, Emily Squires, Bob Story, Mike Thompson, Mike Tierney, Rick Toyer, Abigail & Ricki Toyer, Jon Train, Catherine Tudhope, Stephen Van Dulken, Dave Walsh, Richard Ward, Fiona Werge, Mark Wilkinson, Sarah Wilson, Chris Woods.

❏ POST COVID NOTE

This edition of the guide was researched after the Covid pandemic but is liable to more change than usual. Some of the hotels, cafés, pubs, restaurants and tourist attractions may not survive the further hardships caused by rising fuel prices and inflation. Do forgive us where your experience on the ground contradicts what is written in the book; please email us – info@trailblazer-guides.com so we can add your information to the updates page on the website.

About this book

INTRODUCTION

In devising a walk that would span the north of England from the Cumbrian coast to the North Sea, the legendary fell walker, guide-book writer and illustrator, Alfred Wainwright, created an enduring concept that more than 50 years later continues to inspire hikers in ever-growing numbers.

Despite – until now (see below) – not being an official National Trail with all the support that entails, the Coast to Coast path has almost certainly become the most popular long-distance footpath in England. At about 190 miles it's not the longest in the country and certainly doesn't, as some mistakenly think, cross the country at its widest point. It makes no claim to being especially tough (though we can safely predict that those who attempt it in one go will find it sufficiently challenging). Nor does it, unlike the long-distance paths that run alongside Hadrian's Wall or Offa's Dyke, follow any ancient construction or border.

> It's almost certainly become the most popular long-distance path in England

In truth, the Coast to Coast is but one of an infinite number of routes that could be devised by joining the various footpaths and byways to form a trail across northern England and in doing so providing those who follow it with a snapshot of the country.

But what a magnificent snapshot that is! Around two-thirds of the walk is spent in the national parks of the Lake District (so special, it was awarded UNESCO World Heritage status in 2017), the Yorkshire Dales and the North York Moors. These parks encompass the most dramatic upland scenery in England, from its highest fells to its largest lakes, some of its most beautiful woods and parts of its bleakest, barest moors. The walk also passes through areas alive with some of Britain's rarest wildlife, including red squirrels and otters.

Furthermore, where man has settled on the trail he has, on the whole, worked in harmony with nature to produce some of England's finest villages, from idyllically situated Grasmere to unspoilt Egton Bridge. The trail itself is a further example of this harmony; these paths and bridleways have existed for centuries and though man-

> ❏ A NEW NATIONAL TRAIL
>
> On 12th August 2022 the government announced that the Coast to Coast path had been awarded National Trail status with work on the route due to be completed by 2025. See p92 for route changes. Further information at 🖥 wainwright.org.uk/national-trail.

MR COAST TO COAST – ALFRED WAINWRIGHT

Wainwright's 'AW' monogram on a fingerpost on the North York Moors.

The popular perception of the man who devised the Coast to Coast path is that of a gruff, anti-social curmudgeon with little time for his fellow men, though one who admittedly knew what he was doing when it came to producing guidebooks. It's an unflattering portrait, but one that the man himself did little to destroy. Indeed, many say that he deliberately cultivated such a reputation in order to make himself unapproachable, thus allowing him to continue enjoying his beloved solitary walks without interruptions from the cagoule-clad masses who trudged the fells in his wake. Yet this unflattering and rather dull two-dimensional description disguises a very complex man: artist, father, divorcé, pipe-smoker, accountant, part-time curator at Kendal Museum, TV personality, romantic and cat-lover.

Alfred Wainwright was born in Blackburn on 17 January 1907, to a hardworking, impoverished mother and an alcoholic father. Bright and conscientious, his early years gave little clue to the talents that would later make him famous, though his neat handwriting – a feature of his guidebooks – was frequently praised by his teachers. Leaving school to work in accounts at the Borough Engineer's Office in Blackburn Town Hall, he regularly drew cartoons to entertain his colleagues.

When, in December 1931, he married Ruth Holden, it seemed that Wainwright's life was set upon a course of happy – if humdrum – conformity. Wainwright, however, never saw it like that. In particular, he quickly realised that his marriage had been a mistake. Wainwright felt stifled and bored with his home life; feelings that not even the arrival of a son, Peter, could erase. His wife, though loyal, left Wainwright unfulfilled and any trace of romantic love that had been in the marriage at the beginning quickly drained away. To escape the misery at home, Wainwright threw himself into his new-found hobby, fellwalking. He first visited the Lakes in 1930 and soon after was making detailed notes and drawings on the walks he made. Initially, these visits were few and far between, but a move to Kendal 10 years later to take up a position as an accounting assistant allowed Wainwright to visit the Lakes virtually every weekend. Yet it wasn't until the early 1950s that Wainwright struck upon the idea of shaping his copious notes and drawings into a series of walking guides. The idea wasn't a new one: guides to the Lakes had existed since at least the late 18th century and previous authors had included such literary luminaries as William Wordsworth. Where Wainwright's guides differed, however, was in their detail and the unique charm of their production.

For Wainwright was a publisher's dream: his writing was concise and laced with a wry humour, his ink sketches were delightful, and every page was designed by the author himself, with the text justified on both sides (and without hyphens!) around the drawings. As a result, all the publisher really needed to do was crank up the printing press, load in the paper, and hey presto! They had another bestseller on their hands.

His first seven books, a series of guides to the Lakeland fells, took fourteen years to produce and by the end he had built up quite a following amongst both walkers and those who simply loved the books' beauty. Further titles followed, including one on the Pennine Way (a walk that he seemed to have enjoyed rather less than the others, possibly because at one point he had needed to be rescued by a warden after falling into a bog). As an incentive to walkers, however, he offered to buy a pint for every reader who completed the entire walk, telling them to put it on his bill at the Border

made, do not feel or look like an imposition on the landscape but are very much part of it. While these paths and villages continue to thrive under the steady stream of Coast to Coasters, in other places nature has reclaimed the poignant ruins of mills and mines, ancient Iron Age sites and mysterious stone circles which between them bear witness to thousands of years of human endeavour. They punctuate the path and provide absorbing highlights along the way.

Around two-thirds of the walk is spent in national parks

But the walker on the Coast to Coast path experiences additional, unquantifiable rewards. There is the pleasure of acquiring a developing level of fitness, the satisfaction of unravelling a route-finding conundrum and the relief when a hard-won day finally ends at the doorstep of a cosy B&B. Most memorably, it's the cheery camaraderie shared by your fellow pilgrims bound for Robin Hood's Bay and the window into the lives of the people who live and work in this fabulous landscape that stay with you as you transit the country from coast to coast.

Wainwright's Coast to Coast path

The Coast to Coast path owes its existence to one man: Alfred Wainwright. It was in 1972 that Wainwright, already renowned for his exquisitely illustrated

Hotel at the end of the Pennine Way. The Coast to Coast was the follow-up to the Pennine Way, with the research starting in 1971 and the book published in 1973. It was a project that Wainwright seemed to have derived much greater enjoyment from (though, unfortunately, there was no offer of a free drink this time!).

While all this was going on, however, Wainwright's private life was in turmoil. Though his home life with Ruth remained as cold as ever, Wainwright had found the love of his life in Betty McNally, who had visited him in his office on official matters sometime in 1957. For Wainwright, it was love at first sight, and he began courting Betty soon after. They married eventually in 1970, and by all accounts this union provided Wainwright with the contentment and happiness he had so signally failed to find in his first marriage. She also accompanied Wainwright on his forays into television, where his gruff, no-nonsense charm proved a big hit.

At the time of their marriage Wainwright, already 63, promised Betty 10 happy years. In the event, he was able to provide her with 21, passing away on Sunday, January 20, 1991. His last wish, fulfilled two months later by Betty and his long-time friend Percy Duff, was to have his ashes scattered on Hay Stacks. At the end of his autobiography, *Ex-Fellwanderer*, he sums his life up thus:

I have had a long and wonderful innings and enjoyed a remarkable immunity from unpleasant and unwelcome incidents. ... I never had to go to be a soldier, which I would have hated. I never had to wear a uniform, which I also would have hated. ... I was never called upon to make speeches in public nor forced into the limelight; my role was that of a backroom boy, which suited me fine. I never went bald, which would have driven me into hiding. ... So, all told, I have enjoyed a charmed life, I have been well favoured. The gods smiled on me since the cradle. I have had more blessings than I could ever count.

The start – 'Mile Zero' (**above**) by the Irish Sea near St Bees – is clearly marked. It's become a tradition to collect a pebble, carry it with you as a keepsake to Robin Hood's Bay and return it to the North Sea there.

guides to walking in the Lake District, finally completed a trek across the width of England along a path of his own devising. It was an idea that he had been kicking around for a time: to cross his native land on a route that, as far as he was aware, would 'commit no offence against privacy nor trample on the sensitive corns of landowners and tenants'. The result of his walk, a guidebook, was originally printed by his long-time publishers, *The Westmorland Gazette*, the following year. It proved hugely successful. Indeed, a full 20 years after the book was first published, a television series of the trail was also made in which Wainwright himself starred, allowing a wider public to witness first-hand his wry, abrupt, earthy charm.

Wainwright reminds people in his book that his is just **one of many such trails** across England that could be devised, and since Wainwright's book other Coast to Coast walks have indeed been established. Yet it is still *his* trail that is

INTRODUCTION

by far and away the most popular, and in order to distinguish it from the others, it is now commonly known as Wainwright's Coast to Coast path.

The route has been amended slightly since 1973 mostly because, though careful to try to use only public rights of way, in a few places Wainwright's original trail actually intruded upon private land. Indeed, even today the trail does in places cross private territory and it's only due to the largesse

Above: The Bay Hotel at Robin Hood's Bay marks the eastern end of the Coast to Coast path.

of the landowners that the path has remained near-enough unchanged throughout its course. Route changes are in progress now, however, as the Coast to Coast path becomes a National Trail, with work scheduled to be completed by 2025.

The trail starts and ends on stretches of the England Coast Path, passes through three national parks, crosses the Pennine Way and at times joins both the Lyke Wake Walk and the Cleveland Way.

Below: The wide views in the Lake District are even more impressive if you take one of the higher routes. Here, as you descend from The Cape (Map 21), Ullswater comes into view.

How difficult is the Coast to Coast path?

Undertaken **in one go**, the Coast to Coast path is a long, tough walk. Despite the presence of some fairly steep gradients, every mile is 'walkable' and no mountaineering or climbing skills are necessary. All you need is some suitable clothing, a bit of money, a backpack full of determination and a half-decent pair of calf muscles. In the 190-odd miles from seashore to seashore you'll have ascended and of course descended the equivalent height of Mount Everest.

From seashore to seashore you'll have ascended and of course descended the equivalent height of Mount Everest

That said, the most common complaint we've received about this book, particularly from North American readers, is that it doesn't emphasise how tough it can be. So let us be clear: **the Coast to Coast is a tough trek**, **particularly if undertaken in one go**. Ramblers describe it as 'challenging' and they're not wrong. When walkers begin to appreciate just how tough the walk can be, what they're really discovering is the reality of covering a daily average of just over 14 miles or 23km, *day after day*, for two weeks, in fair weather or foul and while nursing a varying array of aches and pains. After all, how often do any of us walk 14 miles in a day, let alone continuously for *two weeks*?

The Lake District, in particular, contains many steep sections that will test you to the limit; however, there are also plenty of genteel tearooms and places to stay in this section should you prefer to break your days into easier sections.

The topography of the eastern section is less extreme, though the number of places with accommodation drops too, and for a couple of days you may find yourself doing some very long walking days in order to reach a town or village on or near the trail that has somewhere to stay. If the weather is bad it can be quite hard to maintain motivation on this half of the walk.

Regarding safety, there are few places on the regular trail where it would be possible to fall from a great height, save perhaps for the cliff-top walks that book-end the hike. On some of the high-level Lakeland alternatives (see p122 and p132), however, there is a chance of being blown off a ridge. In 2009 a walker suffered this fate and broke his ankle, as did the rescuer who came in a helicopter, though sustaining such a serious injury by being blown over is highly unusual. The greatest danger to trekkers is, perhaps, the likelihood of **losing the way**, particularly in the Lake District with its greater chance of poor visibility, bad weather and, in places, a distinct **lack of signposting** (although this should

RHB 48 MILES
4586 ft ASCENT
111,792 STEPS

ST BEES 132 MILES
18,383 ft ASCENT
307,428 STEPS

change now that it is becoming a National Trail). A compass and knowing how to use it is very useful, as is appropriate clothing for inclement weather and most importantly of all, a pair of boots which you ease on each morning with a smile not a grimace.

Not pushing yourself too hard is important, too, as this leads to fatigue with all its inherent dangers, not least poor decision-making. In case all this deters you from

Above: Isolated YHA Black Sail, England's most remote hostel (see p112).

the walk bear in mind that in 2009 a 71-year-old finished the walk for the 5th time, and that both the 9-year-old son and 7-year-old daughter (in a pair of pink Crocs!) of previous updaters of this book have walked the entire route, and the whole of the Lake District section, respectively. At the same time apparently fit and strong young men with all the right kit have given up for reasons of exhaustion or injury after just a few days.

At the time of writing the record for completing the path is held by a 45-year-old runner from Gloucestershire who ran the route in 39 hours, 18 minutes and 33 seconds, so breaking the previous record (39hrs, 36mins, 52 secs) which had stood since 1991. Breaking the record, he said, had been 'tough' but that he had 'absolutely loved it'; and therein lies an important message: walking the trail *will* be tough but make sure you pace yourself correctly and you will love it too.

How long do you need?

Whilst an athlete may be able to complete the trail in 39 hours, being more realistic we're aware of a walker who managed it in eight days. We also know somebody who did it in 10 and another guy who did four 4-day stages over four years. Continuously or over several visits, for most people, the Coast to Coast trail takes a minimum of 14 walking days; in other words an average distance of just over 14 miles (23km) a day.

Indeed, even with a fortnight in which to complete the trail, many people still find it tough

> **For most people, the Coast to Coast trail takes a minimum of 14 walking days**

going, and it doesn't really allow you time to look around places such as Grasmere or Richmond which can deserve a day in themselves. So, if you can afford to build a couple of rest days into your itinerary or even break it up into shorter stages over several weeks, you'll be very glad you did. Ideally, we'd suggest allowing 18 walking days. This would allow you to break up some of the longer walk days into more manageable sections and give you ample time to make side-trips as well as arrive at your night halt early enough to actually explore and enjoy the village. Remember that you might also lose the odd day to bad weather.

Of course, if you're fit there's no reason why you can't go a little faster if that's what you want to do, though you'll end up having a different sort of trek to most of the other people on the route. For where theirs is a fairly relaxing holiday, yours will be more of a sport as you try to reach the finishing line on schedule. There's nothing wrong with this approach, though you obviously won't see as much as those who take their time. However, what you mustn't do is try to push yourself beyond your body's ability; such punishing challenges often end prematurely in exhaustion, injury or, at the absolute least, an unpleasant time.

See pp36-8 for itineraries covering different walking speeds

When deciding how long to allow for their trek, those intending to camp and carry their own luggage shouldn't underestimate just how much a heavy pack can wear you down. On pp36-8 there are some suggested itineraries covering different walking speeds. If you've only got a few days, don't try to walk it all; concentrate, instead, on one area such as the Lakes or North York Moors. You can always come back and attempt the rest of the walk another time.

When to go

SEASONS

Britain is a notoriously wet country and the north-west of England is an infamously damp part of it. Rare indeed is the trekker who manages to walk the Coast to Coast path without suffering at least one day of rain; three or four days per trek is more likely, even in summer. That said, it's equally unlikely that you'll spend a fortnight in the area and not see any sun at all, and even the most cynical of walkers will have to admit that, during the walking season at least, there are more sunny days than showery ones. That **walking season**, by the way, starts at Easter and builds to a crescendo in August, before quickly tailing off in September. By the end of that month there are few trekkers on the trail, and in late October many places close down for the winter.

Spring

Find a couple of dry weeks in springtime and you're in for a treat. The wild flowers are beginning to come into bloom, lambs are skipping in the meadows and the grass is green and lush. Of course, finding a dry fortnight in spring (around the end of March to mid June) is not easy but occasionally there's a mini heatwave at this time of year. Another advantage will be fewer trekkers on the trail so finding accommodation is easier.

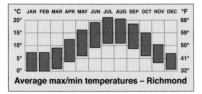
Average max/min temperatures – Richmond

Easter is the exception, the first major holiday in the year when people flock to the Lake District and other national parks. Book accommodation well in advance over Easter.

Summer

Summer, on the other hand, can be a bit *too* busy and, in somewhere like the Lakes over a weekend in August, at times depressingly congested. Still, the chances of a prolonged period of sunshine are of course higher at this time of year than any other, the days are much longer and the heather is in bloom, too, turning the hills a fragrant purple. If you like the company of other trekkers summer will provide you with the opportunity of meeting scores of them, though do remember that you'll need to book your accommodation well in advance or be prepared to camp occasionally. Despite the higher-than-average chance of sunshine, take clothes for any eventuality – it's bound to rain at some point.

Autumn

September can be a wonderful time to walk; many of the families have returned home and the path is clear although accommodation gets filled up in early September by a wave of older visitors who've been waiting for the new school term. The weather is usually sunny, too, at least at the beginning of September. By the end of the month the weather will begin to get a little wilder and the nights will start to draw in. For most mortals the walking season is almost at an end.

Winter

A few people trek the Coast to Coast in winter, putting up with the cold, damp conditions and short days for the chance to experience the trail without other tourists and maybe even under snow. Much of the accommodation will be closed too but whilst it may also be a little more dangerous to walk at this time, particularly on the high-level routes through the Lakes, if you find yourself walking on one of those clear, crisp, wintry days it will all seem absolutely worth it.

RAINFALL

At some point on your walk, it will rain; if it doesn't, it's fair to say that you haven't really lived the full Coast to Coast experience properly. At nearly 5 metres (196 inches), the hills over Borrowdale on Stage 2 record the **highest rainfall in England**; a staggering eight

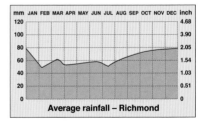

Average rainfall – Richmond

times more than the south-east of England, for example! The question, therefore, is not whether you will be rained on, but how often and how hard. But as long as you dress accordingly and take note of the safety advice on pp80-4, this shouldn't be a problem. Do, however, think twice about tackling some of the high-level alternatives if the weather is bad and visibility poor, and don't do so on your own.

DAYLIGHT HOURS

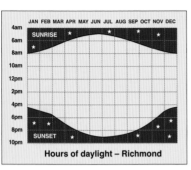

Hours of daylight – Richmond

If walking in autumn, winter or early spring, you must take account of how far you can walk in the available light. It won't be possible to cover as many miles as in summer. Remember though, that you'll get a further 30-45 minutes of usable light before sunrise and after sunset depending on the weather. In June, because the path is in the far north of England there's enough light for walking until at least 10pm.

❏ FESTIVALS AND ANNUAL EVENTS

Thanks largely to its undying appeal with tourists, Grasmere has become something of a mecca for those interested in those peculiarly **Lakeland sports** such as fell running, and Cumberland and Westmorland wrestling.

In addition to the events outlined below, all kinds of **agricultural shows** take place annually in towns and villages on the Coast to Coast trail. These shows are an integral and traditional part of life all over rural England and particularly in the Lake District. Too numerous to list here, details of all the shows can be found by looking at the websites of the places concerned. For further information about events in the southern Lake District see 🖳 applications.southlakeland.gov.uk/eventsearch.

Being aware of the bigger festivals is also useful when planning your walk as there's a good chance that available accommodation will be all the more in demand.

April to June

The villages of Swaledale, which include Keld, Muker, Thwaite, Gunnerside and Reeth, hold an annual music festival, **Swaledale Festival** (🖳 swalefest.org); this usually takes place at the end of May to early June. Another event in June is **Swaledale Marathon** (🖳 www.swaledaleoutdoorclub.org.uk/swaledale-marathon) so accommodation in the area can dry up. Similarly, in early June, **Appleby Horse Fair** (🖳 applebyfair.org) can drain accommodation opportunities in Kirkby Stephen and Orton.

Robin Hood's Bay hosts a **folk music weekend** (🖳 folkclub.rhbay.co.uk), usually on the first or second weekend of June.

July to September

Grasmere Lakeland Sports and Show (🖳 grasmeresports.com) had taken place every year since 1868, except during World Wars I and II, until 2020! It was reinstated in 2022 and is held on August Bank Holiday Sunday. Sports featured include wrestling, tug-of-war, hound-trailing and the more recent addition of mountain-biking.

After the walk many people will head for Whitby to catch a train or bus. If you're there late August consider staying on for **Whitby Folk Week** (🖳 whitbyfolk.co.uk) when the pubs and other venues are abuzz with fiddles and bodhrans.

October to December

If you happen to be in Robin Hood's Bay at the beginning of December, don't miss the **Victorian weekend** (🖳 robin-hoods-bay.co.uk – click on What's on). The town turns out in 19th-century costume, with quizzes, recitals and concerts in aid of charity.

Practical information for the walker

ROUTE FINDING

Currently, the presence of **signposts** and waymarking varies along the path. As work continues on converting the path to a National Trail (2022-25), the waymarking should improve with the use of the familiar acorn symbol as used with other National Trails.

Once over the Pennines and into Yorkshire the trail becomes fairly well signposted and finding the way shouldn't be a problem. In the Lakes, on the other hand, there are few Coast to Coast signposts and you'll have to rely on the descriptions in this book to find the way. For much of the time the path is well trodden and obvious, though of course there are situations where there are several paths to choose from, and other occasions where the ground is so boggy no clear path is visible at all. Misty conditions are another problem, particularly in the Lake District. In these instances a compass or GPS will help you move in the right direction or follow the correct path.

In the Lakes in particular there are some high-level alternatives to the main route and on a clear day fit trekkers should consider taking them. Though obviously more tiring, the rewards in terms of the views and sense of achievement are all worthwhile.

It does pay to **regularly keep track of your position** so when you go wrong you can tell where you've veered off. You're most likely to make a mistake due to fallen or otherwise obscured posts or waymarkers, or while chatting away. Backtracking usually solves that.

For common navigational trouble spots see 'How not to lose your way', pp90-2.

ELECTRONIC NAVIGATION AIDS AND MAPPING APPS

I never carried a compass, preferring to rely on a good sense of direction... I never bothered to understand how a compass works or what it is supposed to do ... To me a compass is a gadget, and I don't get on well with gadgets of any sort.
Alfred Wainwright

While Wainwright's acolytes may scoff, other walkers will accept GPS technology as a well-established navigational aid. With a clear view of the sky, a **GPS receiver** will establish your position as well as elevation in a variety of formats, including the British OS grid system, anywhere on earth to an accuracy of within a few metres.

Most **smartphones** have a GPS receiver built in and mapping apps available to run on it (see box p46).

A modern mobile can receive a GPS signal from space as well as estimate its position often as accurately using mobile data signals from hilltop masts. These signals are two different things: GPS comes free from American, Russian or European satellites and is everywhere all the time but works best outdoors. Much stronger 4- or 5G mobile signals beam off towers up to 40 miles away and are what you pay the phone company for.

Accessing an online map with mobile data (internet via your phone signal, not wi-fi), your position can be pinpointed with great accuracy. But with no signal – as is the case in Britain's remoter upland locales – your phone will use GPS to display your position as a dot on the screen. Except that, *unless you import a map into your phone's internal storage* (which may require an app and even a small financial outlay) without a signal, the kilobit-sized 'tiles' which make up an **zoomable online map** cannot be downloaded. The internet browser's cache may retain a few tiles until the signal resumes or until you walk off that tile's coverage. Much will depend on your service provider. It's said the Vodaphone network works best across rural northern England followed by O2 or EE but check the coverage map on your service provider's website.

The best way to use your mobile as an accurate navigation aid is to download a **mapping app** plus **maps** covering the route (see box p46). That will work with GPS where there is no phone signal. Then download and install a **Coast to Coast Path tracklog** into this app and, ideally, your on-screen location dot will be pulsing right on that track as you walk along.

Unless you happen to own one with a decent sized colour screen, there's little benefit in buying a **handheld GPS** device except that *with decent maps installed*, you can be certain of establishing your location against a map anytime, any place, any where.

❏ **JUST HOW LONG IS WAINWRIGHT'S COAST TO COAST PATH?**

The figure of **191½ miles** has been bandied around for years as this is close to the 190 miles which Wainwright's original edition quoted back in 1972. Disregarding the fact that these days his exact route is no longer followed, for this guidebook each stage was logged using a suitably calibrated GPS odometer and after editing the final tally showed the actual distance walked to be exactly that: 191½ miles (308km). This is via the most used routes and following the alternative route between Bolton-on-Swale and Danby Wiske (as opposed to Wainwright's original route). This, of course, doesn't account for walking to the pub or B&Bs off the track, and even, as some Pythagorians like to consider, the fact that walking up and down hills technically covers more ground than if the terrain was flat. Of course the distance will change again with the proposed route changes due to the path becoming a National Trail.

The precise total length of Wainwright's Coast to Coast (and doubtless many other long-distance paths) is not of great importance in the big picture as you'll walk the walk, but a day's true distance is something worth knowing when psyching yourself up for a long stage. Other guides, maps and local signposts will show differing distances, often constrained to fit the immutable figure estimated by Alfred Wainwright.

Using GPS with this book – tracklog and waypoints

A **tracklog** is a continuous winding line marking the walk from end to end, displayed on your screen; all you have to do is keep on that line. If you lose it on the screen you can zoom out until it reappears and walk towards it. A tracklog can be traced with a mouse off a digital map, or recorded live using a GPS enabled device. When recorded live, tracklogs are actually hundreds of pinged waypoints separated by intervals of either time or more usefully distance (say, around 10 metres). Some smartphones or mapping apps can't display a tracklog with over 500 points so they get truncated into fewer straight lines, resulting in some loss in precision. To download the GPS tracklog on which this book's maps are based, see the Trailblazer website – 🖥 trailblazer-guides.com. Note, however, that as the trail is upgraded to National Trail status (2022-5) there will be route changes (see p92).

Where a tracklog is a continuous line, **waypoints** are single points like cairns. This book identifies key waypoints on the route maps; these waypoints correlate to the list on pp262-5 which gives the OS grid reference and a description. You can download the complete list as a GPS-readable .gpx file of grid references (but with no descriptions) from 🖥 trailblazer-guides.com. As well as an OS grid reference for these waypoints we've now also listed the three-word geocode used by **what3words** (see p261; 🖥 what3words.com) which could be useful in an emergency.

One thing must be understood however: **treating GPS as a complete replacement for maps, a compass and common sense is a big mistake**. Every electronic device is susceptible to battery failure or some electronic malfunction that might leave you in the dark. It's worth repeating that most people who've ever walked the Coast to Coast did so without GPS.

ACCOMMODATION

From one coast to the other, businesses and families alike today owe a lot to Wainwright's inspired concept. Smaller towns and villages as well as isolated farms far from the reliable Lakeland honeypots have come to rely on accommodating and feeding the seasonal flow of coastbound walkers.

The route guide (Part 4) lists a fairly comprehensive selection of places to stay along the trail. The three main options are: camping, staying in hostels/bunkhouses, or using B&Bs/pubs/hotels. Few people stick to just one of these the whole way, preferring, for example, to camp most of the time but spend every third night in a hostel, or perhaps take a hostel where possible but splash out on a B&B or hotel every once in a while.

The table on pp34-5 provides a snapshot of what type of accommodation and services are available in each of the towns and villages, while the tables on pp36-8 provide some suggested itineraries. The following is a brief introduction as to what to expect from each type of accommodation.

Camping

It's possible to camp all along the Coast to Coast path, though few people do so every night. You're almost bound to get at least one night where the rain falls relentlessly, sapping morale; it's then that most campers opt to spend the next night drying out in a hostel or B&B somewhere. There are, however, many advantages with camping. It's more economical, for a start, with most campsites charging £5-15pp. Best of all there's **rarely any need to book**, except possibly in the very high season, and even then you'd be highly unlucky not to find somewhere, even if it means camping discreetly in the woods. The campsites vary and you get what you pay for: some are just pub gardens or a farmer's spare field with basic toilet/shower facilities; others are full-blown caravan sites with security access codes and a sparkling ablutions block and a few spaces put aside for tents. Showers are usually available, occasionally for an additional fee, though more often than not included in the rate. Note that most YHA hostels on the Coast to Coast path now accept campers.

Wild camping (ie camping not in a regular campsite; see also p79) is, strictly speaking, not allowed anywhere in England outside Dartmoor National Park. However, if you have the landowner's permission, it is tolerated in the Lake District; be aware though, that since the influx of wild campers due to the restrictions on foreign travel due to Covid this has become a far more sensitive issue. Some good spots include the level areas surrounding mountain lakes such as Innominate Tarn (on the high route to Borrowdale), Grisedale Tarn (out of Grasmere) and Angle Tarn (two miles from Patterdale). Further east, wild camping is discouraged in both the Yorkshire Dales and the North York Moors. If you do wild camp outside the Lake District, similarly you should always gain permission from the landowner. If that's not possible make sure you camp discreetly, do not make camp fires and leave nothing behind. Woodland areas are your best bet. Steer clear of farmland.

Remember that camping, wild or not, is not an easy option, especially for a solo walker. Walked continuously, the route is wearying enough without carrying the means to sleep and cook with you. Should you decide to camp at campsites, consider using one of the baggage-transfer companies mentioned on pp27-9, though this does mean the loss of spontaneity which is the whole point of camping – and they can't deliver to remote areas eg Angle Tarn; see also box p108!

Bunkhouses, camping pods and shepherd's huts

Bunkhouses can be much more agreeable places, with fluffed-up bedding, bathrooms you'd be happy to show to your parents and even kitchen and lounge areas. The description 'bunkhouse' is often used in place of 'independent hostel' to distinguish a private enterprise from lodgings under the YHA banner (see opposite). **Camping pods** are a relatively new phenomenon that have appeared as part of the craze for '**glamping**'. The specifications for a camping pod vary from site to site but essentially they are stand-alone pods set on a campsite. A few places have **shepherd's huts**, and other variations on glamping; they generally sleep up to two or four people and usually come with bedding and have some facilities.

Hostels

Hostels are plentiful along the Coast to Coast path; whether owned by the Youth Hostel Association (YHA) or independent, they offer some of the best-located and most interesting accommodation along the path. In fact there are now as many independent hostels as YHA ones along the Coast to Coast path, though one YHA hostel is managed independently on a franchise basis.

Despite the name, anyone of any age can join the YHA. This can be done at any hostel, or by contacting the **Youth Hostels Association of England and Wales** (☎ 01629-592700 or ☎ 0800-0191 700, 🖥 yha.org.uk). The cost of a year's membership is £20 for an adult (£15 if you pay by annual Direct Debit). Having secured your membership, YHA hostels are easy to book, either online or by phone. Since members are entitled to a 10% discount (this is valid for a member booking for up to 16 people at the same time and is applicable to both the rate and meals) it is worth joining if you expect to stay in a YHA hostel several times in a year.

Hostels come equipped with a whole range of facilities, from drying rooms to washing machines, televisions to pool tables and fully equipped kitchens. Some have a shop selling a selection of groceries, snacks and souvenirs and most now have internet access; wi-fi is generally available in communal areas. Many offer meals (about £5-10) and several have a licence to sell alcohol. They are also great places to meet fellow walkers, swap stories and compare blisters.

Weighed against these advantages is the fact that even though many hostels now have rooms with two to four beds unless you book a private room you may have to share your night with a heavy snorer. A couple of the hostels also suffer from uncomfortably small dorms when they're full. Some rooms now have en suite facilities but in others you have to share a shower room and in a couple of cases facilities may be limited. Nor is it possible to stay in hostels every night on the trail, for there are some areas where hostels don't exist and when they do they're occasionally at least a mile or two off the path.

At the time of writing it was still not possible to book a bunk in a shared dorm at some hostels, though a few have now opened. Hopefully all hostels will soon have dorm beds again.

❏ **SHOULD YOU BOOK ALL YOUR ACCOMMODATION IN ADVANCE?**

For most of the year but particularly at **weekends** and between **June and August**, unless camping, it's essential you have your night's accommodation secured.

How soon you start booking is up to you but doing so the night before is no longer dependable. If you start booking **up to six months** in advance you'll have a good chance of getting precisely the accommodation you want. Booking so early does leave you vulnerable to changing circumstances of course, but with enough notice it's likely your deposit will be returned as they can easily fill your bed; ask on booking.

Outside the high season and away from weekends, as long as you're **flexible** and willing to take what's offered, you might get away with booking just a couple of weeks or even just days in advance.

If you're planning on staying in **hostels** the same applies, though do be careful when travelling out of high season as many hostels are only available for exclusive hire around November to February. Once again, it's well worth booking in advance.

Campers, whatever the time of year, should always be able to find somewhere to pitch their tent, though at places with only a few pitches it would be worth calling in advance to ensure there would be space.

Note that even in high season some hostels are not staffed during the day and walkers may have to wait until 5pm before checking in, though you may be able to access the kitchen and leave luggage in a secure room before 5pm. It's worth noting that if you are walking with a friend, and therefore would be sharing the cost of a B&B room, the cost of staying in a hostel dorm, once two breakfasts have been added on, is often not that much cheaper than staying in a B&B.

Bed and breakfast

Bed and Breakfasts (B&Bs) are a great British institution and many of those along the Coast to Coast are absolutely charming, with buildings often three or four hundred years old. Older owners often treat you as surrogates for their long-departed offspring and enjoy nothing more than looking after you.

As the name suggests, they provide you with a bed in a private room, and **breakfast** – a hearty, British-style cooked one unless you specify otherwise beforehand – though they range in style enormously (see opposite).

Some B&Bs provide an **evening meal** (usually £10-20); if not, there's often a pub or restaurant nearby and, if it's far, the owner may give you a lift to and from it. **Packed lunches** are almost always available too, for around £5-8.

Rates for B&Bs in this guide start at around £35 per person (assuming two people are sharing a room), and rise to £70 or £80pp for more luxurious places in a popular tourist haunt such as Grasmere. In general, though, most B&Bs charge around £40-45pp. The **single occupancy rate** is usually about £10-15 less than the room rate, though you will sometimes have to pay the room rate.

Guesthouses, hotels, pubs & inns

A **guesthouse** offers B&B but should have a better class of décor and more facilities such as a lounge for guests and is more likely to offer evening meals. All of which makes them sound very much like hotels, of course – except, unlike a hotel, they are unlikely to offer room service. **Pubs & inns** may also offer B&B and tariffs are no more than in a regular B&B (starting from around £35pp). However, you need to be prepared for a noisier environment, especially if your room is above the bar.

❑ **ROOM TYPES – B&B-STYLE ACCOMMODATION**

Rooms usually contain either a double bed (known as a **double room**) or two single beds (known as a **twin room**). Sometimes a **triple room** (usually with one double bed and one single, or occasionally three singles), or **quad room** (usually one double bed and two singles or a bunk bed) are also available. Solo trekkers should take note: **single rooms** are not so easy to find so you'll often end up having to pay a single occupancy supplement (see p32) for use of a room, or even the room rate.

Most places offering B&B-style accommodation on the route have **en suite rooms**; this often means that a shower (or bath) is squeezed into the room. Where a room is advertised as having **private facilities**, it means that the shower and/or bath is in a room reserved solely for the use of the bedroom's occupants and which is usually near the room but not directly connected to it. **Shared facilities** means that the bath or shower facilities are also used by other guests. Since a bath (🛁) is what most walkers prefer at the end of a long day places that have at least one are noted in the route guide.

Hotels cost more (sometimes as much as £100pp, though usually more like £50-60pp), and can occasionally be a little displeased by a bunch of muddy trekkers turning up. That said, most places on this walk, particularly in the quieter towns and villages, are used to seeing trekkers, make a good living from them and welcome them warmly.

Airbnb

The rise and rise of Airbnb (🖳 airbnb.co.uk) has seen private homes and apartments opened up to overnight travellers on an informal basis. While accommodation is primarily based in cities, the concept has spread to tourist hotspots in more rural areas, but do check thoroughly what you are getting and the precise location. While the first couple of options listed may be in the area you're after, others may be far too far afield for walkers. At its best, this is a great way to meet local people in a relatively unstructured environment, but be aware that these places are usually not registered B&Bs, so standards may vary, yet prices may not necessarily be any lower than the norm.

FOOD AND DRINK

Breakfast

Stay in a B&B/guesthouse/hotel and you'll be filled to the gills each morning with a cooked English breakfast. This can consist of a bowl of cereal followed by a plateful of eggs, bacon, sausages, mushrooms, tomatoes, and possibly baked beans or black pudding (a sausage of oats soaked in blood, in case you didn't know, and a constituent of a 'Full *Yorkshire* breakfast'), with toast and butter, and all washed down with coffee, tea and/or juice. Enormously satisfying the first time you try it, by the fourth or fifth morning you may start to prefer the lighter continental breakfast or porridge, which most establishments also now offer; many places also offer gluten free and other options as long as this is requested in advance. Alternatively, and especially if you're planning an early start, you might like to request a packed lunch instead of this filling breakfast and just have a cup of coffee before you leave.

Lunch

Your B&B host or YHA hostel can usually provide a packed lunch at an additional cost, though they usually like this to be requested in advance. Of course there's nothing to stop you preparing your own; there are some fantastic locally made cheeses and pickles that can be picked up along the way, as well as some wonderful bakers still making bread in the traditional manner (the bakeries in Kirkby Stephen and Reeth spring to mind). Alternatively, stop in a pub.

Depending on which routes you take, three or four of the stages in this book are devoid of eateries or shops so **read ahead** about the next day's walk to make sure you never go hungry.

Cream teas

Never miss a chance to avail yourself of the treats on offer in the tea rooms and farmhouses of Cumbria and Yorkshire. Nothing relaxes and revives like a decent pot of tea, and the opportunity to accompany it with a scone served with jam and cream, or a cake or two, is one that should not be passed up.

Evening meals

If your accommodation doesn't do an evening meal you may find that, in many villages, the pub is the only place to eat out. **Pubs** are as much a feature of this walk as moorland, churches and views, and in some cases the pub is as much a tourist attraction as the finest ruined abbey. Most have become highly attuned to the needs of walkers and offer both lunch and evening meals (with often a few regional dishes and usually a couple of vegetarian options), some locally brewed beers, a garden to relax in on hot days and a roaring fire to huddle around on cold ones. The standard of the food varies widely, though portions are usually large, which for some walkers might be all that matters! It's also best not to expect much variety. This is firmly 'meat 'n' two veg' old-fashioned English cuisine country.

That other great British culinary tradition and a favourite of Wainwright's in the bigger towns is the **fish 'n' chip shop**, or 'chippy', which will deep fry your dinner and then slather it in a layer of mushy peas and brown sauce.

Larger towns also have Chinese and Indian **takeaways**, which can make a welcome change from too much pub food and are often the only places still serving food late in the evenings, usually until at least 11pm.

Catering for yourself

The list of village **shops** (often combined with a post office) along the route grows sadly shorter with each edition but those that manage to remain in business have a pretty good selection of foods and your diet will depend on what you can find there. A few even stock **camping gas stove cartridges** (which you can also pick up in the bigger towns such as Grasmere, Kirkby Stephen and Richmond). Part 4 goes into greater detail about what can be found where.

Drinking water

There may be plenty of ways of perishing on the Coast to Coast trail but thirst won't be one of them. Be careful, though, for on a hot day in some of the remoter parts of the Lake District after a steep climb or two you'll quickly dehydrate, which is at best highly unpleasant. Always carry at least **three litres** of water with you no matter what the weather (though on hot days you might need more).

Out of the hills, don't be tempted by the water in the streams you come across in lowland areas where the chemicals from the pesticides and fertilisers used on the farms may become concentrated. It's a lot safer to fill up from taps or high mountain pools and becks. Remember, what makes you ill can't be seen by the naked eye so water from a peat-stained tarn or fellside beck will probably be much less polluted than a dribbling brook in somewhere like the intensively farmed Vale of Mowbray. In all cases, it is sensible to boil and treat your water before you drink it to be sure that it is clean.

An excellent idea is to carry a small portable water filter or water purification tablets with you. There are many different types of filter on the market. We've been especially impressed with LifeStraw (🖳 lifestraw.com) water bottles which make water instantly safe to drink and are light, cheap and ideal for hikers.

MONEY

Banks are very few and far between on the Coast to Coast path. There's now only one in Kirkby Stephen. However, there are **ATMs** in various places.

Post offices, however, provide a very useful service. Most banks in Britain have agreements with the post office allowing customers to make cash withdrawals using their debit card at post offices throughout the country. To find branches and check their services contact the Post Office (🖳 postoffice.co.uk/branch-finder); some post offices also have an **ATM/cashpoint**. Usually you can withdraw cash for free but some may be privately operated and charge £1.25-2 per withdrawal; for further details see 🖳 link.co.uk/consumers/locator. Branches of supermarkets may also have free-to-use ATMs. Non-UK residents take note that foreign bank cards often do not work in such machines so plan ahead.

Another way of getting cash is to use the **cashback** system: find a store that will accept a debit card and ask them to advance cash against the card. A number of the local village stores as well as some pubs will do this, though you'll usually have to spend a minimum of £5 with them first. It pays to ask.

As not all local stores, pubs or B&Bs accept credit/debit cards, it's essential to carry plenty of cash (reckon on £200 per person). For UK residents a **chequebook** could prove useful as a back-up.

INTERNET ACCESS

Most places to stay, cafés and pubs offer **wi-fi** to guests/customers and usually this is free. Some accommodation options, particularly hostels, provide an internet-enabled **computer** for the use of guests; this is usually free. Otherwise, the local **library** is the place to find internet access. Libraries almost always have more than one computer terminal for internet use, which is usually free for a short time (commonly 30 mins) for UK residents.

OTHER SERVICES

Many small villages have a **post office** that doubles as the local store and bank (see Money, above), and nearby you may still find a **phone box**, though be warned that some have now become homes for defribillators or book libraries. Where they do exist, to combat vandalism all accept cards (credit, debit, BT or prepaid), taking a £1.20 connection fee which is charged whether you get an answer or not. Be aware that if you're phoning a mobile from a call box, your £1.20 will last for less than a minute. For cash, calls cost a minimum of 60p (including a 40p connection charge; thereafter 10p a minute); no change is given.

There are **outdoor equipment shops** and **pharmacies** in the larger towns of Grasmere, Kirkby Stephen and Richmond and **tourist information centres** at Kirkby Stephen, Ullswater (near Patterdale), and Richmond.

WALKING COMPANIES

It's possible to turn up with your boots and backpack at St Bees and just start walking, without planning much other than your accommodation (about which, see the box on p21). The following companies, however, are in the business of making your holiday as stress-free and enjoyable as possible.

❑ INFORMATION FOR FOREIGN VISITORS

● **Currency** The British pound (£) comes in notes of £100, £50, £20, £10 and £5, and coins of £2 and £1. The pound is divided into 100 pence (usually referred to as 'p', pronounced 'pee') which come in silver coins of 50p, 20p 10p and 5p and copper coins of 2p and 1p.

● **ATMs/cash machines/cashpoints** Bank ATMs are free to use but others may charge a fee and some, such as Link machines (see p25), **may not accept foreign cards**. ATMs located outside a bank, shop, post office or petrol station are open all the time, but any that are inside will be accessible only when that place is open.

● **Rates of exchange** Up-to-date rates can be found at 🖥 xe.com/currencyconverter.

● **Accommodation booking** Most B&B-style places require a deposit but some places, particularly in rural areas, may not accept card payments or know what information is necessary for foreigners to do a bank to bank transfer. Booking a hotel shouldn't be a problem.

● **Business hours** Most **village shops** are open Monday to Friday 9am-5pm and Saturday 9am-12.30pm, though some open as early as 7.30/8am; many also open on Sundays but not usually for the whole day. Occasionally you'll come across a local shop that closes at lunchtime on one day during the week, usually a Wednesday or Thursday; this is a throwback to the days when all towns and villages had an 'early closing day'. **Supermarkets** are generally open Monday to Saturday 8am-8pm (often longer) and on Sunday from about 9am to 5 or 6pm, though main branches of supermarkets generally open 10am-4pm or 11am-5pm.

Main **post offices** generally open Monday to Friday 9am-5pm and Saturday 9am-12.30pm though where the branch is in a shop post office services are sometimes available whenever the shop is open; **banks** typically open at 9.30/10am Monday to Friday and close at 3.30/4pm, though in some places both post offices and banks may open only two or three days a week and/or in the morning, or limited hours, only.

Pub opening hours have become more flexible – up to 24 hours a day seven days a week – so each pub may have different times. However, most pubs on the Coast to Coast route continue to follow the traditional Monday to Saturday 11am to 11pm, Sunday to 10.30pm and some still close in the afternoon particularly during the week.

The last entry time to most **museums and galleries** is usually half an hour, or an hour, before the official closing time.

● **National (Bank) holidays** Most businesses are shut on 1 January, Good Friday (March/April), Easter Monday (March/April), the first and last Monday in May, the last Monday in August, 25 December and 26 December.

● **School holidays** School holiday periods in England are generally as follows: a one-week break late October, two weeks around Christmas, a week mid February, two weeks around Easter, a week in late May and from late July to early September.

● **Travel/medical insurance** Until the UK left the EU the European Health Insurance Card (EHIC) entitled EU nationals (on production of an EHIC card) to necessary medical treatment under the UK's National Health Service (NHS) while on a temporary

---

Baggage carriers

There are several baggage-transfer companies serving the Coast to Coast route. For all you must book up 6pm (Sherpa Van by 5pm) the previous evening, though earlier is better as it can be cheaper in advance but also to be sure there is space. All baggage forwarders will give an estimated latest time by which you can expect your bags to be delivered, usually 4/4.30pm.

visit here. This is unlikely to be the case for EU nationals once their EHIC card has expired. The latest information can be found at ⌨ nhs.uk/nhs-services (click on: 'NHS services' then 'Visiting-or-moving-to-England') before arrival in the UK. But the EHIC card was never a substitute for proper medical cover on your travel insurance for unforeseen bills and for getting you home should that be necessary. Also consider getting cover for loss or theft of personal belongings, especially if you're staying in hostels, as there may be times when you have to leave your luggage unattended.

● **Weights and measures** In Britain, milk can be sold in pints (1 pint = 568ml) or litres. Beer in pubs is always sold in pints (or half-pints). Most other liquids including petrol (gasoline) and diesel are sold in litres. Distances on road and path signs are given in miles (1 mile = 1.6km) rather than kilometres, and yards (1yd = 0.9m) rather than metres. The population remains split between those who still use inches (1 inch = 2.5cm), feet (1ft = 0.3m) and yards and those who roll with millimetres, centimetres and metres; you'll often be told that 'it's only a hundred yards or so' to somewhere, rather than a hundred metres or so.

Most food is sold in metric weights (g and kg) but the imperial weights of pounds (lb: 1lb = 453g) and ounces (oz: 1oz = 28g) are often displayed too. The weather – a frequent topic of conversation – is also an issue: while most forecasts predict temperatures in Celsius (C), many people continue to think in terms of fahrenheit (F; see temperature chart on p14 for conversions).

● **Time** During the winter the whole of Britain is on Greenwich Mean Time (GMT). The clocks move one hour forward on the last Sunday in March, remaining on British Summer Time (BST) until the last Sunday in October.

● **Smoking** Smoking in enclosed public places is banned. The ban relates not only to pubs and restaurants, but also to B&Bs, hostels and hotels. These latter have the right to designate one or more bedrooms where the occupants can smoke, but the ban is in force in all enclosed areas open to the public – even in a private home such as a B&B. Should you be foolhardy enough to light up in a no-smoking area, which includes pretty well any indoor public place, you could be fined £50, but it's the owners of the premises who suffer most if they fail to stop you, with a potential fine of £2500.

● **Telephones** From outside Britain the international country **access code** for Britain is ☎ 44 followed by the area code minus the first 0, and then the number you require. **Mobile phone reception** is better than you may think; even in the Lakes you're often actually quite close to a town and on high ground where a weak signal can often be picked up. It's said the Vodaphone network works best across rural northern England followed by O2 or EE. If you're using a mobile phone that is registered overseas and doesn't include roaming, consider buying a local SIM card to keep costs down.

● **Emergency services** For police, ambulance, fire and mountain rescue dial ☎ 999.

● **Visas** Despite having left the EU at the time of writing short-term tourist visas were not required by people with a passport from an EU or non-EU Western European country. To check if you need a visa visit ⌨ gov.uk/check-uk-visa.

Note that baggage-transfer companies are usually happy to transfer camping equipment but only to official campsites and/or YHAs. However, they don't go to places that are hard to reach by road such as Ennerdale/YHA Black Sail and YHA Boggle Hole. There may also be a surcharge for places that are off the standard route and the maximum weight per bag may be 20kg (see box below).

These companies also offer **self-guided holidays** (see opposite), long-term car parking and passenger bus services using their baggage vans along the Coast to Coast route. These last two services have two important consequences for trekkers. Firstly, it means that, should you want to skip a walking stage – and subject to availability – you can ride with your luggage on their **passenger bus service** to the next stage. Secondly, you can use Kirkby Stephen (Coast to Coast Packhorse), Richmond (Sherpa Van) or Skipton (Brigantes) as your base, getting a lift in their van to St Bees, and another from Robin Hood's Bay, at the end of the walk, back to their base. However, seating is often limited so you must book well in advance.

You can leave your car at the **secure parking** at their base, which is better than the alternative of leaving it in St Bees and travelling all the way back from the east coast to pick it up again. Or you can buy a return train ticket from your home to one place which may be cheaper and quicker than having to buy one ticket to St Bees, and another from Robin Hood's Bay.

● **Sherpa Van** (☎ 01748 826917, 💻 sherpavan.com; late March to mid October), based in Richmond, is a national organisation that shifts the baggage for their clients and also for many other tour operators. They will transfer (or effectively, store) your excess baggage left at St Bees and deliver it to Robin Hood's Bay for £25. See box below for details of their services.

The Sherpa Van service operates in conjunction with Coast to Coast Packhorse eastwards across the route.

● **Coast to Coast Packhorse** (☎ 017683 71777, 💻 c2cpackhorse.co.uk; see also opposite and p30; late Mar to late Oct), based in Kirkby Stephen. See box below for details of their services.

Packhorse's package customers are welcome to ride on the **daily bus service** with their bags, at no extra cost, should the need arise; this option is also available for baggage-only customers for an extra fee. However, this is subject to availability and must be booked in advance.

❑ **SHERPA VAN AND COAST TO COAST PACKHORSE – NOTES**

Both Sherpa Van and Coast to Coast Packhorse transfer baggage for their clients and also for other Coast to Coast operators. They charge from £14.50 per stage (check website for latest prices) for luggage transfer. They both also have a **secure parking** lot in Kirkby Stephen, where you can leave a car for the duration of your walk for £6.60 per day and also offer a bag store facility for £25 per bag. The cost of travelling direct from Kirkby Stephen to St Bees, or Robin Hood's Bay to Kirkby Stephen, is £40 per person.

One service departs Kirkby Stephen at 8am, arriving at St Bees around 10am, before travelling via the pick-up points back to Kirkby Stephen. A second also leaves Kirkby Stephen at 8am, stopping at the drop-off points before reaching Robin Hood's Bay by 4pm for the direct trip back to Kirkby Stephen, arriving around 6pm. In other words, the buses stop at the various drop-off points only when travelling from west to east.

● **Brigantes Walking Holidays and Baggage Carriers** (☎ 01756 770402, 💻 brigantesenglishwalks.com; Skipton, North Yorkshire; see also below) run a family-operated baggage-transfer service with locally based drivers covering the whole of the north of England.

Contact them or look at their website to get the current prices; bookings must be made by noon the previous day. They have a **secure parking** facility in Kirkby Malham with transport provided to the start of the walk and back from the end.

Self-guided holidays
Self-guided means that the company will organise accommodation, baggage transfer (some contracting out the work to other companies), transport to and from the walk and various maps and bits of advice, but leave you on your own to actually walk the path and cover lunch and dinner.

● **Absolute Escapes** (☎ 0131 610 1210, 💻 absoluteescapes.com) Edinburgh
● **Alpine Exploratory** (☎ 0131 214 1144, 💻 alpineexploratory.com) Edinburgh
● **Badger Adventures** (☎ 01900 516167, 💻 badgeradventurestreks.co.uk; Cumbria)
● **Brigantes Walking Holidays** (see above)
● **British and Irish Walks** (☎ 01242 254353, 💻 britishandirishwalks.com) Glos
● **Coast to Coast Packhorse** (see opposite and p30)
● **Contours Holidays** (☎ 01629 821900, 💻 contours.co.uk) Derbyshire
● **Discovery Travel** (☎ 01983 301133, 💻 discoverytravel.co.uk) UK
● **Footpath Holidays** (☎ 01985 840049, 💻 footpath-holidays.com) Wiltshire
● **Freedom Walking Holidays** (☎ 07733 885390, 💻 freedomwalkingholidays.co.uk) Berkshire
● **Great British Walks** (☎ 01600 713008, 💻 great-british-walks.com) Monmouth
● **Let's Go Walking** (☎ 01837-880075 or ☎ 020-7193 1252, 💻 www.letsgowalking.co.uk) UK
● **Macs Adventure** (☎ 0141 3194532, 💻 macsadventure.com) Glasgow
● **Maximum Adventure** (☎ 01768 371289, 💻 maximumadventure.com) Kirkby Stephen
● **Mickledore** (☎ 017687 72335, 💻 mickledore.co.uk) Keswick, Cumbria
● **Northwestwalks** (☎ 01257 424889, 💻 northwestwalks.co.uk) Wigan
● **Walkers' Britain** (☎ 0800 0087741, 💻 walkersbritain.co.uk) London
● **Walk the Trail** (☎ 01326 567252, 💻 walkthetrail.co.uk) Helston, Cornwall

Group/guided walking tours

If you don't trust your navigational skills or simply prefer the company of other walkers as well as an experienced guide, the following companies will be of interest. Packages nearly always include all meals, accommodation, transport arrangements, minibus back-up and baggage transfer.

Look very carefully at each company's website before booking as each has its own speciality and it's important to choose one that's suitable for you.

● **Alpine Exploratory** (see p29) No specific itineraries but they will arrange a guided tour if requested
● **Badger Adventures** (☎ 01900 516167, 🖳 badgeradventurestreks.co.uk; Cumbria) A family business that offers: 9- to 16-day walks with a trained guide either over the whole route or just in the Lake District.
● **Coast to Coast Packhorse** (see p28 and p29) Offers a number of 14-day/night guided **walks** along the whole path along with a guided **run** over 10 days.
● **Cumbria Tourist Guides** (🖳 cumbriatouristguides.org; Cumbria) The guides have a wealth of local knowledge. If you need one for the whole route, including elevated sections, ensure the guide has a Mountain Leader qualification.
● **Footpath Holidays** (see p29) Runs guided walks in three 4- to 6-day sections from bases (in the Lake District, Yorkshire Dales, and North York Moors) so avoiding the hassle of daily packing. Hikers can book one or all sections.
● **HF Holidays** (☎ 020 3974 8871, 🖳 hfholidays.co.uk; Herts) They run 15-night Coast to Coast guided trail holidays (approx five times a year)
● **Northern Guiding** (☎ 01132 736417, 🖳 northernguiding.co.uk; Leeds) Run by a qualified Mountain Leader who offers private guiding either on your own or in groups and can make bespoke walks.
● **Northwestwalks** (see p29) Operates four 15-day guided holidays a year. Also offers guided holidays for private groups.
● **Walkers' Britain** (see p29) Operates both 15-day (in June and August) and 17-day (May, July and September) Coast to Coast treks.

WALKING WITH CHILDREN

Walking the Coast to Coast with children might seem a recipe for disaster but it can be very rewarding. However, even if you are confident your child/children can physically cope with long walking days – most children above the age of about eight or nine can – there are important points to remember. (If you're worried about how your child might cope consider just doing one stage; a week's walking in the Lakes would be fantastic.)
● **Short walks** Give yourself as long as possible to do the walk; the Relaxed pace B&B/hotel itinerary (see box p38) is ideal as walking days are much shorter which means you can arrive at your destination in plenty of time.
● **Accommodation** This can be a problem: put simply, many accommodation options along the Coast to Coast seem happier to accept dogs than children. Some B&Bs straight out refuse to take children below certain ages and YHA hostels don't allow children to stay in dorms and will insist you rent an entire

dorm (if they don't have suitable private rooms), which quickly makes hostelling as expensive as staying in hotels. You could camp but if you hit an extended period of bad weather this would be hard going with children. Also rooms are not equipped to host families or are prohibitively expensive. So, **book all accommodation in advance**; there would be nothing worse at the end of a long day's walking to arrive in a village with exhausted, hungry children and discover that all the rooms are taken or children aren't welcome.

● **Baggage transfer** Use a baggage-delivery service (see pp27-9) and only carry what you really need for that day's walk.

● **What to take** Good, comfortable **boots** as well as the full array of **suitable clothing**; see pp42-3. Always carry **plenty of snacks** and **water** for them.

● **Rest days** Build in a couple of rest days when your children can do something totally different (boating around Lake Windermere near Grasmere for example). These rest days will help recharge their batteries and give them something to look forward to.

● **Motivation** It can be hard for children to maintain motivation, especially when the weather is bad. Getting them to **map read** and follow the directions in this book helps (though it's probably best that you supervise with this!). Also have **visible targets**, plenty of **breaks** and **play games**.

WALKING WITH A DOG   (see also pp260)

The Coast to Coast is a dog-friendly path, though it's extremely important that dog owners behave in a responsible manner. Although you might love dogs not everyone you pass on the trail does.

If your dog has a habit of running up to strangers (or otherwise intimidating people it doesn't know) keep it on a lead whenever it's in the vicinity of other people. Note, too, that your dog needs to be extremely fit to complete the Coast to Coast path. You may not believe it when you watch it haring around the fields, but they do have a finite amount of energy, so make sure your dog is up to the task of walking for 10-20 miles a day (indeed often much more, considering how far some dogs wander).

When planning your **accommodation** you'll need to check if your dog will be welcome. Places that accept dogs are identified in the route guide by the symbol ☙: some accommodation options charge an extra £5-10 per night (or sometimes per stay) for a dog. Hostels (both YHA and independent) do not permit them unless they are an assistance (guide) dog; smaller campsites tend to accept them, but some of the larger holiday parks do not. Before you turn up always double check whether there is space for them; many places have only one or two rooms suitable for people with dogs. In some cases dogs need to sleep in a separate building; proprietors may also like it if you have a (collapsible) dog crate (see p261) where your dog can sleep.

When it comes to **eating**, most landlords allow dogs in at least a section of their pubs, though few restaurants do. Make sure you always ask first and ensure your dog doesn't run around the pub but is secured to your table or a radiator.

PLANNING YOUR WALK

Budgeting

England is not a cheap place to go travelling and, while the north may be one of the less expensive regions, the towns and villages in the Lakes especially can get all the business they can handle and charge accordingly.

You may think before you set out that you're going to keep your budget to a minimum by camping every night and cooking your own food, but it's a rare trekker who sticks to this. Besides, the B&Bs and pubs on the route are amongst the Coast to Coast's major attractions and it would be a pity not to sample their hospitality from time to time.

If the only expenses of this walk were transport to the route, accommodation and food, budgeting would be a piece of cake. Unfortunately, in addition to these there are all the little **extras** that push up the cost of your trip: for example beer, cream teas, buses or taxis, baggage transfer, laundry, souvenirs.

CAMPING

Most campsites charge £5-15 per person (pp); you can probably survive on less than £20pp per day if you use the cheapest campsites, don't visit a pub, avoid all the museums and tourist attractions in the towns and cook all your own food from staple ingredients. Even then, unforeseen expenses will probably nudge your daily budget up. Include the occasional pint, and perhaps a pub meal every now and then, and the figure will be nearer £30pp per day.

HOSTELS, BUNKHOUSES AND CAMPING BARNS

The charge for staying in a dorm bed in a **hostel** is about £15-25pp per night. Whack on another £6-10 for breakfast, £9-12 for an evening meal, and there's also lunch to consider; packed lunches from a hostel cost £5-7. However, you can use their self-catering facilities for all of these. This means that, overall, it could cost £40-55pp per day, or £50-55pp to live in a little more comfort, enjoy the odd beer and go out for the occasional meal. The few **bunkhouses/camping barns** along the path vary in quality and price, but expect to pay £15-30pp for a bed. A few places offer **glamping pods** and/or **shepherd's huts** for about £35pp for a night.

B&Bs, GUESTHOUSES AND HOTELS

B&B starts at around £35pp per night (for two sharing) but can be at least twice this. Add on the cost of food and you should reckon on at least £70pp per day if walking as a couple or with a friend(s).

Staying in a guesthouse or hotel will cost more. Solo travellers are likely to have to pay a single occupancy supplement (£10-15 less than the room rate), or the full room rate. See also pp22-3.

Itineraries

Most people tackle the Coast to Coast Path from west to east, mainly because this allows them to walk 'with the weather at their back' (most of the time the winds blow off the Atlantic from the south-west). It's also common for people to attempt the walk in one go, though there's much to be said for breaking it up and doing it in sections.

Part 4 of this book has been written from west to east, but there is of course nothing to stop you from tackling it in the opposite direction (see p36). To help plan your walk look at the **planning maps** (at the back of the book) and the **table of village/town facilities** (on pp34-5), which gives a run-down on the essential information you'll need regarding accommodation possibilities and services at the time of writing. You could follow one of the **suggested itineraries** (see boxes p37, p38 and p39) which are based on preferred type of accommodation and walking speeds.

There's also a list of linear **day walks** on pp36-9 which cover the best of the Coast to Coast path, many of which are served by public transport (particularly in the main season) or the Packhorse/Sherpa Van services (see pp27-9). The **public transport** services tables and map are on pp54-6.

Once you have an idea of your approach turn to Part 4 for detailed information on accommodation, places to eat and other services in each village and town on the route. Also in Part 4 you will find summaries of the route to accompany the detailed trail maps.

SUGGESTED ITINERARIES

The itineraries in the boxes on pp37-9 are based on different accommodation types – camping, hostels/bunkhouses/camping barns, and B&B-style accommodation – with each including three options depending on your walking speed (relaxed, medium and fast). They are only suggestions so feel free to adapt them. Don't forget to **add your travelling time** before and after the walk.

And which of these itineraries do we think is the best? Well, the majority of walkers follow the medium-pace walk, but if you can spare the time the relaxed pace is definitely the one to go for.

The slightly shorter walking days will allow you to enjoy the experience more. You can linger longer at viewpoints, include side-trips and explore your host village at the end of the day. We do not suggest the fast pace unless you're attempting the Coast to Coast as an endurance test.

PLANNING YOUR WALK

VILLAGE & TOWN FACILITIES & DISTANCES
St Bees to Robin Hood's Bay

PLACE* & DISTANCE* APPROX MILES / KM	BANK (ATM)	POST OFFICE	INFO	EATING PLACE	FOOD SHOP	CAMP-SITE	HOSTEL BARN	B&B HOTEL
St Bees		✔		𝒲𝒲	✔	✔		𝒲𝒲
Sandwith 4½ / 7.2				(✔)				
Moor Row 3½ / 5.6								
Cleator 1 / 1.6				✔	✔			✔
(Cltr Moor) 1/1.6 (from Cltr) ATM	✔	✔		✔	✔			✔
Ennerdale Bridge 6 / 9.6 (via Dent)				𝒲𝒲	✔	✔	B (Low Cock HF)	𝒲𝒲
Gillerthwaite 5 / 8							Y/H	
Seatoller (& Honister) 9 / 14.5				✔ (Honister)		✔		𝒲
Rosthwaite 2 / 3.2				𝒲𝒲		✔	Y/B	𝒲𝒲
(**Borrowdale Valley**: Longthwaite, Rosthwaite, Stonethwaite)								
Easedale 8½ / 13.7				✔				𝒲𝒲
(Grasmere) 9/14.5 (from Rosthwte) ATM	✔	✔		𝒲𝒲	✔	✔	Y	𝒲𝒲
Patterdale 7½ / 12			TIC	𝒲	✔	𝒲	Y/B	𝒲𝒲
(not Helvellyn routes) (TIC and food shop are at Glenridding, one mile away)								
(Bampton) 1¾ / 2.8				(✔)	✔	(✔) (Burnbanks)		✔
Shap 15½ / 25	ATM	✔		𝒲𝒲	✔	𝒲	B	𝒲𝒲
(Orton 8 / 13 & on to Tebay +3/5)		(✔)		𝒲	✔	✔		𝒲
(Newbiggin-on-Lune) 7 / 11 (from Orton)						(✔) (Bents Farm; 1 mile)		
K'by Stephen 20½/33 (fm Shap) ✔+ATM	✔+ATM		VC	𝒲𝒲	✔	✔	H	𝒲𝒲
Keld 13 / 21 (not Green route)				𝒲		✔	B	𝒲𝒲
(Thwaite) 2 / 3.2 (from Keld)				(✔)				𝒲
(Muker) 3½ / 5.6 (from Keld)				𝒲	✔			
(Gunnerside) 2½ / 4 (from Muker)				𝒲				
Reeth 11 /18 (fm Keld on hi rte) ✔**✔	✔**	✔	NPC	𝒲𝒲	✔	𝒲	Y/B	𝒲𝒲
4 / 6.4 (from Gunnerside on low route)								
Marrick 3½ / 5.6				✔		✔		
Richmond 10½ / 16.9 ATM	ATM	✔	TIC	𝒲𝒲	✔			𝒲𝒲
Colburn 3 / 4.8				✔	✔		✔(+shepherd's hut)	
Brompton-on-Swale 2 / 3.2		✔		𝒲	✔	✔	B	✔
(inc Catterick Bridge)								
Danby Wiske 7½ / 12.1				✔		𝒲		𝒲𝒲
8½ / 13.7 (from Brompton-on-Swale on alternative route)								
Oaktree Hill 2½ / 4 ATM (at Exelby services)	ATM			✔ (at Exelby)			B	✔
Ingleby Cross/Arncliffe 8 / 12.9		(✔)		𝒲				𝒲𝒲
(Osmotherley) 3 / 4.8 (fm Ingleby Cross) (✔)		(✔)		𝒲𝒲	✔	𝒲	Y	𝒲𝒲
Clay Bank Top† 12 / 19.3				𝒲𝒲		𝒲𝒲(½)		𝒲𝒲
Blakey Ridge 8½ / 13.7				✔		✔		𝒲
Glaisdale 10 / 16.1		✔		𝒲	✔			𝒲𝒲
Egton Bridge 2 / 3.2				𝒲				𝒲𝒲
Grosmont 2 / 3.2		(✔)		𝒲	✔			𝒲𝒲
Littlebeck 3½ / 5.6						✔		✔
High Hawsker 7½ / 12				✔		𝒲		
Robin Hood's Bay 4½ / 7.2 ✔**	✔**	✔	VC	𝒲𝒲	✔	𝒲𝒲(½)	Y(1mile)	𝒲𝒲

NOTES *PLACE & DISTANCE Places in **bold** are on the path; places in brackets and not in bold – eg (Bampton) – are a short walk off the path. *DISTANCE is given from the place above that is on the path unless otherwise stated. † **Clay Bank Top** = Chop Gate, Great Broughton & Kirkby-in-Cleveland **B&B/HOTEL** ✔ = one place 𝒲 = two 𝒲𝒲 = three or more

PLACE* & DISTANCE* APPROX MILES / KM	BANK (ATM)	POST OFFICE	INFO	EATING PLACE	FOOD SHOP	CAMP-SITE	HOSTEL BARN	B&B HOTEL
Robin Hood's Bay	✔**	✔	VC	✔✔	✔	✔✔(½)	Y(1mile)	✔✔
High Hawsker 4½ / 7.2				✔		✔		
Littlebeck 7½ / 12						✔		✔
Grosmont 3½ / 5.6		(✔)		✔	✔			✔✔
Egton Bridge 2 / 3.2				✔				✔✔
Glaisdale 2 / 3.2		✔		✔	✔			✔✔
Blakey Ridge 10 / 16.1				✔		✔		✔
Clay Bank Top† 8½ / 13.7				✔✔		✔✔(½)		✔✔
(Osmotherley 11/18 from CBTop, off Map 72)	✔✔	✔		✔	✔	✔	Y	✔✔
Ingleby Cross/Arncliffe 12 / 19.3	(✔)			✔				✔✔
Oaktree Hill 8 / 12.9	ATM (at Exelby services)			✔(at Exelby)			B	✔
Danby Wiske 2½ / 4		✔		✔		✔		✔✔
Brompton-on-Swale 7½ / 12.1	✔	✔		✔	✔	✔	B	✔
(inc Catterick Bridge)								
8½ / 13.7 (from Danby Wiske on alternative route)								
Colburn 2 / 3.2				✔	✔	✔(+shepherd's hut)		
Richmond 3 / 4.8	ATM	✔	TIC	✔✔	✔			✔✔
Marrick 10½ / 16.9				✔		✔		
Reeth 3½ / 5.6	✔**	✔	NPC	✔✔	✔	✔	Y/B	✔✔
(Gunnerside) 4 / 6.4 (from Reeth)				✔✔				
(Muker) 2½ / 4 (from Gunnerside)				✔✔	✔			
(Thwaite) 3½ / 5.6 (from Muker)				(✔)				✔
Keld 11 / 18 (from Reeth on high route)				✔		✔	B	✔✔
2 / 3.2 (from Thwaite)								
K'by Stephen 13 /21 (not Green rte)	✔+ATM	VC		✔✔	✔	✔	H	✔✔
(Newbiggin-on-Lune) 7¾ /12.5 (from K'by S)						(✔)	(Bents Farm; 1 mile)	
(Orton) 7 / 11 & on to Tebay +3/5)	(✔)			✔	✔	✔		✔
Shap 20½/33 (from K'by S)	ATM	✔		✔✔	✔	✔✔	B	✔✔
(Bampton) 1¾ / 2.8				(✔)	✔	(✔)	(Burnbanks)	✔
Patterdale 15½ / 25			TIC	✔	✔	✔✔	Y/B	✔✔
(TIC and food shop are at Glenridding, one mile away)								
Easedale 7½ / 12 (not Helvellyn routes)				✔✔				✔✔
(Grasmere) 1/1.6 (from E'dle)	ATM	✔		✔✔	✔	✔	Y	✔✔
Rosthwaite 8½ / 13.7				✔✔		✔	Y/B	✔✔
(**Borrowdale Valley**: Stonethwaite, Rosthwaite, Longthwaite)								
Seatoller (& Honister) 2 / 3.2				✔(Honister)		✔		✔
Gillerthwaite 9 / 14.5							Y/H	
Ennerdale Bridge 5 / 8				✔✔	✔	✔	B (Low Cock HF)	✔✔
Cleator 6 / 9.6 (via Dent)				✔	✔			✔
(Cltr Moor) 1/1.6 (from Cltr)	ATM	✔		✔	✔			✔
Moor Row 1 / 1.6					✔			
Sandwith 3½ / 5.6				(✔)				
St Bees 4½ / 7.2	✔	✔		✔✔	✔	✔		✔✔

EATING PLACE (✔) = seasonal or open daytime only or only limited days
HOSTEL/BARN Y = YHA hostel H = independent hostel B = Bunkhouse or camping barn
CAMPSITE Bracketed distance eg (½) shows mileage from Coast Path (✔) = basic campsite
INFO TIC = Tourist Info Centre NPC = National Park Centre VC = Visitor Centre
BANK/ATM ATM = ATM only; ATM + ✔ = ATM+bank; ✔** = cashback may be possible

PLANNING YOUR WALK

WHICH DIRECTION?

There are several advantages in tackling the path in a west to east direction, not least the fact that the prevailing winds will, more often than not, be behind you. If you are walking alone but wouldn't mind some company now and again you'll find that most of the other Coast to Coast walkers are heading in your direction, too. However, there is also something to be said for leaving the Lake District – many people's favourite part of the British Isles, let alone the path – until the end of the walk.

DAY AND WEEKEND WALKS

The best day loops and weekend walks on the Coast to Coast

The following suggested trails are for those who don't want to tackle the entire path in one go or just want to get a flavour of the challenge before committing themselves. In our opinion they include the best parts of the Coast to Coast path, and are all described in more detail in Part 4. Day walks bring you back to your starting point, either along other routes not mapped in this book or in some cases using public transport.

PLANNING YOUR WALK

		CAMPING				
Relaxed pace			**Medium pace**		**Fast pace**	
Place	**Approx distance**	**Place**	**Approx distance**	**Place**	**Approx distance**	
Night	miles km		miles km		miles km	
0 St Bees		St Bees		St Bees		
1 Low Cock How*	12½ 20	Ennerdale Br	14 22.5	Ennerdale Br	14	22.5
2 Gillerthwaite#	7½ 12	Borrowdale§	15 24	Borrowdale§	15	24
3 Seatoller	9 14.5	Grasmere	9 14.5	Patterdale	16	26
4 Grasmere	11 18	Patterdale	8½ 13.5	Shap	15½	25
5 Patterdale	7½ 12	Shap	15½ 25	Kirkby Stephen	20½	33
6 Shap	15½ 25	Kirkby Stephen	20½ 33	Reeth	28	45
7 Orton	8 13	Keld	13 21	Colburn	17	27
8 Kirkby Stephen	13 21	Reeth	11 18	Ingleby Cross¡**	20	32
9 Keld	13 21	Colburn	12½ 20	Blakey Ridge	20½	33
10 Reeth	11 18	Danby Wiske¡	10½ 17	Littlebeck(¡)	17	28
11 Marrick	5 8	Osmotherley	12 19.5	R. Hood's Bay	12	19½
12 Brompton-o-S	11½ 19	Blakey Ridge	20½ 33			
13 Danby Wiske¡	8½ 13.5	Glaisdale**(¡)	10 16	*Note that some of this*		
14 Ingleby Cross¡**	9 14.5	Littlebeck(¡)	7 11.5	*accommodation is*		
15 Lordstones	8½ 13.5	R. Hood's Bay	12 19.5	*seasonal: check in advance*		
16 Blakey Ridge	12½ 20					
17 Glaisdale#(¡)	10 16	¡ *Add a mile if taking the alternative route from*				
18 Littlebeck(¡)	7 11.5	*Bolton-on-Swale to Danby Wiske*				
19 R. Hood's Bay	12 19.5	* *Camping available at Low Cock How (see p102)*				

§ *Borrowdale = Longthwaite, Rosthwaite, Stonethwaite*
# / ** *Hostel / B&B only option in Gillerthwaite / Ingleby Cross & Glaisdale*

There is good public transport (see pp54-6) to the start and end points on the suggested weekend walk but no direct service between Reeth and Kirkby Stephen. However, if there are two of you, you can shuttle with two cars, or a car and bike as many walkers do.

St Bees to Sandwith   5 miles/8km (pp93-7)
Get a flavour of the walk by completing the first 2.5% of it! Set out from St Bees and strike off along the red rock sea cliffs; there is no public transport from Sandwith so you will either need to walk back or continue another 5½ miles to Cleator Moor and pick up a bus there.

Around Ennerdale Water   11 miles/18km (pp104-12)
The first truly gorgeous stretch of the Coast to Coast passes along the southern shore of Ennerdale Water to River Liza. You can carry on to Black Sail along an easy track, then take a walk back along the northern access track.

Borrowdale to Grasmere and back   15 miles/24km (pp118-24)
Grasmere for lunch? In good weather it's a great training walk and you'll be able to pin down the Greenup Edge crossing to boot. Warm yourself up on the long climb to the Edge and we recommend you take the regular valley route

PLANNING YOUR WALK

STAYING IN HOSTELS & BUNKHOUSES

	Relaxed pace			Medium pace			Fast pace		
Place	Approx distance		Place	Approx distance		Place	Approx distance		
Night	miles	km		miles	km			miles	km
0 St Bees			St Bees			St Bees			
1 Cleator*	11	18	Cleator*	11	18	Ennerdale Br*14		22.5	
2 Ennerdale Br*	5	8	Ennerdale Br*	5	8	Grasmere	20½	33	
3 YHA Black Sail	8½	13.5	Borrowdale§	10½	17	Shap	23½	38	
4 Borrowdale§	5½	9	Grasmere	10	16	Kirkby Stephen 20½		33	
5 Grasmere	10	16	Patterdale	10	16	Reeth [Grinton] 29		47	
6 Patterdale	10	16	Shap	15½	25	Brompton-o-S 15½		25	
7 Shap	15½	25	Kirkby Stephen 20½		33	Osmotherley	20½	33	
8 Orton	8	13	Keld	13	21	Blakey Ridge*20½		33	
9 Kirkby Stephen	13	21	Reeth [Grinton]12½		20	Grosmont*	13½	2	
10 Keld	13	21	Brompton-o-S	15½	25	R. Hood's Bay 15½		25	
11 Reeth [Grinton] 12½		20	Oaktree Hill¡	10½	17				
12 Brompton-o-S	15½	25	Osmotherley	10	16	*Note that some of this*			
13 Oaktree Hill¡	10½	17	Clay Bank Top*	11	18	*accommodation is*			
14 Osmotherley	10	16	Glaisdale*	19	30.5	*seasonal so you must*			
15 Lordstones*	8	13	R. Hood's Bay	19	30.5	*check in advance*			
16 Blakey Ridge* 12½		20							
17 Glaisdale*	10	16	* No bunkhouses or hostels but alternative						
18 Littlebeck*	7	11.5	accommodation is available						
19 R. Hood's Bay	12	19.5	§ Borrowdale = Longthwaite, Rosthwaite, Stonethwaite						
			¡ Add a mile if taking the alternative route from						
			Bolton-on-Swale to Danby Wiske						

			STAYING IN B&Bs & HOTELS					
Relaxed pace			**Medium pace**			**Fast pace**		
Place	Approx distance		Place	Approx distance		Place	Approx distance	
Night	miles	km		miles	km		miles	km
0 St Bees			St Bees			St Bees		
1 Cleator	11	18	Ennerdale Br	14	22.5	Ennerdale Br	14	22.5
2 Ennerdale Br	5	8	Borrowdale§	15	24	Borrowdale§	15	24
3 Seatoller	14	22.5	Grasmere	9	14.5	Patterdale	17	27
4 Grasmere	10½	17	Patterdale	8½	13.5	Shap	15½	25
5 Patterdale	7½	12	Shap	15½	25	Kby Stephen	20½	33
6 Shap	15½	25	Kirkby Stephen	20½	33	Reeth	28	45
7 Orton	8	13	Keld	13	21	Colburn*	17	27
8 Kby Stephen	13	21	Reeth	11	18	Ingleby Cross¡	20	32
9 Keld	13	21	Richmond	10½	17	Blakey Ridge	20½	33
10 Reeth	11	18	Danby Wiske¡	14	22.5	Littlebeck	17½	28
11 Richmond	10½	17	Osmotherley	12	19.5	R. Hood's Bay	12	19.5
12 Danby Wiske¡	14	22.5	Clay Bank Top†	11	18			
13 Ingleby Cross¡	9	14.5	Blakey Ridge	8½	13.5			
14 Clay Bank Top†	12	19.5	Grosmont	13½	22			
15 Blakey Ridge	8½	13.5	R. Hood's Bay	15½	25			
16 Glaisdale	10	16						
17 Littlebeck	7	11.5	§ *Borrowdale = Longthwaite, Rosthwaite, Stonethwaite*					
18 R. Hood's Bay	12	19.5	* *B&B in a shepherd's hut*					

¡ *Add a mile if taking the alternative route from Bolton-on-Swale to Danby Wiske*
† *Clay Bank Top = Chop Gate, Great Broughton & Kirkby-in-Cleveland (no accommodation at Urra at the time of research)*

down to Grasmere. Rest up, revive yourself in the fleece-wearing capital of the UK, and then take the haul back with the sun to Borrowdale. We don't recommend the high route via Helm Crag unless you're really on form.

Grasmere's Helm Crag loop   8 miles/13km (pp122-4)
A very popular day trip for the more active visitor to Grasmere. It's up to you which direction you take; probably reversing the Coast to Coast by tackling the acute climb up to Helm Crag is best. At the junction at the top of Easedale (Map 17, Wpt 030) you come down the valley. A great day but tougher than you think.

Grasmere to Patterdale and back   16½ miles/26.5km (pp124-37)
A pretty hefty proposition and another great training walk through the heart of the Lakes. The walk takes you up to Helvellyn's summit and along Striding Edge, lunch at the pub and then back either up the valley or along St Sunday Crag (same distance but more climbing on the latter) and back down the other side of Tongue Gill. With very little overlapping, it's easily one of the best days out in the Lakes.

Patterdale to Kidsty Pike and back   13 miles/21km (pp137-42)

Take a 6½-mile walk to the 784-metre (2572ft) summit of Kidsty Pike on the eastern edge of the Lakes and the highest point on the original Coast to Coast route (though Helvellyn and St Sunday are much higher). Have a sandwich and a look around then walk right back down again to Patterdale for a slap-up meal in the pub.

It's a stiff old climb up to Angle Tarn but from there on the gradients just blend in with the surroundings and the views all the way up and down are well worth the effort. Another Lakeland classic that will have you fired up for the real thing.

Kirkby Stephen to Nine Standards and back
12 miles/19.5km (pp165-7)

An easy climb to the mysterious stone cones atop Nine Standards Rigg. From the top you might try a southward link towards Rigg Beck and the Green Route back to town, adding a mile or two, but that can involve some messy bog-trotting.

Keld to Reeth   12½ miles/20km (pp177-91)

Whether you take the high route via a string of evocative mine ruins between breezy moors, or the lowland amble past the hamlets of Upper Swaledale, you're sure to find something you like. If you want to return to Keld you can either take a bus (see pp54-6) or walk back on the alternative route.

Lordstones to Clay Bank Top and back   7½ miles/12km (pp226-31)

On some days a rather too popular run with Teeside dog walkers but the gradients will all be good training for the big day. You need your own transport for this walk, though.

Glaisdale to Grosmont   4 miles/6.5km (see pp241-5)

Not so much a trek as an easy pub crawl, this path takes you along the **Esk Valley** following the course of the river through woodland and along country tracks, via pretty Egton Bridge. At Grosmont there are buses (see pp54-6) back to Glaisdale. Alternatively take a NYMR steam train (see p244) or bus to Whitby.

Little Beck Wood excursion   4½ miles/7km (pp250-1)

A shady afternoon's round trip to Falling Foss waterfall and the adjacent tea room through the lovely Little Beck Wood. You need your own transport for this walk.

Whitby to Robin Hood's Bay   7 miles/11.5km

Not on the Coast to Coast until the last few miles (pp255-7) but a stirring cliff-top tramp nonetheless, ending at the hallowed slipway below Bay Hotel. You won't be the first to pretend you've just finished the entire Coast to Coast, but no one need know. Take the regular bus service (see pp54-6) back to Whitby, which is a fun place too.

PLANNING YOUR WALK

Weekend walks

In addition to the walk described below, some of the day walks can be combined into a two-day trek, particularly in the Lake District.

Kirkby Stephen to Reeth   28 miles/45km (pp165-89)

Anyone who manages to scramble over the Pennines and negotiate the boggy ground down to the old mining village of Keld deserves a reward of some sort, and picturesque Swaledale is just that. As an encore, take Wainwright's high route over the moors to Reeth or the less-demanding stroll down the dale, passing through or near the villages of Muker, Gunnerside and Thwaite to end up in Reeth.

SIDE TRIPS

The Coast to Coast path is long enough and few walkers will be tempted to make side trips. However, Wainwright's series of guides to Lakeland fells describes other walks around the Lake District in further detail and it may be worth making time for an ascent of some of the hills in the area as they give an entirely different perspective of the Lakeland landscape. Old favourites include Great Gable, Striding Edge on Helvellyn, High Street and England's highest mountain, Scafell Pike (3209ft/978m).

What to take

Not ending up schlepping over the fells like an overloaded mule with a migraine takes experience and some measure of discipline. **Taking too much** is a mistake made by first-time travellers of all types, an understandable response to not knowing what to expect and not wanting to be caught short.

By UK standards the Coast to Coast is a long walk but it's not an expedition into the unknown. Experienced independent hill walkers trim their gear to the essentials because they've learned that an unnecessarily heavy pack can exacerbate injuries and put excess strain on already hard-pressed feet. Note that if you need to buy all the gear listed, keep an eye out for the ever-more frequent online **sales** at outdoor gear shops; time it right and you could get it all half price.

❑ NEXT TIME I DO THE C2C...

I will discipline myself to take more time on the trail and to savour the experience of the walking. The metronomic, almost trance-like state that can occur when all you need to do is put one foot in front of the other is rarely achieved when you're focussing on getting to the end. Too often I arrived at my destination by 3pm or even 2pm and although this means more time relaxing in the pub it also means I could have taken more time on the hills, perhaps sitting quietly enjoying a view or taking time to divert from the path to explore the landscape.   **Stuart Greig**

TRAVELLING LIGHT

Organised tours apart, baggage-transfer services tempt walkers to partially miss the point of long-distance walking: the satisfaction of striding away from one coast knowing that you're carrying everything you need to get to the other. But if you've chosen to carry it all you must be ruthless in your packing choices.

HOW TO CARRY YOUR LUGGAGE

Today's **rucksacks** are hi-tech affairs that make load-carrying as tolerable as can be expected. Don't get hung up on anti-sweat features; unless you use a wheelbarrow your back will always sweat a bit. It's better to ensure there is thick padding and a **good range of adjustment**. In addition to hip belts (allied with some sort of stiff back frame/plate), use an unelasticated **cross-chest strap** to keep the pack snug; it makes a real difference.

If camping you'll need a pack of at least 60 or 70 litres' capacity. Staying in hostels 40 litres should be ample, and for those eating out and staying in B&B-style accommodation a 20- to 30-litre pack should suffice; you could even get away with a daypack as many places offer laundry services or if you have quick-drying clothes, you could wash them yourself.

Few backpacks these days claim to be waterproof; use a waterproof **liner** if possible, as well as the elasticated backpack cover like a shower cap that comes with most packs. It's also handy to **compartmentalise** the contents into smaller bags (preferably waterproof ones) so you know what is where. Take a few **(degradable) bags** for wet things, rubbish etc; they're always useful. Finally, pack intelligently with the most frequently used things readily accessible.

FOOTWEAR

Boots

A good pair of boots is vital. Scrimp on other gear if you must – you'll only use waterproofs some days but you'll be walking every mile on every day. Expect to spend up to £150 on quality, three-season footwear which is light, breathable and waterproof, and has ankle support as well as flexible but thick **soles** to insulate your own pulverised soles.

Don't buy by looks or price and avoid buying online until you've been to a shop and tried on an identical pair (and even this can backfire on you). Go to a big outdoor shop on a quiet weekday and spend an hour trying on everything they have in stock that appeals to you.

With modern fabric **breaking in** boots is a thing of the past but arriving in St Bees with an untried pair of boots is courting disaster. You must try them out beforehand, first round the house or office, and then on a full day's walk or two. An old and trusted pair of boots can be resoled and transformed with shock-absorbing after-market **insoles**. Some of these can be thermally moulded to your foot in the shop, but the less-expensive examples are also well worth the investment, even if the need for replacement by the end of the walk is likely. Some walkers wisely carry old trusted boots in their luggage in case their new footwear turns on them – though this can be quite a heavy tactic, of course. Blisters are possible even with a much-loved boot if you walk long and hard enough; for **blister-avoidance strategies** see information on p82.

Boots might be considered over the top for the Coast to Coast; much of the walking is on easy paths and some experienced walkers have turned to trail shoes. They won't last as long as boots, be as tough or crucially, have the height to keep your socks dry in the bogs and streams; but the rewards of nimbleness and greater comfort can transform your walk, just as bad footwear can cast a shadow over it.

Socks
As with all outdoor gear, the humble sock has not escaped the technological revolution (with prices to match) so invest in two or three non-cotton pairs designed for walking. Although cushioning is desirable, avoid anything too thick which will reduce stability. As well as the obvious olfactory benefits, frequent washing will maintain the socks' springiness.

CLOTHES
Tops
The proven system of **layering** is a good principle to follow. A quick-drying synthetic (or the less odiferous merino wool) **base layer** transports sweat away from your skin; the mid layer, typically a **fleece** or woollen jumper, keeps you warm; and when needed, an outer 'shell' or **jacket** protects you from the wind and rain.

Maintaining a comfortable temperature in all conditions is the key. This means not **overheating** just as much as it means keeping warm. Both can prematurely tire you: trudging out of Patterdale on a warm day will soon have you down to your base layer, but any exposed and prolonged descent, or rest on an unsheltered summit such as Kidsty Pike with a strong wind blowing will soon chill you. Although tedious, the smart hiker is forever fiddling with zips and managing their layers and headwear to maintain an optimal level of comfort.

Avoid cotton; as well as being slow to dry, when soaked it saps away body heat but not the moisture – and you'll often be wet from sweat if not rain. Take a change of **base layers** (including underwear), a **fleece** suited to the season, and the best **breathable waterproof** you can afford. **Soft shells** are an alternative to walking in rustling nylon waterproofs when it's windy but not raining.

It's useful to have a **spare set of clothing** so you're able to get changed should you arrive chilled at your destination, but choose **quick-drying clothes** as washing them reduces your payload. Once indoors your body heat will quickly dry out a synthetic fleece and nylon leggings. However, always make sure you have a **dry base layer** in case you or someone you're with goes down with hypothermia. This is why a quality waterproof is important.

Leg wear
Your legs are doing all the work and don't generally get cold so your trousers can be light which will also mean quick-drying. Although they lack useful

pockets, many walkers find leg-hugging cycling polyester **leggings** very comfortable (eg Ron Hill Tracksters). Poly-cotton or microfibre trousers are excellent. Denim jeans are cotton and a disaster when wet.

If the weather's good, **shorts** are very agreeable to walk in, leaving a light pair of trousers clean for the evenings. It also means your lower legs get muddy and not the trousers. On the other hand **waterproof trousers** would only suit people who really feel the cold; most others will find them unnecessary and awkward to put on and wear; quick drying or minimal legwear is better.

> ❏ **WALKING POLES**
> Walking poles are a must for all ages – they saved our knees. They worked for us for a number of reasons from taking some of the weight off our feet, to clearing pathways, supporting our leaps across fast flowing streams and warning off angry looking cattle!
> **Noelle Cox & Chris Foster**

For Lakeland stream crossings and Pennine peat bogs, **gaiters** are a great idea; they also stop irritating pebbles dropping into your footwear. You don't have to wear them all the time.

Headwear and other clothing
Your head is both exposed to the sun and loses most of your body heat so, for warmth, carry a woolly beany that won't blow away and for UV protection a peaked cap; a bandana or microfibre 'buff' makes a good back-up or sweat band too. Between them they'll conserve body heat or reduce the chances of dehydration.

Gloves are a good idea in wintry conditions (carry a spare pair in winter).

TOILETRIES
Take only the minimum: a small bar of **soap** in a plastic container (unless staying in B&Bs); a tiny tube of **toothpaste** and a **toothbrush**; and a roll of **loo paper** in a plastic bag. If you are planning to defecate outdoors you will also need a lightweight **trowel** for burying the evidence (see p78 for further tips).

Less obvious items include: **ear plugs**; high-factor **sun screen**; **moisturiser**; **insect repellent** if camping; and possibly a means of **water purification**. **Liquid soap** is useful; it can also be used for shaving and washing clothes, although a ziplock bag of **detergent** is better if you're laundering regularly.

FIRST-AID KIT
Apart from aching limbs your most likely ailments will be blisters so a first-aid kit can be minimal. **Paracetamol** helps numb pain – although rest, of course, is the only real cure. '**Compeed**', or '**Second Skin**' all treat blisters. An **elastic knee support** is a good precaution for a weak knee as are walking poles (see box above). A tube of Nuun tablets can flavour water and restore lost minerals on the march, and a few sachets of Dioralyte or Rehydrat powders will quickly remedy more serious dehydration.

PLANNING YOUR WALK

Other items worth considering are: **plasters** for minor cuts; a small selection of different-sized **sterile dressings** for wounds; **porous adhesive tape**; **antiseptic wipes**; **antiseptic cream**; **safety pins**; **tweezers**; and **scissors**.

GENERAL ITEMS

Essential

Carry a **compass** (if you know how to use one), **whistle** and **mobile/smart phone** (with the relevant charging device) as well as at least a one-litre **water bottle** or bag; an LED **headtorch**; a thick **transparent plastic bag** to keep this guidebook in (or a waterproof map case on a neck string); **emergency snacks** and a **penknife**.

Useful

If you're not carrying a proper bivvy bag or tent, a compact foil **space blanket** is a good idea in the cooler seasons. Many people take a **camera** (with the relevant **battery**) and **sunglasses**. A **book** is a good way to pass the evenings, especially in mid summer wild camps. A **vacuum flask**, for hot drinks or soup, is recommended if walking in a cooler season. Studies have shown that nothing improves a hilltop view on a chilly day like a hot cup of tea or soup.

SLEEPING BAG & CAMPING GEAR

If you're camping or planning to stay in camping barns you'll need a sleeping bag. Many bunkhouses now offer bedding, some at a nominal cost, but check in advance. All hostels provide bedding and most insist you use it.

A **two-season bag** will do for indoor use, but if you can afford it or anticipate outdoor use, go warmer. The choice over a **synthetic** or **down** filling is a debate without end. Year by year less expensive synthetic-filled bags (typically under £100) approach down's enviable qualities of good compressibility while expanding or 'lofting' fully once unpacked to create maximum warmth. But get a down bag wet (always a risk in the UK) and it clogs up and loses all its thermal qualities; and drying down bags takes half a day at the launderette.

If committed to the exposure of wild camping you'll need a **tent** you can rely on; light but able to withstand the rain and wind. In campsites you may just get away with a cheap tent. Otherwise, a good one-man tent suited to the wilds can cost under £120 and weigh just 1.5kg, with a sub-2kg two-man example costing around £250. An inflatable **sleeping mat** is worth many times its weight.

If you're planning to do some **cooking** along the way, you'll need: a camping stove, a lighter and a box of matches, a set of camping pots, some cutlery, bowls and cups (if your camping pot set doesn't include any) and a cleaning scourer. With all of these, the smaller and lighter the better. It's worth noting, though, that there are plenty of cafés and pubs to eat at along the way so unless you're planning to do some wild camping it's entirely possible to get away without needing to bring any cooking equipment even if you camp every night.

MONEY

ATMs (cash machines) are fairly rare along the Coast to Coast path (and some don't accept foreign cards), but remember holders of most UK bank cards can withdraw cash over the counter at **post offices**. **Banks** are even rarer, with only Kirkby Stephen boasting any. For details see the table of village and town facilities on pp34-5.

Not everybody accepts **debit** or **credit cards** as payment either – though many B&Bs and restaurants now do. As a result, you should always carry plenty of cash with you (particularly if you're relying on a bank card not issued by a UK bank) just to be on the safe side. A **cheque book** from a British bank may be useful in those places where cards are not accepted. Crime on the trail is thankfully rare though it can't hurt to carry your money in a **moneybelt**.

MAPS

The hand-drawn maps in this edition cover the trail at a scale of just under 1:20,000: one mile equals $3\frac{1}{8}$ths of an inch (1km = 5cm). At this generous scale, combined with the notes and tips written on the maps, and the waypoints, they should be enough to stop you losing your way as long as you don't stray too far off the route. That said, a supplementary map of the region – ie one with contours – can prove invaluable should you need to abandon the path and find the quickest route off high ground in bad weather. It also helps you to identify local features and landmarks and devise possible side trips.

In place of their discontinued Outdoor Leisure strip maps, **Ordnance Survey** now have the Explorer series of maps at a scale of 1:25,000 but in order to cover the whole trail you will need eight maps. The trouble here, of course,

---

❑ TIPS FROM A TWO-TIME COAST-TO-COASTER – WHAT TO TAKE

More tips from Geoffrey Simms, who has completed the Coast to Coast Path twice.

A **map-case**, worn as a neck purse inside your shirt, is very useful. So many Coasters walk along clutching your guidebook disintegrating in the rain rather than have it open at the appropriate page under the protection of a map-case. Keep the hands free is my motto. In wet and windy conditions pages can be turned without even removing the guidebook from the case.

Binoculars are also useful. They add not only to your enjoyment of the bird life, but also help with identifying signposts, waymarks, gates and stiles from the top of a slope, or from the entry to a spacious meadow, thereby eliminating the tedious retracing of steps that follows from a false trail.

My calibrated Yamax Digi-walker **pedometer** (🖳 yamax.co.uk) is a faithful friend helping to pinpoint my position. Numerous Coasters walking the 'proper' direction (when I was walking from east to west) were grateful to know the distance to a specific point to which they were heading. As with map-cases and binoculars, I found an almost total absence of pedometer-equipped Coasters.

I am a devotee of **walking poles**, a godsend for my lower back muscles. I reckon they are worth a couple of miles a day. They saved me from hitting the deck on numerous occasions, besides being a great comfort negotiating stepping-stones.

is one of weight and expense and also, **they don't always show the path** and are sometimes out of date with details such as plantations. The details are: Explorer Series 303 (for St Bees); Outdoor Leisure (OL) 4 for the western Lake District; OL5 for the eastern Lake District; OL19 for the upper Eden Valley (Kirkby Stephen); OL30 for Swaledale; Explorer Series 304 (though very occasionally it dips south into 302) for Richmond and the Vale of Mowbray; OL26 for the western North York Moors; and OL27 for the eastern half to Robin Hood's Bay. From the Ordnance Survey website link (⌨ shop.ordnancesurvey.co.uk/os-explorer-wainwrights-coast-to-coast-walk-map-set/) you can buy the nine maps ie with 302 and they include mobile download.

We say again that with a bit of nous many readers manage with the maps in this book, but if any two of the above OS maps are worth getting they are **OL4 and OL5** covering the Lake District where the weather can be bad, the way-marking is worse and the consequences of losing the path vexing in the extreme. By a stroke of luck both these double-sided sheets can be neatly cut in half while still retaining the full extent of the path from west to east.

Unfortunately, the two Outdoor Leisure strip maps produced by Ordnance Survey (see p45) that covered the entire trail at a scale of 1:27,777 went out of print in 2002, and although it may still be possible to get second-hand copies these are increasingly rare (and cost a premium – usually upwards from £30 each – if you can find them); look for sheets OL33 covering the trail from St Bees to Keld and OL34 covering it from Keld to Robin Hood's Bay. The good

---

❏ **DIGITAL MAPPING**   see also pp17-19

There are numerous software packages now available that provide Ordnance Survey (OS) maps for a smartphone, tablet, PC, or GPS unit. Maps are downloaded into an app from where you can view, print and create routes on them.

For a subscription of £4.99 for one month or £28.99 for a year (on their current offer) **Ordnance Survey** (⌨ ordnance survey.co.uk) allows you to download and use their UK maps (1:25,000 scale) on a mobile or tablet without a data connection for a specific period. Their app works well.

Memory Map (⌨ memory-map.co.uk) currently sell OS Explorer 1:25,000 and Landranger 1:50,000 mapping covering the whole of Britain with prices from £19.99 for a one year subscription. **Anquet** (⌨ anquet.com) has the full range of OS 1:25,000 maps covering all of the UK from £28 per year annual subscription.

Maps.me is free and you can download any of its digital mapping to use offline. You can install the Trailblazer tracklog and waypoints for this walk on its mapping but you'll need to convert the .gpx format file to .kml format before loading it into maps.me. Use an online website such as ⌨ gpx2kml.com to do this then email the kml file to your phone and open it in maps.me.

Harvey (⌨ store.avenza.com/collections/harvey-maps) currently use the US Avenza maps app for their *Coast to Coast* map (1:40,000 scale, $15.99).

It is important to ensure any digital mapping software on your smartphone uses pre-downloaded maps, stored on your device, and doesn't need to download them on-the-fly, as this may be expensive and will be impossible without a signal. Remember that battery life will be significantly reduced, compared to normal usage, when you are using the built-in GPS and running the screen for long periods.

news is that electronic copies are available online and could of course be printed off. Have a look at ⌨ walkingplaces.co.uk/c2c.

Coast to Coast Walk (⌨ collins.co.uk/collections/az-adventure-maps; £8.95), part of AZ's Adventure Series for walkers, has been recommended by some walkers. It includes the relevant part of the various OS maps, produced at a scale of 1:25,000, and **has the route highlighted on the map**. It comes in a handy booklet rather than as a series of fiddly fold-out maps and has a useful index.

The alternatives to OS are the strip maps produced by either **Footprint** (⌨ stirlingsurveys.co.uk) or **Harvey Maps** (⌨ harveymaps.co.uk), both of which cover the trail over one or two maps at a scale of around 1:50,000 and 1:40,000 respectively. The problem is that, like our maps, they only cover a narrow strip either side of the trail and consequently give limited opportunities for exploring further afield.

RECOMMENDED READING

Most of the following books can be found in the tourist information centres; the centre at Richmond has a particularly good supply of books about the path and the places en route, as does the Grasmere bookshop. As well as stocking many of the titles listed below, the tourist offices also have a number of books about the towns and villages en route, usually printed by small, local publishers.

Guidebooks, travelogues and DVDs

We have to mention here Wainwright's original book now reprinted: *A Coast to Coast Walk (Wainwright Walkers Edition*, 2017), a veritable work of art.

For the coffee table, *Coast to Coast with Wainwright* (also Frances Lincoln, 2009) marries Wainwright's original text with photos by Derry Brabbs; it makes a great souvenir of the walk as does *The Coast to Coast Walk* (2012) by Karen Frenkel, another beautiful photo collection from the Frances Lincoln stable. *Ancient Feet* (Matador, 2008) by Alan Nolan, is a humourous tale of five friends in their 60s tackling the path. Returning with the Wainwright theme, Hunter Davies's *Wainwright: The Biography* (Orion Press; 2007) is an absorbing account of this complex man.

Generally towards the end of each year Doreen Whitehead produces the latest edition of her long-running publication *Coast to Coast Bed & Breakfast Accommodation Guide* (UK/out of UK £4/6); see ⌨ coasttocoastguides.co.uk.

It's possible you saw *Wainwright Walks Coast to Coast* (DVD; Acorn Media, 2009, 165 mins), the five-part BBC show broadcast as part of a 'Wainwright Walks' series. Julia Bradbury makes an engaging presenter and approaches the task with gusto, interviewing characters along the way (including writer Alan Nolan, see *Ancient Feet* above). Unfortunately, the production hit terrible weather in the Lakes which dampened the impression of that part of the walk; many of the aerial shots were filmed in much better conditions. Rumours circulated on the web and along the trail about body doubles standing in on long shots while she got choppered to the summits looking fresh as a daisy, and whether she walked the entire route. The reality of television as well as of filming outdoors makes the former likely (though she may well have done the walk on another occasion) and watching the parts in quick succession you can't help thinking that it's more fun to walk than to watch.

Downhill (DVD; Crisis Films, 2014, 98 mins) is a Britflick about a group of former schoolfriends reuniting to tackle both the Coast to Coast and their collected midlife crises. It is perhaps best enjoyed after your trip, as you try to spot

---

❏ SOURCES OF FURTHER INFORMATION

Online trail information

💻 **coast2coast.co.uk** Run by Sherpa Van (see p28), this site is crammed full of information and has an online shop for books and maps. They also have a busy Coast to Coast forum, where trekkers share their experiences and others post questions, although it does suffer from a level of flippancy by the 'seen-it-all' regulars who dominate the board. Scrutinise at length before enquiring; it's probably been asked before.

💻 **coasttocoastguides.co.uk** Richmond-based organisation and another excellent website with books and maps for sale and a thorough accommodation guide based on Doreen Whitehead's booklet (see p47).

💻 **walkingplaces.co.uk/c2c** An extensive and cleanly designed website that's not trying too hard to do everything or sell you something. Run by a Coast to Coast enthusiast, there are some excellent resources here that you won't find anywhere else, as well as a tolerant and supportive Coast to Coast forum. The site also hosts blogs (many with lots of photos) by recent walkers, that make interesting reading. There's also a map downloads section; make a donation if you use it.

💻 **wainwright.org.uk** The website of the Wainwright Society, dedicated to 'keeping alive the fellwalking traditions promoted by AW', has a section on the trail.

Tourist information organisations

● **Tourist information centres (TICs)** TICs are based in towns throughout Britain and provide all manner of locally specific information. There are four centres on or near the path: **Ullswater/Glenridding** (near Patterdale, box p138), **Kirkby Stephen** (p162) and **Richmond** (p200).

● **Tourist Boards** Both **Yorkshire Tourist Board** (💻 yorkshire.com) and **Cumbria Tourist Board** (💻 visitlakedistrict.com) oversee the local TICS in each county. Their websites are useful for general information about the county as well as on outdoor activities and local events.

Organisations for walkers

● **Backpackers' Club** (💻 backpackersclub.co.uk) A club aimed at people who are involved or interested in lightweight camping, through walking, cycling, skiing and canoeing. Members receive a quarterly magazine, access to a comprehensive information service (including a library) as well as long-distance path and farm-pitch directories. Membership costs £20 per year, family £30.

● **The Long Distance Walkers' Association** (💻 ldwa.org.uk) Membership includes a journal (*Strider*) three times per year with details of challenge events and local group walks as well as articles on the subject. Membership is offered on a calendar year basis for £18 (£15 via direct debit); if you join in October the cost will include the following calendar year.

● **Ramblers** (💻 ramblers.org.uk) A charity that looks after the interests of walkers throughout Britain and promotes walking for health. Annual membership from £36.60 for an adult (£49 for joint membership) and includes a newsletter, their quarterly *Walk* magazine and an app containing 3000 walking routes and details of their led walks.

❏ **NEXT TIME WE DO THE C2C...**

Take our time. It's a holiday. Forget about the keen types who set off before 8am – let them go. Plan most days at 10-14 miles, that gives plenty of time.

Stay in B&Bs, especially farms. Last time, except for the terrific Langstrath, the pubs and hotels were a bit disappointing while the B&Bs were all good to great.

If we've time, have a rest day in Kirkby Stephen as well as in Richmond. It's welcome after the Lakes. (And there's a launderette!).

Take a lightweight camera, binoculars, a notebook. Make notes at least every evening – it's easy to forget the details, the days merge into one another. Take more notice of the small things: wild flowers, how the dry-stone walls change, curlews. The big things are dramatic, but the small ones are fascinating.

Make sure boots are 100% waterproof. A tiny damp spot on a Sunday stroll in Cheshire is trench foot on Nine Standards Rigg.

Think about going east to west. The Lakes are the highlight but they're hard work at the start. They'd be a great climax starting from the east, when we're more walking-fit. As for the rain-in-your-face argument ... what rain?!   **David Bull**

the locations they've used during and those inevitable 'Hey that's the same chair I sat in!' moments when the action moves into the local pubs.

If you're a seasoned long-distance walker, or even new to the game and like what you see, check out the other titles in the Trailblazer series on p286.

Flora and fauna field guides

Collins *Bird Guide* with its beautiful illustrations of British and European birds continues to be the favourite field guide of both ornithologists and laymen alike. For a guide to the flora you'll encounter on the Coast to Coast path, *The Wild Flower Key* (Warne) by Francis Rose and Clare O'Reilly, is arranged to make it easy to identify unfamiliar flowers. Another in the Collins Gem series, *Wild Flowers*, is more pocket sized and thus more suitable for walkers.

There are also several **field guide apps** for smartphones and tablets, including those that can aid in identifying birds by their song as well as by their appearance. One to consider is: ⌨ merlin.allaboutbirds.org.

Getting to and from the Coast to Coast path

Both St Bees and Robin Hood's Bay are quite difficult to reach on public transport; **St Bees** can only be reached by train and **Robin Hood's Bay** by bus. For this reason, many people who are using the baggage-transfer companies (see pp27-9) opt to start and finish at their bases (Kirkby Stephen, Richmond or Kirkby Malham) as the companies have car parking facilities and then take their transport links to St Bees and Robin Hood's Bay.

If you want to make your own way to/from both St Bees and Robin Hood's Bay see p51; for Kirkby Stephen see p53. Some other parts of the walk can also be reached by train, though nowhere directly on the path; see box on p52.

PLANNING YOUR WALK

NATIONAL TRANSPORT

All **train** timetable and fare information can be found at National Rail Enquiries (☎ 03457 484950, 24hrs; 🖳 nationalrail.co.uk). Alternatively, and to book tickets, you can look on the websites of the train companies concerned (see box below). Timetables and tickets are also available on 🖳 thetrainline.com and 🖳 qjump.co.uk. You are advised to book in advance – it may well save you a small fortune. If your journey involves changes, it's worth checking which train company operates each leg of the journey – you may find you can save money by buying separate tickets for each train company rather than one through ticket for your whole journey.

Coach (long-distance bus) travel is generally cheaper (though with the excellent advance-purchase train fares that is not always true) but takes longer.

PLANNING YOUR WALK

❑ **GETTING TO BRITAIN**

● **By air** Manchester Airport (🖳 manchesterairport.co.uk) remains the nearest major international airport to St Bees. See box on p52 for details of rail services from the airport to St Bees.

Leeds Bradford Airport (🖳 leedsbradfordairport.co.uk) is convenient for Kirkby Stephen and has flights to many European destinations. **Teeside International Airport** (🖳 teessideinternational.com) is 7 miles/11km outside Darlington and useful for Richmond; it also rivals **Newcastle** (🖳 newcastleairport .com) as the nearest airport to Robin Hood's Bay – though with journeys from either airport to Robin Hood's Bay taking at least four hours, neither can be considered convenient for the Coast to Coast's eastern end. Nevertheless, though the services to and from these airports increase year on year, for most foreign visitors one of the London airports (particularly **Stansted, Luton,** and **Heathrow**) remains the most likely entry point to the country. For details about getting from London to St Bees or Robin Hood's Bay, and also for Kirkby Stephen see opposite.

● **From Europe by train** Eurostar (🖳 eurostar.com) operates a high-speed passenger service via the Channel Tunnel between Paris, Brussels, Amsterdam (and some other cities) and London St Pancras International – convenient for both the trains for Carlisle (which leave from nearby Euston) and to the north-east coast (which leave from neighbouring King's Cross).

For more information about rail services from Europe contact your national rail operator, or Railteam (🖳 www.railteam.eu).

● **From Europe by coach** Eurolines (🖳 eurolines.com) have a huge network of long-distance coach services connecting over 600 cities in 36 European countries to London. Check carefully, however: once such expenses as food for the journey are taken into consideration, it often does not work out that much cheaper than taking a flight, particularly when compared to the prices of some of the budget airlines.

● **From Europe by ferry (with or without a car)** Numerous ferry companies operate routes between the major North Sea and Channel ports of mainland Europe and the ports on Britain's eastern and southern coasts as well as from Ireland to ports in both Wales and England. For further information see 🖳 directferries.com.

● **From Europe by car** Eurotunnel (🖳 eurotunnel.com) operates the shuttle train service for vehicles via the Channel Tunnel between Calais and Folkestone taking about an hour between the motorway in France and the motorway in Britain.

The principal coach operator in Britain is **National Express** (☎ 08717 818181, 24 hrs, 🖳 nationalexpress.com). At the time of research National Express were running a limited timetable compared to previous editions; by the time you plan your trek there may be more routes operating than described below. Their up-to-date route map can be found at 🖳 routemap.nationalexpress.com. **Megabus** (🖳 uk .megabus.com) has a more limited service though may be cheaper.

Getting to and from St Bees
● **Train** Carlisle and Barrow-in-Furness are the rail access points for the line to St Bees; see box on p52 for details of Northern's services to these places.

● **Coach/bus** National Express has services to Carlisle from several places in Britain. Services that stop at least once a day in Carlisle include: 590 (London to Glasgow via Birmingham & Penrith); 595 (London to Glasgow via Heathrow); 181 (Birmingham to Glasgow via Manchester and Lancaster) & 182 (Birmingham to Edinburgh via Manchester and Penrith). All travel there once during the day and once overnight. From Carlisle take a train (see box on p52) to St Bees.

● **Car** You can of course drive to St Bees but you will have to find somewhere to park. The nearest motorway is the M6 to Carlisle which joins the M1 just outside Coventry. From the south, leave the M1 at junction 36 (the Southern Lakes turn-off), then take the A590 till it meets the A5092; this then meets the A595 (to Whitehaven) and turn off just before Egremont.

Getting to and from Robin Hood's Bay
● **Train/bus** (see box on p52 and pp54-6 for details) Robin Hood's Bay is, if anything, even harder to reach (or return from) than St Bees. The nearest rail station is at Whitby. LNER operates trains between London King's Cross and Scotland; during the week the most convenient way to reach Whitby is via LNER's direct service to Middlesbrough and then change to a Northern service to Whitby. This would only require one change but the downside is a 90-minute wait at Middlesbrough. Other options, which require two changes, are taking a LNER train to either York or Northallerton then a TransPennine Express (TPEx) train to Middlesbrough and transferring there to a Northern train to Whitby. Alternatively take a LNER train to Darlington and then change to a Northern service to Thornaby or Middlesbrough and then another Northern service to Whitby.

Alternatively for a route involving only one change of train, take a Grand Central Railway (London to Sunderland) train to Hartlepool and then take a Northern train to Whitby; at the time of research there was one connecting service a day. From Whitby Arriva's X93 bus takes about 20 minutes to Robin Hood's Bay.

Another option is to get off an LNER train at York and take one of TransPennine Express's trains to Scarborough then take Arriva's X93 bus to Robin Hood's Bay. The bus journey is longer (about 40 mins) but if coming from London the journey is only around four hours in total.

● **Coach/bus** National Express services calling at Middlesbrough include: 426 (London to Newcastle via Leeds) & 436 (London to Sunderland via York). Other options go to Newcastle (via Middlesbrough) from Manchester (172) &

Birmingham (133; via Nottingham, Sheffield & Leeds). From Middlesbrough take Arriva's No X93 (see box pp54-5) service to Robin Hood's Bay.

● **Car** It's not entirely straightforward to get to Robin Hood's Bay by car either, though compared to public transport it is at least the simplest. From London head up to Doncaster on the M1/A1(M), then the M18/A19 to York. From there you

---

❏ **RAIL SERVICES & OPERATORS** See p56 for map

Avanti West Coast Railway (🖳 avantiwestcoast.co.uk)
● London Euston to Glasgow via Preston, Oxenholme Lake District, Penrith North Lakes & Carlisle, Mon-Sat 1/hr, Sun approx 1/hr but not all services stop at Oxenholme or Penrith and some stop at Crewe
● London Euston to Edinburgh via Birmingham, Preston, Oxenholme Lake District, Penrith North Lakes & Carlisle, Mon-Fri 6/day, Sat & Sun 3-4/day
Note: not all services stop at all stations and there are additional services from Birmingham and connecting services from Preston
Note: At the time of research Avanti's franchise was only valid for a few more months and their services had been very limited so it is essential to check before travel.

Grand Central Railway (🖳 grandcentralrail.com)
● London King's Cross to Sunderland via York, Thirsk, Northallerton, Eaglescliffe & Hartlepool, daily 3-5/day

London North Eastern Railway (LNER; 🖳 lner.co.uk)
● London King's Cross to Newcastle/Edinburgh via York, Northallerton & Darlington, daily 1-2/hr to Northallerton Mon-Fri and fewer at the weekend. However, there are additional services if change at York and weekend services may require a change at York.
● London King's Cross to Middlesbrough via York & Thornaby, Mon-Fri 1/day

Northern (☎ 0800 200 6060, 🖳 northernrailway.co.uk)
● Carlisle to Barrow-in-Furness via Whitehaven & **St Bees**, daily 8-10/day (plus approx 4/day Carlisle to Whitehaven in the evening)
● Manchester Airport to Barrow-in-Furness via Manchester Piccadilly, Preston, Lancaster & Carnforth, Mon-Sat 10/day, Sun 8/day
● Manchester Airport to Windermere via Manchester Piccadilly, Lancaster, Oxenholme Lake District & Kendal, Mon-Sat 6/day, Sun 4/day; additional services for Windermere start at Oxenholme Lake District, daily approx 1/hr
● Leeds to Carlisle via Skipton, Settle & **Kirkby Stephen** (🖳 settle-carlisle.co.uk), Mon-Sat 9/day, Sun 6/day
● Middlesbrough to Whitby (Esk Valley Railway; 🖳 eskvalleyrailway.co.uk) via Danby, Lealholm, **Glaisdale**, **Egton** & **Grosmont**, Mon-Sat 4-5/day, Sun 4/day
For more information about getting to: St Bees see p51; to Whitby (for Robin Hood's Bay) see p51; and to Kirkby Stephen see opposite.

TransPennine Express (🖳 tpexpress.co.uk)
● York to Scarborough, approx 1/hr (some services start at Manchester Airport, Liverpool, Leeds or York)
● Manchester Airport to Glasgow or Edinburgh via Manchester, Preston, Lancaster, Oxenholme Lake District & Carlisle, daily approx 1/hr
● Manchester Airport to Redcar via Manchester, Leeds, York, Northallerton, Thornaby & Middlesbrough, daily approx 1/hr
Note: See p244 for details of North York Moors railway services.

can head north-east to Scarborough on the A64, then follow the A171 heading towards Whitby, turning off on the B1447 for Robin Hood's Bay. If coming from Manchester take the M62 north-east to Leeds, then the A64 all the way to Scarborough, from where you pick up the A171 as outlined above.

Getting to Kirkby Stephen

● **Train** Kirkby Stephen is a stop on Northern's Carlisle to Settle/Leeds line (see box opposite for details). Coming from London King's Cross either take an LNER train to Leeds and then catch a Northern train to Kirkby Stephen. There are 3-5 connecting services a day and the whole journey takes about 4½-5¼ hours.

Alternatively take an Avanti West Coast train from London Euston to Carlisle then a Northern train to Kirkby Stephen; the journey takes approximately 4½-5½ hours.

● **Coach/train** The best option is to take a National Express coach to Carlisle (see p51) then a Northern train to Kirkby Stephen.

● **Car** The A685 runs through the town and the trans-Pennine A66 crosses the A685 just four miles north of the town. The nearest motorway, the M6, is 22 miles west of the A66 interchange. (See pp27-9 for information about long-stay parking facilities operated by the baggage-transfer companies.)

LOCAL TRANSPORT SERVICES

Public transport is limited along the Coast to Coast path. While most places have some sort of bus service, these may be irregular and just 1-2/day or even 1/week. Usually the choice of destination is limited too, often the nearest big town.

To check the current bus timetables, visit **traveline** (🖳 traveline.info), which has public transport information for the whole of the UK. This is usually easier than contacting the operator direct as many bus services are run by more than one operator. From the Cumbria County Council website (🖳 cumbria.gov .uk/buses) you can search details of buses, trains and ferries in the county. For information about services in North Yorkshire visit 🖳 dalesbus.org, or 🖳 north yorks.gov.uk/public-transport.

Details of local rail/bus services and operators as well as public transport maps are shown on the following pages. Please note:

● Service details were as accurate as possible at the time of writing but it is essential to check before travel

● Services on Bank Holiday Mondays are usually the same as Sunday services; Monday to Saturday services generally don't operate on Bank Holiday Mondays

● Services generally operate at the same frequency in both directions

● Be aware that where routes are serviced by more than one operator (usually during the peak season), the different operators may not accept each other's tickets

● In rural areas it is usually possible to 'hail and ride' a passing bus though it is important to stand where visibility is good and also somewhere where it would be safe for the driver to stop

● See pp27-9 for details of **Packhorse**'s and **Sherpa Van**'s services along this route.

PLANNING YOUR WALK

☐ BUS SERVICES & OPERATORS – CUMBRIA (see below for North Yorkshire)   SEE p56 FOR MAP

No	Operator	Route and frequency details
30	Stagecoach	Maryport to Frizington via Whitehaven & **Cleator Moor**, Mon-Sat 2/hr, Sun 4/day from Whitehaven
30	Stagecoach	Maryport to Thornhill via Whitehaven & Egremont, Mon-Sat 2/hr, Sun 3/day
77/77A	Stagecoach	(Honister Rambler) Keswick to **Seatoller** circular route via Honister (Slate Mine) & **Rosthwaite**, Easter to Oct daily approx 1/hr
78	Stagecoach	Keswick to **Seatoller** via **Borrowdale** & **Rosthwaite**, daily 2/hr
106	CCC	**Tebay** to Penrith via **Orton** & **Shap**, Tue & Fri 1/day
111	FVB	Penrith to Kendal via **Tebay**, **Orton** & **Shap**, Tue & Fri 1/day
300	Stagecoach	Penrith to **Burnbanks Village**, Thur only 1/day
508	Stagecoach	Whitehaven to Carlisle, Sun 10/day (via Workington, some services start from Whitehaven as service 30)
555	Stagecoach	Penrith to Windermere via Glenridding, **Patterdale** & Bowness on Windermere, daily 6-10/day
570	CCC	Lancaster to Keswick via Kendal, Windermere, Bowness Pier, Ambleside & **Grasmere**, Mon-Sat approx 1/hr plus 8/day fast between Lancaster & Kendal, Sun 4/day plus 7/day Kendal to Keswick
571	CCC	Ravenstonedale to Kendal via **Shap**, **Orton**, Old Tebay & **Tebay**, Thur 1/day
599	Stagecoach	Brough to Kendal via **Kirkby Stephen** & **Tebay**, Mon 1/day
S5	Western Dales	Bowness Pier to **Grasmere** via Windermere, Ambleside & Rydal, Apr-Oct daily 2-3/hr (early morning services start/end in Kendal), Nov-Mar 9/day
S6	Western Dales	**Kirkby Stephen** to Penrith via Ravenstonedale, **Newbiggin-on-Lune** & **Tebay**, Thur only 3/day (1/day starts/ends in Sedbergh)
		Kirkby Stephen to Penrith, Tue only 3/day (1/day starts/ends in Sedbergh)

BUS SERVICES & OPERATORS – NORTH YORKSHIRE

No	Operator	Route and frequency details
M3	Moorsbus*	Darlington to Pickering via Middlesbrough, Guisborough, Danby Lodge Visitor Centre, **(Lion Inn) Blakey**, Hutton le Hole & Kirkbymoorside
M4	Moorsbus*	Saltburn to **Sutton Bank** via Redcar, Guisborough, Great Ayton, Stokesley, **Chop Gate**, **Great Broughton**, Rievaulx & Helmsley
M5	Moorsbus*	Stockton to Helmsley, Stokesley, **Ingleby Cross/Ingleby Arncliffe**, Northallerton, Thirsk & Coxwold

M6	Moorsbus	York to Danby Lodge Visitor Centre via Norton, Malton, Pickering, Rosedale Abbey & Ralph Cross (a 1½-mile walk north from (**Lion Inn**) **Blakey**, some of which is on the CtoC path)

* **Note**: Moorsbus is a volunteer, not for profit, transport provider and they hope to operate all services at weekends and on bank holidays 1- to 2-/day (though 3- to 4-/day inside North York Moors national park) between early June and September though it is possible not all will operate on a Saturday so it is essential to check their website before travel.

X26	Arriva NE	Colburn to Darlington via Catterick Garrison & **Richmond**. Mon-Sat 2/hr, Sun 1/hr starts in Scotton
X27	Arriva NE	Scotton to Darlington via Catterick Garrison & **Richmond**. Mon-Sat 1/hr
29	Hodgsons	Darlington to **Richmond**. Mon-Sat 5-6/day
30	Little White Bus	(Swaledale Shuttle; circular route) **Keld** to **Richmond** via **Thwaite, Muker, Gunnerside,** Low Row, **Reeth,** Grinton & Hudswell. Mon-Sat 3-4/day (Hudswell 2/day), but check the website as some stops must be booked in advance
34	Hodgsons	**Richmond** to Darlington via **Brompton-on-Swale,** Catterick Village, Marne Barracks & Scorton. Mon-Sat 4/day plus 2/day to Marne Barracks
55	Hodgsons	**Richmond** to Northallerton via **Brompton-on-Swale,** Scorton & **Bolton-on-Swale.** Mon-Sat 3/day
80	Abbotts of L	Stokesley to Northallerton via **Ingleby Cross & Osmotherley.** Mon-Sat 3-4/day
89	Abbotts of L	Stokesley to Northallerton via Great Broughton, Kirkby-in-Cleveland, **Ingleby Cross & Osmotherley.** Mon-Sat 3/day
X93/X94	Arriva NE	Scarborough to Whitby via Fylingthorpe, **Robin Hood's Bay & Hawsker,** daily 1-2/hr

Note that one service an hour starts from/continues to **Middlesbrough** (see below) via **Guisborough** and no change of bus is needed; some services are X94.

95	Arriva NE	Whitby to Lealholm via **Grosmont, Egton Bridge & Glaisdale.** Mon-Sat 5-6/day
830	NDales Bus	Preston to **Richmond** via Lancaster, Ribblehead, Hawes, **Muker, Gunnerside, Reeth,** Grinton & Swaleview, Sun & Bank Holidays mid May to late Oct 1/day
831	Arriva NE	**Middlesbrough** to Kirkby Lonsdale via **Richmond, Reeth, Gunnerside, Muker, Thwaite & Keld.** early June-late Oct Sun & Bank Holidays 1/day

Operator contact details

● **Cumbria: Cumbria Classic Coaches** (CCC; ☎ 015396 23254, ▢ cumbriaclassiccoaches.co.uk); **Fellrunner Village Bus** (FVB; ☎ 07734 529432, ▢ fellrunnerbus.co.uk); **Stagecoach** (▢ stagecoachbus.com); **Western Dales** (▢ westerndalesbus.co.uk; services operated by volunteers)
● **North Yorkshire: Abbotts of Leeming** (Abbotts of L; ☎ 01677 422858, ▢ abbottscoaches.co.uk; note both the 80 and 89 services were up for tender at the time of research so check in advance); **Arriva North East** (▢ www.arrivabus.co.uk/north-east); **Hodgsons** (☎ 01833 630730, ▢ hodgsonsbuses.com); **Northern Dalesbus** (NDales Bus▢ dalesbus.org); **Little White Bus** (☎ 01969 667400, ▢ littlewhite bus.co.uk); **Moorsbus** (☎ 01751 477216, ▢ moorsbus.org)

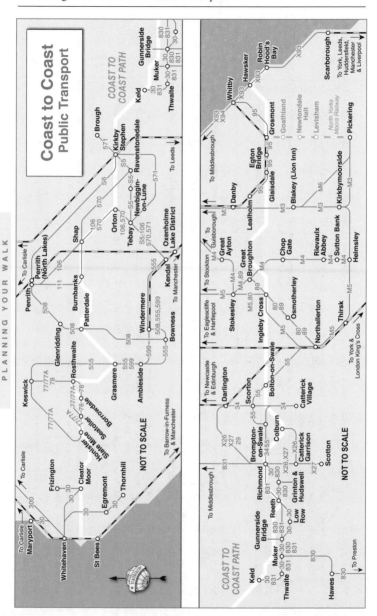

Coast to Coast Public Transport

THE ENVIRONMENT & NATURE

2

Conserving the Coast to Coast path

With a population of over 66 million Britain is a densely populated island and England is the most crowded part of it. As such, the English countryside has suffered a great deal of pressure from both over-population and the activities of an ever more industrialised world. Thankfully, there is some enlightened legislation to protect the surviving pockets of forest and heathland.

Apart from these, it is interesting to note just how much man has altered the land that he lives on. Whilst the aesthetic costs of such intrusions are open to debate, what is certain is the loss of biodiversity that has resulted. The last wild boar was shot near the Coast to Coast trail a few centuries ago; add to that the extinction of bear, wolf and beaver (now being reintroduced in selected pockets in Scotland and Dorset) as well as, far more recently, a number of other species lost or severely depleted over the decades and you get an idea of just how much of an influence man has over the land, and how that influence is all too often used negatively.

There is good news, however. In these enlightened times when environmental issues are quite rightly given more precedence, many endangered species, such as the otter, have increased in number thanks to the active work of voluntary conservation bodies. There are other reasons to be optimistic. The environment is no longer the least important issue in party politics and this reflects the opinions of everyday people who are concerned about issues such as conservation on both a global and local scale.

GOVERNMENT AGENCIES AND SCHEMES

Natural England
Natural England (🖵 gov.uk/government/organisations/natural-eng land) is responsible for enhancing biodiversity, landscape and wildlife in rural, urban, coastal and marine areas; promoting access, recreation and public well-being; and contributing to the way natural resources are managed. One of its roles is to identify, establish and manage national trails (see box p58), national parks, areas of outstanding natural beauty (AONBs), national nature reserves (NNRs),

sites of special scientific interest (SSSIs), and special areas of conservation (SACs) and to enforce regulations relating to these sites.

The highest level of landscape protection is the designation of land as a **national park** which recognises the national importance of an area in terms of landscape, biodiversity and as a recreational resource. This designation does not signify national ownership and these are not uninhabited wildernesses, making conservation a knife-edged balance between protecting the environment and the rights and livelihoods of those living in the parks. At the time of writing there were 10 national parks in England; see ⊟ nationalparksengland.org.uk. Three of these are bisected by the Coast to Coast path: Lake District (⊟ lakedistrict .gov.uk), Yorkshire Dales (⊟ www.yorkshiredales.org.uk) and North York Moors (⊟ northyorkmoors.org.uk). At the time of writing none of these had much in the way of specific Coast to Coast trail information on their websites, though this may change due to the path's forthcoming National trail status.

The second level of protection is **area of outstanding natural beauty** (AONB). The only AONB (see box opposite) passed on the Coast to Coast trail covers the very southern extremity of the North Pennines as you pass Nine Standards Rigg and before you enter the Yorkshire Dales. The primary objective for an AONB is conservation of the natural beauty of a landscape. As there is no statutory administrative framework for their management, this is the responsibility of the local authority within whose boundaries they fall. Some AONBs, including the North Pennines, have also been designated **geoparks** (⊟ euro peangeoparks.org), a European Union initiative originally set up as a socio-economic project to help the development and management of deprived areas which nevertheless benefited from a rich geological heritage, defined as both unique and important. The concept has since moved on, with today's geoparks designed to raise awareness of an area and to educate the general public.

National nature reserves (NNRs) are places where the priority is protection of the wildlife habitats and geological formations. There are currently 224 (including Smardale in Cumbria) in England and they are either owned or managed by Natural England, or by approved organisations such as wildlife trusts.

Local nature reserves (LNRs) are places with wildlife or geological features that are of special interest to local inhabitants; there are 10 in Cumbria and 15 in North Yorkshire. However, these are designated by local councils.

❏ NATIONAL TRAILS

These are Britain's flagship long-distance paths which grew out of the post-war desire to protect the country's special places, a movement which also gave birth to National Parks and AONBs. National Trails in England are largely funded by Natural England and are managed on the ground by a National Trail Officer. They coordinate the maintenance work undertaken by either the local highway authority, or the National Trust, where it crosses their land, and ensure that the trail is kept up to nationally agreed standards.

The Coast to Coast Path will become a National Trail when the upgraded sections of the path (see p92) open in 2025.

❑ **OTHER GOVERNMENT AGENCIES AND BODIES**

● **Historic England** (🖳 historicengland.org.uk) Non departmental public body with a central aim of ensuring that the historic environment of England is properly maintained; over 400,000 places (inc buildings, monuments and parks) are listed.
● **Forestry England** (🖳 forestryengland.uk) Government department for establishing and managing forests for a variety of uses.
● **National Association of Areas of Outstanding Natural Beauty** (🖳 landscapes forlife.org.uk); for further information on the North Pennines AONB visit 🖳 www.northpennines.org.uk.

Sites of Special Scientific Interest (SSSIs) range in size from little pockets protecting wild flower meadows, important nesting sites or special geological features, to vast swathes of upland, moorland and wetland. SSSIs, of which there are over 4100 in England, are a particularly important designation as they have some legal standing. They are managed in partnership with the owners and occupiers of the land who must give written notice before initiating any operations likely to damage the site and who cannot proceed without consent from Natural England. Many SSSIs are also either a NNR or a LNR.

Special Area of Conservation (SAC) is an international designation which came into being as a result of the 1992 Earth Summit in Rio de Janeiro, Brazil. This European-wide network of sites is designed to promote the conservation of habitats, wild animals and plants, both on land and at sea. Every land SAC is also an SSSI.

CAMPAIGNING AND CONSERVATION ORGANISATIONS

These voluntary organisations started the conservation movement in the mid 19th century and are still at the forefront of developments. Independent of government but reliant on public support, they can concentrate their resources either on acquiring land, which can then be managed purely for conservation purposes, or on influencing political decision-makers by lobbying and campaigning.

Managers and owners of land include well-known bodies such as the RSPB, NT and CPRE. The **Royal Society for the Protection of Birds** (**RSPB**; 🖳 rspb.org.uk), has over 150 nature reserves and more than a million members. There are two reserves on the Coast to Coast path, both of great significance. St Bees Head, at the very start of the trail, and Haweswater, at the eastern end of the Lake District; see p144.

The **National Trust** (**NT**; 🖳 nationaltrust.org.uk) is a charity with over three million members which aims to protect, through ownership, threatened coastline, countryside, historic houses, castles and gardens, and archaeological remains for everyone to enjoy. On the Coast to Coast trail, the NT's properties are concentrated in the Lakes where they look after such beauty spots as: Ennerdale, supposedly England's wildest valley; parts of Ullswater; and 4925 hectares (12,170 acres) of Grasmere and Great Langdale including, curiously, the bed of Grasmere Lake, Johnny Wood and Bay Ness (see Map 93).

THE ENVIRONMENT & NATURE

CPRE The Countryside Charity (formerly **Campaign to Protect Rural England**; 🖥 cpre.org.uk) exists to promote the beauty and diversity of rural England by encouraging the sustainable use of land and other natural resources in both town and country.

English Heritage (🖥 www.english-heritage.org.uk) is now a charity that is independent from government and which looks after over 400 historic buildings, monuments and sites; in this respect it often overlaps the work of National Trust. See also Historic England (box p59).

The umbrella organisation for the 47 wildlife trusts in the UK is **The Wildlife Trusts** (🖥 www.wildlifetrusts.org); the two branches relevant to the Coast to Coast path are **Cumbria Wildlife Trust** (🖥 cumbriawildlifetrust.org .uk) and **Yorkshire Wildlife Trust** (🖥 ywt.org.uk).

Woodland Trust (🖥 woodlandtrust.org.uk) restores woodland throughout Britain for its amenity, wildlife and landscape value.

BEYOND CONSERVATION

Pressures on the countryside grow year on year. Western society, whether directly or indirectly, makes constant demands for more oil, more roads, more houses, more cars. At the same time awareness of environmental issues increases, as does the knowledge that our unsustainable approach to life cannot continue. Some governments appear more willing to adopt sustainable ideals, others less so.

Yet even the most environmentally progressive of governments are some way off perfect. It's all very positive to classify parts of the countryside as National Parks and Areas of Outstanding Natural Beauty but it will be of little use if we continue to pollute the wider environment, the seas and skies. For a brighter future we need to adopt that sustainable approach to life. It would not be difficult and the rewards would be great.

The individual can play his or her part. Walkers in particular appreciate the value of wild areas and should take this attitude back home with them. This is not just about recycling the odd green bottle or two and walking to the corner shop rather than driving, but about lobbying for more environmentally sensitive policies in local and national government.

The first step to a sustainable way of living is in appreciating and respecting this beautiful, complex world we live in and realising that every one of us plays an important role within the great web. The natural world is not a separate entity. We are all part of it and should strive to safeguard it rather than work against it. So many of us live in a way that seems far removed from the real world, cocooned in centrally heated houses and upholstered cars. Rediscovering our place within the natural world is both uplifting on a personal level and important regarding our outlook and approach to life.

THE ENVIRONMENT & NATURE

Flora and fauna

The beauty of walking from one side of England to the other is that you pass through just about every kind of habitat this country has to offer. From woodland and grassland to heathland, bog and beach, the variety of habitats is surpassed only by the number of species of flower, tree and animal that each supports.

The following is not in any way a comprehensive guide – if it were, you would not have room for anything else in your rucksack – but merely a brief guide to the more commonly seen flora and fauna of the trail, together with some of the rarer and more spectacular species.

MAMMALS

The Coast to Coast path is alive with all manner of native species and the wide variety of habitats encountered on the way means that the wildlife is varied too. Unfortunately, most of these creatures are shy and many are nocturnal, and walkers can consider themselves extremely lucky if during their trek they see more than three or four species.

One creature that you will see everywhere along the walk, from the cliffs at St Bees to the fields outside Robin Hood's Bay, is the **rabbit** (*Oryctolagus cuniculus*). Timid by nature, most of the time you'll have to make do with nothing more than a brief and distant glimpse of their white tails as they stampede for the nearest warren at the first sound of your footfall. Because they are so numerous, however, the laws of probability dictate that you will at some stage get close enough to observe them without being spotted; trying to take a decent photo of one of them, however, is a different matter.

If you're lucky you may also come across **hares**, often mistaken for rabbits but much larger, more elongated and with longer back legs and ears.

Rabbits used to form one of the main elements in the diet of the **fox** (*Vulpes vulpes*), one of the more adaptable of Britain's native species. Famous as the scourge of chicken coops, their reputation as indiscriminate killers is actually unjustified: though they will if left undisturbed kill all the chickens in a coop in what appears to be a mindless and frenzied attack, foxes will actually eat all their victims, carrying off and storing the carcasses in underground burrows for them and their families to eat at a later date. These days, however, you are far more likely to see foxes in towns, where they survive mostly on the scraps and leftovers of the human population, rather than in the country. While generally considered nocturnal, it's not unusual to encounter a fox during the day too, often lounging in the sun near its den.

One creature that is strictly nocturnal, however, is the **bat**, of which there are 17 species in Britain, all protected by law. Your best chance of spotting one is just after dusk while there's still enough light in the sky to make out their flitting forms as they fly along hedgerows, over rivers and streams and around street lamps in their quest for moths and insects. The most common species in Britain is the pipistrelle (*Pipistrellus pipistrellus*).

The Lakes offer one of the few chances in England to see the rare **red squirrel** (*Sciurus vulgaris*), particularly around Patterdale and Haweswater. While elsewhere in the country these small, tufty-eared natives have been usurped by larger North American cousins, the **grey squirrel** (*Sciurus carolinensis*), in the Lakes the red squirrel maintains a precarious foothold.

Patterdale offers walkers on the Coast to Coast their best chance of seeing the **badger** (*Meles meles*). Relatively common throughout the British Isles, these nocturnal mammals with their distinctive black-and-white-striped muzzles are sociable animals that live in large underground burrows known as setts. They appear after sunset to root for worms and slugs. One creature which you almost certainly won't encounter, though they are said to exist in the Lakes, is the **pine marten** (*Martes martes*). Extremely rare in England since being virtually wiped out during the 19th century for their pelts and their reputation as vermin, there are said to be a few in the valley of Ennerdale, though the last positive identification was in 2011. In addition to the above, keep a look out for other fairly common but little-seen species such as the carnivorous **stoat** (*Mustela erminea*), its smaller cousin the **weasel** (*Mustela nivalis*), the **hedgehog** (*Erinaceus europaeus*) – these days, alas, most commonly seen as roadkill – and a number of species of **voles**, **mice** and **shrews**.

One of Britain's rarest creatures, the **otter** (*Lutra lutra*), is enjoying something of a renaissance thanks to concerted conservation efforts. Though more common in the south-west, otters are still present in the north of England. At home both in salt and freshwater, they are a good indicator of a healthy unpolluted environment. Don't come to the north expecting otter sightings every day though. If you see one at all you should consider yourself *extremely* fortunate, for they remain rare and very elusive. There are said to be some in Swaledale and their numbers are growing.

A surprisingly large number of trekkers encounter deer on their walk. Mostly this will be the **roe deer** (*Capreolus capreolus*), a small native species that likes to inhabit woodland, though some can also be seen grazing in fields. As with most creatures, your best chance of seeing one is very early in the morning, with sightings particularly common in Ennerdale, the upper end of Swaledale and the Vale of Mowbray.

Britain's largest native land mammal, the **red deer** (*Cervus elaphus*), is rarely seen on the walk though it does exist in small pockets around the Lakes.

BIRDS

The Coast to Coast is rich with birds and you don't have to be an expert to connect with them.

There's a real treat at the very start of the trail, north-west England's only seabird cliffs at the RSPB's St Bees Nature Reserve (Map 2). In spring and summer neat black and white auks jostle for space on the narrow ledges, whirr to

and fro on tiny wings and bob about on the sea, their natural element. **Guillemots** (*Uria aalge*) have long pointed beaks and **razorbills** (*Alca torda*) flattened beaks. Look for England's only **black guillemots** (*Cepphus grille*), coal black with a white patch on their side, on the sea; they nest hidden in crevices.

Kittiwakes (*Rissa tridactyla*), small gulls with 'dipped in ink' wingtips loudly call their name, while grey **fulmars** (*Fulmarus glacialis*), relatives of the albatross, circle on stiff wings. Listen for the 'cronk' of big black, wedge-tailed **ravens** (*Corvus corax*) and look out for the grey shape of a perched or hunting **peregrine falcon** (*Falco peregrinus*).

BLACK GUILLEMOT
L: 350MM/13.5"

RSPB's Haweswater Reserve (Maps 28-29) has many of the birds you'll encounter along the path – but sadly not its iconic golden eagles (*Aquila chrysaetos*), for many years the only ones in England. Never managing to raise young, the last female died in 2004, followed by the male in 2016. But there is still lots to see. In the oak woods look out for the red flash of a **redstart's** (*Phoenicurus phoenicurus*) tail, or the neat black-and-white **pied flycatcher** (*Fidecula hypoleuca*), as well as more familiar **tits** (*Parus* species), **treecreepers** (*Certhia familiaris*), and, in big old trees the attractive grey and apricot **nuthatch** (*Sitta europea*). Conifers along the path may have bright red **crossbills** (*Loxia curvirostra*) sitting on the spiky treetops, or tiny green **siskins** (*Carduelis spinus*) making their distinctive song flight. Out in the open, the **ring ouzel** (*Turdus torquata*) is the moorland blackbird, distinguished by the white band across its chest, whilst the much smaller **wheatear** (*Oenanthe oenanthe*) flashes a white rump in flight. **Stonechats** (*Saxicola torquata*), neat in black and orange, sit atop gorse bushes. Look out for the smart, low white flanks and deep green head of a male **goosander** (*Mergus merganser*) on Haweswater, and later in the season the delightful fluffballs of tiny chicks following their chocolate-headed mother.

Eagles may have gone but in 2001, in the middle of the Foot and Mouth outbreak which was a particularly severe disaster for the Lake District, **ospreys** (*Pandion haliaetus*) returned naturally to nest on Bassenthwaite Lake, the first in hundreds of years for England – and over a million people have seen them from the osprey-viewing platforms established by the Lake District Osprey Project.

Skylarks (*Alauda arvensis*) will be with you all along the trail in spring and summer, carrolling high overhead, whilst in the lower farmland there'll be lots of brightly coloured cock **pheasants** (*Phasianus colchicus*) and their duller females. Introduced from China, pheasants are now released in their thousands for shooting.

Along the rushing mountain streams you'll see **dippers** (*Cinclus cinclus*), portly chocolate brown with a white breast. Related to the **wren** (*Troglodytes troglodytes*), they literally walk under water to find their prey. **Common sandpipers** (*Actitis hypoleucos*) bob at the water's edge and the **grey wagtail** (*Motacilla cinerea*) is a beautiful dove grey contrasting with bright lemon yellow.

Even more dramatic – and noisy – are piping black and white **oystercatchers** (*Haematopus ostralegus)* with their stunning orange bills.

The bubbling call of the **curlew** (*Numenius arquata),* brown with the longest curved beak, is the true sound of the moors, along with tumbling, round winged, deep green and white **lapwing** (*Vanellus vanellus*), calling their popular name, 'peewit'. Jumpy **redshank** (*Tringa totanus*) with their red legs and cryptic brown **snipe** (*Gallinago gallinago*), zigzagging away in panicky flight, nest in wetter places but it is the tiny **dunlin** (*Calidris alpina*), a miniature curlew with its curved beak that braves the highest, wettest ridges of the Pennines. There are beautiful **golden plover** (*Pluvialis apricaria*), too – their name says it all, piping their thin call from behind a tussock as they guard their young.

LAPWING/PEEWIT
L: 320MM/12.5"

But the heather moors belong to the **red grouse** (*Lagopus lagopus*) – sturdy, an attractive red-brown, with their iconic 'go-back, go-back' call and whirring flight that makes them such a challenge to shooters. The patchwork of heather, so characteristic of much of the path's landscape, is created by burning to provide the different habitats the grouse need. They are also one of the few birds to stay on the moors through the winter – golden plover move to wet lowland grasslands, dippers move lower down their stream whilst common sandpiper migrate all the way to Africa. You're less likely to see the rare **black grouse** (*Tetrao tetrix*) which are much less numerous.

One bird you will be lucky to see is the beautiful dove-grey **hen harrier** (*Circus cyaneus*), quartering the moors on long black-tipped wings. Reduced to as few as two pairs by systematic and illegal persecution because they eat grouse, the near extinction of this stunning species in England has cast a big question mark over the future of grouse shooting.

Nondescript **meadow pipits** (*Anthus pratensis*) are everywhere on the moors – small, long-tailed, brown with a weak flight and thin piping call, yet able to tough it out in the harshest environment. Dashing grey **merlins** (*Falco columbarius*), miniature peregrines, hunt them fast and low – in contrast to **kestrels** (*Falco tinnunculus*) which hover for voles far below, or the slow circling of broad-winged, eagle-like **buzzards** (*Buteo buteo*).

REPTILES

© Henry Stedman

The **adder** is the only common snake in the north of England, and the only venomous one of the three species in Britain. They pose very little risk to walkers – indeed, you should consider yourself extremely lucky to see one, provided you're a safe distance away. They bite only if provoked, preferring to hide instead. The venom is designed to kill small mammals such as mice, voles and shrews, so deaths in humans are very rare, but a bite can be extremely unpleasant and occasionally dangerous to children or the elderly. You are most likely to encounter them in spring when they come out of hibernation and during the summer when pregnant females warm themselves in the sun. They are easily identified by the striking zigzag pattern on their back. Should you be lucky enough to encounter one, enjoy it but leave it undisturbed.

Gorse
Ulex europaeus

FLOWERS

Spring is the time to come and see the spectacular displays of colour on the Coast to Coast path. Alternatively, arrive in August and you'll see the heathers carpeting the moors in a blaze of purple flowers.

The coastal meadows
The coastline is a harsh environment subjected to strong, salt-laced winds. One plant that does survive in such conditions, and which will probably be the first you'll encounter on the path, is **gorse** (*Ulex europaeus*) with its sharp-thorned bright yellow, heavily scented flowers. Accompanying it are such cliff-top specialists as the pink-flowering **thrift** (*Armeria maritima*) and white **sea campion** (*Silene maritima*) and **fennel** (*Foeniculum vulgare*), a member of the carrot family which grows to over a metre high.

Thrift (Sea Pink)
Armeria maritima

Woodland and hedgerows
From March to May **bluebells** (*Hyacinthoides nonscripta*) proliferate in the woods along the Coast to Coast, providing a wonderful spectacle. Little Beck (see p250) and Clain (see p224) woods are particularly notable for these displays. The white **wood anemone** (*Anemone nemorosa*) and the yellow **primrose**

Sea Campion
Silene maritima

THE ENVIRONMENT AND NATURE

Dog Rose
Rosa canina

Forget-me-not
Myosotis arvensis

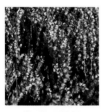

Heather (Ling)
Calluna vulgaris

(*Primula vulgaris*) also flower early in spring. **Red campion** (*Silene dioica*), which flowers from late April, can be found in hedge banks along with **rosebay willowherb** (*Epilobium angustifolium*) which also has the name fireweed due to its habit of colonising burnt areas.

In scrubland and on woodland edges you'll find **bramble** (*Rubus fruticosus*), a common vigorous shrub, responsible for many a ripped jacket thanks to its sharp thorns and prickles. **Blackberry** fruits ripen from late summer into autumn. Fairly common in scrubland and on woodland edges is the **dog rose** (*Rosa canina*) which has a large pink flower, the fruits of which are used to make rose-hip syrup.

Other flowering plants common in wooded areas and in hedgerows include the tall **foxglove** (*Digitalis purpurea*) with its trumpet-like flowers, **forget-me-not** (*Myosotis arvensis*) with tiny, delicate blue flowers and **cow parsley** (*Anthriscus sylvestris*), a tall member of the carrot family with a large globe of white flowers which often covers roadside verges and hedge banks.

Heathland and scrubland

There are three species of heather. The most dominant one is **ling** (*Calluna vulgaris*), with tiny flowers on delicate upright stems. The other two species are **bell heather** (*Erica cinerea*), with deep purple bell-shaped flowers, and **cross-leaved heath** (*Erica tetralix*) with similarly shaped flowers of a lighter pink, almost white colour. Cross-leaved heath prefers wet and boggy ground. As a result, it usually grows away from bell heather which prefers well-drained soils.

Heather is an incredibly versatile plant which is put to many uses. It provides fodder for livestock, fuel for

THE ENVIRONMENT AND NATURE

Bell Heather
Erica cinerea

Foxglove
Digitalis purpurea

Bluebell
Hyacinthoides non-scripta

Common Dog Violet
Viola riviniana

Heartsease (Wild Pansy)
Viola tricolor

Common Vetch
Vicia sativa

Lousewort
Pedicularis sylvatica

Primrose
Primula vulgaris

Ox-eye Daisy
Leucanthemum vulgare

Rowan (tree)
Sorbus aucuparia

Common Hawthorn
Crataegus monogyna

Red Campion
Silene dioica

Rosebay Willowherb
Epilobium angustifolium

Yarrow
Achillea millefolium

Hogweed
Heracleum sphondylium

THE ENVIRONMENT AND NATURE

Bird's-foot trefoil
Lotus corniculatus

Germander Speedwell
Veronica chamaedrys

Tormentil
Potentilla erecta

Early Purple Orchid
Orchis mascula

fires, an orange dye and material for bedding, thatching, basketwork and brooms. It is still sometimes used in place of hops to flavour beer, and the flower heads can be brewed to make good tea. It is also incredibly hardy and thrives on the denuded hills, preventing other species from flourishing. Indeed, at times, highland cattle are brought to certain areas of the moors to graze on the heather, allowing other species a chance to grow.

Not a flower but worthy of mention is the less attractive species, **bracken** (*Pteridium aquilinum*), a vigorous non-native fern that has invaded many heathland areas to the detriment of native species.

Grassland

There is much overlap between the hedge/woodland-edge habitat and that of pastures and meadows. You will come across **common bird's-foot trefoil** (*Lotus corniculatus*), **Germander speedwell** (*Veronica chamaedrys*), **tufted** and **bush vetch** (*Vicia cracca* and *V. sepium*) and **meadow vetchling** (*Lathyrus pratensis*) in both.

Often the only species you will see in heavily grazed pastures are the most resilient. Of the thistles, the three most common species are **creeping thistle**, **spear thistle** and **marsh thistle** (*Cirsium arvense, C. vulgare* and *C. palustre*). Among them you may find **common ragwort** (*Senecio jacobaea*), **yarrow** (*Achillea millefolium*), **sheep's** and **common sorrel** (*Rumex acetosella* and *R. acetosa*), and **white** and **red clover** (*Trifolium repens* and *T. pratense*).

Other widespread grassland species include **harebell** (*Campanula rotundifolia*), delicate yellow **tormentil** (*Potentilla erecta*) which will often spread up onto the lower slopes of mountains along with **devil's-bit scabious** (*Succisa pratensis*). Also keep an eye out for orchids such as the **fragrant orchid** (*Gymnadenia conopsea*) and **early purple orchid** (*Orchis mascula*).

TREES

It seems incredible that, before man and his axe got to work, most of the bleak, empty moors and windswept Lakeland fells were actually covered by trees. Overgrazing of land by sheep and, to a lesser extent, deer, which eat the young shoots of trees, has ensured that the ancient forests have never returned. These days, the biggest areas of tree cover are the ghastly pine plantations of Ennerdale and other places in the Lakes. Yet

Ramsons (Wild Garlic)
Allium ursinum

Meadow Buttercup
Ranunculus acris

Marsh Marigold (Kingcup)
Caltha palustris

Meadow Cranesbill
Geranium pratense

Water Avens
Geum rivale

Scarlet Pimpernel
Anagallis arvensis

Harebell
Campanula rotundifolia

Herb-Robert
Geranium robertianum

Cotton Grass
Eriophorum angustifolium

Common Ragwort
Senecio jacobaea

Hemp-nettle
Galeopsis speciosa

Cowslip
Primula veris

THE ENVIRONMENT AND NATURE

there are still small patches of indigenous woodland on the Coast to Coast path. Perhaps the most interesting are the Atlantic Oakwoods at Borrowdale, including Johnny Wood (see Map 14) on the way to Longthwaite. The woods are cared for by the National Trust and are actually correctly known as temperate rainforest, the moist Atlantic climate creating a landscape of boulders covered by liverworts and ferns, under **oaks** (*Quercus petraea*) dripping in moss and lichen.

There are other areas of woodland in the Lakes, including Easedale Woods on the way into Grasmere and Glenamara Park, just before Patterdale, which has some truly spectacular mature trees. One interesting thing about oak trees is that they support more kinds of insects than any other tree in Britain and some of these insects affect the oak in interesting ways. The eggs of the gall-fly, for example, cause growths on the leaves, known, appropriately enough, as galls. Each of these contains a single insect. Other kinds of gall-flies lay eggs in stalks or flowers, leading to flower galls – growths the size of currants.

Oak woodland is a diverse habitat and not exclusively made up of oak. Other trees that flourish in oak woodland include **downy birch** (*Betula pubescens*), its relative the **silver birch** (*Betula pendula)*, **holly** (*Ilex aquifolium*), and **hazel** (*Corylus avellana*) which has traditionally been used for coppicing (where small trees are grown for periodic cutting). Further east there are some examples of limestone woodland. **Ash** (*Fraxinus excelsior*) and oak dominate, along with **wych elm** (*Ulmus glabra*), **sycamore** (*Acer*) and **yew** (*Taxus*). **Hawthorn** (*Crataegus monogyna*) also grows on the path, usually in isolated pockets on pasture. These species are known as pioneer species and play a vital role in the ecosystem by improving the soil. It is these pioneers, particularly the **rowan** (*Sorbus aucuparia*) and hawthorn, that you will see growing all alone on inaccessible crags and ravines. Without interference from man, these pioneers would eventually be succeeded by longer-living species such as oak. In wet, marshy areas and along rivers and streams you are more likely to find **alder** (*Alnus glutinosa*).

Colour photos (following pages)

● **Opposite**: Looking back from Grisedale Tarn down the trail to Grasmere. At Grisedale Tarn there's a choice of routes to Patterdale. Easiest is the **Grisedale Valley route**, the **St Sunday Crag route** is a hard climb but with superb views and for the **Helvellyn route** you'll need a very good head for heights for the Striding Edge ridge walk (see next page).

● **pp72-3 Top – left**: The St Sunday Crag route (west to east) ascends to The Cape (Map 21). **Centre**: Allan Bank's walls are adorned with giant portraits of previous residents, including the Romantic poets, Wordsworth and Coleridge (p125). **Right**: Striding Edge (© HS).
Middle – left to right: 1. Grisedale Tarn. 2. Behind St Oswald's in Grasmere, you can visit Wordsworth's grave. 3. Minding the bar in the White Lion, Patterdale (Map 25).
Bottom – left to right: 1. This sculpture stands at the seven-mile mark (Map 4). 2. Wordsworth's Dove Cottage (p125) in Grasmere. 3. Take a steamer trip on beautiful Ullswater (p138).

● **pp74-5 Clockwise from top left**: 1. The trail takes you into the North York Moors National Park (Stage 11). 2. On the idyllic Swaledale Valley route (Stage 8). 3. Try to catch a performance at Richmond's Theatre Royal, the most complete Georgian theatre in the country, dating back to 1788 (p200; © BT). 4. The mysterious Nine Standards (p169) mark the boggy transit of the Pennines (© BT). 5. The ruins of Richmond Castle rise above the River Swale (Map 61). 6. East Gill Force waterfall (Map 50).

MINIMUM IMPACT & OUTDOOR SAFETY

Minimum impact walking

ENVIRONMENTAL IMPACT

A walking holiday in itself is an environmentally friendly approach to tourism, but here are some ideas on how to further minimise your impact on the environment while walking the Coast to Coast.

Use public transport whenever possible

Public transport along the trail is not bad, with many places served by at least one bus or train a day. Public transport is always preferable to using private cars; it benefits visitors, locals and the environment.

Never leave litter

'Pack it in, pack it out'. Leaving litter is antisocial so carry a degradable bag for all your rubbish, organic or otherwise and even other people's too, and pop it in a bin in the next village. Better still, reduce what you take with you by getting rid of packaging in advance.

● **Is it OK if it's biodegradable?** Not really. Apple cores, banana skins, orange peel and the like are unsightly, encourage flies, ants and wasps, and ruin a picnic spot for others; they can also take months to decompose. Either bury them or take them away with you.

Buy local

Buying local produce not only reduces the amount of pollution and congestion that food transportation creates, so-called 'food miles', it also ensures that you are supporting local farmers and producers.

Erosion

● **Stay on the main trail** The effect of your footsteps may seem minuscule but when multiplied by several thousand walkers each year they become rather more significant. Avoid taking shortcuts, widening the trail or taking more than one path, especially across hay meadows and ploughed fields. At the time of writing this was particularly true on the boggy Pennine stage, which is divided into three trails to be used for four months a year (see pp169-72), so reducing

---

(Opposite) Above: Trail's end is at Robin Hood's Bay. Reward yourself with a pint or an icecream – or several of both – at the Bay Hotel (see p259). **Below**: Beautiful Little Beck Wood (p250) offers welcome respite from the moors. You'll pass the hollowed out boulder known as The Hermitage (**bottom**) and Falling Foss Waterfall (**left**), with its tea garden nearby. **Centre**: Fat Betty (p241).

erosion on any one trail. However, this may change due to the National Trail work.

● **Consider walking out of season** The high season for walkers coincides with the time of year when nature wants to do most of its growth and repair, meaning the trail is often prevented from recovering. Walking at less busy times eases this pressure while also generating year-round income for the local economy. It may also make the walk a more relaxing experience with fewer people on the path and less competition for accommodation.

Respect all flora and fauna

Care for all wildlife you come across along the path; it has as much right to be there as you. Tempting as it may be to pick wild flowers, leave them so the next people who pass can enjoy them too. Don't break branches off trees.

If you come across wildlife keep your distance and don't watch for too long. Your presence can cause considerable stress, particularly if the adults are with young, or in winter when food is scarce. Young animals are rarely abandoned. If you come across young birds keep away so that their mother can return.

The code of the outdoor loo

'Going' in the outdoors is a lost art worth reclaiming, for your sake and everyone else's. As more and more people discover the joys of the outdoors this is becoming an important issue. In some parts of the world where visitor pressure is higher than in Britain, walkers and climbers are required to pack out their excrement. This might one day be necessary here. Human excrement is not only offensive to our senses but, more importantly, can infect water sources.

● **Where to go** Wherever possible **use a toilet**. Public toilets are marked on the trail maps in this guide; you'll also find toilets in pubs, cafés and campsites. If you do have to go outdoors, avoid ruins which can otherwise be welcome shelter for walkers, as well as sites of historic or archaeological interest, and choose a place that is at least **30 metres away from running water**. Use a stick or trowel to **dig a small hole** about 15cm (6") deep to bury your excrement. It decomposes quicker when in contact with the top layer of soil or leaf mould. Stirring loose soil into your deposit speeds up decomposition. Do not squash it under rocks as this slows down the composting process. If you have to use rocks to cover it make sure they are not in contact with your faeces.

● **Toilet paper and tampons** Toilet paper takes a long time to decompose whether buried or not. It is easily dug up by animals and may then blow into water sources or onto the path. The best method for dealing with it is to **pack it out**. Put the used paper inside a paper bag which you then place inside a degradable plastic bag. Then simply empty the contents of the paper bag at the next toilet you come across and throw the bag away. If this is too much bother, light your used toilet paper and watch it burn until the flames are out; you don't want to start a wild fire. Pack out **tampons** and **sanitary towels**; they take years to decompose and may also be dug up and scattered about by animals.

Wild camping

Strictly speaking, wild camping is not allowed anywhere in England apart from in Dartmoor National Park. If you do wild camp anywhere on the C2C path, you must always ask the landowner for permission. In most cases this is impractical so don't camp on farmland at all, but on uncultivated land or in forests, and follow these suggestions:

● **Be discreet** Camp alone or in small groups, spend only one night in each place, pitch your tent late and leave early.

● **Never light a fire** Accidental fire is a great fear for farmers and foresters. Never make a camp fire; take matches and cigarette butts out with you to dispose of safely. The deep burn caused by camp fires, no matter how small, damages turf which can take years to recover. Cook on a camp stove instead.

● **Don't use soap or detergent** There is no need to use soap; even biodegradable soaps and detergents pollute streams. You won't be away from a shower for more than a couple of days. Wash up without detergent; use a plastic or metal scourer, or failing that, a handful of fine pebbles or some bracken or grass.

● **Leave no trace** Endeavour to leave no sign of having been there: no moved boulders, ripped up vegetation or dug drainage ditches. Before departing, pick up any litter and leave the place in the same state you found it in, or better.

❏ THE COUNTRYSIDE CODE

The Countryside Code, originally described in the 1950s as the Country Code, was revised and relaunched in 2004, in part because of the changes brought about by the CRoW Act (see p80); it has been updated several times since, the last time in 2022. The Code seems like common sense but sadly some people still appear to have no understanding of how to treat the countryside they walk in. A summary of the latest Code (🖥 gov.uk/government/publications/the-countryside-code), launched under the banner 'Respect. Protect. Enjoy.', is given below.

Respect other people
● be considerate to those living in, working in and enjoying the countryside
● leave gates and property as you find them
● do not block access to gateways or driveways when parking
● be nice, say hello, share the space
● follow local signs and keep to marked paths unless wider access is available

Protect the natural environment
● take your litter home – leave no trace of your visit
● do not light fires and only have BBQs where signs say you can
● always keep dogs under control and in sight
● dog poo – bag it and bin it – any public waste bin will do
● care for nature – do not cause damage or disturbance

Enjoy the outdoors
● check your route and local conditions
● plan your adventure – know what to expect and what you can do
● enjoy your visit, have fun, make a memory

ACCESS

Britain is a crowded island with few places where you can wander as you please. Most of the land is a patchwork of fields and agricultural land and the terrain through which this path marches is no different. However, there are countless public rights of way, in addition to this path, that criss-cross the land. This is fine, but what happens if you feel a little more adventurous and want to explore the moorland, woodland and hills that can also be found near the walk?

Right to roam

The Countryside & Rights of Way Act 2000 (CRoW), or 'Right to Roam' as dubbed by walkers, came into effect in 2005 after a long campaign to allow greater public access to areas of countryside in England and Wales deemed to be uncultivated open country; essentially moorland, heathland, downland and upland areas. Some land is covered by restrictions (high-impact activities such as driving, cycling and horse-riding are not permitted) and some land is excluded (gardens, parks, cultivated land). Full details are on the Natural England website (see p41).

> ❏ **LAMBING**
>
> Lambing takes place from mid March to mid May when dogs should not be taken along the path. Even a dog secured on a lead can disturb a pregnant ewe. If you see a lamb or ewe that appears to be in distress contact the nearest farmer. Also, be aware of cows with calves.

With more freedom in the countryside comes a need for more responsibility from the walker. Remember that wild open country is still the workplace of farmers and home to wildlife. Have respect for both and avoid disturbing either.

Outdoor safety

AVOIDANCE OF HAZARDS

With good planning most hazards can be avoided. Always make sure you have suitable **clothing** (pp42-3) to keep warm and dry, whatever the conditions, and a change of inner clothes. Carrying plenty of food and water is vital.

The **emergency signal** is six blasts on the whistle or six flashes with a torch, best done when you think someone might see or hear them.

Safety on the Coast to Coast path

Sadly every year people are injured while walking the Coast to Coast path. The most dangerous section is the Lake District, where the visitor numbers, elevation, lack of signage (at the time of writing) and sometimes extreme weather all combine to imperil walkers. Locally based mountain-rescue teams, such as the ones in Patterdale and Kirkby Stephen, are staffed by volunteers who are ready 24 hours a day, 365 days of the year. In an emergency phone ☎ 999 and the police will activate the service. Rescue teams rely on donations. All rescue teams should be treated as very much the last resort, however, and it's vital you take every precaution to ensure your own safety:

● Avoid walking on your own if possible, particularly on the Lakeland fells.
● Make sure that somebody knows your plans for every day that you're on the trail. This could be a friend or relative whom you have promised to call every night, or the place you plan to stay in at the end of each day's walk. That way, if you fail to turn up or call that evening, they can raise the alarm.
● If the weather closes in suddenly and mist descends while you're on the trail, particularly on the moors or fells, and you become uncertain of the correct trail, do not be tempted to continue. Just wait where you are and you'll find that mist often clears, at least for long enough to allow you to get your bearings. If you're still uncertain, and the weather does not look like improving, return the way you came to the nearest point of civilisation.
● Fill up with water at every opportunity and carry some high-energy snacks.
● Always carry a torch, compass, map, whistle, phone and wet-weather gear.
● Wear sturdy boots, not trainers. ● Be extra vigilant if walking with children.

Dealing with an accident
● Use basic first aid to treat the injury to the best of your ability.
● Work out exactly where you are. If possible leave someone with the casualty while others go to get help. If there are only two people, you have a dilemma. If you decide to get help leave all spare clothing and food with the casualty.
● In an emergency dial ☎ 999 (or the EU standard number ☎ 112). Don't assume your mobile won't work up on the fells. However, before you call work out exactly where you are; on the app What3words (🖥 what3words.com) the world is divided into three-metre squares and each has its own three-word geocode so it makes it easy to tell people where you are. **See p261 for the what3words refs for the waypoints in this book**.

WEATHER FORECASTS

The Coast to Coast suffers from very unpredictable weather so try to find out what the weather is going to be like before you set off for the day, especially if heading for high routes in the Lakes. Many hostels and tourist information centres will have pinned up somewhere a summary of the weather forecast.

The **Mountain Weather Information Service** (🖥 mwis.org.uk) gives detailed online forecasts for the upland regions of Britain including the Lake District and Yorkshire Dales. Forecasts are also available at 🖥 metoffice .gov.uk. Pay close attention to the forecast and consider altering your plans accordingly. That said, even if a sunny day is forecast, always assume the worst and pack some wet-weather gear in your rucksack.

BLISTERS

It's essential to try out new boots before embarking on your long trek. Make sure they're comfortable and once on the move try to avoid getting them wet on the inside and remove small stones or twigs that get in the boot. Air and massage your feet at lunchtime, keep them clean, and change your socks regularly.

As soon as you start to feel any hot spots developing, stop and apply a few strips of low-friction zinc oxide tape. Leave it on until your foot is pain free or the tape starts to come off. As you're walking continuously the chances are it won't get better, but it won't get worse so quickly. If you know you have problems apply the tape pre-emptively. If you've left it too late and a blister has developed you should apply a plaster such as Compeed. Many walkers have Compeed to thank for enabling them to complete their walk; they can last for up to two days even when wet and work with a combination of good adhesive, a gel pad and a slippery outer surface. Popping a blister reduces the pressure but can lead to infection. If the skin is broken keep the area clean with antiseptic and cover with a non-adhesive dressing material held in place with tape.

Blister-avoiding strategies include rubbing the prone area with Vaseline or wearing a thin and a thick sock as well as adjusting the tension of your laces. All are ways of reducing rubbing and foot movement against the inside of the boot.

HYPOTHERMIA

Also known as exposure, hypothermia occurs when the body can't generate enough heat to maintain its normal temperature, usually as a result of being wet, cold, unprotected from the wind, tired and hungry. It's usually more of a problem in upland areas such as in the Lakes and on the moors.

Hypothermia is easily avoided by wearing suitable clothing, carrying and consuming enough food and drink, being aware of the weather conditions and checking the morale of your companions. Early signs to watch for are feeling cold and tired with involuntary shivering. Find some shelter as soon as possible

---

❏ TIPS FROM A TWO-TIME COAST-TO-COASTER – BLITZING BLISTERS

My local podiatry unit of the NHS recommended **Pedigel elasticated gel** (🖳 foot caresupplies.com). I bought a strip to cut into the appropriate lengths to slip over specific toes; in my case, the two smallest on each foot, as a preventative measure right from the start. This product appears indestructible, requiring no replacement for the entire C2C. It is easily slipped off before showering, and at night, and appears to retain its preventive properties indefinitely. I completed the entire walk without the trace of a blister!

I am also grateful to your guidebook for introducing me to **zinc oxide tape** for toe protection. One roll lasts for ever, it seems. I applied the tape to my middle toes. After two or three showers (bathroom not rainfall) the tape needs renewing.

I was also comforted by a supply of **Compeed plasters** in my washbag just in case. The cheaper alternatives to Compeed I have found a false economy.

This prompts me to mention footwear. In 2014 I bought a pair of approach shoes for Offa's Dyke. I used them for a walk from Suffolk to Dover. As summer footwear they are extremely comfortable and sufficiently rugged to protect feet and toes in most conditions. But then I wore them for my second C2C walk. Despite the Gore-Tex protection, fabric topped boots or shoes are not sufficiently waterproof, and are too low-cut around the ankles, for the bogs on C2C. Traditional **leather walking boots** seemed almost universal among my fellow Coasters. Quite right, too!

Geoffrey Simms

and warm the victim up with a hot drink and some chocolate or other high-energy food. If possible give them another warm layer of clothing and allow them to rest until feeling better. If allowed to worsen, erratic behaviour, slurring of speech and poor co-ordination will become apparent and the victim can very soon progress into unconsciousness, followed by coma and death. Quickly get the victim out of wind and rain, improvising a shelter if necessary.

Rapid restoration of bodily warmth is essential and best achieved by bare-skin contact: someone should get into the same sleeping bag as the patient, both having stripped to the bare essentials, placing any spare clothing under or over them to build up heat. Send or call urgently for help.

HYPERTHERMIA

Not an ailment that you would normally associate with the north of England, hyperthermia (heat exhaustion and heatstroke) is a serious problem nonetheless. Symptoms of **heat exhaustion** include thirst, fatigue, giddiness, a rapid pulse, raised body temperature, low urine output and, if not treated, delirium and finally a coma. The best cure is to drink plenty of water.

Heatstroke is another matter altogether, and even more serious. A high body temperature and an absence of sweating are early indications, followed by symptoms similar to hypothermia such as a lack of co-ordination, convulsions and coma. Death will follow if treatment is not given instantly. Sponge the victim down, wrap them in wet towels, fan them, and get help immediately.

SUNBURN

It can happen, even in northern England and even on overcast days. The only surefire way to avoid it is to stay wrapped up or smother yourself in sunscreen (with a minimum factor of 30) and apply it regularly throughout the day. Don't forget your lips, nose and the back of your neck.

COLLAPSE OF MORALE

This is not something that can be quickly treated with medication, but is probably the biggest cause of abandoned attempts on the Coast to Coast walk. Weather and injury which add up to exhaustion might be presumed to be the most common culprit but, as we know, plenty manage the walk in monsoonal conditions and hobble into Robin Hood's Bay with a great experience behind them. Others though, can suddenly think: 'what's the point, I'm not enjoying this'.

What it all boils down to is this: knowing your limitations and addressing your motivation; matching expectations with your companions; avoiding putting yourself under stress and being flexible rather than insisting on hammering out every last mile without repetition, hesitation or deviation. You can add having good equipment to that list too.

Above all, settle on a **realistic schedule** with at least one, if not two, rest days over the full trek. Even then, it's amazing how sore muscles and feet can recover overnight, especially if you can at least start the day in sunshine. Don't assume a rest day has to be in a town such as Kirkby Stephen or Richmond. A big room in a lone moorland farmhouse or even two nights in a holiday cottage with a telly or a fat book may suit those who find the bigger towns an intrusion on the spirit of the walk. It's not fashionable to admit it, but not every day on the Coast to Coast will necessarily be a winner. It's one reason why many people go on to do the walk again and again; the first time is often looked back on as an eye-opening reconnaissance.

Perhaps the best way to avoid the risk of getting fed up is not to tackle the full 190 or so miles in one go. Wainwright certainly didn't. Thirteen days non-stop on the trail, come rain or shine, really is a bit much for most people (a schedule which at first glance the 13 stages of this book may seem to encourage). Some days end up as nothing more than forced marches or gritty lessons in pain management because, for many, our prized vacation time is treated as an extension of our busy work life where we must make the most of every minute, 24/7.

At Trailblazer we propose: turn on, tune in and slow down.

Using this guide

The route is described from west to east and divided into 13 stages. Though each of these roughly corresponds to a day's walk between centres of accommodation, it's not necessarily the best way to structure *your* trek. There are enough places to stay – barring a couple of stretches – for you to pretty much divide the walk up however you want.

On pp36-8 are tables to help you plan an **itinerary**. To provide further help, **practical information** is presented on the trail maps, including waypoints (WPT) and walking times, places to stay, camp and eat, as well as shops from which to buy provisions.

Further **service details** are given in the text under the entry for each settlement. See box pp90-2 for **navigation trouble spots**. For **map profiles** and cumulative **distance chart** see the colour pages at the end of the book.

TRAIL MAPS   [see key map inside cover; symbols key p84]

Scale and walking times

The trail maps are to **a scale of 1:20,000** (1cm = 200m; 3¹/₈ inches = one mile). Each full-size map covers about two miles but that's a very rough estimate owing to variety of terrain.

Walking times are given along the side of each map; the arrow shows the direction to which the time refers. Black triangles indicate the points between which the times have been taken. These times are merely a tool to help you plan and are not there to judge your walking ability.

After a couple of days you'll know how fast you walk compared with the time bars and can plan your days more accurately as a result. **See note on walking times in the box below**.

❏ **IMPORTANT NOTE – WALKING TIMES**

Unless otherwise specified, **all times in this book refer only to the time spent walking**. You should add 20-30% to allow for rests, photos, checking the map, drinking water etc, not to mention time simply to stop and stare. When planning the day's hike count on 5-7 hours' actual walking.

Up or down?

The trail is shown as a red dashed line. An arrow across the trail indicates the slope; two arrows show that it is steep. Note that the arrow points towards the higher part of the trail. If, for example, you are walking from A (at 80m) to B (at 200m) and the trail between the two is short and steep it would be shown thus: A – – – >> – – – – B. Reversed arrow heads indicate a downward gradient. Note that the *arrow points uphill*, the opposite of what OS maps use on steep roads. A good way to remember our style is '**front pointing on crampons up** a steep slope' and 'open arms – Julie Andrews style – **spreading out to unfold the view down** below.'

Other features

The numbered GPS waypoints refer to the list of **OS grid references** on pp262-5 and the list of **what3words references** on p261. Other features are marked on the map when they are pertinent to navigation. A red triangle ⚠ indicates either **1)** an area of navigational difficulty: advice written directly below the symbol, or **2)** possible route changes proposed in the area as the trail is upgraded to National Trail status (2022-5); watch for new signs.

ACCOMMODATION

Accommodation marked on the map is either on or within easy reach of the path. Many B&B proprietors based a mile or two off the trail will offer to collect walkers from the nearest point on the trail and take them back next morning.

Details of each place are given in the accompanying text. The number of **rooms** of each type is given at the beginning of each entry, ie: **S** = Single, **T** = Twin room, **D** = Double room, **Tr** = Triple room and **Qd** = Quad. Note that many of the triple/quad rooms have a double bed and one/two single beds thus in a group of three or four, two people would have to share the double bed but it also means the room can be used as a double or twin.

Your room will either have **en suite** (bath or shower) facilities, or a **private** or **shared** bathroom or shower room just outside/near the bedroom.

Rates quoted for B&B-style accommodation are **per person (pp)** based on two people sharing a room for a one-night stay; rates are usually discounted for longer stays. Where a single room **(sgl)** is available the rate for that is quoted if different from the rate per person. The rate for single occupancy **(sgl occ)** of a double/twin is generally higher and may be the room rate; the per person rate for three/four sharing a triple/quad is usually lower. At some places the only option is a **room rate**; this will be the same whether one or two people (or more if permissible) use the room. See p22 for more information on rates.

The text also indicates whether the premises have: **WI-FI** (WI-FI); if a bath (◗) is available either as part of en suite facilities, or in a separate bathroom – for those who prefer a relaxed soak at the end of the day; if a **packed lunch** (Ⓛ)

❑ **Opening days and hours** for pubs, restaurants and cafés are as accurate as possible but check in advance, especially if there are few eating places in the area.

ROUTE GUIDE AND MAPS

can be prepared, subject to prior arrangement; and if **dogs** (— see also p31) are welcome, again subject to prior arrangement, in at least one room. The policy on charging for dogs varies; many places make an additional charge per day or per stay, while some may require a refundable deposit against any potential damage or mess.

ST BEES   see map p89

Situated close to the county's westernmost point, the ancient village of St Bees makes a fine starting point to your walk. Sleepy for the most part – except for the rowdy Friday nights when the workers from Sellafield come to let off some steam – St Bees has just enough facilities and services to set you on your way. The village is agricultural in origin; many of the buildings along the main street were once farms dating back to the 17th century and, on Outrigg, there's even an ancient **pinfold** – a circular, stone-walled enclosure once used to house stray livestock recovered from the surrounding hills. The livestock would remain in the pinfold until the farmer could afford to pay a fine to retrieve them.

The town's main sight is its distinctive red sandstone **Priory Church**, once part of a thriving 12th-century Benedictine priory dedicated to the saints Bega (see box below) and Mary. Original Norman features include the impressively elaborate Great West Door and, standing opposite, the curious carved Dragon Stone, a door

lintel also from the 12th century. The church is believed to stand on a site that had been holy to Christians for centuries prior to the monastery's foundation and has seen over eight hundred years of unbroken worship since then. Not even the dissolution of the monasteries ordered by Henry VIII in 1538, which led to the closure of this and every other priory you'll come across on the Coast to Coast path, could stop the site from being used by the villagers as their main centre of worship even though Henry's commissioners had removed the lead from the roof and for much of the 16th century the whole building was left open to the elements. Restoration began in the early 17th century, with a major overhaul of the building taking place in the 19th. Thankfully, however, the architects preserved much of the church's sturdy Norman character.

As with several of the larger churches on the route, there's a table just inside the door with various pamphlets on the history of both the church and the village. Don't

ROUTE GUIDE AND MAPS

❑ WHO WAS ST BEES?

St Bees is actually a corruption of **St Bega**, an Irish princess who fled her native country sometime between the 6th and 9th centuries to avoid an arranged marriage with a Norwegian prince. Landing on England's north-west coast, St Bega lived as a hermit and became renowned for her good deeds. Legends grew up around her over the centuries. In the most famous of these, St Bega approached Lord Egremont to ask for some land for a convent she wished to found.

Egremont promised St Bega all the land covered by snow the next day; which, as it was to be midsummer's day, was not as generous an offer as it first appeared. Miraculously, however, snow did fall that day and St Bega was able to build her convent, around which the village was founded.

St Bega statue, St Bees

© Joel Newton

miss the glass case in the southern aisle displaying a shroud and a lock of woman's hair unearthed in the excavation of a 14th-century grave; and the graveyard to the north of the church, where you'll find the shaft of a stone cross from the 10th century (in other words, older than every other part of the church), with its Celtic decorations still visible.

St Bees School across the road from the church is one of the most venerable in Cumbria, having been founded by **Edmund Grindal** on his deathbed in 1583. Grindal rose to become Archbishop of Canterbury during the reign of Elizabeth I and his birthplace, on the junction of Finkle St and Cross St, is the oldest surviving house in St Bees. The school itself, the alma mater of Rowan Atkinson amongst other luminaries, was forced to close in 2015 due to financial difficulties, but it re-opened in September 2018 in partnership with a Chinese education group.

Services

There's some **tourist information** on the town's website (🖳 stbees.org.uk).

St Bees Post Office (☎ 01946 822343; **fb**; Mon-Fri 9am-5.30pm, Sat to 2pm) offers banking facilities for anyone with a UK-issued card. However, it may be more useful for the **shop** (daily 7am-8pm) which has a decent selection of groceries and toiletries plus hot pies, wine and beer, and Coast to Coast maps and souvenirs.

You can also buy provisions, books and maps in **Hartley's Beach Shop & Tea Room** (see Where to eat). There's also a **public phone** by the station.

Two things the town lacks are an outdoor shop and a pharmacy, but a 10-minute train ride north to **Whitehaven** will deliver you alongside a huge Tesco as well as both a Millets and a Boots on King St, 10 minutes' walk into town. Alternatively, you have to wait until you reach Grasmere.

Transport (see also p52 & pp54-6)

There are no bus services to St Bees so the only public transport option for getting here is by **train**; St Bees is on Northern's Carlisle to Barrow-in-Furness line. However, Stagecoach's 30 bus service goes to Whitehaven (from Carlisle), which is then just a 7-minute train ride from St Bees.

For a **taxi**, try Sterling Cabs (☎ 01946 823000), based in Egremont, or White Line Taxis (☎ 01946 66111, 🖳 whitelinetaxis-cumbria.co.uk), in Whitehaven.

Where to stay

On the front behind the RNLI lifeboat station and owned by the adjacent hotel (see opposite) are the serried cabins of ***Seacote Caravan Park*** (☎ 01946 822777, 🖳 seacote.com; WI-FI; 🐕; Mar/Apr to early Nov). Pitches cost from £10 for a hiker & tent, £15-18 for 2- to 5-man tents. They recommend booking in peak season though will always try to accommodate Coast to Coast walkers.

Stonehouse Farm (☎ 01946 822224, 🖳 stonehousefarm.net; 1S/2D/1D or T/1T/1Tr, all en suite; 🛁; WI-FI; Ⓛ; 🐕), where you can fall asleep to the hiss of the barn owl, is a long-established and reliable **B&B**; it is situated just 30 metres from the railway station and is the only working farm within St Bees. Most of the rooms are in its Georgian farmhouse, though they also have a self-contained apartment (1D) in the courtyard. There are additional apartments but they are holiday lets. B&B costs from £45pp (£55/70 sgl/sgl occ).

Set inside the old Station House, ***Lulu's Guesthouse*** (☎ 01946 822600, 🖳 loumorland1975@yahoo.co.uk; 2D/1D or T/1Qd, all en suite; 🛁; WI-FI; Ⓛ) offers

SYMBOLS USED IN TEXT

🛁 Bathtub in, or for, at least one room; WI-FI means wi-fi is available
Ⓛ packed lunch available if requested in advance
🐕 Dogs allowed subject to prior arrangement (see p31)
fb signifies places that have a Facebook page (for latest opening hours)

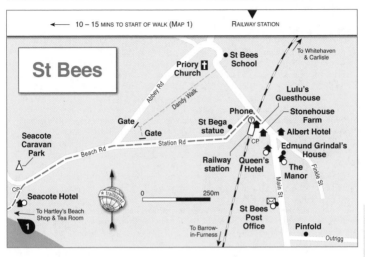

St Bees

To Whitehaven & Carlisle

St Bees School

Priory Church

Lulu's Guesthouse

Abbey Rd   Dandy Walk

Phone   Stonehouse Farm

Gate   St Bega statue   Albert Hotel

Gate   Station Rd   CP   Edmund Grindal's House

Seacote Caravan Park   Beach Rd   Railway station   Queen's Hotel   The Manor

Finkle St

Seacote Hotel   Main St

To Hartley's Beach Shop & Tea Room   0   250m   St Bees Post Office   Pinfold

To Barrow-in-Furness   Outrigg

ROUTE GUIDE AND MAPS

B&B from £42.50pp (sgl occ £75) with a continental breakfast. The quad is a two-room flat.

Further along Main St, the 17th century pub, **Queen's Hotel** (☎ 01946 822287, 🖳 queenshotel.stbees@hotmail.com; 2S/6D/2T, all en suite; ✆; WI-FI; Ⓛ) charges from £40pp (sgl/sgl occ £55/67.50) for B&B. **The Manor** (☎ 01946 820587; 6D/3T, all en suite; ✆; WI-FI; Ⓛ; 🐾) is another pub with B&B, charging from £40pp (sgl occ room rate). Online booking is available through 🖳 booking.com for both of these.

A third pub with rooms is **Albert Hotel** (☎ 01946 822345, 🖳 alberthotel-stbees .co.uk/index.htm; 2D/2T all en suite; ✆; WI-FI; Ⓛ), at 1 Finkle St; it has B&B for £32.50-37.50pp (sgl/sgl occ from £35/45). There are great views from some of the rooms.

The large **Seacote Hotel** (☎ 01946 822300, 🖳 seacote.com; 2S and 68D/T/Tr or Qd, all en suite; ✆; WI-FI; Ⓛ; 🐾) has a mixture of rooms, though all are a bit uninspiring. Some of the upper-storey rooms have sea views. B&B costs from £27.50pp (sgl from £45 occ room rate).

Where to eat and drink
The Manor (see Where to stay; food Mon-Fri noon-2.30pm & 5-8pm, Sat noon-8pm, Sun noon-4pm & 5-8pm) is a reliable pub with a comprehensive menu (mains £10-20, sandwiches from £5.50) and a Sunday lunch (roast only £9.95, two/three courses £12.95/15.95) served all day on Sunday. It's advisable to book in advance for evening meals here, especially at weekends.

On the other side of the road, *Queen's Hotel* (see Where to stay; food Tue-Sun 5-8pm) has a good-value menu and a bar known for its real ales and malt whiskies.

For sea views, cream teas and excellent ice-cream made on the premises, call in at *Hartley's Beach Shop & Tea Room* (Map 1, p94; ☎ 01946 820175; **fb**; shop summer school hols daily 9am-8pm, Nov to Easter winter to 4pm, rest of year to 5pm, café daily 9am-4pm, hot food till 3.30pm) on the foreshore, just a short walk before Mile Zero.

At nearby *Seacote Hotel* (see Where to stay) there's a bar serving pub grub (daily noon-8.30pm). The food is cheap (mains from £6.50), but you get what you pay for.

If it's just a snack you want, the pies in **St Bees Post Office** (see Services) are excellent.

❏ HOW NOT TO LOSE YOUR WAY

Although it improves incrementally, the Coast to Coast path has been the least well signposted of Britain's popular long-distance trails. Principally this is because it wasn't originally designated a 'National Trail' with all the funding benefits that involves such as consistent and effective signage or slabs over bogs that the less-popular Pennine Way got years ago. The trail also passes through the Lake District – a UNESCO World Heritage Site – where the national park authorities have elected not to sully the upland trails with signposts. This, combined with occasions of low visibility, may in places give problems with navigation. However, as the Coast to Coast is now in the process of becoming a National Trail signage should improve.

The minute you step out of the Lake District National Park signage by local authorities, local landowners or well-wishers, improves in places, all the way across much of the Pennines into Yorkshire. Here, among other signs, North Yorkshire County Council's yellow waymark discs are used towards the North Yorkshire Moors and the North Sea. Elsewhere, wooden 'Coast to Coast' fingerposts point the way – though not always accurately.

In 2012 the Wainwright Society announced agreements had been made to mark fingerposts at public road crossings with a special C2C logo featuring Wainwright's 'AW' monogram; if walking west to east they will become far more prevalent the further you progress along your walk.

Consistency aside, what is actually needed are *additional* marker posts and directional waymarks across the trouble spots listed overleaf, as well as a few other places. In many places supportive farmers have taken it upon themselves to fulfill this task.

A few tips

Our advice is to **study the book's maps closely** and read through the entire day's stage before you start it, making a note of possible tricky spots (we have made a list of these to help you – see opposite. Once on the move it's easy to get distracted, be it blindly following others who may be on some other walk or simply following the obvious trail while engrossed in a natter, so you end up missing an obscure but crucial turn off. It's a nuisance, but the C2C being what it is, you'll have to consult the book frequently to keep on track.

Keep this book readily accessible come rain or shine; at times you'll be referring to it several times an hour. A large pocket will do in the dry, but overall a waterproof **map case** on a neck string works best. In pelting rain you'll probably want to get your head down and press on, but the book's maps may still need frequent attention.

This guidebook's maps depict only a narrow strip along the trail. Depending on your experience in reading maps as well as the location of the accommodation you may use, getting **Ordnance Survey sheets OL4, OL5 and OL19** covering the Lake District and the Pennines might be worthwhile or the Coast to Coast Walk AZ Adventure Atlas (see p47). Even then, a **compass** helps on the occasions when you're not sure the path you're following is heading in the same direction as the one you think you're on according to the book.

Trailblazer tracklog and GPS waypoints

The absolute bombproof way to identify the Coast to Coast route is to refer to a **GPS tracklog**, displayed as a continuous line on either a GPS unit or a smartphone running GPS. Ground-based mobile location signals aren't the same and anyway, don't cover remote areas or even some lakeland valleys. The **C2C requires a GPS satellite signal** which on a smartphone eats battery power.

Clearly you won't depend on a tracklog every step of the way, so save the batteries on either unit by merely activating them when in need. To download the GPS tracklog on which the maps are based, see the Trailblazer website. In addition, **GPS waypoints** are listed on pp262-5. These GPS waypoints are also downloadable from the website. They can be imported into a device or simply manually keyed from the back of the book into a GPS or plotted on an OS map to pin down a location.

Common navigational trouble spots

These are the well-known trouble spots on the Coast to Coast path. The list may well be rendered obsolete by improvements in waymarking and signage, and in some cases, drainage – or by simply making use of the book's GPS data.

On our maps we've also highlighted the places where people frequently get lost with a **warning triangle** to emphasise the need for vigilance; note them well. That's not to say that you won't get lost elsewhere, but we think in most places you'll recognise your error within less than a mile.

● **Stanley Pond** (Maps 3 & 4) Just after the railway tunnel the route is often waterlogged, causing walkers to detour to the south, get disoriented and so take the wrong route on reaching the woods. At the woods (WPT 004) head north-east (diagonally) up the field to the tunnel, as the map suggests.

● **Dent Hill** (Maps 5 & 6) This shouldn't be a problem as long as you remember to look out for the signpost (to 'Dent Fell') to your left (and often half obscured by the trees) taking you off the forestry trail (although note that you can simply follow the forestry trail for an easier, less boggy route to the top). A few metres away a second signpost points you rightwards, straight up the hill. As you leave the trees you join a wall and cross over an A-frame stile, the wall taking you virtually to Dent's summit before stones across some boggy patches help keep you on the right path. Continue in the same direction until a right turn brings you to the tall ladder stile leading to Raven Crag hill. If the weather/visibility are terrible on your Dent Hill day, consider taking the quiet road from Black How Farm (WPT 008) to Ennerdale Bridge.

● **Leaving Black Sail Hostel** (Map 12) Take the higher, more northerly **and barely visible** path even though the majority of walkers – including many C2Cers foolish enough to have a different guidebook – will take the obvious path heading southeast to Great Gable. Don't worry about striking out alone; after a few metres the path is obvious and you'll see the others below you negotiating the boggy ground while you skip merrily over and above the drumlins.

And when you hit Loft Beck, it's you who'll find it straightforward finding the trail that climbs alongside it – for your path will lead you straight onto it after you've crossed the beck – while those who took the lower path will have to ford Loft Beck before they can even think about tackling the climb.

● **Top of Loft Beck** (Map 12) Clear as a bell in good conditions, in poor visibility some lose their way here and OS maps aren't much help. If you miss the massive, beck-top cairn (WPT 022) and arrive at the fence in the bogs, just follow it east and south to the gate (WPT 023), then carry on towards Grey Knotts (Map 13).

● **Greenup Edge** (Map 16) The 'edge' is actually a broad col preceded by bogs crossed by an indistinct path marked by hard-to-see cairns on low outcrops. Even in perfect visibility hitting the right fence post and nearby twin cairns (WPT 029) takes some luck as other, more prominent fenceposts along the col's rim can lure you astray. Aim resolutely for the southern side of the col at a point where a track begins to ascend to Low White Stones to the south.   *(cont'd overleaf)*

ROUTE GUIDE AND MAPS

❏ **HOW NOT TO LOSE YOUR WAY**   *(cont'd from p91)*

Or, do as many do and hit the Edge early to avoid the mired cairned path, then follow it south-east to WPT 029. Having located the twin cairns, the route down to the next key junction at the top of Easedale is clearer.

● **Boredale Hause** (Map 25) Several converging paths can make this grassy junction confusing; take the most used one bending right (ie S-E) then south to Angle Tarn.

● **High Street** (off Map 27) From Angle Tarn (Map 26) to The Knott is these days a single, clear path and short of a white-out, it's hard to think what the problem is at High Street other than simply missing the flattened trackside cairn (WPT 048) before the col. The cairn is small, but marks the start of another clear track running north-east to Kidsty Pike, the route's high point.

● **South of Oddendale** (Map 36) Some walkers experience a brief route finding wobble here even though there are poles and good landmarks. Leave the main track for WPT 061 at the southern corner of the strip plantation, then head up to the wall-like rim of limestone pavements (WPT 062) and use the 'two trees' landmark.

● **Sunbiggin Tarn** (Maps 39 & 40) Locate the clear path off the road (WPT 065) curving south of the tarn and over a wooden bridge (WPT 067), then at the southern edge of a walled pen aim uphill for the reservoir head on a hilltop, just over a minor road.

● **Nine Standards routes** (Maps 45, 46 & 47) In very thick mist seeing the myste-rious cairns (Map 46 Nine Standards; WPT 082) before they see you can be tricky as can continuing from there south past the trig point to the key Red and Blue route junc-tion (Map 47; WPT 085, half a mile away) while avoiding bogs on the way.

But the real problems lie further on; see pp169-71 for more details and help with wayfinding. If you get to this junction, the Blue route has posts leading to Whitsundalebeck valley; the Red route has less frequent landmarks and great care is required to find the right path – especially as there is no actual 'path'. This ruined sec-tion is in dire need of Pennine-Way-like paving. Many people get confused here and end up cutting across the road and just following that into Keld. It might be less glam-orous, but at least it gets you there safely… The lower Green route is easier to follow and much less of a mire.

● **Graystone Hills** (Maps 91 & 92) Even in clear weather, the fact that there are so few of the fingerposts marking the way when crossing this final stretch of very boggy moorland makes this a tricky route to follow – even though you can see the cars on the nearby A171. Then once off the moor, getting the 500m from WPT 144 to the start of the rocky/muddy trail may take some intuition. Watch your orientation closely or use GPS.

⚠COAST TO COAST PATH NATIONAL TRAIL – ROUTE CHANGES ⚠

On the maps in this book we've used the red warning triangle to indicate possible route changes as the trail is upgraded to National Trail status (2022-5). Watch for new signs in the following areas:

Map 4 (route through Moor Row); Map 5 (route up Dent Hill); Map 8 (route to Ennerdale Water); Map 17 (route down Easedale); Map 18 (route approaching Grasmere); Maps 55 & 56 (route entering Reeth); Map 57 (route near Marrick Priory); Maps 88 & 89 (route over Sleights Moor and across A169).

❏ THE ENGLAND COAST PATH

As opposed to 'simply' crossing England from St Bees to Robin Hood's Bay you could take the long way around and follow the England Coast Path, although this would add hundreds of miles to your journey, require many more OS maps, and probably more than one set of boots! It's estimated, when finished, it will be 2795 miles (4498km) long. Indeed, when completed the new national trail will be the longest coastal path in the world.

At the time of writing the England Coast Path wasn't fully open but the sections that bookend the Coast to Coast path – following the sea away from St Bees and into Robin Hood's Bay – are.

The idea for such a project had been discussed amongst ramblers' groups for many years but it was the Marine and Coastal Access Act (2009), which finally set out the powers that would be needed in order to create such a route, responsibility for its planning and creation being delegated to Natural England (see p41). The first stretch between Weymouth Bay and Portland Harbour opened in 2012 to coincide with the Olympics but progress since has stalled somewhat. In 2014, the government's plan was to have the trail finished by 2020. However, politics, economics, and a pandemic have inevitably had their impact on that ambition. Further details on the path's progress and the sections which are currently open can be found at 🖳 nation altrail.co.uk/en_GB/trails/england-coast-path and 🖳 gov.uk/government/publica tions/england-coast-path-overview-of-progress.

STAGE 1: ST BEES TO ENNERDALE BRIDGE   MAPS 1-7

Introduction

There is a lot of variety in this **14-mile (22.5km, 6¼hr)** stage, beginning with a cliff-top walk along the Irish Sea and ending (weather permitting) with a high-level view from Dent Hill across to the brooding western fells of the Lake District.

Most will find this first day a bit of a struggle, particularly the haul up and over Dent Hill into Ennerdale Bridge. If you think this may include you, pace yourself while you have a choice and consider stopping at or near Cleator, before continuing on the second day to the hostels at High Gillerthwaite or even Black Sail. In a couple of days, you may be glad you did.

The route

As far as we and most other walkers are concerned, '**Mile Zero**' (WPT 001) on the path is at the Coast to Coast monument by the RNLI lifeboat station facing

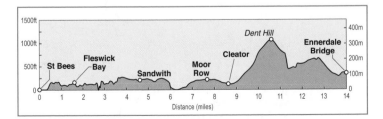

ROUTE GUIDE AND MAPS

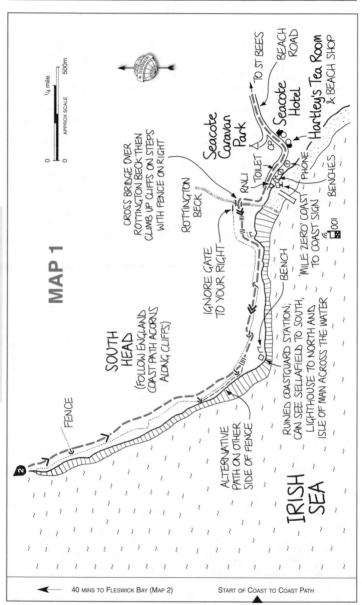

MAP 1

¼ mile

APPROX SCALE

0   500m

SOUTH HEAD
(FOLLOW ENGLAND COAST PATH ACROSS ALONG CLIFFS)

FENCE

CROSS BRIDGE OVER ROTTINGTON BECK THEN CLIMBS UP CLIFFS ON STEPS WITH FENCE ON RIGHT

ROTTINGTON BECK

IGNORE GATE TO YOUR RIGHT

TO ST BEES

BEACH ROAD

Seacote Hotel

Hartley's Tea Room & BEACH SHOP

Seacote Caravan Park

TOILET

RNLI

PHONE

BENCHES

'MILE ZERO COAST TO COAST SIGN'

BENCH

ALTERNATIVE PATH ON OTHER SIDE OF FENCE

RUINED COASTGUARD STATION; CAN SEE SELLAFIELD TO SOUTH, LIGHTHOUSE TO NORTH AND ISLE OF MAN ACROSS THE WATER

IRISH SEA

2

← 40 MINS TO FLESWICK BAY (MAP 2)

START OF COAST TO COAST PATH ▲

the Irish Sea. To get to Mile Zero follow Beach Rd to the shore, baptise your boots in the surf and take a photo by the sign with its steel adornment showing the entire C2C elevation profile. Some walkers even collect a small pebble as a keepsake to drop into the North Sea at the end of the walk. Suitably initiated, turn north-west, steel yourself for the adventure about to unfold, and climb up the steep path to the clifftop. You're now on the Coast to Coast path, with a

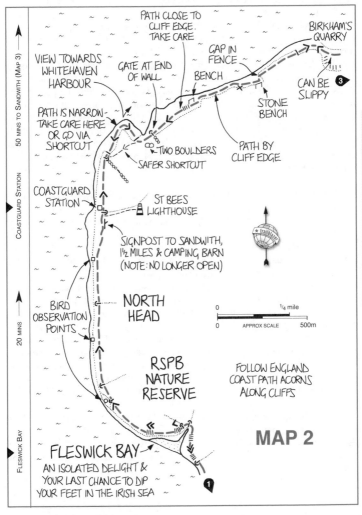

ROUTE GUIDE AND MAPS

fence on one side and what becomes a 300ft (90m) drop on the other. Until the trail turns inland and east it's recently been befriended by the England Coast Path (see box p93). The ECP's National Trail acorns point you in the right direction along the cliffs, although the route couldn't be simpler to follow.

The cliffs themselves are made of red St Bees sandstone, used in the construction of many of the buildings in the vicinity since medieval times and part of a broad sedimentary bed which you'll encounter again in the Vale of Eden on the far side of the Lakes.

The first notable landmark is the cleft of **Fleswick Bay** (Map 2) composed of a secluded pebble beach surrounded by red sandstone cliffs with some unusually weathered boulders on the shore.

This bay marks the dividing line between the constituent parts of St Bees Head: **South Head**, which you've been on up to now, and **North Head** (Map 2), which you now climb up to from the bay. Two features distinguish this latter part of St Bees Head: the three **RSPB observation points**, to the left of the path, which allow you to peer safely over the cliffs and observe the seabirds nesting there (including puffins, terns and England's only colony of black guillemots); and **St Bees Lighthouse**, a little way inland from the path but clearly visible since South Head. After the lighthouse the path continues to the tip of **North Head** before curving east along the coast and eventually turning inland at **Birkham's Quarry**.

Fifteen minutes later you arrive in the village of **Sandwith** (Map 3; pronounced 'Sanith'). This is the first settlement of note on the trail; it's almost five miles/8km along the path from St Bees (though only two miles/3km as the crow flies!).

The village pub, ***Dog and Partridge*** (☎ 01946 592177; WI-FI) is open Thursday to Sunday (from 3.30pm on Thur & Fri) and does **food** (Thur & Fri 3.30-8.30pm, Sat noon-8.30pm, Sun noon-4pm).

Taking the road past the pub, the path crosses Byerstead Rd and, just over half a mile (0.8km) later, the B5345 linking Whitehaven to St Bees.

From the tunnel beneath the railway line at the foot of the hill, the trail crosses waterlogged fields around what was **Stanley Pond** (with possible navigation issues; see box p92) and a small stream (**Scalegill Beck**; Map 4), before passing underneath a disused railway. We, however, advise you to take the steps on your right up the side of the tunnel onto the disused railway track; take a left here and follow the 'track' to Moor Row. **Moor Row** lacks the village-green charm of Sandwith and at the time of writing it had no services useful for walkers.

Following the uncomfortably narrow and busy road south out of Moor Row (signposted to Egremont), you're relieved to get off it soon and head into a field. A series of **kissing gates** follows before you join up with a track that takes you past a cricket ground and on over a river bridge, before arriving alongside St Leonard's Church in Cleator.

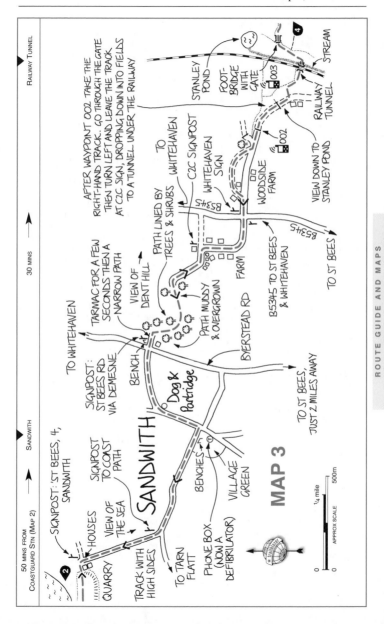

MAP 3

¼ mile

APPROX SCALE

0 · · · · · 500m

TO WHITEHAVEN

SIGNPOST: 'ST BEES, 4, SANDWITH

HOUSES

VIEW OF THE SEA

SIGNPOST TO COAST PATH

QUARRY

TRACK WITH HIGH SIDES

TO TARN FLATT

PHONE BOX (NOW A DEFIBRILATOR)

BENCHES

VILLAGE GREEN

SANDWITH

Dog & Partridge

BENCH

SIGNPOST: ST BEES RD VIA DEMESNE

TARMAC FOR A FEW SECONDS THEN A NARROW PATH

VIEW OF DENT HILL

PATH MUDDY & OVERGROWN

PATH LINED BY TREES & SHRUBS

BYERSTEAD RD

TO ST BEES, JUST 2 MILES AWAY

B5345 TO ST BEES & WHITEHAVEN

FARM

TO ST BEES

B5345

WOODSIDE FARM

WHITEHAVEN SIGN

TO WHITEHAVEN

C2C SIGNPOST

VIEW DOWN TO STANLEY POND

STANLEY POND

FOOTBRIDGE WITH GATE

003

002

RAILWAY TUNNEL

STREAM

AFTER WAYPONT 002 TAKE THE RIGHT-HAND TRACK. GO THROUGH THE GATE THEN TURN LEFT AND LEAVE THE TRACK AT C2C SIGN, DROPPING DOWN INTO FIELDS TO A TUNNEL UNDER THE RAILWAY

CLEATOR   **MAP 4; MAP 5, p100**

As with Moor Row before it, it's clear that Wordsworth's lyrical ballads never reached out to immortalise the grim, pebbledashed, terraces of Cleator.

Remnants of 12th-century masonry in the **church** (St Leonard's; Map 4) attest to the village's venerability, but the abiding impression dates from a 19th-century iron-ore mining boom when Irish migrants flooded into the area (as the many Celtic house names suggest). The mining collapsed in the latter half of the 19th century and the nearby settlements followed suit; a familiar story repeated across west Cumbria. It's ameliorated today by the ongoing decommissioning of the ageing Sellafield nuclear plant, offering work to the 10,000 who want it.

Cleator Stores (also known as **Cleator Pie Shop;** ☎ 01946 810038; summer Mon-Fri 5.30am-4pm, Sat 8am-2pm, Sun 8.30-10.30am; in the winter the hours depend in part on demand) has a limited range of food items. Don't be surprised if a sign outside it says 'No Pies'. The shop is actually locally famed for its pies and, despite the negativity of the sign, they often do have pies but prefer not to advertise them because, as the shop owner gleefully told us: 'We've had brawls in here with people fighting over slices of our pies.' If a pie here is set to be a highlight of your trip call them to order one when you are nearby and don't pass through over the weekend as the pies are only available between Monday and Friday.

Alternatively, **Cleator Moor**, the regional hub with many grand 19th-century edifices, some once painted by Lowry, is a mile to the north, and has an **ATM** and **post office** in the **Co-op** (Mon-Sat 7am-10pm,

Sun 10am-4pm), as well as corner shops and several junk-food outlets.

Stagecoach's No 30 Frizington **bus** service calls at Cleator Moor; see pp54-6 for details.

Where to stay and eat

Nine miles along the Coast to Coast path from St Bees, Cleator can make a very good destination after a weary first day's walk.

Set in the former council offices, **Ennerdale Country House Hotel** (☎ 01946 813907, ▣ bespokehotels.com/ennerdale hotel; 3S/18D/3T/7Tr, all en suite; ✆; WI-FI; ℚ; ✿) has very pleasant rooms done out in a pseudo medieval-style that doesn't quite work. **B&B** starts at £40pp (sgl £70, sgl occ room rate). It's very comfortable – some rooms have four-poster beds, others are suites, while all bathrooms have bath-tubs as well as showers – and is the closest place to the path. Some of the better hotel restaurant **food** on the Coast to Coast is served daily (sandwiches & soup/chips noon-2pm, evening meal 5-8.30pm) in both the restaurant and the bar.

In **Cleator Moor** (off Map 5), two miles north of Cleator along the A5086, is **Parkside Hotel** (☎ 01946 811001, ▣ the parksidehotel.co.uk; **fb**; 2D/4Tr, all en suite; WI-FI; ℚ) with **B&B** from £37.50pp (sgl occ room rate). **Food** (daily 4.30-9pm) is available in their bar/restaurant. It's a dreary roadside schlep up from Cleator to Parkside Hotel so it's better to follow the quieter cycleway directly from Moor Row (Map 4) north-east for two miles via Cleator Moor to the hotel. Alternatively they are happy to arrange a transfer through a local taxi company though there will be a charge.

From Cleator it's possible to take the road route north and east to Ennerdale Bridge, so avoiding Dent Hill, either off the A5086 or at Black How Farm just before you enter the Dent-side plantation. Either way is said to be not too bad for traffic, though unless the weather is positively treacherous, or you're intent on saving energy, take the high route. It would be a shame to miss the summit of Dent Hill (Map 5) and the trickling tranquillity of Nannycatch Beck (Map 6) that lies hidden away at its foot.

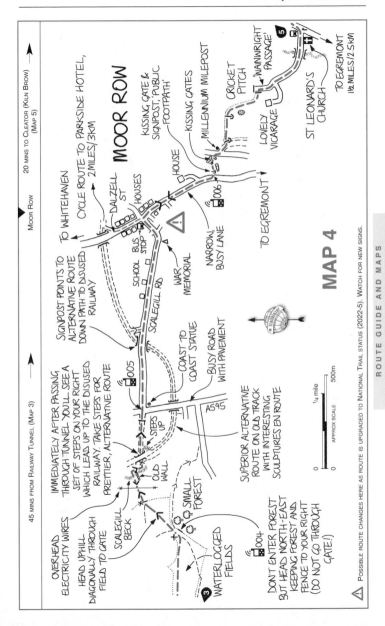

MOOR ROW

MAP 4

CYCLE ROUTE TO PARKSIDE HOTEL, 2 MILES/3KM

TO WHITEHAVEN

SIGNPOST POINTS TO ALTERNATIVE ROUTE DOWN PATH TO DISUSED RAILWAY

IMMEDIATELY AFTER PASSING THROUGH TUNNEL YOU'LL SEE A SET OF STEPS ON YOUR RIGHT WHICH LEAD UP TO THE DISUSED RAILWAY. TAKE STEPS FOR PRETTIER, ALTERNATIVE ROUTE

OVERHEAD ELECTRICITY WIRES

HEAD UPHILL DIAGONALLY THROUGH FIELD TO GATE

SCALEGILL BECK

OLD WALL

SMALL FOREST

WATERLOGGED FIELDS

DON'T ENTER FOREST BUT HEAD NORTH-EAST KEEPING FOREST AND FENCE TO YOUR RIGHT (DO NOT GO THROUGH GATE!)

STEPS UP

COAST TO COAST STATUE

BUSY ROAD WITH PAVEMENT

A595

SUPERIOR ALTERNATIVE ROUTE ON OLD TRACK WITH INTERESTING SCULPTURES EN ROUTE

DALZELL ST

HOUSES

SCHOOL

BUS STOP

SCALEGILL RD

WAR MEMORIAL

NARROW, BUSY LANE

HOUSE

KISSING GATE & SIGNPOST, 'PUBLIC FOOTPATH'

KISSING GATES

MILLENNIUM MILEPOST

CRICKET PITCH

'WAINWRIGHT PASSAGE'

LONELY VICARAGE

ST LEONARD'S CHURCH

TO EGREMONT

TO EGREMONT 1½ MILES/2.5KM

¼ mile

500m

APPROX SCALE

ROUTE GUIDE AND MAPS

⚠ POSSIBLE ROUTE CHANGES HERE AS ROUTE IS UPGRADED TO NATIONAL TRAIL STATUS (2022-5). WATCH FOR NEW SIGNS.

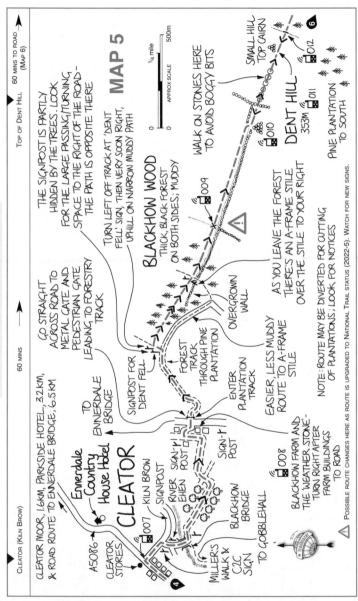

CLEATOR (KILN BROW)

60 MINS

TOP OF DENT HILL

60 MINS TO ROAD (MAP 6)

MAP 5

APPROX SCALE

0 — 500m

0 — ¼ mile

CLEATOR MOOR, 1.6KM, PARKSIDE HOTEL, 3.2KM, & ROAD ROUTE TO ENNERDALE BRIDGE, 6.5KM

A5086

Ennerdale Country House Hotel

CLEATOR

CLEATOR STORES

KILN BROW SIGNPOST

🏠 007

RIVER EHEN

MILLER'S WALK
C2C SIGN

TO GOBBLEHALL

BLACKHOW BRIDGE

SIGN-POST

SIGN-POST

🏠 008

BLACKHOW FARM AND THE 'WEATHER STONE'- TURN RIGHT AFTER FARM BUILDINGS TO ROAD

TO ENNERDALE BRIDGE

SIGNPOST FOR DENT FELL

ENTER PLANTATION TRACK

FOREST TRACK THROUGH PINE PLANTATION

OVERGROWN WALL

EASIER, LESS MUDDY ROUTE TO A-FRAME STILE

GO STRAIGHT ACROSS ROAD TO METAL GATE AND PEDESTRIAN GATE LEADING TO FORESTRY TRACK

THE SIGNPOST IS PARTLY HIDDEN BY THE TREES. LOOK FOR THE LARGE PASSING/TURNING SPACE TO THE RIGHT OF THE ROAD – THE PATH IS OPPOSITE THERE

TURN LEFT OFF TRACK AT 'DENT FELL' SIGN, THEN VERY SOON RIGHT, UPHILL ON NARROW MUDDY PATH

BLACKHOW WOOD
THICK, BLACK FOREST ON BOTH SIDES; MUDDY

🏠 009

⚠

AS YOU LEAVE THE FOREST THERE'S AN A-FRAME STILE OVER THE STILE TO YOUR RIGHT

NOTE: ROUTE MAY BE DIVERTED FOR CUTTING OF PLANTATIONS; LOOK FOR NOTICES

WALK ON STONES HERE TO AVOID BOGGY BITS

🏠 010

DENT HILL
353M 🏠 011

PINE PLANTATION TO SOUTH

SMALL HILL TOP CAIRN

🏠 012

6

💧

⚠ POSSIBLE ROUTE CHANGES HERE AS ROUTE IS UPGRADED TO NATIONAL TRAIL STATUS (2022-5). WATCH FOR NEW SIGNS.

4

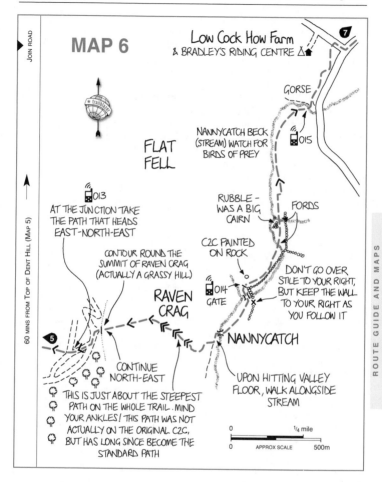

The long and sweaty climb to **Dent Hill summit** takes about an hour from Cleator. At the base of the hill keep an eye out for the 'weather stone' (which can also predict earthquakes) outside Blackhow Farm. If the meteorological stone has been feeling generous then from the top of Dent Hill there could be views to the Lakeland fells ahead and the sea behind, with the gigantic plant of Sellafield to the south-west and, on a good day, the silhouette of the Isle of Man and Galloway (Scotland) across the Solway Firth.

After the hilltop the Coast to Coast path signpost points left to a gate from where you contour and then descend **Raven Crag** hill (Map 6). Although very steep, it's become the *de facto* path now, contrary to Wainwright's original instructions. Maybe he had a point – when we say steep we mean it; poles may help and irate readers still write in and complain about the gradient down Raven Crag hill but trust us, it's a lot quicker, good for the quads and more scenic.

From **Nannycatch**, which is a delightful meadow beside a stream and an ideal picnic or rest stop, head due north along the pretty beck, following the course of the water to the road into Ennerdale Bridge. Here you'll find *Low Cock How Farm* (Bradley's Riding Centre; Map 6; ☎ 01946 861354, 💻 www.theultimategavin.co.uk/bradleys; 3D or T/1Tr, shared facilities; WI-FI; Ⓛ; 🐾), a year-round riding centre with **B&B** from £50pp (sgl occ £50). There is also a well-equipped 8-berth **bunkhouse** (from £35pp with breakfast) as well as **camping** (from £12pp). There are shower and cooking facilities in the bunkhouse and separate facilities for campers. Breakfast for campers costs £6 and must be booked by the night before. Evening meals are not available but anyone can order a home delivery; there are various menus to choose from. Horse-riding (£40 per hr) is also available.

ENNERDALE BRIDGE   MAP 7

Ennerdale Bridge is the first of the self-consciously pretty Lakeland villages, occupying a wonderful location spanning River Ehen in one of Britain's least-developed valleys.

Where to stay and eat

Lottery-funded and volunteer-run, *The Gather* (☎ 01946 862453, 💻 thegatherennerdale.com; **fb**; WI-FI; 🐾) is a fabulous **shop** and *café* (summer Mon-Sat 9am-5pm, Sun 10am-4pm, winter daily 10am-4pm) with tasty food (bacon rolls, scones & good strong coffee), hiker-handy products (groceries, maps, toiletries, plasters) and delightful, locally made handicrafts (sheepswool keyrings, Cumbrian bookmarks). They cater for various dietary requirements eg vegan and gluten free. It also has attached **shower facilities** (£3pp), which are sparkling clean, have plenty of space, and can be used by passing hikers when The Gather is open.

Barely 100 metres away, the friendly *Fox and Hounds* (☎ 01946 861373, 💻 foxandhoundsinn.org; 1T/1D/1Tr, all en suite; 💬; WI-FI; Ⓛ; 🐾) is the hub of the village come evening. It serves excellent **food** (Mon-Sat noon-9pm, Sun to 8pm, winter hours variable) – booking is recommended – and some fine local ales. **B&B** costs from £57.50pp (sgl occ £95). You can also **camp** (🐾) for £8pp in their small garden. Campers can use the toilet in the pub when it's open, or walk 100 metres up the road to use the shower facilities at The Gather (see column opposite) when that is open. As long as some B&B guests are staying a takeaway breakfast is generally available for campers.

In the centre of the village proper, *Shepherd's Arms Hotel* (☎ 01946 861249, 💻 shepherdsarms.com; 2D/1T/3D or T, all en suite, 1D/1T private bathroom; 💬; WI-FI; Ⓛ; 🐾) offers B&B from £60pp (sgl occ £81-86). **Food** is served daily (Apr-Oct noon-9pm, Nov-Mar Mon-Wed 5-9pm, Thur-Sun noon-9pm). Main meals cost from £9.95.

Near **Kirkland**, 1½ miles from Ennerdale Bridge, is *Ghyll Farm B&B* (☎ 01946 861330, 💻 ghyllfarm.co.uk; 2D or T/1Tr, all en suite; WI-FI; Ⓛ). B&B costs from £65pp (sgl occ £116) and each room has a pleasant outdoor seating area. To get here, head for Kirkland; half a mile after you leave the village of Ennerdale Bridge take the first right turn down a single-track road. There are signs at the junction but look for the remains of an old barn and a timber footpath signpost on the corner of the main road and the lane (don't take the first unmade track a quarter of a mile outside the village); follow the single-track road for a further half-mile where there's a sign for the farm and it's a further half mile to the top of the hill.

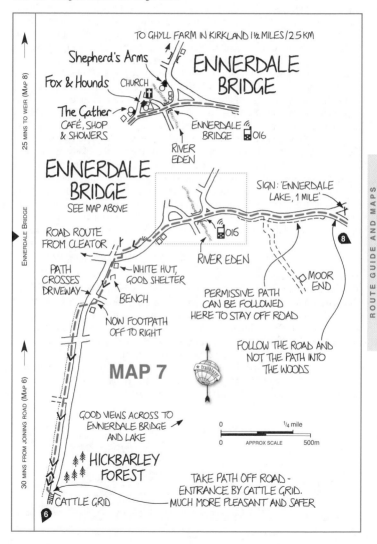

25 MINS TO WEIR (MAP 8)

ENNERDALE BRIDGE

30 MINS FROM JOINING ROAD (MAP 6)

ROUTE GUIDE AND MAPS

TO GHYLL FARM IN KIRKLAND 1½ MILES/2.5 KM

Shepherd's Arms

Fox & Hounds   CHURCH

ENNERDALE BRIDGE

The Gather
CAFÉ, SHOP
& SHOWERS

ENNERDALE
BRIDGE   016

RIVER
EDEN

ENNERDALE
BRIDGE
SEE MAP ABOVE

SIGN: 'ENNERDALE
LAKE, 1 MILE'

ROAD ROUTE
FROM CLEATOR

016

8

PATH
CROSSES
DRIVEWAY

WHITE HUT,
GOOD SHELTER

RIVER EDEN

BENCH

MOOR
END

NOW FOOTPATH
OFF TO RIGHT

PERMISSIVE PATH
CAN BE FOLLOWED
HERE TO STAY OFF ROAD

MAP 7

trailblazer

FOLLOW THE ROAD AND
NOT THE PATH INTO
THE WOODS

GOOD VIEWS ACROSS TO
ENNERDALE BRIDGE
AND LAKE

0   ¼ mile

0   500m
APPROX SCALE

HICKBARLEY
FOREST

CATTLE GRID

TAKE PATH OFF ROAD -
ENTRANCE BY CATTLE GRID.
MUCH MORE PLEASANT AND SAFER

6

STAGE 2: ENNERDALE BRIDGE TO BORROWDALE   MAPS 7-14

Introduction

As with any day in the Lakes, the enjoyment of this **15-mile (24km, 6½hr** via low route) stage depends largely on the weather. And be warned you are heading towards the spot which records the highest rainfall in England; the wryly named **Sprinkling Tarn** just south of Seathwaite receives an average of 196 inches (over 5m) of rain a year, a phenomenal amount. Lakeland is known for its wash-outs (eg Dec 2015) and at the time of writing Seathwaite still has the record for the highest rainfall over both 3- and 4-day periods. Indeed if it's raining horizontally with waterfalls running off the crags, chances are the path along the **southern edge of Ennerdale Water** will be one long stream with occasional fords rising halfway up your shins. Unless you like splashing about in such weather the access track along the northern shore may be a better option.

If the weather is fine, however, the southern pathway is preferable as it hugs the lakeside more closely and is for walkers only. Beyond the lake's end, in clear conditions even the high route via Red Pike can get busy, but be warned it's a fair old climb and you can still enjoy great views down to Buttermere from the top of Loft Beck or Grey Knotts on the standard route. If the weather is closing in, it would be foolhardy to attempt the fell-top alternative. It's a long walk from Ennerdale Bridge, your first real stage in the Lakes, although you can rearrange this day at any of the four hostels spaced out along the route. Slower walkers – or those wishing just to pause and relish the views – might find it a push to walk all the way from Ennerdale to Borrowdale via the high-route in one day.

The route

The stage's first half involves a walk along the southern side of the attractive **Ennerdale Water** (Map 8) and though it's not quite the dreamy lakeside stroll you may have imagined (the rocky terrain can be a bit of a pain under foot), navigation couldn't be simpler. At one point the path rises over the outcrop of **Robin Hood's Chair** (take the easier right route at the top of the crag) to enter mossy light woodland as you near the eastern extremity of the lake.

Family-friendly *Low Gillerthwaite Field Centre* (Map 10; ☎ 01946 861229, 🖳 lgfc.org.uk; **fb**; limited satellite WI-FI) has comfortable **hostel** accommodation (2x4-, 1x8-, 1x10-, 1x14-bed rooms)...   *(cont'd on p108)*

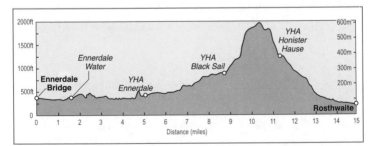

ROUTE GUIDE AND MAPS

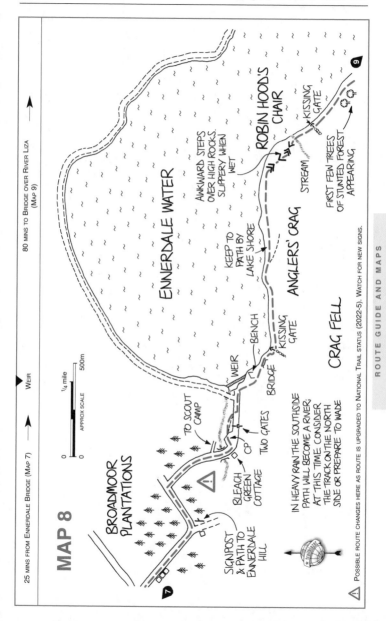

25 MINS FROM ENNERDALE BRIDGE (MAP 7) ▶ WEIR ▶ 80 MINS TO BRIDGE OVER RIVER LIZA (MAP 9)

MAP 8

BROADMOOR PLANTATIONS

SIGNPOST & PATH TO ENNERDALE HILL

7

BLEACH GREEN COTTAGE

TO SCOUT CAMP

CP

TWO GATES

WEIR

BENCH

BRIDGE

KISSING GATE

ENNERDALE WATER

KEEP TO PATH BY LAKE SHORE

AWKWARD STEPS OVER HIGH ROCKS. SLIPPERY WHEN WET

ROBIN HOOD'S CHAIR

STREAM

KISSING GATE

9

FIRST FEW TREES OF STUNTED FOREST APPEARING.

ANGLERS' CRAG

CRAG FELL

IN HEAVY RAIN THE SOUTHSIDE PATH WILL BECOME A RIVER, AT THIS TIME CONSIDER THE TRACK ON THE NORTH SIDE & PREPARE TO WADE

⚠ POSSIBLE ROUTE CHANGES HERE AS ROUTE IS UPGRADED TO NATIONAL TRAIL STATUS (2022-5). WATCH FOR NEW SIGNS.

0 ¼ mile
0 APPROX SCALE 500m

ROUTE GUIDE AND MAPS

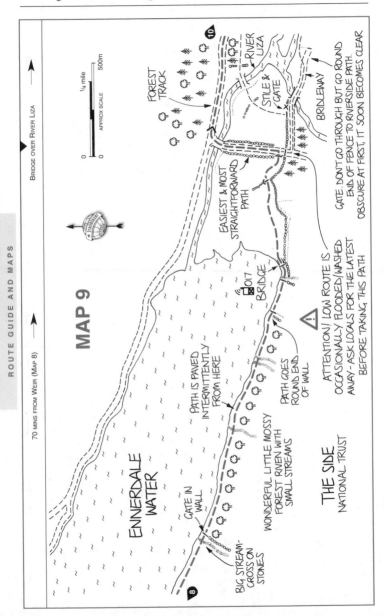

← 70 MINS FROM WEIR (MAP 8) →

BRIDGE OVER RIVER LIZA →

MAP 9

10

8

RIVER LIZA

FOREST TRACK

STILE & GATE

BRIDLEWAY

GATE. DON'T GO THROUGH BUT GO ROUND END OF FENCE TO RIVERSIDE PATH. OBSCURE AT FIRST, IT SOON BECOMES CLEAR

EASIEST & MOST STRAIGHTFORWARD PATH

¼ mile

APPROX SCALE

0   500m

1017 BRIDGE

ATTENTION! LOW ROUTE IS OCCASIONALLY FLOODED/WASHED AWAY - ASK LOCALS FOR THE LATEST BEFORE TAKING THIS PATH

ENNERDALE WATER

PATH IS PAVED INTERMITTENTLY FROM HERE

PATH GOES ROUND END OF WALL

THE SIDE
NATIONAL TRUST

WONDERFUL LITTLE MOSSY FOREST RIVEN WITH SMALL STREAMS

GATE IN WALL

BIG STREAM-CROSS ON STONES

8

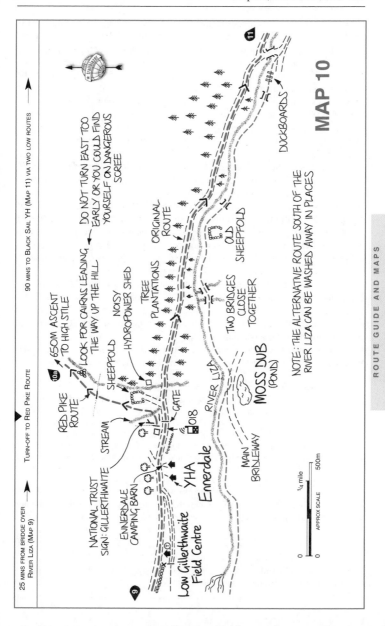

(cont'd from p104) and charges from £18pp. A sleeping bag or sleeping sheet is needed and also a pillow if you want one as due to COVID they are no longer providing them. There is a well-equipped kitchen, a dining room, a drying room and two lounges with wood fires as well as good shower and toilet facilities. Note that if a group is in residence (which is not unusual) you may not be allowed to stay so call ahead. It is generally self-catering only – and the nearest shop is back at Ennerdale Bridge – so come prepared (although you can sometimes buy farm eggs and locally brewed beer here). However, if booked in advance the warden will prepare a meal (from £8 for 2 courses). Note that mobile phone signals are notoriously poor here (though they now have limited reception for O2).

Up the track a bit the small, and very convivial, *YHA Ennerdale* (Map 10; ☎ 0345 371 9116, 🖳 yha.org.uk/hostel/yha-ennerdale; 2x4-, 2x6-bed rooms; dorm beds from £12pp, private rooms from £39 for up to two sharing, some en suite rooms; ⒧; mid Mar to end Oct), at High Gillerthwaite, has good facilities and a lovely location. Copious but not especially tasty meals are available for guests only, though these should be booked in advance. The hostel is licensed and has a slick self-catering kitchen and cosy lounge. It also generates its own hydro-powered electricity. Reception opens at 5pm (not a moment earlier!). Note that there is no mobile phone signal or wi-fi available here.

Next door, and run by the same YHA management, is **Ennerdale Camping Barn** (aka **High Gillerthwaite Camping Barn**; contact details same as YHA Ennerdale). However, at the time of research, the camping barn was open for exclusive hire only and that is likely to stay the same till at least 2025. Contact the YHA to check for any changes to this.

Just beyond the camping barn is the start of the alternative trail up to Red Pike, High Stile and Hay Stacks. The low route continues on p112.

The Red Pike, High Stile & Hay Stacks route
Maps 10 p107, 10a, 10b p110 & 12 p113

'All I ask for, at the end, is a last, long resting place by the side of Innominate Tarn, on Haystacks where the water gently laps the gravelly shore and the heather blooms and Pillar and Gable keep unfailing watch. A quiet place, a lonely place. I shall go to it, for the last time, and be carried: someone who knew me in life will take me there and empty me out of a little box and leave me there alone. And if you, dear reader, should get a bit of grit in your boot as you are crossing Haystacks in the years to come, please treat it with respect. It might be me'.

Alfred Wainwright *Memoirs of an Ex-Fellwanderer*

In his *Coast to Coast* guide Wainwright describes this route as suitable only for 'very strong and experienced fellwalkers' in clear weather.   *(cont'd on p112)*

❑ BAGGAGE-TRANSFER BLACK SPOTS
Note, that YHA Ennerdale and YHA Black Sail are beyond the reach of the baggage carriers (see pp27-9), so you'll need to plan ahead.

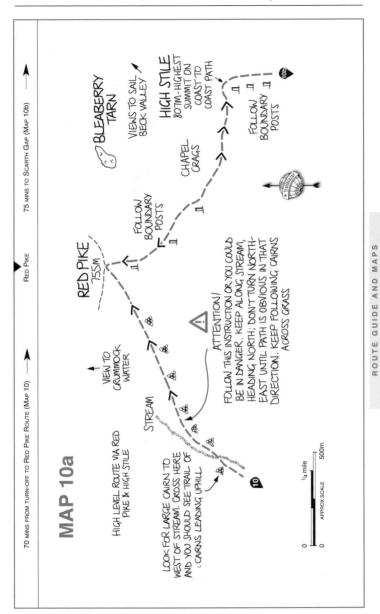

MAP 10a

HIGH LEVEL ROUTE VIA RED
PIKE & HIGH STILE

RED PIKE
755M

BLEABERRY
TARN

VIEWS TO SAIL
BECK VALLEY ↗

HIGH STILE
807M - HIGHEST
SUMMIT ON
COAST TO
COAST PATH

CHAPEL
CRAGS

FOLLOW
BOUNDARY
POSTS

FOLLOW
BOUNDARY
POSTS

10b

VIEW TO CRUMMOCK
WATER ↗

STREAM

ATTENTION!
FOLLOW THIS INSTRUCTION OR YOU COULD
BE IN DANGER. KEEP ALONG STREAM,
HEADING NORTH; DON'T TURN NORTH-
EAST UNTIL PATH IS OBVIOUS IN THAT
DIRECTION. KEEP FOLLOWING CAIRNS
ACROSS GRASS

LOOK FOR LARGE CAIRNS TO
WEST OF STREAM. CROSS HERE
AND YOU SHOULD SEE TRAIL OF
CAIRNS LEADING UPHILL

10

0   ¼ mile
APPROX SCALE
0   500m

ROUTE GUIDE AND MAPS

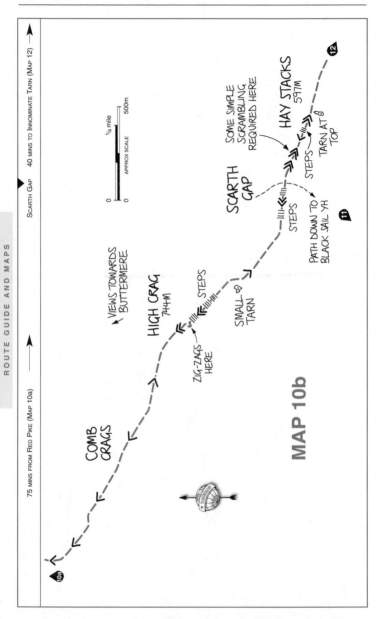

ROUTE GUIDE AND MAPS

75 MINS FROM RED PIKE (MAP 10a) →

← SCARTH GAP   40 MINS TO INNOMINATE TARN (MAP 12) →

COMB CRAGS

VIEWS TOWARDS BUTTERMERE

HIGH CRAG
744M

ZIG-ZAGS HERE

STEPS

SMALL TARN

SCARTH GAP

STEPS

SOME SIMPLE SCRAMBLING REQUIRED HERE

HAY STACKS
597M

STEPS

TARN AT TOP

PATH DOWN TO BLACK SAIL YH

MAP 10b

APPROX SCALE
0 — ¼ mile
0 — 500m

10a

11

12

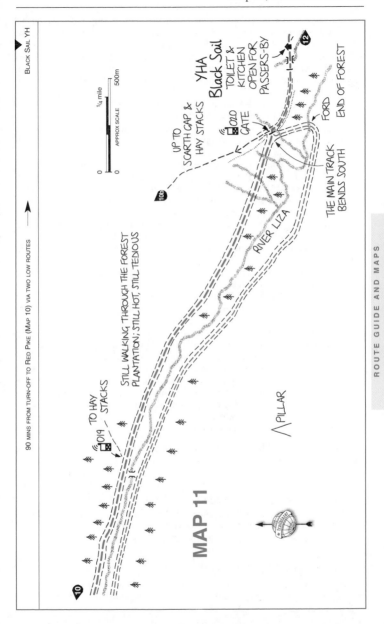

BLACK SAIL YH

90 MINS FROM TURN-OFF TO RED PIKE (MAP 10) VIA TWO LOW ROUTES

MAP 11

10

Ǝ019 TO HAY STACKS

STILL WALKING THROUGH THE FOREST PLANTATION; STILL HOT, STILL TEDIOUS

PILLAR

RIVER LIZA

10b

UP TO SCARTH GAP & HAY STACKS

Ǝ010 GATE

THE MAIN TRACK BENDS SOUTH

FORD

END OF FOREST

YHA Black Sail
TOILET & KITCHEN OPEN FOR PASSERS-BY

12

APPROX SCALE

¼ mile

500m

(cont'd from p108) While we don't think the group of people who can do this walk is quite as exclusive as Wainwright suggests, we certainly agree that the weather needs to be clear, if only because the views possible at the top – in particular across Buttermere to the north and to Great Gable and Pillar in the south – benefit from it. (If the weather takes a significant turn for the worse up there, you can drop down from Scarth Gap on steps to the YHA Black Sail hostel; see Map 10b.)

There are no technically difficult parts, though there are some steep ascents and particularly descents which will hammer the knees, and route finding on the way up to Red Pike can be tricky. This alternative route should add about 1½ **miles** (**2.5km, 1¾hrs**) to this stage, all in all making it a pretty tough day so early in the walk.

The high-level route takes in a number of summits, including Red Pike (755m), High Stile (807m, the highest summit on the Coast to Coast path), High Crag (744m) and Hay Stacks (597m), the lowest but the most interesting. The place where some err from the path is on the initial climb up to Red Pike where it's tempting to branch off eastwards too early: make sure that, having crossed the stream, you continue north-east (following cairns) until you're firmly on the grassy upper reaches of Red Pike (Map 10a). There are *just* enough cairns to show the way, though if in doubt, your motto should be: head up the slope rather than along it.

Having gained the ridge the path becomes clear and you'll find yourself ticking off one peak after another as you make your way to **Innominate Tarn** (Map 12). From there, Wainwright recommends ignoring the obvious path that continues in an easterly direction to the north of **Blackbeck Tarn**, instead continuing in a south-easterly direction to an unmarked reunion with the low route near the top of **Loft Beck**. Though you'll struggle to follow any clear path in the ground, this trail is marked on Map 12. However, it's said that few trekkers actually manage to successfully rejoin the low route and instead forge their own path to **Honister Slate Mine**. If you wish to try, the best tactic from Innominate Tarn is to aim for **Brandreth Fence** to the south and continue along it until you come to a reunion with the regular route at the gate in the fence (WPT 023). Otherwise, the easiest solution is to continue on the clear trail to Blackbeck, from where you can follow the wide track down to Honister (see p116). Just make sure you don't start to descend to Buttermere.

Continuing on the **low route** up the valley, just over 90 minutes after joining the forest track you emerge at the head of Ennerdale and reach the wonderfully isolated bothy that is now *YHA Black Sail* (Maps 11/12; ☎ 0345 371 9680, 🖳 yha.org.uk/hostel/yha-black-sail; 2x4-, 1x8-bed rooms; WI-FI in communal area; ⓛ; mid Mar to end Oct), the country's most remote YHA hostel. Basic but comfortable and with magical views along the valley who could not wish to wake up here on a sunny morning? Meals are available (book in advance) and the hostel is licensed; note that debit and credit cards aren't accepted at the hostel. The

---

❑ **IMPORTANT NOTE – WALKING TIMES**

All times in this book refer only to the time spent walking. You will need to add 20-30% to allow for rests, photography, checking the map, drinking water etc.

MAP 12

THIS IS EXTREMELY BOGGY IN PLACES AND THERE IS NO PATH. INSTEAD, KEEP TO THE FENCE, MOVING AWAY TO AVOID THE BOGGY SECTIONS, IGNORING THE STILES UNTIL THE CORRECT ONE IS FOUND, WITH CAIRN-LINED PATHS LEADING AWAY ON BOTH SIDES

MAIN PATH GOING DOWN TO BLACKBECK TARN. PATH ALSO LEADS TO HOPPER QUARRY- A USEFUL, SIMPLER PATH TO THE 'ORIGINAL' C2C ROUTE

ATTENTION! AT BOGGY SADDLE, 022, TURN EAST AND CLIMB PATH MARKED BY CAIRN TO A GATE IN FENCE

DUBS QUARRY

INNOMINATE TARN

10b

SUDDENLY FIND YOU'RE ON A RIDGE WALK WITH VIEWS TO BUTTERMERE TO THE NORTH-WEST

BRANDRETH FENCE

RED PIKE ALTERNATIVE

BLACKBECK TARN

JUNCTION NOT OBVIOUS

024

13

YHA Black Sail

THIN BUT DEFINITE PATH

021

GATE IN BRANDRETH FENCE

023

PATHS JOINING FROM RIGHT

CAIRNS MARK THE WAY HERE

11

TO GREAT GABLE

DRUMLINS (HILLOCKS)

LOW LEVEL ROUTE

LOFT BECK

STEPS FOLLOWING STREAM UP STEEP HILL

BRANDRETH FENCE

ATTENTION! PATH GOES OFF EASTISH FROM YH- DO NOT TAKE THE MUCH MORE OBVIOUS PATH HEADING SOUTH-EAST

STEEP PATH IS CORRECT ROUTE

TONGUE BECK

0   ¼ mile
0   500m
APPROX SCALE

communal areas of the hostel are left open during the day for passing hikers, providing welcome shelter, use of the toilets, and the chance to make a cup of tea, or even a full lunch, in the kitchen. There's an honesty box for anything you consume. Incidentally, if the weather clears, just before the hostel are some steps leading up to Scarth Gap (Map 10b) on the high route (see p112).

From the hostel things can get a little tricky. You need to follow the correct path east (take the path that goes straight on past the hostel, rather than the more obvious path that bears off slightly to the right) to meet the climb up the side of **Loft Beck** and from there the path to Grey Knotts from where the long descent to Honister Hause and Borrowdale begins. Armed with this advice, in fine weather the way is crystal clear, but unfortunately such conditions are infrequent in these parts, particularly in the afternoon when most attempt the climb. At the top of Loft Beck follow Map 12 carefully to negotiate this section and have a compass or GPS at hand. At worst, at the top of the Beck blunder north over the boggy saddle to the **Brandreth Fence** and follow it east (right) to the gate at Wpt 023.

From the gate in Brandreth Fence, an initially indistinct path rises to contour around the western face of Brandreth and **Grey Knotts** (Map 13), with

ROUTE GUIDE AND MAPS

❑ HONISTER SLATE MINE

The story of mining at Honister began 400 million years ago when volcanic ash, combined with water and subsequent compression, formed the fine-grained rock now called slate. When the glaciers of the last Ice Age retreated up Gatesgarthdale they exposed three parallel veins of slate along the steep sides of the valley and sporadic mining may have taken place before the Roman era. Certainly by the early 1700s slate was being quarried here on an industrial scale and, as well as the disused tramway you walk down, there were roads and aerial ropeways to take the slate to the road. The workers who split and finished the slate lived in barracks in Honister during the week; the adjacent YHA hostel is a former quarry workers' building. After closing in the 1980s, the mine (along with the nearby quarry) re-opened in 1997 and has since developed into a slick, tourist-oriented facility backed by small-scale mining operations.

The **Visitor Centre** (Map 13; ☎ 01768 777230, 🖳 honister.com; daily 9am-5pm) is well worth a look. There are guided tours into the mine – contact them for details. For those with energy to spare they've also set up a *via ferrata*. Common in the Dolomites of northern Italy, a via ferrata, or 'iron way', is essentially a series of fixed iron ropes, ladders and other climbing aids to help non-climbers reach places that would otherwise be inaccessible. The one at Honister, for which a guide is compulsory, takes climbers through the quarry up to Fleetwith Pike on what they claim is the old miners' route to work. The cost is from £45, including equipment hire. Book via the website.

Attached to the visitors centre is the popular *Sky High Café* (also known as *Sky Hi Café*; 🐾; daily 8.30am-5pm), which does a mean bacon buttie (£4) as well as coffee, cakes and ice-creams. There's also a **gift shop** full of slate-based souvenirs, from great slabs that have been fashioned into coffee tables, to smaller chippings sold by the bagful. Some of the stuff is lovely but think twice before leaving with a full-size slate coffee table on your back; it's still a long way to Robin Hood's Bay. Something small such as a Coast to Coast coaster may be more appropriate.

60 MINS FROM TOP OF LOFT BECK (MAP 12) → ▶ HONISTER SLATE MINE → 60 MINS TO SEATOLLER (MAP 14) →

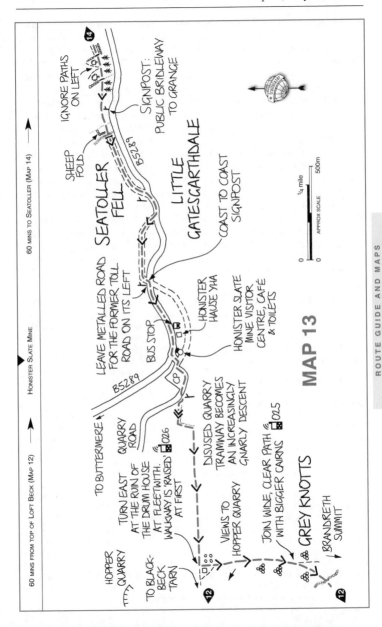

IGNORE PATHS ON LEFT

SHEEP FOLD

SEATOLLER FELL

SIGNPOST: PUBLIC BRIDLEWAY TO GRANGE

LITTLE GATESGARTHDALE

COAST TO COAST SIGNPOST

LEAVE METALLED ROAD FOR THE FORMER TOLL ROAD ON ITS LEFT

B5289

BUS STOP

HONISTER HAUSE YHA

HONISTER SLATE MINE VISITOR CENTRE, CAFÉ & TOILETS

¼ mile

500m

0

0

APPROX SCALE

TO BUTTERMERE

B5289

QUARRY ROAD

CP

MAP 13

DISUSED QUARRY TRAMWAY BECOMES AN INCREASINGLY GNARLY DESCENT

HOPPER QUARRY

TO BLACK-BECK TARN

TURN EAST AT THE RUIN OF THE DRUM HOUSE AT FLEETWITH. WALKWAY IS RAISED AT FIRST

026

VIEWS TO HOPPER QUARRY

JOIN WIDE, CLEAR PATH WITH BIGGER CAIRNS

025

GREY KNOTTS

BRANDRETH SUMMIT

12

12

ROUTE GUIDE AND MAPS

occasional cairns along the way. The working Hopper Quarry can be seen in the distance to the north. The path soon joins the larger path (WPT 025) coming down from Brandreth and Great Gable and drops gently to **Drum House**, now little more than a massive pile of stones and slate. The path's arrow-straight course betrays its previous incarnation as a quarry tramway; Drum House's original purpose was to house the cable that operated the tramway that ran to the cutting sheds. At the bottom of the steep and rather precarious tramway track is **Honister Hause**, and the hullabaloo surrounding **Honister Slate Mine Visitor Centre** (see box p114) at the crest of the notoriously steep Honister Pass road which many a caravanner has regretted tackling. Unfortunately, **YHA Honister Hause** (Map 13; ☎ 01768 777267 or ☎ 0345 371 9522, 💻 yha.org.uk/hostel/yha-honister-hause), which is next door, is operating on an exclusive hire only basis and is likely to continue to do so till 2025 at least; contact the YHA to check the latest. However, you have the option during the day of eating at the *café* (see box p114) attached to the slate mine's visitor centre next door. Stagecoach's 77/77A **bus** services calls at Honister Slate Mine (see pp54-6).

From Honister the path either parallels or is on the B5289 to Little Gatesgarthdale. Down in the valley the path loops back on itself to join the road at **Seatoller** (Map 14), although for a nifty short cut avoiding this village and saving you half a mile, see the map.

SEATOLLER   MAP 14

The National Trust village of Seatoller has a couple of places proving B&B accommodation, camping, an outdoor activity centre, a public phone box, a post box and a bus stop: Stagecoach's No 77/77A & 78 **bus** call here (see pp54-6 for details).

Where to stay and eat

You're now well and truly among the Lakeland honeypots with B&B prices which can make hostelling seem not such a bad idea after all. In the village centre *Seatoller House* (☎ 01768 777218, 💻 seatollerhouse.co.uk; 2D/2Tr all en suite, 3D or T/1Tr/2Qd private facilities; ➸; WI-FI; ⓛ; 🐾; Mar-mid Nov) is a 300-year-old building that's been a guesthouse for over a century. The rate for B&B is from £80pp (sgl occ £100); add £35 for a four-course dinner (fixed menu) served at 7pm every day except Tuesday. Generally, one-night stops are not an option, but if you're already in need of a rest day, or content in taking your time long the C2C, there are certainly worse places you could find yourself spending a couple of nights.

Right opposite, *Seatoller Farm* (email contact is preferred – for the address see their website 💻 seatollerfarm.co.uk; **fb**) is a working National Trust hill farm that allows **camping** (🐾; late Apr-late Oct). The rate (from £11pp) includes use of a shower; booking is essential. There is no wi-fi or phone signal. Wood-fired pizzas (late Apr-end Sep Fri & Sat 6-8pm), but not gluten free, are sold at the farm. They may have a small shop selling essentials from 2023.

Just outside the village, *Glaramara Hotel* (☎ 01768 777222, 💻 glaramara.co.uk; 8S/6D/19D or T, all en suite; ➸; WI-FI; ⓛ; 🐾) is a hotel and outdoor activity centre. Despite the slightly institutional atmosphere it's a great place to stay with good food and it's well set up for walkers. Facilities include a spacious residents' lounge with log fires, bar, and drying room. B&B costs from £82pp (sgl £82, sgl occ £107); but rates may be discounted in quiet periods. Three-course evening meals (from £30 if booked a week in advance or £39 if not) are also available. Non-residents can use the hotel during the day for teas and coffees as well as **light lunches** (daily noon-3pm).

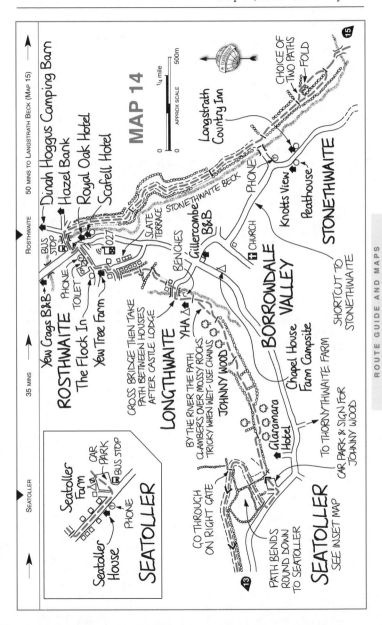

From Seatoller the trail wends its way through **Johnny Wood** (see p70), joining the short cut mentioned on p116 and passing the YHA hostel into Borrowdale Valley (Map 14).

BORROWDALE VALLEY
MAP 14, p117

Borrowdale Valley is made up of three separate settlements: Longthwaite, Rosthwaite and Stonethwaite. Small, picturesque and composed largely of slate-roofed, white-washed stone farm cottages, these are the iconic Lake District hamlets that tourists from around the world flock to see.

Longthwaite

The first building you come to in Borrowdale is the excellent *YHA Borrowdale* (☎ 0345 371 9624, ☐ yha.org .uk/hostel/yha-borrowdale; 3x2-, 2x3-, 5x4-, 6x6- & 1x8-bedded rooms; WI-FI; ☾; open all year), a spacious and well-run lodge with a laundry and drying room. Meals are available if pre-booked (non residents welcome too), and there is a large self-catering kitchen. They even have their own bar serving cask ales! Dorm beds weren't available at the time of writing but hopefully this will have changed by the time you begin your trek; private rooms start from £29 for 2 sharing but in peak season expect to pay £99. You can also **camp** (from £8pp; ☾) here and there are the now ubiquitous options for **glamping** (2-4 people; £59-129; ☾). Credit cards are accepted.

Longthwaite also plays host to *Gillercombe B&B* (☎ 01768 777602; 1S/1D/2T, shared bathroom; ☾; ☾; Mar-Oct). The friendly owner, Rachel Dunckley, is a mine of useful local information and local gossip, and her B&B offers a comfortable and convenient place to stay right in the heart of Borrowdale. B&B rates are from £50pp (inc for sgl/sgl occ). However, it is essential to book well in advance, as it's very popular.

A hop and a skip down the road is *Chapel House Farm Campsite* (☎ 01768 777256, ☐ chapelhousefarmcampsite.co .uk; ☾; generally Mar-Oct but check their website) where you can pitch your tent (from £9pp) in a roadside field. Facilities are basic – a clean and simple toilet and

shower block (50p for a 'hot' 4-minute shower). They always have space for walkers but they don't offer breakfast or packed lunches now.

Rosthwaite

The biggest settlement of the three is Rosthwaite to the north. Stagecoach's No 77/77A & 78 **bus** services call here; see pp54-6 for details.

Providing a first-rate service for walkers, *Yew Tree Farm* (☎ 01768 777675, ☐ borrowdaleyewtreefarm.co.uk; 1D/1T, both en suite; ☾; WI-FI; ☾; Mar-late Oct/early Nov) charges from £55pp (sgl occ £75). As well as selling their own produce, they also run a quirky little tearoom, *The Flock In* (Feb-late Oct/early Nov; daily 10am-5pm), opposite the main building, where the tea is served in pints or half pints. All their dishes are home-made, many using produce from the farm! Particularly recommended are the Herdwick Stew served with a cheese scone (£7.95) and the Herdwick lamb pasty & chutney (£5.50) – they are famous for both.

The Royal Oak Hotel (☎ 01768 777214, ☐ royaloakhotel.co.uk; 1S/2T/8D/ 2D or T/4Tr/1Qd, all en suite; ☾; WI-FI; ☾; ☾) once hosted the poet William Wordsworth. Rates for B&B vary a lot and there may be special offers so contact them for details but expect to pay from £75pp for two sharing (sgl/sgl occ from £80). They also offer a four-course meal for £31.50 (daily 6.30-8pm). The majority of rooms are in the main hotel but some are in a converted barn across the farmyard. There is also an **apartment** sleeping up to four (£140 per night inc breakfast) and two **bunkhouses** (1 x 4- and 1 x 6- bed rooms with separate facilities) from £120 for the 4-bunk room inc breakfast.

Next door is *Scafell Hotel* (☎ 01768 777208, ☐ scafell.co.uk; 3S/10D/7T/3Tr, all en suite; ☾; WI-FI mainly in public areas; ☾; ☾), a large place which has served as a coaching inn since 1850 – some rooms are furnished with antiques. B&B costs from £90pp (sgl £90, sgl occ room rate) but it's worth checking online for offers and always booking direct. The menu is extensive and the **food** good. The restaurant is open daily 6.30-9pm but booking is essential. Their ***Riverside Bar*** (food daily noon-2.30pm & 6-9pm) has cheaper bar meals, including burgers, steak and local trout.

Yew Craggs B&B (☎ 017687 77348, 🖳 yewcraggsborrowdale.co.uk; 1D/2D or T, all en suite; WI-FI; Ⓛ) charges from £57.50pp (sgl occ £110) for one-night stops. Evening meals (from £18 for two courses) are available if 72 hours' notice is given.

Just off the path, ***Hazel Bank Country House*** (☎ 01768 777248, 🖳 hazelbankhotel.co.uk; 4D/3D or T, all en suite; ▼; WI-FI; Ⓛ; Feb-Nov) is a very comfortable, award-winning hotel set in extensive grounds. B&B costs £100-120pp (dinner, bed & breakfast £142-162pp; sgl occ B&B from £190) and bookings for a Saturday night are normally two-night minimum stay and DB&B only.

Nearby is ***Dinah Hoggus Camping Barn*** (☎ 01768 777689, 🖳 lakelandcampingbarns.co.uk; mid Feb-end Nov), a very simple but attractively rustic place sleeping 12 people. At the weekend it is almost always booked by groups but during the week they may take bookings (booking is essential and the minimum group size is four people). There's a cooking and eating area with a kettle, microwave and electric hob, and a toilet and shower. They charge from £15pp (mattresses provided, but no bedding so you need to have a sleeping bag).

Stonethwaite

Just under a mile (about 1.6km) to the south and away from the relative clamour of Rosthwaite, Stonethwaite nestles in its own little world at the end of a road running parallel to the beck that shares its name. Although frequently rained upon, it's among the prettiest of the Lakeland hamlets with an attractive little **church**.

Knotts View (☎ 01768 777604; 1D/2D or T, shared facilities; WI-FI; Ⓛ) charges from £50pp (sgl occ £50) for **B&B**. The building is 450 years old and, with its low ceilings, it feels like it. Under the same ownership is ***Peathouse Tea & Coffee Shop*** (usually Apr-end Oct daily, but with flexible opening hours) next door. However, at the time of research and due to COVID they were offering takeaway only. Incidentally, if you're not familiar with the nature of peat, by the time you get to Greenup Edge tomorrow you'll be an expert.

Best of all has long been ***The Langstrath Country Inn*** (☎ 01768 777239, 🖳 thelangstrath.co.uk; 5D/6D or T, all en suite; ▼; WI-FI; Ⓛ; 🐕; Feb-Nov Tue-Sun), indeed some trekkers say it has the best restaurant on the whole trail. Their menu (Feb-Nov Tue-Sun noon-2.30pm & 6-8.30pm, 2.30-4pm light bites only) may include locally sourced produce such as herb-roasted local pork loin; mains cost from £14.25. The rooms are undoubtedly worthy of praise: B&B costs from £62.50pp (sgl occ room rate). Note that they don't usually accept advance bookings for single-night stays on Fridays or Saturdays.

STAGE 3: BORROWDALE TO GRASMERE — MAPS 14-18

Introduction

In good weather this **9-mile (14.5km, 4-5½hr high route)** stage is a Lakeland classic; a straightforward climb up past Lining Crag to Greenup Edge, followed by the high-level ridge walk we recommend (see p122) or a less adventurous and slightly shorter plod down the valley to the edge of Grasmere. Wainwright combines this stage with the next one to Patterdale, adding up to at least a 17-mile (27.5km) hike, and a few walkers do just that. Sticking to the valley routes as Wainwright did, it's not too demanding. If doing so, we recommend you take

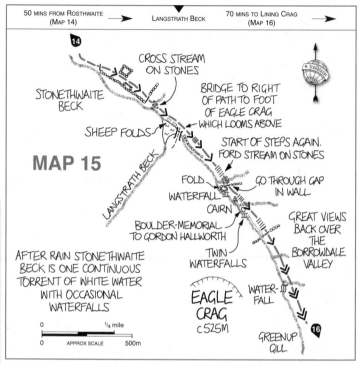

50 MINS FROM ROSTHWAITE (MAP 14) →

LANGSTRATH BECK

70 MINS TO LINING CRAG (MAP 16) →

14

CROSS STREAM ON STONES

STONETHWAITE BECK

BRIDGE TO RIGHT OF PATH TO FOOT OF EAGLE CRAG WHICH LOOMS ABOVE

SHEEP FOLDS

MAP 15

START OF STEPS AGAIN. FORD STREAM ON STONES

LANGSTRATH BECK

FOLD

WATERFALL

CAIRN

GO THROUGH GAP IN WALL

BOULDER-MEMORIAL TO GORDON HALLWORTH

GREAT VIEWS BACK OVER THE BORROWDALE VALLEY

AFTER RAIN STONETHWAITE BECK IS ONE CONTINUOUS TORRENT OF WHITE WATER WITH OCCASIONAL WATERFALLS

TWIN WATERFALLS

WATER- FALL

EAGLE CRAG c 525M

0   ¼ mile

0   APPROX SCALE   500M

GREENUP GILL

16

at least one of the high-level options on either stage; this is the Lake District after all. Taking on the high routes in one long day – not least via Helvellyn and Striding Edge which will add **two miles and up to two hours** – may leave you a little drained for the 15½-miler from Patterdale to Shap which follows and along which there are no easy gradients. Our advice? Do one of the two high routes and don't rush. This is one of the highlights of the Coast to Coast.

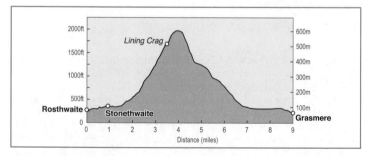

The route

The stage begins with a level amble through the fields alongside **Stonethwaite Beck** (Map 14), with **Eagle Crag** a looming presence across the water. It looks massive but by the time you get to Greenup Edge (Map 16) you'll be looking *down* on Eagle Crag. At the bridge by Langstrath Beck you join **Greenup Gill** (Map 15), which after heavy rain becomes one long torrent of white water and waterfalls, with views back down to Borrowdale growing more impressive with every upward step.

The path's gradient picks up a notch past Eagle Crag, drops into a basin of *drumlins* (mounds created by glacial action) and a stepped climb up onto the top of **Lining Crag** (Map 16) from where, weather permitting, views reach over towards Scafell Pike, England's highest summit at 3210ft (978m).

Look to the south and you'll also make out the beginning of the path to the broad col of **Greenup Edge**. This next section is where some lose their way, the boggy ground and indistinct cairns obscuring the correct direction even in ideal conditions. As you near the col look out for the old fence posts which once

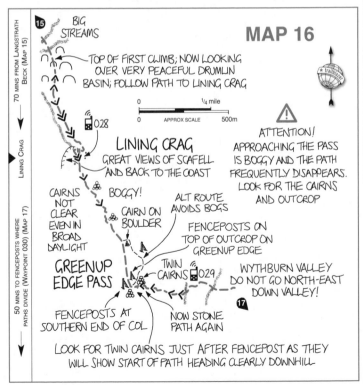

ROUTE GUIDE AND MAPS

15 BIG STREAMS

MAP 16

TOP OF FIRST CLIMB; NOW LOOKING OVER VERY PEACEFUL DRUMLIN BASIN; FOLLOW PATH TO LINING CRAG

0   ¼ mile
0   APPROX SCALE   500m

028

LINING CRAG
GREAT VIEWS OF SCAFELL AND BACK TO THE COAST

CAIRNS NOT CLEAR EVEN IN BROAD DAYLIGHT

BOGGY!

CAIRN ON BOULDER

ALT ROUTE AVOIDS BOGS

ATTENTION!
APPROACHING THE PASS IS BOGGY AND THE PATH FREQUENTLY DISAPPEARS. LOOK FOR THE CAIRNS AND OUTCROP

FENCEPOSTS ON TOP OF OUTCROP ON GREENUP EDGE

GREENUP EDGE PASS

TWIN CAIRNS 029

WYTHBURN VALLEY DO NOT GO NORTH-EAST DOWN VALLEY!

17

FENCEPOSTS AT SOUTHERN END OF COL

NOW STONE PATH AGAIN

LOOK FOR TWIN CAIRNS JUST AFTER FENCEPOST AS THEY WILL SHOW START OF PATH HEADING CLEARLY DOWNHILL

70 MINS FROM LANGSTRATH BECK (MAP 15)

LINING CRAG

50 MINS TO FENCEPOSTS WHERE PATHS DIVIDE (WAYPOINT 030) (MAP 17)

stretched up and over to Low White Stones, the hill south of the col; see box p91. If you see one on an outcrop, aim to the south of it to a less conspicuous fence post at ground level and, a few metres further on, the key twin **cairns** (WPT 029) from where the descent from the Edge commences across the head of **Wythburn Valley**. You cross the upper basin of Wyth Burn on clearer tracks to the 'gateposts' on Map 17 (WPT 030) marking its neighbour, **Far Easedale**. From here you choose the valley route or the more demanding high route which most hikers take these days, along with casually clad day-trippers out of Grasmere who commonly combine both into a loop.

The ridge-walk alternative to Grasmere via Helm Crag
Map 17 & Map 18, p124

The high-level route takes in **Calf Crag**, **Gibson Knott** and **Helm Crag** amongst others. The ground is often saturated but the climbs up to the various summits take only a few minutes and give some great viewpoints down to Easedale Gill and Easedale Tarn glistening below. It's a long hard walk with rocky steps and bogs; allow at least 90 minutes from the 'fenceposts' to Lancrigg Woods. That is the price of surveying Castle, Lang and Silver Hows (hills) behind you to the south-west, and Helvellyn and Great Rigg beyond. By the time you've reached Helm Crag overlooking the following stage, the steep descent to the north-western outskirts of Grasmere may well finish you off!

Whichever route you take, when you reach the bottom and Easedale it's worth a diversion through **Lancrigg Woods** along **Poet's Walk** (Map 18), a tranquil delight that may soothe sore feet. It comes as no surprise to find that the Lakeland poets enjoyed it; indeed, they planted many of the trees that grow in the woods. Along the way is an inscription, in Latin, describing how Wordsworth's sister Dorothy would sit at this spot while her brother walked up and down composing verses. The path crosses the croquet lawn of Lancrigg Hotel (see below) and a minute later passes Thorney How. Here at the road the trail continues north-east for the climb over to Patterdale. To the south a 20-minute walk leads to Grasmere, the Lake District's busiest tourist village.

EASEDALE   MAP 18, p124
Picturesque Easedale has a few places to stay and eat right on the path if you aren't diverting into Grasmere.

Where to stay and eat
If you stick to the path via Poet's Walk you'll walk right past *Lancrigg* (☎ 015394 35317, ☐ lancrigg.co.uk; 11D/2D or T/2T/1Qd, all en suite; ☞; WI-FI; Ⓛ; 🐾), a large country-house hotel with parts dating back to the 17th century. **B&B** costs from £60pp (sgl occ room rate). **Food** (restaurant daily 12.30-3.30pm & 6-7pm) is available to non-residents; mains at lunch are £7.50-15.95.

On the A591 is a pub, *The Traveller's Rest* (☎ 015394 35604, ☐ lakedistrict inns.co.uk/travellers-rest; 8D/2T, all en suite; ☞; WI-FI; Ⓛ; 🐾). B&B costs from £30pp to £80pp (sgl occ room rate). **Food** is served daily (noon-3pm & 5-8.45pm) and includes hearty portions of mainly local dishes.

A couple of hundred metres along the road, towards Grasmere, *Chestnut Villa* (☎ 015394 35218, ☐ chestnutvilla.com; 6D, all en suite; ☞; WI-FI; Ⓛ) charges £62.50-90pp (sgl occ £100-120) offers accommodation but on a room-only basis.

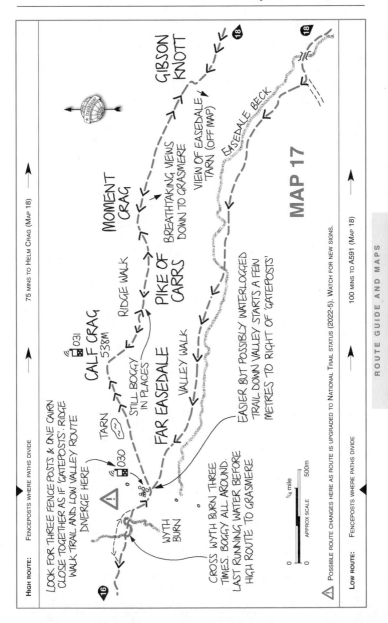

HIGH ROUTE: FENCEPOSTS WHERE PATHS DIVIDE

75 MINS TO HELM CRAG (MAP 18)

LOOK FOR THREE FENCE POSTS & ONE CAIRN CLOSE TOGETHER AS IF 'GATEPOSTS'. RIDGE WALK TRAIL AND LOW VALLEY ROUTE DIVERGE HERE

CALF CRAG
538M

TARN

STILL BOGGY IN PLACES

RIDGE WALK

MOMENT CRAG

GIBSON KNOTT

BREATHTAKING VIEWS DOWN TO GRASMERE

VIEW OF EASEDALE TARN (OFF MAP)

PIKE OF CARRS

FAR EASEDALE

VALLEY WALK

EASEDALE BECK

MAP 17

EASIER BUT POSSIBLY WATERLOGGED TRAIL DOWN VALLEY STARTS A FEW METRES TO RIGHT OF 'GATEPOSTS'

⚠

WYTH BURN

CROSS WYTH BURN THREE TIMES. BOGGY ALL AROUND. LAST RUNNING WATER BEFORE HIGH ROUTE TO GRASMERE

16

18

18

030

031

¼ mile

APPROX SCALE

500m

0

0

⚠ POSSIBLE ROUTE CHANGES HERE AS ROUTE IS UPGRADED TO NATIONAL TRAIL STATUS (2022-5). WATCH FOR NEW SIGNS.

LOW ROUTE: FENCEPOSTS WHERE PATHS DIVIDE

100 MINS TO A591 (MAP 18)

ROUTE GUIDE AND MAPS

GRASMERE   see map p127

Wordsworth called this valley 'the fairest place on earth' and his association with Grasmere has done so much to popularise the place that on some days you might wish you'd not paused here in your wandering o'er the hills and vales. Fleece-clad hordes stream in all summer to mill about or grab a lunch and masses of coach-tour groups pause to take selfies before puttering off, but looking out to the glorious hills surrounding the village, you can see why. And with facilities and services that include discount hiking outlets, an ATM and, unlike other places along the walk, more than one shop, it can all add up to a worthwhile stopover.

HIGH ROUTE: 75 MINS FROM FENCEPOSTS (MAP 17) → HELM CRAG → 55 MINS VIA GOODYBRIDGE FARM → A591 →

LOW ROUTE: 100 MINS FROM FENCE-POSTS (MAP 17) → A591 →

17

★ trailblazer

MAP 18

032
HELM CRAG
360° VIEWS OVER THE FELLS

START OF BRIDLEWAY UP TO GRISEDALE TARN

TO KESWICK

WPT 033: EASILY MISSED SHORT CUT FOR THOSE HEADING ONTO PATTERDALE BYPASSING GRASMERE

19

A591

17

AT WALL TURN RIGHT THEN LEFT ONTO STONY TRACK

STEPS

CAIRN

POET'S WALK

THORNEY HOW

MILL BRIDGE

Traveller's Rest

LANCRIGG WOODS
Lancrigg Hotel

033

034

Chestnut Villa

FARMHOUSE

SLATE TRACK

GOODY BRIDGE

PYE LANE

EASEDALE BECK

JACKDAW COTTAGE

EASEDALE

EASEDALE FOREST

GOODYBRIDGE FARM

YHA Grasmere Butharlyp Howe

FOOTPATH TO GRASMERE, 20MINS - FAR NICER THAN FOLLOWING THE ROAD

EASEDALE RD

ALLAN BANK (NT)
(SEE TOWN PLAN)

GRASMERE

0   ¼ mile
0   APPROX SCALE   500m

⚠ POSSIBLE ROUTE CHANGES HERE AS ROUTE IS UPGRADED TO NATIONAL TRAIL STATUS (2022-5). WATCH FOR SIGNS.

ROUTE GUIDE AND MAPS

Though Wordsworth lived in Grasmere for only nine years, it was a productive period and he wrote many of his best-known works here. (All together now: '*I wandered lonely as a cloud...*') His cottage is the main sight in the village and his grave is in the grounds of St Oswald's Church (see column opposite), one of the more peaceful spots in Grasmere's often overcrowded centre.

More spacious than the preceding valley settlements, to the west the large farmhouses and grand homes share the undulating land with forests of mature deciduous trees and flocks of dozy sheep and through the busy jumble of buildings in the centre flows River Rothay, a tranquil haven for ducks and other waterfowl; to the south lies brooding Grasmere Lake, flanked by steep, forested hills.

What to see and do

William Wordsworth lived in the beautiful **Dove Cottage** (off map p127; ☎ 015394 35544, 🖳 wordsworth.org.uk; Tue-Sat 10am-5pm; £14 for cottage, museum & garden orchard, £11 without the cottage) for fewer than ten years, yet its importance in both his development as a poet and his life was enormous. Many of his best-loved and most powerful works were written here and this was his first home with his wife Mary Hutchinson and where three of his children were born. The cottage is, by the standards of the Lake District, relatively large, containing eight rooms rather than the more typical three or four, thus betraying its origins as a 17th-century pub. One of Wordsworth's frequent visitors was that other well-known literary figure (and opium fiend) Thomas de Quincey. De Quincey declared the house to be a fortuitous one for writers and when the Wordsworths vacated it in 1808 the de Quinceys moved in, thus continuing the cottage's literary connections. The **museum** next door contains original manuscripts by the Wordsworths, and there's an on-site *café* (Tue-Sun 10am-5pm). Dove Cottage is about 500m south-east from The Green, just off the A591.

A 10-minute stroll from The Green, **Allan Bank** (Map 18, opposite; ☎ 015394 35143, 🖳 nationaltrust.org.uk/allan-bank; days/hours vary so check the website; £6.50, free for National Trust members) is another of Wordsworth's onetime residences in the area. For two years fellow Romantic poet, Samuel Taylor Coleridge lived with the Wordsworths in the house. Blighted by opium addiction (which Wordsworth disapproved of) their friendship deteriorated (a rift that never healed) and they left the property behind, Wordsworth moving to Grasmere rectory. Over 100 years later, Allan Bank became home to Canon Hardwicke Rawnsley, one of the founders of the National Trust. The walls inside the house are now adorned with giant portraits of Wordsworth, Coleridge, and Rawnsley, completed by local artist Sarah Jackman. The views from the house alone make Allan Bank well worth a visit. As well as the house there's also garden and woodland trails to be explored, and if you're lucky there may be live music in the garden. All very tranquil indeed.

● **Other sights** Before you leave, you may like to pay a visit to **Wordsworth's family grave** around the back of **St Oswald's**, a 13th-century church named after the 7th-century king of Northumbria who preached on this site. Wordsworth's prayer-book is on display in the church.

Standing by the side entrance to the church grounds is the 150-year-old **Gingerbread Shop** (☎ 015394 35428, 🖳 grasmeregingerbread.co.uk; **fb**; daily 9.15am-5.30pm, closing hours may vary in the winter), a tiny 'factory' that used to be the local school; it is said that Wordsworth taught here occasionally. The secret recipe for the gingerbread was created by Sarah Nelson back in 1854 and is so highly treasured that it's kept inside the Windermere branch of NatWest Bank. You'll do well to find better-tasting gingerbread anywhere on this planet, let alone in Grasmere, and it is sold in small, individual pieces (90p, or 6/12 for £4.50/7.95) that can be easily slipped into rucksack pockets. However, beware the queue.

Opposite is **Storyteller's Garden** (🖳 taffythomas.co.uk) which hosts several events throughout the year – see the website for details. Around the village centre are a number of **galleries** displaying works by local artists.

Near the church is the small **Wordsworth Daffodil Garden**, an attractive landscaped park filled with shady broadleaf trees and, in spring, lots of the namesake daffodils. It's free to enter.

Make sure, too, that you check out Lancrigg Woods and Poet's Walk (Map 18, p124), the start of which you walked past on your way into Grasmere.

Services

There's a free **ATM** at the **Co-op** (daily 7am-10pm), the best place to stock up on provisions.

You can also withdraw money with most UK bank cards at the **post office** (Mon-Fri 9.30am-5pm, Sat-Sun 10am-5pm, winter 10.30am-4pm) which is housed inside a gift shop on Stock Lane.

Grasmere has an excellent bookshop, **Sam Read Bookseller** (☎ 015394 35374, 🖥 samreadbooks.co.uk; generally daily 10am-1pm & 1.30-5pm, Jan-Feb Fri-Mon though) that has been trading since 1887. There's a surprisingly wide range of books in this tardis of a shop and when you've found something to read you can pick up a coffee from *Lucia's* (see Where to eat) next door.

Close to the Co-op is a **pharmacy** (Mon-Fri 9am-5.30pm, Sat to 1pm) if your Compeed supply is running perilously low. There are numerous **trekking/outdoor shops** dotted around the town centre.

Transport   (see also pp54-6)

Stagecoach's No 555 and their No 599 'Lakesider' **bus** call at Windermere railway station (approx 36 mins) where you can pick up a Northern train to Oxenholme Lake District and from there connect to other stations in Britain. On sunny summer days they use an open-top bus for the service. Buses leave from Broadgate.

Where to stay

This is merely a selection of the many places to stay here. Being Grasmere, with all the tourist business it can handle, B&Bs are very reluctant to accept a one-night-only booking on summer weekends. Either stay for two nights and spend a day enjoying the town and surrounds or try to avoid the high-season weekends. Single occupancy may well mean paying the room rate.

Hostels *YHA Grasmere Butharlyp Howe* (☎ 0345 371 9319, 🖥 yha.org.uk/hostel/yha-grasmere-butharlyp-howe; 6x2-, 10x4-, 2x6-, 2x8-bed rooms; private rooms from £59 for two sharing; WI-FI in public areas; Ⓛ) enjoys a central location and is housed in a Victorian mansion in attractive grounds. Note that it is bookable at weekends year-round by individuals and on a 60-day rolling release for stays midweek; also dorm beds weren't available to book at the time of writing. It's well facilitated with an alcohol licence, a smart self-catering kitchen, a large drying room, laundry facilities, a games room and three lounges. There is a large grassy lawn for **camping** (from £10pp; 🐾) and there are also two **tipis** and two **land-pods** (mid Apr to end Oct; sleeping up to four; £79-119) to consider spending the night in; ensure you book in advance though. The meals are okay here too, especially when you consider the cost of eating out in Grasmere; there are 'supper club' options (2 courses, eg, lasagne and fruit salad) and pizzas in the evenings, as well as breakfast baps. A continental/cooked breakfast costs £5.95/9.95. Credit cards are accepted and there's 24hr access.

B&Bs On the approach into Grasmere, *Glenthorne* (☎ 015394 35389, 🖥 glenthorne.org; 4S/13T/5D, all en suite, 3S/1T share facilities; 🛆; WI-FI; Ⓛ; Feb-Nov) is a Victorian, Quaker-owned (though folk of any creed can stay) country house/conference centre near another of Wordsworth's old houses, Allan Bank (see p125). Though the place feels like a hostel when you first walk in – perhaps owing to the wonderfully informal atmosphere – the rooms are quite smart. Overriding everything, however, is the hospitality here, with trays of cakes and tea laid out for guests each day (4.30-5/5.30pm). Evening meals (7pm;

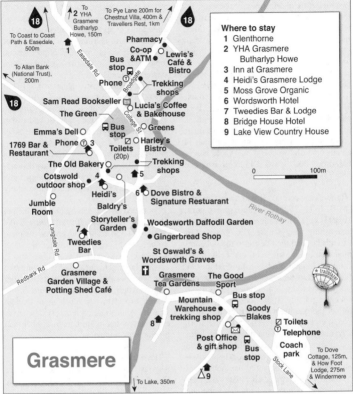

Grasmere

To Coast to Coast Path & Easedale, 500m

To 2 YHA Grasmere Butharlyp Howe, 150m

To Pye Lane 200m for Chestnut Villa, 400m & Travellers Rest, 1km

To Allan Bank (National Trust), 200m

18

Easedale Rd

Pharmacy
Co-op &ATM
Lewis's Café & Bistro
Bus stop
Phone
Broadgate
Trekking shops

Sam Read Bookseller
The Green
Lucia's Coffee & Bakehouse
College St

Emma's Dell
Bus stop
Greens
Phone 3
Harley's Bistro
1769 Bar & Restaurant
Toilets (20p)

The Old Bakery
Trekking shops
Cotswold outdoor shop
4
5
Dove Bistro & Signature Restaurant
6
Heidi's
Jumble Room
Baldry's
Langdale Rd
Storyteller's Garden
Woodsworth Daffodil Garden

7
Tweedies Bar
Gingerbread Shop
St Oswald's & Wordsworth Graves

Redbank Rd
Grasmere Garden Village & Potting Shed Café
Grasmere Tea Gardens
The Good Sport
Bus stop

Mountain Warehouse trekking shop
Goody Blakes
Toilets
Telephone

8
Post Office & gift shop
Bus stop
Coach park
To Dove Cottage, 125m, & How Foot Lodge, 275m & Windermere
Stock Lane

9
To Lake, 350m

River Rothay

trailblazer

0 — 100m

Where to stay
1 Glenthorne
2 YHA Grasmere Butharlyp Howe
3 Inn at Grasmere
4 Heidi's Grasmere Lodge
5 Moss Grove Organic
6 Wordsworth Hotel
7 Tweedies Bar & Lodge
8 Bridge House Hotel
9 Lake View Country House

ROUTE GUIDE AND MAPS

from £25pp) must be booked 48hrs in advance; all they ask is a few seconds' silence before eating. B&B rates are per person: from £63/75pp for a non en suite/en suite room).

In the centre of the village itself, *Heidi's Grasmere Lodge* (☎ 015394 35248, ☐ heidisgrasmerelodge.co.uk; 4D/1D or T, all en suite; ☕; WI-FI; (Ⓛ)), above **Heidi's café** (see Where to eat), is an award-winning boutique-like B&B with charming, individually designed rooms, one of which has its own private roof terrace and another has a private balcony. B&B costs £60-82.50pp (sgl occ room rate) but at weekends in high season they often

insist on a two-night minimum stay if booking in advance.

Lake View Country House (☎ 07783 759617, ☐ lakeview-grasmere.com; 1D/4Tr/1Qd, two up to five, all en suite; ☕; WI-FI; 🐾) is, as its name suggests, one of the few places to stay from where you can actually see the lake (from the first floor). It's a lovely place near the centre of Grasmere but quietly tucked away at the end of a lane. Three of the largest rooms have self-catering facilities and one has a roof terrace too. B&B costs £75-112.50pp, room only £62.50-100pp (sgl occ room rate); breakfast is served at The Good Sport (see p128). If booking in advance stays of two nights are often required except in winter. There's direct access to the lakeshore which could be useful for people with dogs; though all dogs need to be kept on a lead, particularly as there's a badger sett in the garden!

South of Grasmere, 150m beyond Dove Cottage is *How Foot Lodge* (☎ 015394 35366, 🖥 howfootlodge.co.uk; 4D/2T, all en suite; ✆; WI-FI; ⓛ; mid Feb-end Nov) though only one room a night is available for one-night stays in the summer and they don't accept one-night bookings in advance for the weekend but would nearer the time. B&B costs £45-50pp (sgl occ £85-95).

Hotels Very central, *Moss Grove Organic* (☎ 015394 35251, 🖥 mossgrove.com; 10D/1D or T, all en suite; ✆; WI-FI; 🐾) is a smashing place whose strict green ethos extends beyond the kitchen to their accommodation, with some of the beds made from reclaimed timber sitting atop oak floors from sustainable forests. All this, and yet the building still retains its original Victorian charm. The prices, however, do reflect the quality, with B&B costing from £65pp up to £145pp (sgl occ £15 discount). One reader wrote saying it was worth it for the luxurious bed alone (they stayed in Room 5). Breakfast is organic where possible; there is no restaurant or bar though it is possible to buy organic chocolates and truffles as well as bottles of organic wine and beer. Note that if booking in advance, stays of two nights are usually required over a Saturday night.

The Inn at Grasmere (☎ 015394 35456, 🖥 theinnatgrasmere.co.uk; 2S/42D or T/5T, all en suite; ✆; WI-FI; ⓛ; 🐾) is also right in the centre of town. It lacks a little of the charm of some of the other places around here, but the rooms are smart. B&B costs £65-87.50pp (sgl/sgl occ from £115).

Tweedies Bar & Lodge (☎ 015394 35300, 🖥 tweediesgrasmere.com; 14D/2D or T, all en suite; ✆; WI-FI; ⓛ; 🐾) is a huge, rambling place. An old-fashioned-looking pile on the outside, inside it is all polished floorboards and original tilework

mixed with striking colour schemes, with each bedroom individually decorated. The three acres of sprawling gardens are another attraction, as is its location in the heart of town. B&B costs from £72.50pp (sgl occ room rate). There is a two-night minimum stay at weekends.

The Wordsworth Hotel (☎ 015394 35592, 🖥 thewordsworthhotel.co.uk; 24D or T/7D, 4 suites, all en suite; ✆; WI-FI; ⓛ; 🐾) was formerly the smartest address in the centre of town; a large attractive hotel with facilities including pool, sauna, Jacuzzi and cocktail bar. B&B costs from £90pp (sgl occ £159) but rates vary depending on demand. Advance bookings for a one-night stay on a Saturday aren't usually accepted.

Owned by the same company behind The Inn at Grasmere, *Bridge House Hotel* (☎ 015394 35425, 🖥 bridgehousegrasmere .co.uk; 21D/5D or T, all en suite; ✆; WI-FI; ⓛ; Feb-end Oct, rest of year Thur-Sun) is another large place near the river, with two acres of gorgeous grounds. B&B is from approximately £80pp (sgl occ from £150), though expect to pay much more in high season (sgl occ rate on request). They generally accept one-night bookings other than for Saturday nights.

Where to eat and drink

As you'd expect for a major tourist centre like Grasmere, cafés and restaurants are plentiful throughout the village, though there are few **pub**-type places. It's worth noting that for an evening meal you would be wise to book your table as far ahead as possible.

The Good Sport (☎ 07724 330722, 🖥 grasmerepub.com; **fb**; WI-FI; 🐾; food daily breakfast 9-10.30am, from 9.30am in winter, & 11am-8.30pm) serves beers and a cider brewed at Grasmere Brewery which is in the grounds of Lake View Country House – and gin (plain and flavoured) and vodka are also distilled there. The beer garden here goes down to the river. One satisfied walker reported: 'They serve very good food and a nice home brewed pint which we could recommend after a long day on the path'. Despite the name, they do not show sport. However, their Grasmere Herdwick lamb dishes including a burger (£18) will more than compliment or make up for the lack of large noisy screens.

Otherwise *Tweedies Bar* (see Where to Stay; food generally daily noon-3pm & 6-9pm) is recommended. You could also try *1769 Bar & Restaurant* (food daily noon-9.30pm, restaurant 6-9pm) at **The Inn at Grasmere** (see Where to stay).

In contrast, you'll be tripping over **cafés**: for excellent Fairtrade coffee there's *Lucia's Coffee + Bakehouse* (**fb**; Mon-Sat 9am-4.30pm), beside the bookshop; the banana bread they occasionally have on sale is delicious.

The Old Bakery (daily 9am-4.30pm; WI-FI) is a café that's neither old, nor a bakery, but does do breakfasts, pastries and pies as well as takeaway sandwiches. A few steps on, *Heidi's* (see Where to stay; 🐾; daily 9.15am-3pm) serves light lunches and welcomes dogs with well-behaved owners.

Baldry's (☎ 015394 35301, 🖥 baldrys-grasmere.com; WI-FI; 🐾; daily 10am-4.30pm), across the road, is a genteel tea-room; a Lakeland breakfast (served until 11.30am) costs £12.45 (vegetarian £11.45) and a scone, jam & cream (£3.75).

Opposite The Green, *Emma's Dell* (☎ 015394 35234, 🖥 www.emmasdell.uk; **fb**; summer Mon-Thur 10am-4pm, Fri-Sun to 4pm, winter days/hours variable; WI-FI; 🐾) is a fine place to enjoy a sweet or savoury crêpe (from £5.50) or a scone (from £3.25).

A number of cafés vie for position near the bridge over River Rothay. Best located is *Grasmere Tea Gardens* (☎ 015394 35590; WI-FI; daily 10am-4pm, winter to 3pm), with a back terrace overlooking the river. It's been in business since 1889.

At **Grasmere Garden Village** (☎ 015394 35255, 🖥 grasmeregardens.com) there's *Potting Shed Café* (Mon-Sat 10am-4.30pm, Sun to 4pm; WI-FI; 🐾). The menu includes home-made soups (£5.95) and sandwiches (from £8.95), plus a full-English breakfast (£10.50, vegetarian £8.95) till 11.30am.

The rather plush *Dove Bistro* (daily 6-8.45pm, Sat & Sun noon-2pm), part of

Wordsworth Hotel (see Where to stay) serves mains from £16.75 as well as afternoon tea (daily noon-5pm, £18.95pp; Champagne afternoon tea £23.95pp). You'd be advised to pre-book. Their *Signature Restaurant* (daily 12.30-4.30pm & 6-8.45pm) has an à la carte menu and a four-course dinner with canapés for £47.

On the same street, but more down to earth, is *Greens* (☎ 01539 435790; **fb**; mid Feb-mid Nov 9.30am-4pm but check on Facebook page as days can vary; WI-FI; 🐾), a contemporary café-bistro with a warm atmosphere and healthy food including gluten-free, vegetarian and vegan options.

On Broadgate, *Lewis's Café & Bistro* (☎ 015394 35266, 🖥 lewissofgrasmere.co.uk; Mar-end Nov Tue-Sun 5.30-9pm; 🐾) is a family-run bistro serving locally sourced Cumbrian food, with a few Italian and Thai dishes thrown in for good measure.

Goody Blakes (☎ 07947 823710; generally 6-9pm but days vary so call to check; 🐾; WI-FI), Stock Lane, serves smashing food in a relaxed atmosphere and is the go-to place for a steak (local sirloin/fillet £22.95/27.95).

Most unusual of all is *The Jumble Room* (☎ 015394 35188, 🖥 thejumble room.co.uk; Mar-Oct Thur-Sat 4.30-10pm, Nov-Feb Fri-Sat 5.30-9.30pm; booking advisable) on Langdale Rd. The décor looks less of a jumble with each passing year but this quirky little place still gets rave reviews. The menu changes frequently and includes dishes from all four corners of the globe with a few extra corners you never knew about. Look out for their Baja fish tacos, with Jumble Room dirty fries (£18.50; vegan tacos, and other vegan dishes are also available).

What was the Methodist church is now *Harley's Bistro* (☎ 015394 35533; **fb**; food Sun-Thur 9.30am-5pm, Fri & Sat 9.30am-7.30pm; WI-FI; 🐾): the church's features remain although the style of service has obviously changed; reviews are mixed, but it's a cheaper option compared to many of Grasmere's other eateries (Cumbrian burger £16.95, pizzas from £10.95).

STAGE 4: GRASMERE TO PATTERDALE   MAPS 18-25

Introduction

Ignoring the alternative routes for the moment, this is the shortest of the stages. Short, but no less sweet for it's another classic hike along which walkers can enjoy some great views back to Grasmere and, once over the pass, down across Grisedale to Patterdale, another gorgeous valley with the lake of Ullswater twinkling away to the north.

The most direct routes avoiding Striding Edge are a mere **8½ miles (13.5km, 3-4hrs)** and deliver a simple walk up to **Grisedale Pass (Hause)** and either down the valley or – more satisfyingly – up along the ridge of St Sunday Crag. The longer route ascends the 950-metre bulk of Helvellyn, returning to the valley via the stirringly named Striding Edge ridge walk; an additional distance of around **two miles** and a considerable amount of climbing and at times, exposure. Both the high routes are described on p132 and p134. You can delay your choice on which path to take until Grisedale Tarn, where the three paths go their separate ways.

The route

First of all you need to reach the heights of Grisedale Tarn, which involves a climb up a bridleway running off the A591, reached either by walking up the A591 to the bridleway, if coming from Grasmere or, as we've mapped it (Map 18, p124) by picking up the original Coast to Coast path near Thorney How.

At a footbridge or ford the bridleway divides at the foot of **Great Tongue** (Map 19) into a steeper route alongside **Little Tongue Gill**, or a mildly steadier gradient to the east of Great Tongue along **Tongue Gill** which is slabbed for part of its length.

Soon you arrive at the pretty mountain lake of **Grisedale Tarn** (Map 20) with the trail zigzagging up **Dollywaggon Pike** towards Helvellyn. Keeping to the easier path down Grisedale valley, the descent is as uncomplicated as the ascent, with the **Brothers' Parting Stone** just below the tarn (so-called because

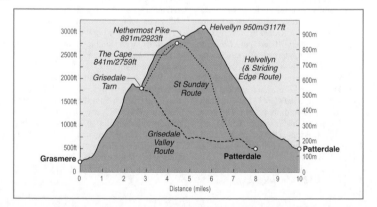

it's said that here in 1800 Wordsworth last met with his brother John, who died at sea a few years later). Just under a mile further on by **Ruthwaite Beck**, Ruthwaite Lodge, a climbers' hut, is usually locked up. The path continues down the valley and briefly joins a tarmac road (Map 24) where the

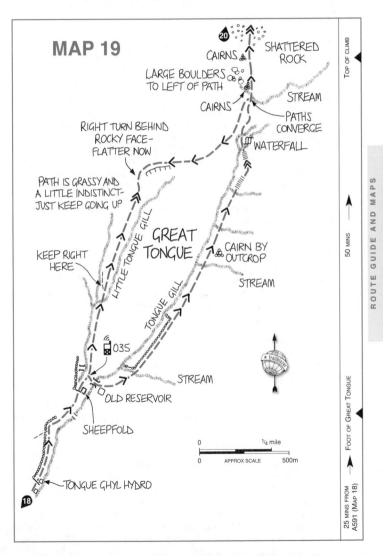

MAP 19

20

SHATTERED ROCK

CAIRNS

LARGE BOULDERS TO LEFT OF PATH

CAIRNS

STREAM

PATHS CONVERGE

WATERFALL

RIGHT TURN BEHIND ROCKY FACE – FLATTER NOW

PATH IS GRASSY AND A LITTLE INDISTINCT – JUST KEEP GOING UP

KEEP RIGHT HERE

LITTLE TONGUE GILL

GREAT TONGUE

CAIRN BY OUTCROP

STREAM

TONGUE GILL

035

STREAM

OLD RESERVOIR

SHEEPFOLD

TONGUE GHYL HYDRO

18

0   1/4 mile

0   APPROX SCALE   500m

TOP OF CLIMB

50 MINS

ROUTE GUIDE AND MAPS

FOOT OF GREAT TONGUE

25 MINS FROM A591 (MAP 18)

Helvellyn/Striding Edge route comes in. You then leave the road to the right to enter the National Trust's **Glenamara Park** (and where the St Sunday Crag route converges), with some wonderful views over Patterdale and beyond to Ullswater (Norse for 'Water with a Bend').

All being well, you'll drop onto the road by Patterdale Hotel about two hours after leaving Grisedale Tarn.

The high-level options: Helvellyn & Striding Edge; St Sunday Crag
If weather conditions allow, one of these two high-level routes should be seriously considered. After all, it would be a shame on this, the penultimate stage in the Lake District, if you didn't try to climb as many peaks as possible.

Helvellyn & Striding Edge   Map 20; Maps 22-24 pp135-6
IMPORTANT NOTE! Since the descent via Striding Edge is precarious and, given the sheer drops on either side, **can be very dangerous indeed** even in calm weather with little wind, this route is only for people experienced in such conditions and certainly not for anyone who suffers at all from vertigo.
Of the two high-level options, **Helvellyn**, at 950m (3113ft) the third highest peak in England after Scafell Pike and Scafell, is understandably the more popular. The climb is arduous and, having reached the top, you then face a nerve-tingling drop on a crumbling slope above **Red Tarn**, followed by a knife-edge walk along **Striding Edge ridge** to reach the trail dropping to Patterdale. A memorial plaque to Robert Dixon who was killed here in 1858 whilst following his fox hounds during a hunt does little to calm the nerves – and there are many more recent victims of this vertiginous trail. But with a steady head and light winds the sense of achievement is ample reward for your efforts.
Wainwright waxes lyrical about this side trip, describing the notorious Striding Edge as the 'best quarter mile between St Bees and Robin Hood's Bay'. He visited Helvellyn on his first trip to the Lakes in 1930, and it was this trip that inspired his passion for the Lakes. He approached the peak from the opposite direction to that given here and he edged along it 'in agonies of apprehension'. This route takes about 3¼ hours from Grisedale Tarn to Patterdale, though that assumes you take the lower path just below the knife-edge crest of Striding Edge which can be traversed in as little as 20 minutes. However, with the inevitable waiting that needs to be done to let people coming the other way go by (at least at weekends), expect it all to add up to 4 hours from the tarn. You won't regret the extra time – it is truly exhilarating.

St Sunday Crag   Map 20, Map 21 p134, Map 24 p136
It's said that better views, if fewer thrills, lie in wait on the southern side of the valley along St Sunday Crag. Indeed, for many people these are the best views on the entire route, particularly those towards Ullswater. What's more, the effort required to climb up to St Sunday Crag is, by the standards of the lakes, fairly negligible, a steady plod away from the Tarn followed by a reasonably steady descent, at least until the sudden drop into Glenamara Park. It takes about **2¾ hours** (walking time only) from Grisedale Tarn to Glenamara Park.
   Soon after leaving Grisedale Tarn, you'll see a trail rising away from the lake, soon joined by the usual path from the tarn's mouth. You join the ridge at Deepdale Hause, where the path from Fairfield summit feeds in from the right, and soon arrive at the high point known as **The Cape** (841m/2759ft). All along

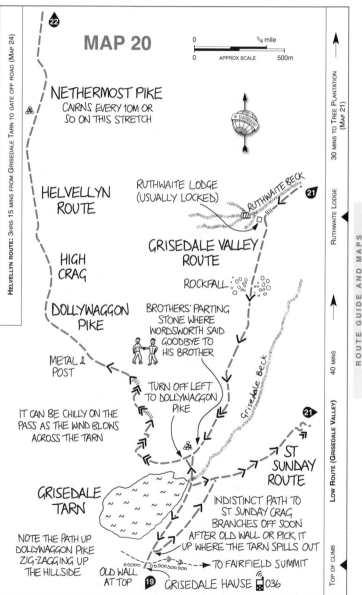

MAP 20

0   ¼ mile

0   APPROX SCALE   500m

★ trailblazer

NETHERMOST PIKE
CAIRNS EVERY 10M OR
SO ON THIS STRETCH

**HELVELLYN
ROUTE**

RUTHWAITE LODGE
(USUALLY LOCKED)

RUTHWAITE BECK

21

**GRISEDALE VALLEY
ROUTE**

**HIGH
CRAG**

ROCKFALL

**DOLLYWAGGON
PIKE**

BROTHERS' PARTING
STONE WHERE
WORDSWORTH SAID
GOODBYE TO
HIS BROTHER

METAL
POST

Grisedale Beck

TURN OFF LEFT
TO DOLLYWAGGON
PIKE

IT CAN BE CHILLY ON THE
PASS AS THE WIND BLOWS
ACROSS THE TARN

21

**ST
SUNDAY
ROUTE**

**GRISEDALE
TARN**

INDISTINCT PATH TO
ST SUNDAY CRAG
BRANCHES OFF SOON
AFTER OLD WALL OR PICK IT
UP WHERE THE TARN SPILLS OUT

NOTE THE PATH UP
DOLLYWAGGON PIKE
ZIG-ZAGGING UP
THE HILLSIDE

TO FAIRFIELD SUMMIT

OLD WALL
AT TOP

19 GRISEDALE HAUSE 036

HELVELLYN ROUTE: 3HRS 15 MINS FROM GRISEDALE TARN TO GATE OFF ROAD (MAP 24)

30 MINS TO TREE PLANTATION (MAP 21)

RUTHWAITE LODGE

40 MINS

LOW ROUTE (GRISEDALE VALLEY)

TOP OF CLIMB

ROUTE GUIDE AND MAPS

you've fine views of the next stage; a ramp rising steadily past briefly glimpsed Angle Tarn to Kidsty Pike and the unseen depths of Haweswater beyond.

From The Cape make sure you walk briefly north and not east for Gavel Pike. Then at a **cairn** (WPT 038) the path continues north-east before dropping off the ridge and tumbling down to Glenamara Park, where you meet up with the low-level route and enter Patterdale.

TREE PLANTATION

30 MINS FROM RUTHWAITE LODGE (MAP 20)

LOW ROUTE (GRISEDALE VALLEY)

ROUTE GUIDE AND MAPS

WALLED ENCLOSURE OF TREES - THE CROSSING PLANTATION

23

2 MILES TO PATTERDALE SIGN

BOARDS ACROSS STREAMS

VIEWS TOWARDS ULLSWATER - THE BEST PANORAMA ON THE C2C?

GRISEDALE BECK

GRISEDALE VALLEY ROUTE

ATTENTION! LEAVE THE CAPE TO THE NORTH, NOT NORTH-EAST

24

20

038

LOOK FOR CAIRNS TO SHOW YOU THE PATH FROM THE TOP OF THE CAPE

DO CROSS THIS BRIDGE HOWEVER!

DON'T BE TEMPTED BY THE PRETTY BRIDGE JUST TO YOUR LEFT - KEEP STRAIGHT ON!

THE CAPE 037
841M

GRISEDALE BECK

CAIRNS

ST SUNDAY ROUTE TIMING
FROM GRISEDALE TARN (MAP 20) TO GLENAMARA PARK (MAP 24), 2HRS 45MINS

ST SUNDAY CRAG

trailblazer

PATH CLIMBS UP TO COL ON RIDGE

NOW ON RIDGE. NOT NARROW LIKE STRIDING EDGE, BUT IT IS OFTEN VERY, VERY WINDY

MAP 21

20

JOIN MAIN RIDGE PATH AT DEEPDALE HAUSE

RIDGE PATH FROM FAIRFIELD SUMMIT

0   1/4 mile
0   APPROX SCALE   500m

ST SUNDAY CRAG ROUTE: 2 HRS 45 MINS FROM GRISEDALE TARN (MAP 20) TO GLENAMARA PARK (MAP 24)

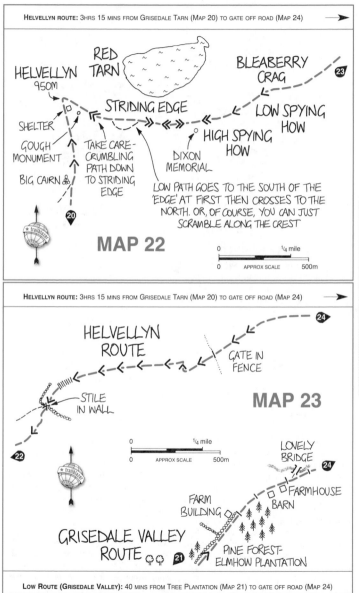

RED TARN

HELVELLYN
950M

BLEABERRY CRAG

23

STRIDING EDGE

LOW SPYING HOW

SHELTER

HIGH SPYING HOW

GOUGH MONUMENT

TAKE CARE - CRUMBLING PATH DOWN TO STRIDING EDGE

DIXON MEMORIAL

BIG CAIRN

LOW PATH GOES TO THE SOUTH OF THE 'EDGE' AT FIRST THEN CROSSES TO THE NORTH. OR, OF COURSE, YOU CAN JUST SCRAMBLE ALONG THE CREST

20

MAP 22

| 0 | | ¼ mile |
| 0 | APPROX SCALE | 500m |

ROUTE GUIDE AND MAPS

HELVELLYN ROUTE

GATE IN FENCE

24

STILE IN WALL

MAP 23

22

| 0 | | ¼ mile |
| 0 | APPROX SCALE | 500m |

LOVELY BRIDGE

24

FARMHOUSE

FARM BUILDING

BARN

GRISEDALE VALLEY ROUTE

21

PINE FOREST - ELMHOW PLANTATION

HELVELLYN ROUTE: 3HRS 15 MINS FROM GRISEDALE TARN (MAP 20)   GATE OFF ROAD →

HELVELLYN ROUTE

23

BRAESTEADS FARM

TARMAC

GRISEDALE VALLEY ROUTE

HARRISON CRAG

23

ST SUNDAY ROUTE TIMING FROM GRISEDALE TARN (MAP 20) TO GLENAMARA PARK (MAP 24), 2HRS 45MINS

039

21

ST SUNDAY CRAG ROUTE

25

TURN RIGHT THROUGH GATE, OFF ROAD FROM HERE

25

HEAD SOUTH-EAST FROM OAK TREE 040

CROSS STREAM ON STEPPING STONES

GLENAMARA PARK

* trailblazer

MAP 24

0 .... ¼ mile
0   APPROX SCALE   500m

LOW LEVEL (GRISEDALE)   40 MINS FROM TREE PLANTATION   GATE OFF ROAD →
ROUTE: (MAP 21)

PATTERDALE   MAP 25

Patterdale is little more than a meandering collection of houses strung along the A592. Normally valleys this beautiful would be full of souvenir shops and tearooms. But Patterdale, while not exactly undiscovered, is mercifully free of the 'Lakeland Babylon' found in Grasmere. The valley is also something of a **wildlife** haven, including a population of red squirrels – some of the last remaining in England. We saw one playing on the grassy roof at the YHA during a past visit.

The **fountain of St Patrick** (off Map 25) – Patterdale is a corruption of St Patrick's Dale – is an ornate Victorian construction set in a bank by the side of the road just outside Glenridding, and is said to mark the spot where the saint baptised the locals.

Services

Sadly, Patterdale Village Store, the first shop to sell Wainwright's guidebooks, closed in 2021, meaning that the nearest **shop** is now R&R Corner Shop (☎ 079287 92565, 🖥 cornershop.uk.com; **fb**; daily

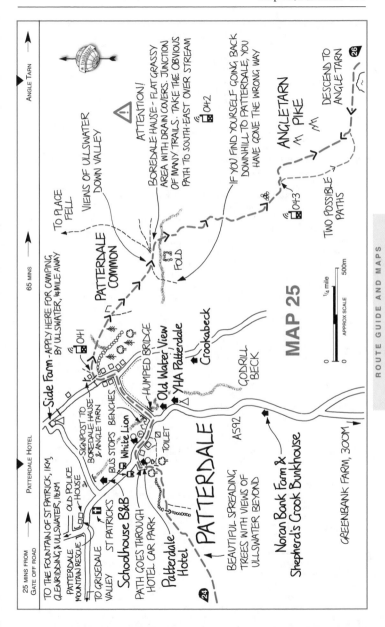

ANGLE TARN →

65 MINS →

PATTERDALE HOTEL

25 MINS FROM GATE OFF ROAD

TO THE FOUNTAIN OF ST PATRICK, 1KM, GLENRIDDING & ULLSWATER, 1½KM

PATTERDALE MOUNTAIN RESCUE

OLD POLICE HOUSE

TO GRISEDALE VALLEY

ST PATRICKS

Schoolhouse B&B

SIGNPOST TO BOREDALE HOUSE & ANGLE TARN

BUS STOPS BENCHES

White Lion

TOILET

Side Farm — APPLY HERE FOR CAMPING, BY ULLSWATER, ¼ MILE AWAY

041

VIEWS OF ULLSWATER DOWN VALLEY

TO PLACE FELL

PATTERDALE COMMON

ATTENTION!
BOREDALE HAUSE — FLAT GRASSY AREA WITH DRAIN COVERS. JUNCTION OF MANY TRAILS. TAKE THE OBVIOUS PATH TO SOUTH-EAST OVER STREAM

042

IF YOU FIND YOURSELF GOING BACK DOWNHILL TO PATTERDALE, YOU HAVE GONE THE WRONG WAY

ANGLETARN PIKE

043

TWO POSSIBLE PATHS

DESCEND TO ANGLE TARN

26

HUMPED BRIDGE

Old Water View
YHA Patterdale

Crookabeck

GODRILL BECK

MAP 25

0 — ¼ mile
0 — 500m
APPROX SCALE

FOLD

PATTERDALE

A592

PATH GOES THROUGH HOTEL CAR PARK

Patterdale Hotel

24

BEAUTIFUL SPREADING TREES WITH VIEWS OF ULLSWATER BEYOND

Noran Bank Farm & Shepherd's Crook Bunkhouse

GREENBANK FARM, 300M

7am-7pm, closes earlier in winter) approximately one mile away in Glenridding (off Map 25). The shop is well-stocked and if you've time it's only a short stroll from there to the shore of Ullswater.

Note that walking to Glenridding and back will add a couple of miles to your total for the day. However, Stagecoach's **bus** No 508 (Patterdale Bus) calls here and in Glenridding (see pp54-6) so that could save the walk.

Where to stay and eat

There's a range of **accommodation** in Patterdale, though this being the Lakes, booking ahead is vital if you don't want to end up sleeping in a ditch with a red squirrel for a duvet. Remember, the next stage to Shap is commonly agreed to be the toughest on the Coast to Coast walk, so you'll want to be on form. If you run out of luck in Patterdale, there's more accommodation in Glenridding (see box below).

Campers have two choices in Patterdale itself (though there are other campsites along the banks of Ullswater): either camp at the YHA, or across Goldrill Beck at *Side Farm* (☎ 01768 482337, ☎ 077961 28897; from £12pp; ☼ kept on lead; Easter to Oct). You can't pre-book tent pitches, but genuine Coast to Coast walkers will always be accepted (even if the sign says they're full). But in summer one reader recommends getting here before 4pm or you may struggle to find a flat pitch for your tent. The rate includes use of the toilets and (hot) showers; there are also laundry facilities (additional charge). It actually lies a little way beyond the farm on the edge of the lake but they insist you check-in at the farm first. However, considering they have a *tearoom* (Easter to Oct daily 10am-5pm; ☼ kept on lead), it's a great place to recuperate before pitching your tent. And just in case you thought you'd heard the last of him, it's said our old friend Wordsworth was a regular visitor to Side Farm.

At the other end of the village, *YHA Patterdale* (☎ 0345 371 9337, 🖳 yha.org .uk/hostel/patterdale; 1S, 4x2-, 7x8-, 2x10-bed rooms; WI-FI in public areas; ⓛ; Mar-Oct) is on the main road. The 1970s' building may not win any design awards, but its

ROUTE GUIDE AND MAPS

🖳 ULLSWATER AND GLENRIDDING

I wandered lonely as a cloud,
That floats on high o'er vales and hills,
When all at once I saw a crowd,
A host of golden daffodils,
Beside the lake, beneath the trees,
Fluttering and dancing in the breeze.
    William Wordsworth, *Daffodils*

It is said that Wordsworth was inspired to write these words after a trip to Ullswater. Certainly it's a beautiful lake and unlike neighbouring Grasmere and Haweswater there's plenty to do *on* the water too.

It takes about 20 minutes to walk to the lake from Patterdale. There is a **tourist information centre** (Apr-Oct daily 9.30am-5.30pm, Nov-Mar Sat & Sun to 3.30pm; WI-FI) in the main car park in Glenridding.

Boats (motorboats) can be hired (see 🖳 lakelandboathire.co.uk) though don't try to emulate Donald Campbell, who broke the 200mph water speed record on Ullswater in 1955. For something more sedate, hire a rowing boat, or you can take a cruise on a **steamer** (☎ 017684 82229, 🖳 ullswater-steamers.co.uk). There have been steamers on the lake since 1859 and two of the five boats currently in service, *Lady of the Lake* and *Raven*, have been operating since the late 19th century with the former believed to be the oldest working passenger vessel in the world. Services operate year-round (3-9/day) to Howton, Pooley Bridge and back although during strong winds services will be cancelled.

For further details of accommodation, activities and events around Ullswater see 🖳 ullswater.co.uk.

eco-friendly grass roof does sometimes attract red squirrels, and inside it has been refitted comfortably with spacious common areas. The building is open all day, although reception opens at 5pm. As with most YHAs, meals are available (pre-book) and it is licensed. There is a drying room and laundry facilities. Credit cards are accepted. Dorm beds cost from £15 and private rooms for up to two sharing from £25. They also usually offer **camping** (🐾; from £5pp).

A short walk from here, at **Noran Bank Farm** (☎ 01768 482327, 🖳 noran bank.co.uk), you'll find the very comfortable *Shepherd's Crook Bunkhouse* (WI-FI; Ⓛ; 🐾) with two rooms; one has a bunk bed and en suite shower (from £25pp), the other sleeps up to six (also in bunks; £25pp) and has separate shower facilities. It's open all year, has a fully equipped kitchen – a DIY breakfast costs £6 – and all bed linen is provided. Noran Bank Farm also has two rooms in its *Farmhouse B&B* (1T/1Tr with shared facilities; 🛏; Ⓛ; WI-FI; 🐾; Mar-Oct) from £32.50pp (enquire for sgl occ rates), though unlike the bunkhouse, the B&B rooms aren't available through the winter months. There's a two-night minimum stay on weekends and bank holidays. At over 400 years old the farm is older than quite a few countries.

Other B&Bs include one long-standing establishment, just before the YHA hostel. *Old Water View Country Inn* (☎ 01768 482175, 🖳 oldwaterview.co.uk; 2D/1T/3Tr, all en suite; 🛏; WI-FI; Ⓛ) is a wonderful place and was a favourite of Wainwright's. The rooms are comfortable – B&B costs from £65pp (sgl occ £125) – and they open the outdoor bar (approx noon-8pm but when the weather is good) so guests – as well as non residents – can enjoy a beer in the garden; they also serve baked potatoes, sandwiches & (hot) baguettes. They also have a 'Herdy hut' available for **glamping** (1T; from £45pp, sgl occ £85); it's not en suite but does have its own private bathroom in the house. The proprietors are keen walkers and know the Coast to Coast well. Spot 'Rachael – The Chain Lady', one of the C2C's 'iconic pieces of artwork' hiding in the garden.

Just north of the path is *Schoolhouse B&B* (☎ 01768 482887, 🖳 schoolhouse patterdale.co.uk; 1D en suite with private sitting room, 1S/1D shared bathroom; 🛏; WI-FI; Ⓛ) which charges from £57.50pp (sgl occ £90) for the en suite room and from £47.50pp (sgl/sgl occ £62/80) for the other rooms. Both double rooms have four-poster beds. There's also a drying room.

The smartest and most expensive lodgings in the village are at *Patterdale Hotel* (☎ 01768 482231, 🖳 patterdalehotel.co.uk; 4S and 48D/T or Qd, all en suite; 🛏; WI-FI; Ⓛ). Part of a chain, it's an enormous establishment and their reluctance to accept bookings for less than two-/three-night stays may deter C2Cers. However, they will take one-night bookings if there is a vacancy near the time; bookings must be through central reservations ☎ 01253 293122 option 1. For B&B expect to pay from £62/55pp (sgl from £50, sgl occ room rate) for a room with/without a view of Lake Ullswater. For rates which include dinner and special offers check the website. The restaurant is generally for hotel residents only. The bar also serves hot **food** and snacks (daily noon-5pm) and is open to non-residents.

South of the village, on the road to Noran Bank Farm, *Greenbank Farm* (☎ 01768 482292, 🖳 greenbankfarmpatter dale.co.uk; 1D/1T/1D or T, shared shower facilities; WI-FI; Ⓛ; Apr-early Oct) is a working sheep farm; they charge from £32.50pp (sgl occ £40) for B&B and from £12 for an evening meal (book in advance).

Crookabeck B&B (☎ 07979 345630, 🖳 crookabeck.com; 2D or T/1T, all en suite; WI-FI; Ⓛ) has a shared lounge area (TV, sink & fridge) – breakfast is eaten here – and superb views. B&B costs from £55pp (sgl occ £100).

Very close to the path and the focus of the village is the wonderful 19th-century *White Lion* pub (☎ 017684 82214, 🖳 whitelionpatterdale.com; 1S/1D private facilities, 2D/3T all en suite; WI-FI; Ⓛ; 🐾), which offers **B&B** from £45pp (sgl occ generally room rate) as well as serving good, hearty pub **food** (daily noon-8pm) and fine cask ales (including Wainwright's).

STAGE 5: PATTERDALE TO SHAP   MAPS 25-34

Introduction

Today is the day you leave the Lake District and it is true that, as a rule, once the Lakes are behind you the wayfinding becomes easier and the gradients kinder. But the crags, knotts, pikes and fells that have been your high-level chums for the past few days won't let you go without a struggle.

Be prepared to feel very tired at the end of this **15½-mile (25km, 6½hr)** stage. The long climb up to Kidsty Pike, the trickily steep descent down to Haweswater (see box p144) and the undulating stage above the lake's shore add up to well over **1300 metres** (4400ft) of ascent. Together it all conspires to make the seemingly harmless spin down over field and farmland to Shap enough to curse the very name of Wainwright.

With no accommodation directly on the route nor, indeed, any shops, tea-rooms or pubs, you have little choice but to grit your teeth and knuckle down. To shorten the day, a few walkers now take a 1¼-mile (2km) detour to **Bampton** (see p143). An option for campers is Aragon at **Burnbanks** (see opposite).

The route

You'll have spotted the ramp rising up from the far side of Patterdale. After much huffing and puffing it drops you down to the grassy platform known as **Boredale Hause** (Map 25) where the correct way is (for once!) actually the most obvious continuing south-east, by one trail or another, to the scalloped shoreline of **Angle Tarn** (Map 26) with its two little islands.

The gradient levels off for a while until another haul leads up around **The Knott** (Map 27) before you reach a small cairn, telling you to turn sharp left along the ridge that leads to **Kidsty Pike**, which at a modest 784m (2572ft) is the high point on the original Coast to Coast route.

From the top, looking west, you can see the Pillar looking down onto Ennerdale Water from all those days ago, and Scafell Pike, Helvellyn and St Sunday from the previous stage. To the south lie unknown lands including the deep cleft of Riggindale in whose crags England's last golden eagle once lived. The biggest descent on the walk now follows – at times you'll need your hands

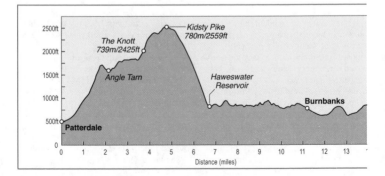

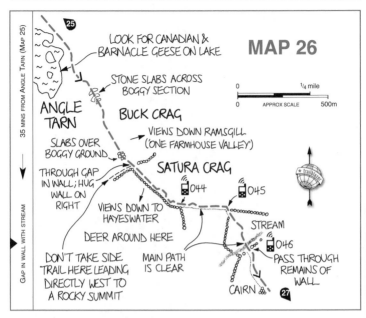

– to the very shores of **Haweswater Reservoir** (Map 28; see box on p144, but a lakeside amble while spinning your dainty parasol is sadly not on the cards. Instead you're soon panting like a hippo on a treadmill high above the shore, measuring each streaming gill until the waters terminate at the wooded glade along **Haweswater Beck** (Map 30).

The 'model' village of **Burnbanks** is little more than a huddle of 18 houses at the head of the reservoir. Fellrunner's limited (Thur only) No 111 **bus** service calls here (see pp54-6). You can **camp** year-round at the basic *Aragon* (Map

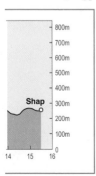

30; ☎ 01931 713629, 🖳 chizzer@homecall.co.uk; well-behaved 🐕) for £10pp (inc shower). Follow the trail from Burnbanks for five minutes and turn left where the path crosses the lane at Naddle Bridge. It's quiet riverside woodland; look out for red squirrels though there aren't as many as there used to be.

☐ **IMPORTANT NOTE – WALKING TIMES**

All times in this book refer only to the time spent walking. You will need to add 20-30% to allow for rests, photography, checking the map, drinking water etc.

40 MINS FROM GAP IN WALL WITH STREAM (MAP 26) ▶ THE KNOTT ▶ 60 MINS TO BRIDGE OVER STREAM BY HAWESWATER (MAP 28) ▶

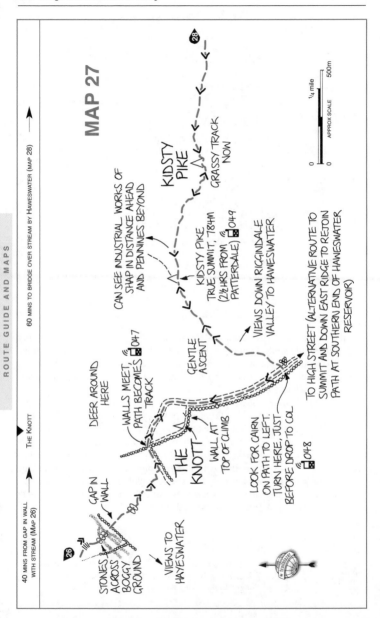

MAP 27

28

KIDSTY PIKE

GRASSY TRACK NOW

CAN SEE INDUSTRIAL WORKS OF SHAP IN DISTANCE AHEAD AND PENNINES BEYOND

KIDSTY PIKE TRUE SUMMIT, 784M (2½ HRS FROM PATTERDALE) 📱049

VIEWS DOWN RIGGINDALE VALLEY TO HAWESWATER

GENTLE ASCENT

WALLS MEET, PATH BECOMES TRACK 📱047

DEER AROUND HERE

THE KNOTT

WALL AT TOP OF CLIMB

LOOK FOR CAIRN ON PATH TO LEFT. TURN HERE, JUST BEFORE DROP TO COL 📱048

TO HIGH STREET (ALTERNATIVE ROUTE TO SUMMIT AND DOWN EAST RIDGE TO REJOIN PATH AT SOUTHERN END OF HAWESWATER RESERVOIR)

GAP IN WALL

26

STONES ACROSS BOGGY GROUND

VIEWS TO HAYESWATER

¼ mile
0   500m
APPROX SCALE
0

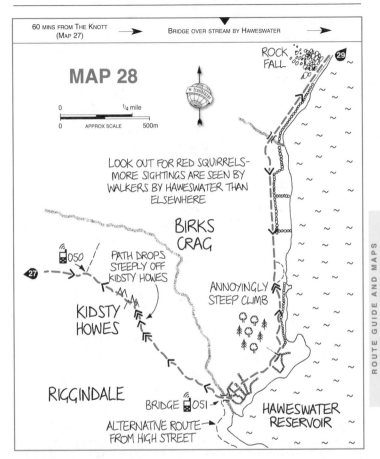

60 MINS FROM THE KNOTT (MAP 27) →   BRIDGE OVER STREAM BY HAWESWATER →

MAP 28

0   ¼ mile
0   APPROX SCALE   500m

LOOK OUT FOR RED SQUIRRELS-
MORE SIGHTINGS ARE SEEN BY
WALKERS BY HAWESWATER THAN
ELSEWHERE

ROCK FALL

BIRKS CRAG

PATH DROPS STEEPLY OFF KIDSTY HOWES

050

ANNOYINGLY STEEP CLIMB

KIDSTY HOWES

RIGGINDALE

BRIDGE 051

ALTERNATIVE ROUTE FROM HIGH STREET

HAWESWATER RESERVOIR

ROUTE GUIDE AND MAPS

BAMPTON off MAP 30, p145

For a B&B that seems to supply your every need, there's ***Bampton Shop & Tea Room*** (☎ 01931 713351, 🖳 bamptonvillageshop .co.uk; **fb**). **Rooms** (1D/1 room sleeping up to five, both en suite; 🛏; WI-FI; 🐾) are available but they now only accept bookings for a minimum two-night stay and the rate from £37.50pp (sgl occ room rate) doesn't include breakfast. The **shop** (Mon-Tue & Thur-Sat 8.30am-4.30pm, Wed to noon, Sun 10am-2pm) is well stocked and houses the village **post office** (same hours). Their *café* (Mon-Tue & Thur-Sat noon-4pm) does soups, sandwiches and home-made cakes.

Back on the trail it now feels a relief to be walking on the level, soft grass for miles at a time and, free of the national park's edicts, helpful 'Coast to Coast' signposts reappear too. Wall follows stile follows field follows stile until,

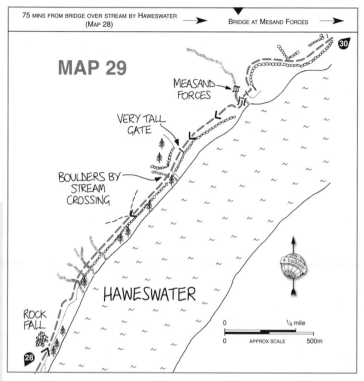

MAP 29

MEASAND FORCES

VERY TALL GATE

BOULDERS BY STREAM CROSSING

HAWESWATER

ROCK FALL

28

30

0 · 1/4 mile

0 · APPROX SCALE · 500m

ROUTE GUIDE AND MAPS

❑ HAWESWATER RESERVOIR

What is now one of Cumbria's largest bodies of water was once a small and fairly unassuming lake stuck on the eastern edge of the Lake District national park. In 1929, however, a bill was passed authorising the use of Haweswater as a reservoir to serve the needs of the population of Manchester. A concrete dam, 470m wide and 35m high, was constructed at the northern edge of the lake, raising the depth of the lake by over 30m and increasing the surface area to four miles long by half a mile wide (6km by 1km).

This project was not without its opponents; many protested at the loss of the settlements such as Mardale Green on Haweswater's eastern shore (near the pier). Before the village was flooded, coffins were removed from the graveyard and buried elsewhere and the 18th-century Holy Trinity Church was pulled down. Some of the windows from this church are now in the reservoir tower. Even today, during times of drought when the water level is low, the walls of Mardale emerge from the reservoir.

Despite man's interference the lake is still something of a wildlife haven. Swimming in the waters are wild brown trout, char, gwyniad and perch, while **Riggindale** is an RSPB haven, with wheatear, raven, ring ouzel and peregrine.

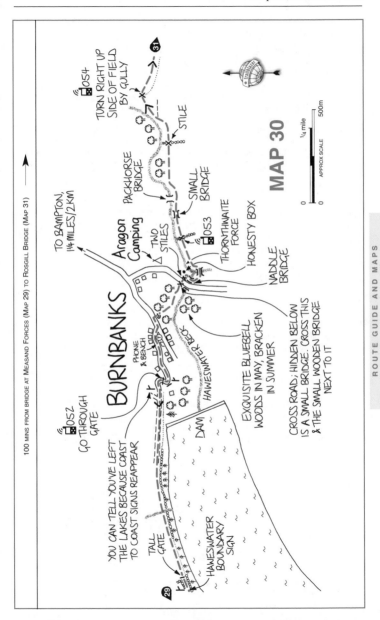

100 MINS FROM BRIDGE AT MEASAND FORCES (MAP 29) TO ROSGILL BRIDGE (MAP 31) →

31

☐054+ TURN RIGHT UP SIDE OF FIELD BY GULLY

STILE

PACKHORSE BRIDGE

SMALL BRIDGE

MAP 30

¼ mile

0   500m

0   APPROX SCALE

TO BAMPTON, 1¼ MILES/2KM

Aragon Camping

TWO STILES

☐053

THORNTHWAITE FORCE

HONESTY BOX

NADDLE BRIDGE

BURNBANKS

PHONE & BENCH

HAWESWATER BOX

EXQUISITE BLUEBELL WOODS IN MAY, BRACKEN IN SUMMER

CROSS ROAD; HIDDEN BELOW IS A SMALL BRIDGE. CROSS THIS & THE SMALL WOODEN BRIDGE NEXT TO IT

☐052 GO THROUGH GATE

YOU CAN TELL YOU'VE LEFT THE LAKES BECAUSE COAST SIGNS REAPPEAR

DAM

HAWESWATER BOUNDARY SIGN

TALL GATE

29

ROUTE GUIDE AND MAPS

❏ **SHAP ABBEY**

Shap Abbey (see Map 32) has the distinction of being the last abbey to be founded in England, in 1199. It was built by the French Premonstratensian order founded by St Norbert at Prémontré in Northern France, who were also known as the White Canons after the colour of their habits. The abbey was also the last to be dissolved by Henry VIII, in 1540. Presumably Henry's henchmen would have had plenty of practice in plundering monasteries by this time, which is perhaps why the abbey is today in such a ruinous state. The best-preserved section is the **western belltower**, built around 1500.

Since its demise, the abbey has had to suffer the commonplace indignity of having some of its best-carved stonework purloined by the locals for use in their own buildings. The cottage by the abbey clearly used some in its construction, albeit to good effect, while Shap's 17th-century market hall is built largely from abbey stone. Even some of the local stone walls contain abbey stones.

towards the end of the stage, you descend on **Shap Abbey** (see box above and Map 32), an atmospheric ruin set in a peaceful spot by River Lowther. It's just regrettable that, by the time you get here, you'll probably be somewhat of a ruin yourself, your thoughts having long ago turned from holy orders to hors d'oeuvres following a hot bath. From the abbey, all that remains is to tick off the road or parallel paths presaging your triumphant entry into **Shap**.

SHAP   MAP 33, p148

Shap is a long, narrow village lining a wide street, the A6, once the north-west's main route to Scotland and still the highest main road in the country as it passes over Howgill Fells. The road used to supply Shap's traders with enough passing trade to make a living and the village prospered. But then they built the M6 and things have been

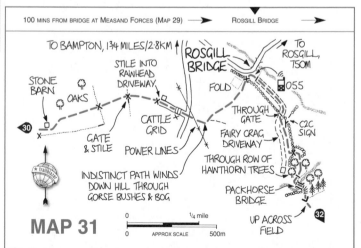

100 MINS FROM BRIDGE AT MEASAND FORCES (MAP 29) ⟶   ROSGILL BRIDGE   ⟶

TO BAMPTON, 1¾ MILES/2·8KM

ROSGILL BRIDGE

TO ROSGILL, 750M

STILE INTO RAWHEAD DRIVEWAY

STONE BARN

OAKS

FOLD

055

THROUGH GATE

CATTLE GRID

C2C SIGN

30

FAIRY CRAG DRIVEWAY

GATE & STILE

POWER LINES

THROUGH ROW OF HAWTHORN TREES

INDISTINCT PATH WINDS DOWN HILL THROUGH GORSE BUSHES & BOG

PACKHORSE BRIDGE

UP ACROSS FIELD

32

MAP 31

0   ¼ mile

0   APPROX SCALE   500m

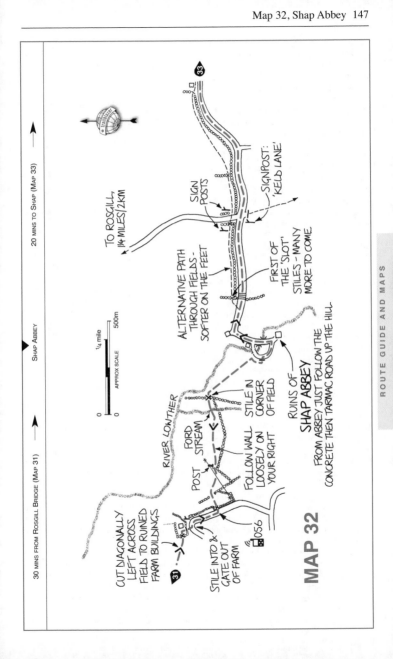

30 MINS FROM ROSGILL BRIDGE (MAP 31) ⟶   SHAP ABBEY   ⟶   20 MINS TO SHAP (MAP 33) ⟶

33

TO ROSGILL, 1¼ MILES/2KM

SIGN POSTS

SIGNPOST: 'KELD LANE'

ALTERNATIVE PATH THROUGH FIELDS — SOFTER ON THE FEET

FIRST OF THE 'SLOT' STILES — MANY MORE TO COME

N
* trailblazer *

¼ mile
0   500m
APPROX SCALE

RIVER LOWTHER

FORD STREAM

STILE IN CORNER OF FIELD

POST

FOLLOW WALL LOOSELY ON YOUR RIGHT

RUINS OF SHAP ABBEY

FROM ABBEY JUST FOLLOW THE CONCRETE THEN TARMAC ROAD UP THE HILL.

CUT DIAGONALLY LEFT ACROSS FIELD TO RUINED FARM BUILDINGS

STILE INTO & GATE OUT OF FARM

056

31

MAP 32

ROUTE GUIDE AND MAPS

pretty quiet since, bar the presence of a couple of quarries and cement factories. That said, you have to admire the sense of community in Shap – you'll notice pretty much everyone knows everyone else.

There are some attractive features in town, including a 17th-century **market hall** built with masonry from the **abbey** (see box on p146), but overall the place is not exactly Las Vegas on New Year's Eve. However, now you're out of the Lakes you don't have to fight over the great accommodation, plus there's a chippy, a grocery store, three pubs, a post office and even an outdoor heated **swimming pool** (end May to early Sep) which, at over 900ft above sea level (274m), is England's highest open-air heated pool.

Services

There's a **newsagent** (Mon-Fri 5am-5pm, Sat 5am-12.30pm) at the southern end of town which now hosts the **post office** (same hours). The decent-sized **Lakes and Dales Co-operative** (daily 7am-10pm) has a free-to-use **ATM** outside it and also does cashback (UK bank cards only). The **library** (Mon 10am-1pm, Fri 2-5pm, Sat 10am-2pm) in the Old Courthouse has **internet access**. The village has its own website (🖳 shapcumbria.co.uk).

Cumbria Classic Coaches 106 & 570 **bus** services call here (see pp54-6).

Where to stay

Being out of the Lakes, many B&B owners need to make more of an effort to attract custom, and with most of their guests being Coast to Coasters, it's something that is appreciated by many of our readers. There's none of that 'two nights minimum stay at weekends' malarkey or overpricing you've put up with on previous days.

As you come into town *New Ing Lodge* (☎ 01931 716719, 🖳 newinglodge .co.uk; 2D/3Tr/2Qd, all en suite, 2D with private facilities; 🛏; WI-FI; ⓛ; 🐾) is one of our favourite B&Bs on the entire Coast to Coast. This friendly place offers a variety of accommodation, including **B&B** rooms (from £44pp, sgl occ £69), two 4-bed **bunk-bed rooms** (from £35pp exc breakfast), and a large **camping** space (from

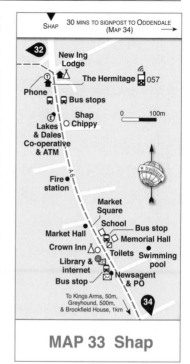

MAP 33 Shap

£7.50pp, inc shower). **Breakfast** (£12) is available if requested in advance, and there's a small bar serving local ales. Note that breakfast and packed lunches are only available March to the end of October.

Camping is also available in the pub garden at *Crown Inn* (☎ 01931 716562; WI-FI in pub only; ⓛ; 🐾). There's only space for six **tents** (from £7pp), but they also have two **camping pods** (sleeping up to two/three people; from £10pp). The pods have nothing inside them other than a strip of carpet, so you'll need your own sleeping bag, but they're ideal for campers who don't fancy pitching a tent in the rain. A laundry service (£10 per load) is available as is breakfast (from £5.50; from 8.30am) if requested in advance. For campers there's a shower (inc in the rate) in the outhouse toilet (Apr-Oct/Nov).

Over the road from New Ing Lodge, *The Hermitage* (☎ 01931 716671, 🖳 jean jackson_hermitage@btopenworld.com; 1T private bathroom, 1D/1Tr both en suite; ☞; WI-FI; Ⓛ) continues to be highly recommended. The beautiful house itself is over 300 years old but the rooms come with all mod cons. **B&B** costs from £50pp (sgl occ usually room rate, but worth enquiring).

There are three more B&B options at the southern end of town. Few begrudge the walk to *Brookfield House* (Map 34; ☎ 01931 716397, 🖳 brookfieldshap.co.uk; 3D or T all en suite; ☞; WI-FI; Ⓛ; Easter-mid Oct) which has become a legend among Coast to Coasters and is frequently cited as the best stay on the entire walk. Nothing is too much trouble for Margaret, who charges £50-57.50pp (sgl occ from £100). Their breakfasts and packed lunches are renowned. They have a bar, lounge, and drying facilities.

The King's Arms (Map 34; ☎ 01931 716277, 🖳 kingsmsshap.co.uk; 1D/2T/ 2Tr, all en suite, 1Tr/1Qd both with private facilities; ☞; WI-FI; Ⓛ; 🐾) charges from £49.50pp (sgl occ £79).

The Greyhound Hotel (Map 34; ☎ 01931 716718, 🖳 greyhoundshap.co.uk; **fb**; 6D or T/2T/1Qd, all en suite; ☞; WI-FI; 🐾; Feb-Dec) dates back to 1680 but has recently been renovated. B&B costs £32.50-55pp (sgl occ room rate).

Where to eat and drink
There's fairly standard **pub food** to be had at both *Crown Inn* (see Where to stay; food daily noon-8pm) and *The King's Arms* (see Where to stay; food Mon-Sat noon-2pm, Sun to 3pm, daily 5-8.30pm, winter hours variable).

The award-winning *Shap Chippy* (☎ 01931 716060, 🖳 shapchippy.co.uk; Tue-Sat noon-1.30pm & 4-7.30pm, Sun 4-7.30pm) does excellent fish & chips either to eat in (to 1pm or 7pm) or take away.

At *The Greyhound Hotel* (see Where to stay; bar Mon-Fri 3-11pm, Sat & Sun from noon, food Wed-Fri 5-8.30pm, Sat noon-8.30pm, Sun to 8pm) the menu includes vegan, vegetarian and gluten-free dishes and a roast on Sunday.

STAGE 6: SHAP TO KIRKBY STEPHEN　　　　MAPS 34-43

Introduction
Those who struggled over the previous stages may be less than delighted to learn that, at **20½ miles (33km, 7hrs)**, today's hike across the **Westmorland plateau** is even longer. But the good news is that prolonged gradients and rocky sole-mashing trails have been replaced by grassy strolls across the well-drained limestone bedrock, making it something of a 'recovery day' and, with your fitness now improving, rather satisfying in its own right. Many people find the sudden and dramatic change of scenery from the Lakeland hills to rolling, barren moorland and agricultural land pleasantly satisfying as well. Before you unrolls a steady, undulating transit over field and moorland as you flank the enigmatic Howgill Fells to the south and approach the peat-sodden ridge they call the Pennines.

If you're not convinced a fine day's walk lies ahead, there's a chance to break it in two by taking the short diversion into Orton, only eight miles from Shap. It's coming across 'lost' villages such as Orton that is part of the appeal of the Coast to Coast walk. Stranded far from well-established tourist trails (and, until 2016, most of these villages were outside of a national park too, though many have now been incorporated within the newly enlarged Yorkshire Dales National Park), they're simply what they are; places where people live but in a manner and locale that for most of us is long past. It's then that it dawns on you that, away from the coach-tour honeypots, the forgotten corners of rural England are full of these charming places, scraping by with a shop, a pub, a church and maybe even a bus.

This stage is also replete with **prehistoric sites**, though it's fair to say that none of them will make your jaw drop in amazement; unforewarned you'd probably pass by none the wiser but still cheered by a surprisingly great day aboard the Coast to Coast path.

30 MINS FROM SHAP (MAP 33) ⟶   SIGNPOST TO ODDENDALE ⟶

33

BRIDGE OVER RAILWAY
SIGNPOSTS
OVERHEAD CABLES
GO STRAIGHT AT 3-WAY JUNCTION
Kings Arms
SHAP
STEPS OVER WALL
TO JCT 40 FOR PENRITH
M6 MOTORWAY
THE WEDGE OF KIDSTY PIKE IS VISIBLE 7 MILES TO THE WEST
GATE & STEPS
MUDDY FIELD WITH RABBITS
SHAP, KENDAL MOTORWAY SIGN
Greyhound
A6
AFTER PASSING THROUGH WALL, HEAD DIAGONALLY LEFT
058
LOW CRAG
HAWTHORN TREES, HORSEFIELD
FARM
SIGN TO ODDEN-DALE
Brookfield House
OVERHEAD CABLES
TO JCT 39 FOR SHAP
059
35
TO KENDAL, 15 MILES/26KM
MAP 34
CEMENT WORKS
CONTOURING ROUND HILL WITH OCCASIONAL TREE LEFT & RIGHT

0   ¼ mile
0   APPROX SCALE   500m

trailblazer

1000ft
Shap   Oddendale   Robin Hood's Grave   Turn for Orton   Sunbiggin Tarn
500ft
0
0   1   2   3   4   5   6   7   8   9   10   11   12   13   14
Distance (miles)

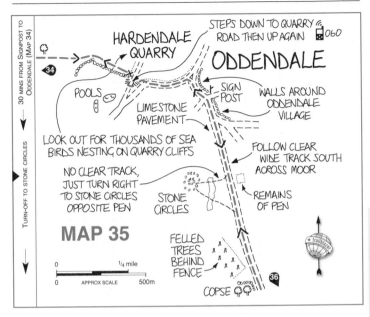

The route

With over 20 miles to cover, you leave Shap to cross first the railway then the motorway (M6) which funnel through north-west England. They are soon forgotten as you skirt the hidden, walled hamlet of **Oddendale** (Map 35) and cross the boundary of Yorkshire Dales National Park; it was extended in 2016. (You'll leave the national park just before Kirkby Stephen and won't re-enter it until past Nine Standards). Just a few minutes off the path to the west lie two concentric **stone circles** dating back nearly 6000 years.

Continue south to cut past a strip of felled plantation and head over more limestone pavements (Map 36) and down into **Lyvennet Beck**. Now you turn north-east, passing **Robin Hood's Grave** (Map 37), a large cairn in a shallow fold in the moor and certainly not the grave of the man who gives his name to the bay that is the ultimate destination on this path. Eventually, with the

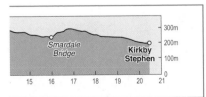

Howgills bubbling up ahead, the trail drops down to a road and follows it south to the B6260, before leaving the tarmac to drop left down again past a well-preserved **limekiln** above Broadfell Farm. Those bound for **Orton**, whose church

ROUTE GUIDE AND MAPS

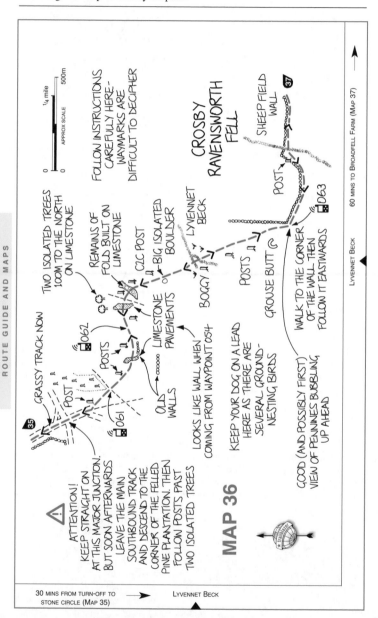

MAP 36

CROSBY RAVENSWORTH FELL

FOLLOW INSTRUCTIONS CAREFULLY HERE - WAYMARKS ARE DIFFICULT TO DECIPHER

TWO ISOLATED TREES 100m TO THE NORTH ON LIMESTONE

REMAINS OF FOLD BUILT ON LIMESTONE

C2C POST

GRASSY TRACK NOW

062

POSTS

LIMESTONE PAVEMENTS

OLD WALLS

061

POST

BIG ISOLATED BOULDER

LYVENNET BECK

BOGGY

POSTS

GROUSE BUTT

POST

SHEEP FIELD WALL

37

063

WALK TO THE CORNER OF THE WALL THEN FOLLOW IT EASTWARDS

⚠ ATTENTION! KEEP STRAIGHT ON AT THIS MAJOR JUNCTION. BUT SOON AFTERWARDS LEAVE THE MAIN SOUTHBOUND TRACK AND DESCEND TO THE CORNER OF THE FELLED PINE PLANTATION. THEN FOLLOW POSTS PAST TWO ISOLATED TREES

35

LOOKS LIKE WALL WHEN COMING FROM WAYPOINT 054

KEEP YOUR DOG ON A LEAD HERE AS THERE ARE SEVERAL GROUND-NESTING BIRDS

GOOD (AND POSSIBLY FIRST) VIEW OF PENNINES BUBBLING UP AHEAD

¼ mile
500m
APPROX SCALE

60 MINS TO BROADFELL FARM (MAP 37)

LYVENNET BECK

30 MINS FROM TURN-OFF TO STONE CIRCLE (MAP 35) → LYVENNET BECK

tower has been clearly visible since the brow of the hill, should continue down through the farm from here; the rest march resolutely on to join the farm's driveway and continue east round **Orton Scar**.

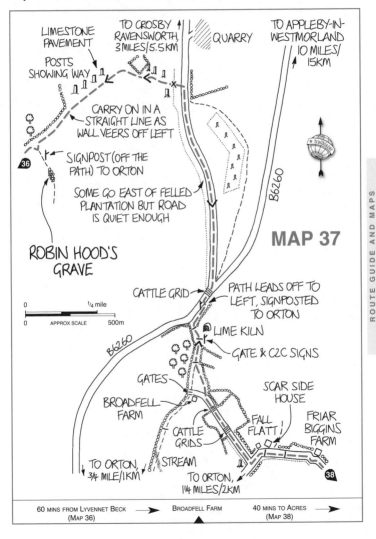

LIMESTONE PAVEMENT

POSTS SHOWING WAY

TO CROSBY RAVENSWORTH, 3 MILES/5.5 KM

QUARRY

TO APPLEBY-IN-WESTMORLAND 10 MILES/ 15KM

CARRY ON IN A STRAIGHT LINE AS WALL VEERS OFF LEFT

36

SIGNPOST (OFF THE PATH) TO ORTON

SOME GO EAST OF FELLED PLANTATION BUT ROAD IS QUIET ENOUGH

B6260

MAP 37

ROBIN HOOD'S GRAVE

0   ¼ mile

0   500m
APPROX SCALE

B6260

CATTLE GRID

PATH LEADS OFF TO LEFT, SIGNPOSTED TO ORTON

LIME KILN

GATE & C2C SIGNS

GATES

SCAR SIDE HOUSE

BROADFELL FARM

CATTLE GRIDS

FALL FLATT

FRIAR BIGGINS FARM

38

TO ORTON, ¾ MILE/1 KM

STREAM

TO ORTON, 1¼ MILES/2 KM

ROUTE GUIDE AND MAPS

60 MINS FROM LYVENNET BECK
(MAP 36) →

BROADFELL FARM

40 MINS TO ACRES →
(MAP 38)

ORTON   see map

Orton is typical of the quaint 'unknown' villages in which the Coast to Coast specialises, but one with a couple of surprises in store for walkers.

For one thing there's the **church** (All Saint's) dating back to 1293 below which are the remains of some **pillories** or stocks once used to punish wrongdoers; perhaps they were spending too much time round the back of **Kennedy's chocolate factory** (see column opposite). Popping in here you may think you've been transported to a chocolaterie in some upmarket Parisian suburb but no, this is Orton, east Cumbria.

Services

The well-stocked **village store** (☎ 015396 24225; Mon 9am-6pm, Tue-Sat 8am-6pm, Sun 10am-noon; **post office** Tue & Thur 9am-5pm, Sat to 4pm) is nearby, in rude health we're pleased to report and with enough provisions to restock your travelling larder.

Cumbria Classic Coaches No 106 & 570 **bus** services stop in the village; see pp54-6 for details.

Where to stay and eat

Camping is available at *New House Farm* (Map 38; ☎ 015396 24324; from £10pp; 🐾; Mar-Nov) though facilities are basic.

The George Hotel (☎ 01539 624071, 🖳 thegeorgehotelorton.co.uk; **fb**; 3D or T/1Qd all en suite, 1S/1T share bathroom; 🛏; WI-FI; Ⓛ) is in the centre of town. B&B costs from £50pp (sgl/sgl occ £50) and they have a drying room. They also offer **camping** space for 4 to 5 tents in part of the beer garden (from £5 per tent, plus £3pp for a shower). **Food** is served daily 6-8.30pm and Sat & Sun noon-2.30pm; the bar opens at 3pm in the summer and 5pm in the winter.

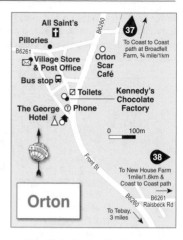

All Saint's
Pillories
B6261
Village Store & Post Office
Bus stop
The George Hotel
☑ Toilets
ⓣ Phone
Orton Scar Café
Kennedy's Chocolate Factory
To Coast to Coast path at Broadfell Farm, ¾ mile/1km
B6260
37
0   100m
38
To New House Farm 1mile/1.6km & Coast to Coast path
Front St
B6260
To Tebay, 3 miles
B6261 Raisbeck Rd
Orton

For **food** there's also the spacious *Orton Scar Café* (**fb**; Mar-Sep Mon-Sat 9am-5pm, Sun to 4pm, Oct-Feb Tue-Sun 9am-4pm; WI-FI; 🐾 outside only), a lovely place on the edge of the village. You can sit inside or out; they serve sandwiches, jacket potatoes, and all-day breakfasts, scones and cakes as well as a roast lunch on Sunday (small/large £9.95/11.95; booking advised).

You can't leave Orton without sampling the chocolate at *Kennedy's* (☎ 01539 624781, 🖳 kennedyschocolates.co.uk; shop Mon-Sat 9am-5pm, Sun 10am-5pm). Though specialising in chocolate-based goodies, ordinary stuff (toasties, sandwiches, coffee and ice-cream are also available), but for a chocoholic overdose, their chocolate cake washed down with a hot chocolate ought to hit the mark. Note that at the time of research everything was takeaway only.

TEBAY   off Orton map, above

About three miles south of Orton, *The Old School* (☎ 015396 24286, 🖳 oldschooltebay.co.uk; 1S/1D/1Qd/2x6-bed room, all en suite; WI-FI; Ⓛ; 🐾) charges from £47.50pp (sgl £45, sgl occ rate on request) for B&B. Since they are a little way out of Orton they are happy to pick walkers up if arranged at the time of booking.

Cumbria Classic Coaches No 106, 570 & 571 and Western Dales' S5 **bus** services stop here (see pp54-6 for details).

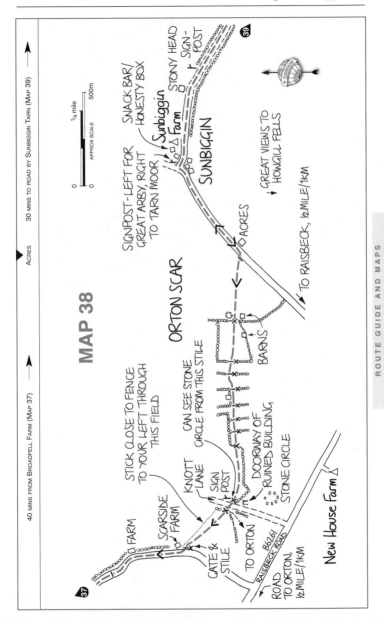

40 MINS FROM BROADFELL FARM (MAP 37)   ACRES   30 MINS TO ROAD BY SUNBIGGIN TARN (MAP 39)

MAP 38

ORTON SCAR

STICK CLOSE TO FENCE TO YOUR LEFT THROUGH THIS FIELD

CAN SEE STONE CIRCLE FROM THIS STILE

KNOTT LANE

SIGN POST

DOORWAY OF RUINED BUILDING

STONE CIRCLE

SCARSIDE FARM

FARM

GATE & STILE

TO ORTON

B6261 RAISBECK ROAD

ROAD TO ORTON, ½MILE/1KM

New House Farm

BARNS

SIGNPOST - LEFT FOR GREAT ASBY, RIGHT TO TARN MOOR

SNACK BAR/ HONESTY BOX

Sunbiggin Farm

STONY HEAD SIGN- POST

SUNBIGGIN

ACRES

GREAT VIEWS TO HOWGILL FELLS

TO RAISBECK, ½MILE/1KM

37

39

¼ mile   500m
0   APPROX SCALE   0

ROUTE GUIDE AND MAPS

There's a second and more impressive **stone circle** (see Map 38) a mile to the east of Orton on the Coast to Coast path. Those who *did* visit Orton can rejoin this track at the stone circle by taking Raisbeck Road east and heading up Knott Lane. At **Sunbiggin** there's camping at *Sunbiggin Farm* (Map 38; ☎ 07979 648974 (WhatsApp message preferred), 🖳 sunbiggin-camping.mailchimpsites .com; Apr-Oct, WI-FI; 🐾) from £10pp. There's also a *snack bar* in a summer house; it is sometimes locked but if not there is a fridge, a kettle, some chairs and a selection of sandwiches, cakes and scones with payment on an honesty basis – rave reviews have been received for the cake especially. Across the road they have *bunkhouse* accommodation with four beds £20 per bed or £70 sole occupancy. There are washing and drying facilities; showers and a shared kitchen. Bedding and towels can be rented and there's home-made frozen food available.

After this, the trail continues east across walled fields and on to **Tarn Moor** (Map 39). All being well you'll emerge from the moor on a back road alongside **Sunbiggin Tarn**, an important bird sanctuary. Here you turn briefly south and then cut directly east across the heather-clad **Ravenstonedale Moor**; you'll have seen the sign boards indicating the course, a path the Coast to Coast shares with the Dales Way. You reach another lane on the far side of the moor.

The little village of **Newbiggin-on-Lune** (off Map 40) nestles at the foot of Howgill fells and is about 1¼ miles south of the point where the path crosses a lane after Ravenstonedale Moor. However, at the time of writing the two B&Bs there had closed and the only service there now is Western Dales' (Thur only) S5 **bus** (see pp54-6). You reach another lane on the far side of the moor. To continue on the Coast to Coast don't follow the lane but cross it, head past the hill top, but underground, reservoir and continue east. *(cont'd on p160)*

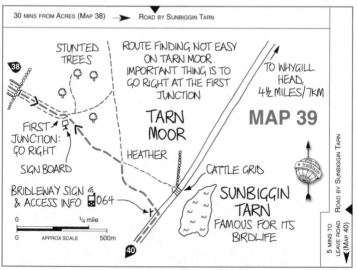

30 MINS FROM ACRES (MAP 38) ⟶ ROAD BY SUNBIGGIN TARN

STUNTED TREES

ROUTE FINDING NOT EASY ON TARN MOOR. IMPORTANT THING IS TO GO RIGHT AT THE FIRST JUNCTION

TO WHYGILL HEAD, 4½ MILES/7KM

MAP 39

FIRST JUNCTION: GO RIGHT

SIGN BOARD

TARN MOOR

HEATHER

CATTLE GRID

BRIDLEWAY SIGN & ACCESS INFO 064

SUNBIGGIN TARN FAMOUS FOR ITS BIRDLIFE

★ trailblazer

0 ... ¼ mile
0 ... APPROX SCALE ... 500m

ROAD BY SUNBIGGIN TARN

5 MINS TO LEAVE ROAD (MAP 40)

40

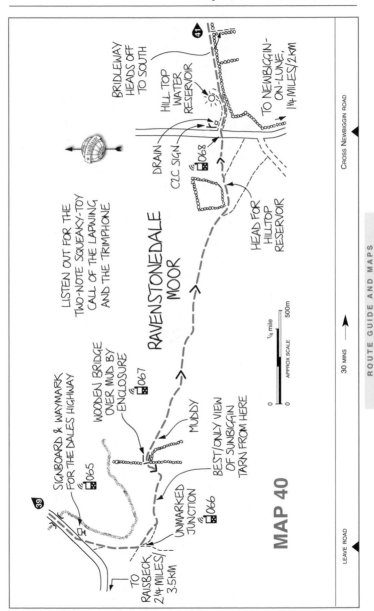

MAP 40

RAVENSTONEDALE MOOR

LISTEN OUT FOR THE TWO-NOTE SQUEAKY-TOY CALL OF THE LAPWING, AND THE TRIMPHONE

SIGNBOARD & WAYMARK FOR THE DALES HIGHWAY 📷 065

WOODEN BRIDGE OVER MUD BY ENCLOSURE 📷 067

MUDDY

BEST/ONLY VIEW OF SUNBIGGIN TARN FROM HERE

UNMARKED JUNCTION 📷 066

TO RAISBECK, 2¼ MILES/ 3.5KM

39

BRIDLEWAY HEADS OFF TO SOUTH

HILL TOP WATER RESERVOIR

DRAIN

C2C SIGN

📷 068

HEAD FOR HILLTOP RESERVOIR

TO NEWBIGGIN-ON-LUNE, 1¼ MILES/2KM

41 8

0   ¼ mile
0   500m
APPROX SCALE

30 MINS

LEAVE ROAD

CROSS NEWBIGGIN ROAD

ROUTE GUIDE AND MAPS

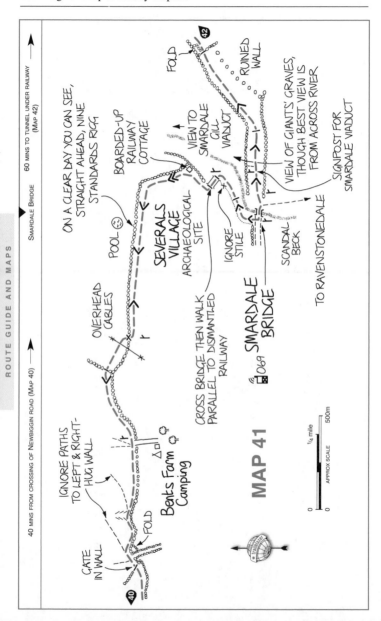

40 MINS FROM CROSSING OF NEWBIGGIN ROAD (MAP 40) ——→

SMARDALE BRIDGE

60 MINS TO TUNNEL UNDER RAILWAY (MAP 42)

GATE IN WALL

IGNORE PATHS TO LEFT & RIGHT– HUG WALL

FOLD

Bents Farm Camping

OVERHEAD CABLES

ON A CLEAR DAY YOU CAN SEE, STRAIGHT AHEAD, NINE STANDARDS RIGG

POOL

BOARDED-UP RAILWAY COTTAGE

SEVERALS VILLAGE ARCHAEOLOGICAL SITE

CROSS BRIDGE THEN WALK PARALLEL TO DISMANTLED RAILWAY

SMARDALE BRIDGE
069

MAP 41

¼ mile
500m
APPROX SCALE

VIEW TO SMARDALE GILL VIADUCT

IGNORE STILE

SCANDAL BECK

TO RAVENSTONEDALE

FOLD

RUINED WALL

VIEW OF GIANTS' GRAVES, THOUGH BEST VIEW IS FROM ACROSS RIVER

SIGNPOST FOR SMARDALE VIADUCT

42

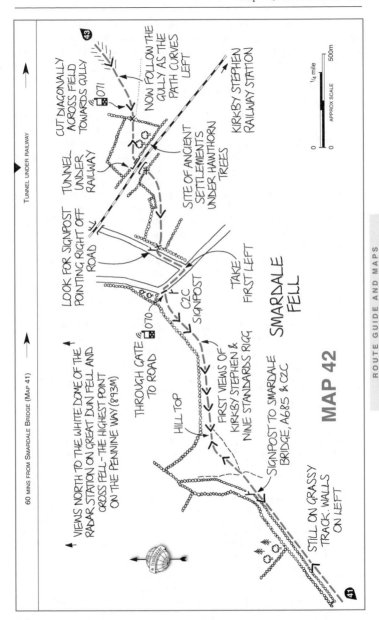

60 MINS FROM SMARDALE BRIDGE (MAP 41) →

TUNNEL UNDER RAILWAY

VIEWS NORTH TO THE WHITE DOME OF THE RADAR STATION ON GREAT DUN FELL AND CROSS FELL – THE HIGHEST POINT ON THE PENNINE WAY (893M)

LOOK FOR SIGNPOST POINTING RIGHT OFF ROAD

TUNNEL UNDER RAILWAY

CUT DIAGONALLY ACROSS FIELD TOWARDS GULLY

071

NOW FOLLOW THE GULLY AS THE PATH CURVES LEFT

SITE OF ANCIENT SETTLEMENTS UNDER HAWTHORN TREES

KIRKBY STEPHEN RAILWAY STATION

THROUGH GATE TO ROAD

070

C2C SIGNPOST

TAKE FIRST LEFT

SMARDALE FELL

HILL TOP

FIRST VIEWS OF KIRKBY STEPHEN & NINE STANDARDS RIGG

SIGNPOST TO SMARDALE BRIDGE, A685 & C2C

MAP 42

STILL ON GRASSY TRACK. WALLS ON LEFT

0   APPROX SCALE   500m
0   ¼ mile

43

41

ROUTE GUIDE AND MAPS

(cont'd from p156) Tracking a thread of dry-stone walls (see box p188) below Great Ewe Fell will bring you past the beautifully located **Bents Farm** (Map 41; ☎ 015396 23681) which offers basic (toilet and drinking water; no showers) **camping** from £5pp. Booking isn't required.

The next prehistoric site lies a short way past the farm where, having crossed a stile, a signpost used to urge you to stick to the recognised path so as not to disturb the archaeological site. This'll probably come as something of a surprise because, no matter how hard you look, there seems to be nothing remarkable. Satellite imagery reveals that what you're actually looking at is the **Severals Village settlement**, said to be one of the most important prehistoric sites in Britain. The fact that it remains unexcavated does nothing to quell archaeologists' enthusiasm for the place. Without leaving the path, look for irregular or unnatural depressions and bumps in the land here; it's these undulations that have so excited archaeologists.

On the opposite side of **Scandal Beck** lies the final ancient site on this stage: the so-called **Giants' Graves** (called 'pillow mounds' on 25k OS maps) are a series of long narrow mounds which, some say, may have been prehistoric rabbit enclosures.

Dropping down to **Smardale Bridge** across Scandal Beck, more recent archeological evidence can be spied in the form of the distant **Smardale Gill viaduct** along a former railway that once joined Kirkby Stephen to what is now the M6 corridor. Climbing to the crest of **Smardale Fell** (Map 42), on a clear day the Pennines rise before you like a standing wave with the cairns on Nine Standards Rigg just visible beyond the quarry west of Kirkby Stephen. Looking north across Eden valley, with less difficulty you may also spot the white dome of the radio station atop Great Dun Fell and to the left, Cross Fell, at 893m (2930ft), the highest point on the Pennine Way – but that's a walk for another day.

By now, those nearing **Kirkby Stephen** will not be mindful of such distant prospects, as slowly the town's churches and then other buildings rise from the wooded vale below.

KIRKBY STEPHEN   map p163

Kirkby Stephen (pronounced 'Kirby' Stephen) vies with Richmond as the biggest town on the route, though don't let that fool you into thinking that this place is a metropolis. In fact, Kirkby Stephen is a pleasant and prosperous market town built along the A685 with a population of around 1800, a figure that's swollen considerably during the summer months by walkers, runners, cyclists and other outdoor *bon viveurs*. If you're due a rest after the Lakeland stages, a day off in town is the tonic to numerous woes.

There've been **markets** in Kirkby Stephen since at least 1361 when it was granted a market charter. Note the cobbled outline on the market square's floor; it marks the outer limits of a former bull baiting area, a popular pastime in the town until 1820 when a bull broke free and ran amok, killing a number of bystanders.

The principal tourist attraction in Kirkby Stephen is the 13th-century **church**, which is known locally as the Cathedral of the Dales. The distinctive red sandstone church (part of the same formation found at St Bees) is separated from the market square by the peaceful lawn of the **cloisters**. On entering the main gate, on your right is **Trupp Stone**, where until 1836 the

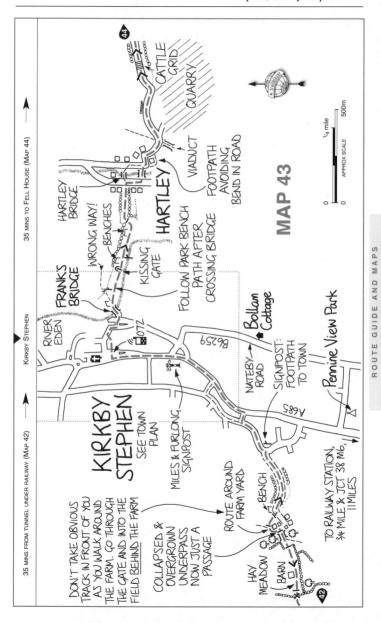

35 MINS FROM TUNNEL UNDER RAILWAY (MAP 42) — KIRKBY STEPHEN — 35 MINS TO FELL HOUSE (MAP 44)

MAP 43

DON'T TAKE OBVIOUS TRACK IN FRONT OF YOU AS YOU WALK AROUND THE FARM. GO THROUGH THE GATE AND INTO THE FIELD BEHIND THE FARM

COLLAPSED & OVERGROWN UNDERPASS NOW JUST A PASSAGE

ROUTE AROUND FARM YARD

KIRKBY STEPHEN

SEE TOWN PLAN

MILES & FURLONG SIGNPOST

BENCH

HAY MEADOW

BARN

TO RAILWAY STATION, ¾ MILE & JCT 38 M6, 11 MILES

NATEBY ROAD

SIGNPOST: FOOTPATH TO TOWN

A685

Bollam Cottage

B6259

Pennine View Park

RIVER EDEN

FRANKS BRIDGE

WRONG WAY!

BENCHES

KISSING GATE

HARTLEY BRIDGE

HARTLEY

FOLLOW PARK BENCH PATH AFTER CROSSING BRIDGE

VIADUCT

FOOTPATH AVOIDING BEND IN ROAD

CATTLE GRID

QUARRY

0   ¼ mile

0   APPROX SCALE   500m

ROUTE GUIDE AND MAPS

locals' tithes were collected. Take half an hour or so to wander around inside the church. It is built on the site of a Saxon church, though the earliest feature (the nave) of the present structure dates only to 1220. Features to look out for include the 17th-century **font**, a great stone lump at the rear of the church, and the nearby **bread shelves**, used for distributing bread to the poor. There's also a **Norman coffin** by the north wall, unearthed in 1980 during restoration work, and a glass display cabinet housing old Bibles and, curiously, a **boar's tusk**, said to belong to the last wild boar shot in England. The church's most interesting feature, however, is the 8th-century **Loki Stone** facing the main door, a metre-high block carved by the Vikings with the horned figure of the Norse god Loki.

Other Kirkby Stephen sites of note include the old and much-photographed **signpost** at the southern end of town, where the distances are given in miles and furlongs; and the curious but attractive **stone seats** in the form of sheep that stand by the door of the visitor centre. Carved by artist Keith Alexander, they're reputed to increase the fertility of any who sit upon them, ovine or otherwise. **Frank's Bridge** is a pretty double-arched stone footbridge, a quiet place to sit by the grassy riverbank and feed the ducks. It's thought to be named after a local brewer, Frank Birkbeck, who lived here in the 19th century.

One other item of note is the flock of **parrots** that fly around town during the day before returning home to their owner, a local resident, at dusk. Since the first edition of this guide we've been writing about these birds, without ever seeing them and beginning to think we'd either been the victim of a hoax or, if they had really existed at one time, we could be fairly certain that they did no longer. However, on a recent trip we finally saw three beautiful blue and yellow parrots in the trees near the Pennine View campsite. So keep your eyes peeled!

Services

Kirkby Stephen has become the spiritual (if not *quite* the geographical) heart of the

Coast to Coast path. Packhorse (see pp28-9) operate out of the town and those who opt to take advantage of their 'taxi' service will spend the night in Kirkby Stephen before being shuttled to St Bees the next morning. If you've left your car here, the Packhorse van arrives back in town from Robin Hood's Bay at around 6pm.

The **Upper Eden visitor centre** (☎ 017683 71199, ☐ www.visiteden.co.uk; Easter to Oct daily 10am-4pm, Nov to Easter Mon, Wed, Fri & Sat 11am-3pm) is crammed with brochures and the (volunteer) staff are knowledgeable and have information about accommodation. The Visit Eden website focuses on information about the Upper Eden area; for general information about Kirkby Stephen visit ☐ kirkby-stephen.com. Nearby is the **bookshop** (Mon/Wed/Fri/Sat 10am-4pm).

By the church is the **library** (Mon & Wed 10am-noon & 1-3pm, Sat 10am-1pm but check website as these may change) with free **wi-fi** and **internet**. There's also a **bank** with an **ATM**.

On the way into town there's a well-stocked Spar (Mon-Sat 8am-10.30pm, Sun 9am-10.30pm). Diverting from the town centre there's a large Co-op (Mon-Sat 7am-10pm, Sun 10am-4pm), set back from North Rd. There's a **launderette** (Fri-Mon 9.30am-6.30pm) just off Market St.

Eden Outdoors (☎ 017683 72431, ☐ eden-outdoors.business.site; Mon-Wed & Fri-Sat 8.30am-4pm, winter from 9am) is very well stocked with outdoor gear, maps and books. A bigger rival, **Mad About Mountains** (☎ 017683 72879, ☐ madaboutmountains.co.uk; **fb**; Mon-Sat 9am-5pm) is further down the road on the opposite side.

Blister kits and other medications are on sale at Green Tree **pharmacy** (Mon-Fri 9am-5.30pm, Sat 9am-1pm).

Transport   (see also pp54-6)

Kirkby Stephen is on Northern's Carlisle to Settle/Leeds railway line. The **railway station**, the only one apart from St Bees on the first half of the C2C path, lies over a mile south of the town. **Bus** services here are very limited: Western Dales' S5 (Thur only)

& S6 (Tue only) and Cumbria Classic Coaches No 571 (Mon only) call here.

For a **taxi** call Prima Taxis (☎ 017683 72557).

Where to stay

Pennine View Park (Map 43; ☎ 017683 71717, 🖥 pennineviewpark.co.uk; 🐕; WI-FI; Mar-early Nov) is a secure, manicured, no-nonsense caravan and camping park just

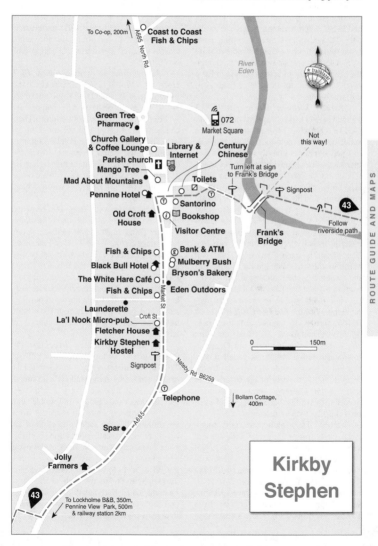

To Co-op, 200m

Coast to Coast Fish & Chips

A685 North Rd

River Eden

🎈 trailblazer

Green Tree Pharmacy

📶 072
📱 **Market Square**

Church Gallery & Coffee Lounge

Library & Internet

Century Chinese

Not this way!

Parish church

Mango Tree

Mad About Mountains

Toilets

Turn left at sign to Frank's Bridge

Pennine Hotel

Santorino

Signpost

Old Croft House

Bookshop

43

Visitor Centre

Frank's Bridge

Follow riverside path

Fish & Chips

Bank & ATM

Black Bull Hotel

Mulberry Bush

The White Hare Café

Bryson's Bakery

Fish & Chips

Eden Outdoors

Market St

Launderette

La'l Nook Micro-pub

Croft St

Fletcher House

0   150m

Kirkby Stephen Hostel

Signpost

Nateby Rd B6259

Telephone

Bollam Cottage, 400m

A685

Spar

Jolly Farmers

Kirkby Stephen

43

To Lockholme B&B, 350m,
Pennine View Park, 500m
& railway station 2km

ROUTE GUIDE AND MAPS

on the southern outskirts of town. Camping costs from £10.50pp for backpackers, with a large, flat grassy area set aside for tents away from the motorhomes and caravans. It has a clean ablutions block (use of the shower facilities is included in the rate), a laundry room, a small campers' kitchen, and a bar where evening meals are available. They also have three **camping pods** (with beds for up to five but no bedding) from £45 for one or two sharing, though they are unlikely to accept bookings for a single-night stay for these over bank holiday weekends.

Kirkby Stephen Hostel (☎ 07812 558525, 🖳 kirkbystephenhostel.co.uk; 1T/1Tr/1Qd/3x6-, 1x8-bed rooms all en suite, 1Qd shower facilities; WI-FI; 🐾) is an independent hostel grandly housed in a former Methodist chapel in the centre of town. It can be decidedly spooky when there aren't any other guests. A bed in any room costs from £26.50 but if you want a private room, you must pay for all the beds in that room. There are decent self-catering facilities, a large communal living area as well as a drying room. Check-in time is variable. The hostel is open year-round, but call ahead to check for availability in winter as the owners may be reluctant to turn on the heating for just one passing hiker.

For **B&B**, we've received many recommendations for *The Old Croft House* (☎ 017683 71638, 🖳 theoldcrofthouse.co.uk; 1S private bathroom, 2D/1T all en suite; 🍺; WI-FI; 🅛). It's a lovely old Georgian townhouse with a warm, oak-panelled interior full of books, made all the better by the warmth and generosity of the owners who know what Coasters want, welcoming guests with freshly baked cakes and even providing foot spas on request! Easily one of the best B&Bs along the entire route. B&B costs from £55pp (sgl £60, sgl occ room rate).

Next to the hostel and a favourite with many readers is *Fletcher House* (☎ 017683 71013, 🖳 fletcherhouse.co.uk; 2D/2T, all en suite; 🍺; WI-FI; 🅛); they have spacious, well-equipped rooms and offer B&B from £57.50pp (sgl occ £80). There's also a dry-

ing room, guest lounge, and this is another place that provides a foot spa.

Towards the southern end of town at 63 High St *The Jolly Farmers Guest House* (☎ 017683 71063, 🖳 thejollyfarmers.wordpress.com; 4D/5T, all en suite; 🍺; 🅛; WI-FI; 🐾) is a converted pub that welcomes guests with tea and home-made scones on arrival and offers a laundry service (£15). B&B costs from £57.50pp (sgl occ £70-75).

At the time of writing **Black Bull Hotel** (☎ 017683 72803, 🖳 blackbullkirkbystephen.co.uk; 5D/3T/1Tr, all en suite; 🍺; WI-FI; 🐾), at 38 Market Sq, had recently been taken over by new people. They charge from £42.50pp (sgl occ room rate).

There's also pub-like hotel accommodation at the small *Pennine Hotel* (☎ 017683 74997, 🖳 penninehotel.com; 1S/3D/1T all en suite, 1D with private facilities; 🍺; WI-FI; 🅛). B&B costs from £40pp (sgl occ £60).

A 5-minute walk from the heart of town, on Nateby Rd, is lovely *Bollam Cottage* (Map 43; ☎ 07580 165045, 🖳 bollamcottage.co.uk; 2D or T/1D, all en suite; 🍺; WI-FI; Easter-end Sep), with oak beams and a wood burner. B&B costs from £57.50pp (sgl occ £105). They have drying facilities for rain-soaked gear. Guests also have a separate lounge with wood-burning stove and fell views. Check-in is 4-6pm unless another time has been arranged in advance.

Lockholme Bed and Breakfast (☎ 07808 166380, 🖳 lockholme.co.uk; 2D or T/1T all en suite; WI-FI; 🅛), 48 South Rd, is recommended by some walkers who found it to be: 'well appointed, very comfortable and spotless' and 'most comfortable and run by welcoming hosts'. It is not far from the trail and has the added attraction of an excellent view (weather permitting!) of the Nine Standards. You can enter at the back and go into a boot/drying room so you can get rid of wet clothes and boots (they are also happy to do laundry – about £15 for a medium load). B&B costs from £57.50pp (sgl occ £95). They also have a guest lounge overlooking the garden.

Where to eat and drink

To make up a picnic, you'll find fair value and a mouthwatering range of speciality breads and sandwiches at **Bryson's Bakery** (☎ 017683 71958, 🖳 brysonsofkeswick.co .uk; Mon-Sat 8am-4pm, Sun 9am-3pm). They've been in business since 1947 so you can be assured they know what they're doing!

As for tearooms, *The White Hare Café* (**fb**; Mar-late Oct Wed-Sat 9am-4.30pm, Sun 9.30am-4.30pm, late Oct-Mar Thur-Fri 10am-4pm, Sat & Sun from 9.30am; WI-FI; 🐕) gives you a great big pot of tea and there's a good range of cakes and light lunches. They also have folders full of useful information for Coast-to-Coasters.

Mulberry Bush (☎ 017683 71572; **fb**; summer daily 9am-5pm, winter Fri-Wed 9am-5pm but if it is quiet they may close earlier) is another popular café.

Church Gallery & Coffee Lounge (☎ 017683 72395, 🖳 church-gallery.co.uk; Mon-Sat 9am-5pm, Sun 11am-5pm; WI-FI; 🐕) at the top end of town is a bit of a find: it's both a gift shop and a small, great-value self-service café with drinks and cakes. They also have a nice little outdoor area facing the church.

On the main street there are no fewer than three **fish & chip places** including, at the northern end, *Coast to Coast* (☎ 017683 71194; Fri & Sat 11.45am-1.45pm, Thur-Sun 4.30-7.30pm) dating from 1929 and said to be Wainwright's favourite.

For Chinese, there's **Century Chinese Restaurant** (☎ 017683 72828; **fb**; Tue-Sun 5-10pm), at the back of Market Square, serving unusually good classic Chinese takeaway meals. Nearby, *Santorino* (☎ 017683 72323; Sun-Thur 4-11pm, Fri-Sat to 1am) is Kirkby Stephen's fast-food shack. No British town is complete without a curryhouse and Kirkby Stephen's *Mango Tree* (☎ 017683 74960; daily 5-10.30/11pm) is one of the best places to eat here. It's right in the middle of town by Market Square; dishes start from around £9.

For pub food, *The Black Bull* (see Where to stay; food Mon-Thur noon-8pm, Fri & Sat 1.30-8pm, Sun noon-5pm) serves mains from £12, local ales such as Black Sheep.

Pub grub is also served in the bar and restaurant at *The Pennine Hotel* (see Where to stay; Mon-Thur noon-3pm & 5-8pm, Fri & Sat same but to 8.30pm, Sun to 4pm; 🐕).

La'L Nook (☎ 07506 075625; **fb**; Fri 4-11pm, Sat noon-11pm, Sun 1-10pm; 🐕; WI-FI), Croft St, is a micro pub that ale aficionados may not want to miss.

STAGE 7: KIRKBY STEPHEN TO KELD   MAPS 43-50

Introduction

This **13-mile (21km, 5-6hrs via the high routes)** stage is something of a redletter day. Not only do you cross the **Pennines** – the so-called backbone of the British Isles across whose flanks the Industrial Revolution gathered pace 200

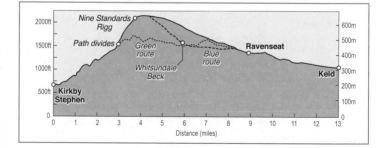

years ago – but in doing so you cross the **watershed** on the Coast to Coast. From the summit at Nine Standards Rigg all rivers, including the infant head-waters of the Swale which you'll track for the next few days, flow eastwards to drain into the North Sea. In a flush of optimism, you could say it's downhill all the way (but don't be fooled – it's not!).

You also pass from the county of Cumbria into **Yorkshire**, your home for the rest of the trek and finally, by the end of this stage by our reckoning you're very close to the halfway point, having completed over 90 miles of the 190-odd total.

Yet in spite of these significant landmarks, the one thing that most walkers remember about the transit of the Pennines is the **peat bogs** they have to nego-tiate along the way. The maps point out the boggiest sections and, on the high-er of the **three colour-coded routes** (see pp169-72), it's a good time to don gaiters if you have them. It's not so bad on the way up to Nine Standards. But afterwards it's like a different route, the path (or rather 'paths', there being three of them) all but disappearing and the waymarking minimal, and only really vis-ible by someone with excellent eyesight on a clear day. And then there are the

ROUTE GUIDE AND MAPS

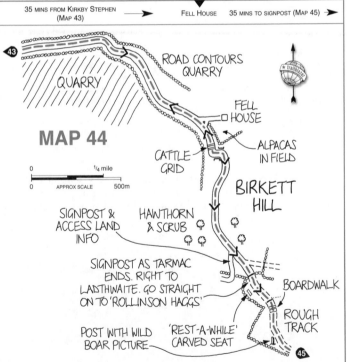

35 MINS FROM KIRKBY STEPHEN (MAP 43) ⟶   FELL HOUSE   35 MINS TO SIGNPOST (MAP 45) ⟶

ROAD CONTOURS QUARRY

QUARRY

FELL HOUSE

MAP 44

ALPACAS IN FIELD

CATTLE GRID

0   ¼ mile
0   APPROX SCALE   500m

BIRKETT HILL

SIGNPOST & ACCESS LAND INFO

HAWTHORN & SCRUB

SIGNPOST AS TARMAC ENDS. RIGHT TO LADTHWAITE. GO STRAIGHT ON TO 'ROLLINSON HAGGS'

BOARDWALK

ROUGH TRACK

POST WITH WILD BOAR PICTURE

'REST-A-WHILE' CARVED SEAT

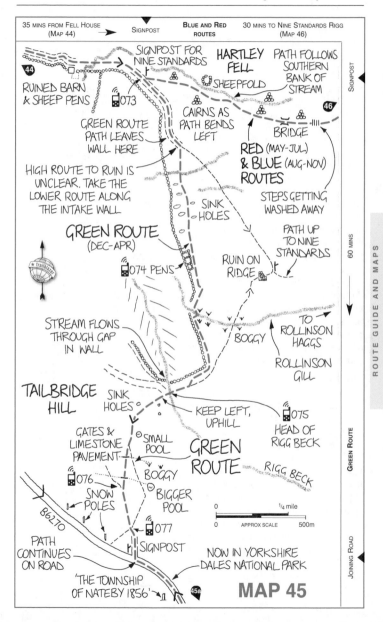

35 MINS FROM FELL HOUSE (MAP 44) → SIGNPOST ▼ BLUE AND RED ROUTES 30 MINS TO NINE STANDARDS RIGG (MAP 46)

44 RUINED BARN & SHEEP PENS

SIGNPOST FOR NINE STANDARDS

HARTLEY FELL

PATH FOLLOWS SOUTHERN BANK OF STREAM

SIGNPOST ▶

SHEEPFOLD

073

GREEN ROUTE PATH LEAVES WALL HERE

CAIRNS AS PATH BENDS LEFT

46

BRIDGE

RED (MAY-JUL) & BLUE (AUG-NOV) ROUTES

HIGH ROUTE TO RUIN IS UNCLEAR. TAKE THE LOWER ROUTE ALONG THE INTAKE WALL

STEPS GETTING WASHED AWAY

GREEN ROUTE (DEC-APR)

SINK HOLES

PATH UP TO NINE STANDARDS

60 MINS

074 PENS

RUIN ON RIDGE

STREAM FLOWS THROUGH GAP IN WALL

BOGGY

TO ROLLINSON HAGGS

ROLLINSON GILL

TAILBRIDGE HILL

SINK HOLES

KEEP LEFT, UPHILL

075 HEAD OF RIGG BECK

GATES & LIMESTONE PAVEMENT

SMALL POOL

GREEN ROUTE

BOGGY

076

SNOW POLES

BIGGER POOL

RIGG BECK

0   ¼ mile
0   APPROX SCALE   500m

B6270

077

PATH CONTINUES ON ROAD

SIGNPOST

NOW IN YORKSHIRE DALES NATIONAL PARK

'THE TOWNSHIP OF NATEBY 1856'

45a

MAP 45

ROUTE GUIDE AND MAPS

GREEN ROUTE

JOINING ROAD

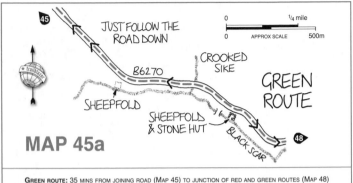

JUST FOLLOW THE
ROAD DOWN

CROOKED
SIKE

GREEN
ROUTE

B6270

SHEEPFOLD

SHEEPFOLD
& STONE HUT

BLACK SGAR

MAP 45a

0   ¼ mile
0   APPROX SCALE   500m

GREEN ROUTE: 35 MINS FROM JOINING ROAD (MAP 45) TO JUNCTION OF RED AND GREEN ROUTES (MAP 48)

bogs themselves, where many a trekker
has been injured and many more have
lost boots, dignity – and even the will to
carry on – in the moist, tenacious
embrace of these silent dangers. If you
do succumb to the mires, cheer yourself
up with the thought that at the end of
this stage you'll spend the night in the
gentle pastoral scenery of **Swaledale**,
the most northerly of Yorkshire's Dales
and some say its loveliest.

The route
From Kirkby Stephen you cross the
Eden river at **Frank's Bridge** (Map 43)
and continue up to **Hartley** village.

From here follow the lane uphill
past the huge **quarry** – a strenuous start
to the day. At the end lies a wide **dirt
track** (Map 44) up Hartley Fell where,
three miles from town, the path divides
(Map 45, WPT 073): the **red** and **blue**
routes head east up the hill to Nine
Standards, while the **green route** parallels a stone wall before striking off over
a rising moorland path to the quiet
(B6270) Kirkby Stephen–Keld road.
The three routes are described in more
detail opposite.

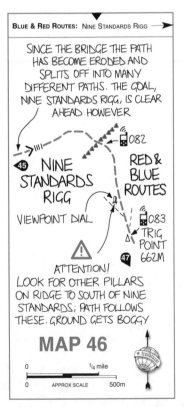

BLUE & RED ROUTES: NINE STANDARDS RIGG →

SINCE THE BRIDGE THE PATH
HAS BECOME ERODED AND
SPLITS OFF INTO MANY
DIFFERENT PATHS. THE GOAL,
NINE STANDARDS RIGG, IS CLEAR
AHEAD HOWEVER

082

45 NINE
STANDARDS
RIGG

RED &
BLUE
ROUTES

VIEWPOINT DIAL

083
TRIG
POINT
662M

47

⚠ ATTENTION!
LOOK FOR OTHER PILLARS
ON RIDGE TO SOUTH OF NINE
STANDARDS; PATH FOLLOWS
THESE. GROUND GETS BOGGY

MAP 46

0   ¼ mile
0   APPROX SCALE   500m

ROUTE GUIDE AND MAPS

The three routes over the moors Due to severe erosion of the peat by walkers as well as a lack of investment to do something about it, there are **three colour-coded paths** across the Pennines to Keld, the exact route you take depending on the time of year or weather conditions, though most walkers continue to ignore the seasonal guidelines. These routes are marked on Maps 45, 45a, 46 and 47. They initially diverge at a signpost for Nine Standards (Map 45, WPT 073) at which point boggy episodes set in whichever route you take. As we mentioned before, the waymarking is terrible – particularly on the Red and Blue routes – so follow our instructions carefully. Furthermore, the junction where the red and blue paths separate really has been ravaged by erosion from your predecessors' footwear and gets worse year by year. If ever there was a part of the Coast to Coast path that needed lining with stone slabs or duckboards, it's here at the southern end of Nine Standards Rigg which looks like a scene from the Somme, circa 1916.

The **blue and red** high routes are about the same length (4 miles from Nine Standards to the point where all three paths converge just west of Ravenseat). The low-level **green route** is about half a mile shorter (adding up to 12½ miles for this stage) and, with a couple of miles of road, takes about an hour less.

The advice seems to be: if you can't see Nine Standards (WPT 073) due to low cloud or mist, you'll see even less when you're up there and may even get lost, so take the green route.

It's possible to have your cake and eat it up here. Should you arrive at Nine Standards and the weather turns on you, follow a path south for three-quarters of a mile and then head west from the cairns, passing to the west of Rollinson Haggs to pick up Rollinson Gill and so the green route (see p172) before it reaches the head of Rigg Beck (WPT 075). From there follow the green route all the way to Keld.

● **Blue route (Aug-Nov; Maps 45-49; 3hrs 20mins from where the green route separates)** Weather permitting, this is the route to choose to get the full Pennine experience (or should that be immersion?). Up to Nine Standards (WPT 082), just 30 minutes from the junction with the green route it matches the red route.

Heading south past the **trig point** (662m; Map 46; WPT 083) and the low ruins to the end of the ridge, at the key junction marked by the mire-bound signpost (WPT 085) this route then takes an eastern course down to Whitsundale Beck (Map 47). Irregular and ageing posts daubed with forensic traces of light blue paint guide you east down to the Beck, but if you can't rely on seeing them, a compass bearing of 100° or so will do the same job. Once down in the Beck follow its winding course south to a reunion with the other two paths (Map 49), and just 15 minutes from refreshments at Ravenseat Farm (see p172), if the farm is open.

● **Red route (May-July; Maps 45-49; 3hrs 35mins from where the green route separates)** In clear conditions this route is straightforward enough. From the boot-ravaged divergence with the blue route (WPT 085; Map 47) things can get a little boggier still and there are no waymarkers as the route rolls south over the barely noticeable crest of **White Mossy Hill**.   *cont'd on p172)*

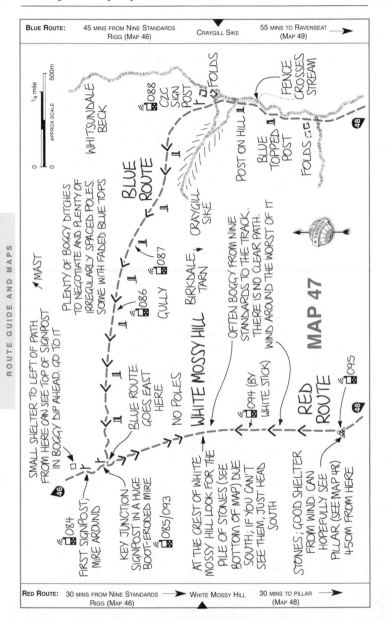

BLUE ROUTE

WHITSUNDALE BECK

C2C SIGN POST 088

FOLDS

FENCE CROSSES STREAM

POST ON HILL

BLUE TOPPED POST

FOLDS

48

MAST

PLENTY OF BOGGY DITCHES TO NEGOTIATE AND PLENTY OF IRREGULARLY SPACED POLES. SOME WITH FADED BLUE TOPS

087

086 GULLY

CRAYGILL SIKE

BIRKDALE TARN

WHITE MOSSY HILL

NO POLES

BLUE ROUTE GOES EAST HERE

SMALL SHELTER TO LEFT OF PATH FROM HERE CAN SEE TOP OF SIGNPOST IN BOGGY DIP AHEAD. GO TO IT

46

FIRST SIGNPOST, MIRE AROUND

084

KEY JUNCTION SIGNPOST IN A HUGE BOOT-ERODED MIRE

085/093

AT THE CREST OF WHITE MOSSY HILL LOOK FOR THE PILE OF STONES (SEE BOTTOM OF MAP) DUE SOUTH; IF YOU CAN'T SEE THEM, JUST HEAD SOUTH

OFTEN BOGGY FROM NINE STANDARDS TO THE TRACK. THERE IS NO CLEAR PATH. WIND AROUND THE WORST OF IT

MAP 47

094 (BY WHITE STICK)

RED ROUTE

095

48

STONES; GOOD SHELTER FROM WIND. CAN HOPEFULLY SEE PILLAR (SEE MAP 48) 450M FROM HERE

¼ mile
APPROX SCALE 500m

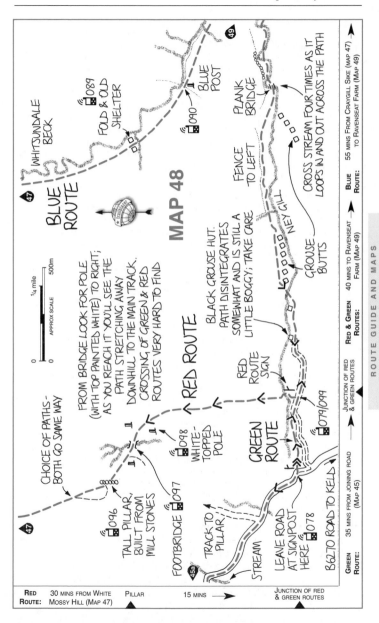

MAP 48

BLUE ROUTE

WHITSUNDALE BECK

089 FOLD & OLD SHELTER

BLUE POST

090

PLANK BRIDGE

FENCE TO LEFT

CROSS STREAM FOUR TIMES AS IT LOOPS IN AND OUT ACROSS THE PATH

NEY GILL

GROUSE BUTTS

47

CHOICE OF PATHS – BOTH GO SAME WAY

FROM BRIDGE LOOK FOR POLE (WITH TOP PAINTED WHITE) TO RIGHT; AS YOU REACH IT YOU'LL SEE THE PATH STRETCHING AWAY DOWNHILL TO THE MAIN TRACK. CROSSING OF GREEN & RED ROUTES VERY HARD TO FIND

← RED ROUTE

BLACK GROUSE HUT. PATH DISINTEGRATES SOMEWHAT AND IS STILL A LITTLE BOGGY; TAKE CARE

RED ROUTE SIGN

GREEN ROUTE

098 WHITE-TOPPED POLE

097 FOOTBRIDGE

096 TALL PILLAR, BUILT FROM MILL STONES

079/099

45a

TRACK TO PILLAR

LEAVE ROAD AT SIGNPOST HERE 078

STREAM

B6270 ROAD TO KELD

¼ mile
APPROX SCALE
0 500m

¼ mile

ROUTE GUIDE AND MAPS

(cont'd from p169) From here you should be able to make out a large **pile of stones** (resembling a ruin) to the south; once there you hope to be able to see a tall stone **pillar** (WPT 096) to the south-south-east.

At this point you drop south-east over a small **footbridge** and then south down towards the green route where you turn east onto a track and continue on to the farm at Ravenseat (see below). Note that on both these higher routes it's well worth taking your time to **avoid the worst bogs** by all means possible: backtracking, taking a running jump, using a pole, letting your partner go first (always a sensible tactic) or even using them as a plank; whatever works for you. One Trailblazer updater got a bit blasé here and sank down over his knees, while during another update we met a women on the trail with a broken wrist – caused, so it transpired, by getting her arm caught in the loop of her trekking pole which in turn got caught in the mud. Perhaps those tales of calf-swallowing Pennine bogs were not so exaggerated after all.

● **Green route (Dec-Apr; Maps 45, 45a, 48-49; 3½hrs from where the route separates from the red and blue routes)** This is the simplest route and in inclement weather the best one to take, regardless of the season. Note that we found the more-used path from the junction post at WPT 073 no longer squelches pointlessly halfway up to Rollinson Haggs only to drop down again (as shown on OS maps).

The more practical route follows the intake wall to the moderately impressive **head of Rigg Beck** which meanders away down its valley.

After Rigg Beck there follows a rise to gates and a section of weathered **limestone pavement** before you join the B6270. Note too that later on, the point where the green route *officially* leaves the B6270 (Map 48, WPT 078) at a right-hand bend seems to be another pointless hiding to nothing, this time up a gully on all fours and then straight into a bog with no obvious path exiting it. Instead, continue along the road for another minute or so (Map 48) and turn north up the car track. The official path – such as it is – soon joins it. Shortly you'll pass the bootworn scar of the red route coming down from the pillar to join your track (WPT 079), and soon the track ends by a black grouse hut.

From here you follow, and occasionally cross, **Ney Gill** as it wends its way towards the blue route junction at Whitsundale Beck just out of Ravenseat (WPT 080). All in all, on a rainy day keeping below 1700ft (530m) the green route need not be regarded as a 'consolation prize'. Although it's a shame to miss out the mysterious cairns, it's a fine moorland walk in its own right, getting lost is not too great a risk and the road stage along Birkdale is a fine way to appreciate the peaty wastelands without necessarily sinking into them. In really bad weather it's probably sensible if, once you hit the B6270 road to just stay on it all the way into Keld. Of course, it's not the proper Coast to Coast route, but at least it will get you into the village safely.

Whichever way you've come over the moors, many readers have confirmed that by the time they get to ***Ravenseat Farm*** (Map 49; 🖥 yorkshireshepherdess .com) they're unable to resist a sit down for some **refreshments** (including afternoon cream teas served most days between mid May and September noon-4pm). The owner, and mother of nine children, Amanda Owen (aka The Yorkshire Shepherdess), is something of a celebrity round these parts, and has

WHITSUNDALE BECK

BLUE ROUTE

TO TAN HILL, 3 MILES/5KM

Ravenseat Farm
CREAM TEAS

48 091

RED & GREEN ROUTES FOLD

48

092/080

CROSS STREAM, GO UP TRACK

WATER FALL

WHITSUNDALE BECK

BARN

SMALL GATE INTO FIELD & SIGNPOST TO KELD

TWO BARNS

RUINED WALL

VERY MUDDY AROUND HERE

GAP IN WALL

SIGNPOST

BOUNDARY WALL

WOODED RAVINE

TO B6270

SIGNPOST TO KELD

EDDY FOLD

0   ¼ mile
0   APPROX SCALE   500m

MAP 49

50

RAVENSEAT FARM

70 MINS TO KELD (MAP 50)

ROUTE GUIDE AND MAPS

written books about her young family's life in the Dales. Hollywood has even bought the rights for the film apparently.

From Ravenseat the path tracks south alongside the engorged chasm of **Whitsundale Beck**, punctuated with some impressive waterfalls and the finely restored but otherwise unused '*laithes*' (stone barns for housing hay and live-stock) which are a feature of Swaledale. Passing the farmhouse of **Smithy Holme** (Map 50), you can join the B6270 immediately by crossing the bridge, or take the path above the riverside cliff of **Cotterby Scar**. (For once we rec-ommend the road, as it allows you to visit Wainwath Force.) These two paths reunite by the bridge just by *Keld Bunk Barn* (see p174), at Park House, from where it's a gentle half-mile stroll to what passes for Keld village centre. The tough first half of the Coast to Coast is now behind you; hopefully your feet are keeping up with the pace.

KELD   **MAP 50, opposite**

Keld sits at the head of Swaledale where the Coast to Coast bisects the longer, north-bound Pennine Way. Today it's a tiny – and very pretty – hill village of solid stone buildings huddled against the often inclement weather. However, in common with the rest of Swaledale, in the mid 19th century Keld stood at the heart of a local lead-mining industry. Many of the buildings including the two **chapels** were constructed at this time, as a quick survey of the construction dates carved on the houses' lintels will confirm.

Another old building, the former Literary Institute, has been converted into the unstaffed **Keld Countryside & Heritage Centre** (⌨ keld.org.uk; Apr-Oct 8am-9pm, Nov-Mar 8.30am-5pm) which has displays and photographs of local history and farming heritage. One neat little feature allows you to press buttons to hear the thoughts of local residents including a farmer and a historian.

Keld is more about water than lead today. The name means 'spring' in Norse and the **Swale River**, dyed brown by the peat, rushes past the village. Do take the opportunity to visit some of the numerous nearby waterfalls – more accurately called cascades or, locally, **forces** (another Norse word) – including Catrake Force, just above the village, and East Gill Force under a bridge below it. Being not only a tiny village at the crossroads of two major long-distance paths, but also being situated in the ever-popular Swaledale, accommodation options in Keld dry up fast if you leave it too late in the high season. Further down the valley the B&Bs in Thwaite and Muker (on the 'low level' route to Reeth) are no less popular. Indeed, such are the charms of Swaledale's rolling scenery, dotted here and there with the distinctive 'laithes' that many hikers forego Wainwright's high route (see pp177-81) via Swinner and Gunnerside gills in favour of the gentle stroll down the Swale valley to Reeth.

Services

The only services in Keld are a **public toilet** and a **phone box**. For more details on Keld and the rest of Swaledale visit ⌨ swaledale.net.

However, **Bus** No 30 (AKA the community-run Little White Bus) and Northern DalesBus No 831 (early June-late Oct) call here (see pp54-6).

Where to stay and eat

You'll have walked past *Keld Bunk Barn & Swaledale Yurts* (☎ 01748 886549 or ☎ 01748 886159, ⌨ keldbunkbarnandyurts .com), at Park House, on the way into the village; it is now owned and run by the Halls. The site is a wonderful place to stay, with helpful hosts, excellent facilities and its very own fearsome waterfall – **Raiby Force** – gushing past the back door (you can swim in the pool beneath it in summer). Some details (WI-FI; Ⓛ; ⚐; Feb-end Nov) apply to both the barn and yurts. Tea and coffee are available as is breakfast; options (from £4) are a hot breakfast baguette with bacon and egg, a bowl of porridge, two croissants and also cafetière coffee. Home-cooked evening meals (24hrs' notice required; menu on website) are served and they have an alcohol licence. There's even a hot tub for up to six people for hire (60 mins; £20 for two people plus £5pp). Note the two-night minimum stay if booking a Saturday night (and three-nights for bank holiday weekends for the Yurts) and it is possible the bunk barn will have been booked for sole occupancy.

Rates (inc bedding and towel) in the **bunk barn** (1D/1Tr/1Qd) are from £79 for the en suite double room (sgl occ room rate) or from £90/120 in the triple/quad (shared facilities). As bunkhouses go it's about as comfortable as you can get with a kitchen, a small drying room, a dining area and a cosy lounge with a TV. **Swaledale Yurts** comprises five Mongolian yurts; each sleeps up to five people (from £109, or from £149 at peak times, per night for two sharing plus £20 per additional person; sgl occ full rate). Incredibly cosy, bedding is provided and each has a wood-burning stove. Each yurt has a separate private shower, which has some kick to it, and washing facilities.

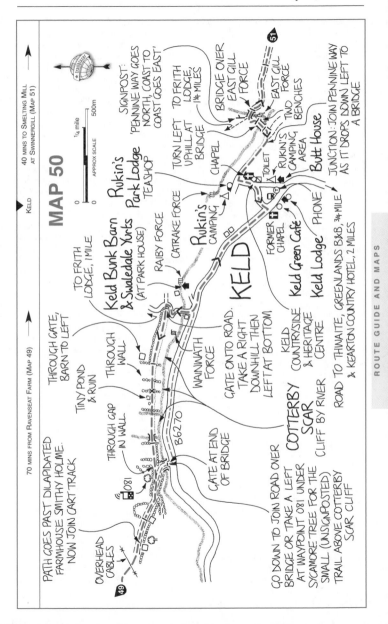

MAP 50

¼ mile
APPROX SCALE
500m

49

OVERHEAD CABLES

PATH GOES PAST DILAPIDATED FARMHOUSE SMITHY HOLME. NOW JOIN CART TRACK

THROUGH GATE, BARN TO LEFT

TINY POND & RUIN

THROUGH WALL

TO FRITH LODGE, 1 MILE

Keld Bunk Barn & Swaledale Yurts (AT PARK HOUSE)

RAIBY FORCE

CATRAKE FORCE

Rukin's Park Lodge TEASHOP

SIGNPOST: 'PENNINE WAY GOES NORTH, COAST TO COAST GOES EAST'

TO FRITH LODGE, 1¼ MILES

TURN LEFT UPHILL AT BRIDGE

CHAPEL

BRIDGE OVER EAST GILL FORCE

EAST GILL FORCE

51

TWO BENCHES

THROUGH GAP IN WALL

081

WAINWATH FORCE

GATE ONTO ROAD. TAKE A RIGHT DOWNHILL THEN LEFT AT BOTTOM

Rukin's CAMPING

KELD COUNTRYSIDE & HERITAGE CENTRE

KELD

TOILET

Rukin's CAMPING AREA

Butt House

FORMER CHAPEL

Keld Green Café

Keld Lodge PHONE

JUNCTION: JOIN PENNINE WAY AS IT DROPS DOWN LEFT TO A BRIDGE

GATE AT END OF BRIDGE

B6270

COTTERBY SCAR
CLIFF BY RIVER

GO DOWN TO JOIN ROAD OVER BRIDGE OR TAKE A LEFT AT WAYPOINT 081 UNDER SYCAMORE TREE FOR THE SMALL (UNSIGNPOSTED) TRAIL ABOVE COTTERBY SCAR CLIFF

ROAD TO THWAITE, GREENLANDS B&B, ¾ MILE & KEARTON COUNTRY HOTEL, 2 MILES

Rukin's Park Lodge (☎ 01748 886274, 🖥 www.rukins-keld.co.uk) is at the bottom of the village, though their actual **campsites** (Easter to end Sep; 🐾; walkers from £8pp) are in three different areas: one is below Butt House and the other right by the river. There is a shower-and-toilet block shared by all. They don't take bookings but walkers will always be accepted. They also have a lovely little **teashop** (WI-FI but only outside; 🐾; Easter to end Sep daily 8.30am-5.30pm, to 6pm peak season) in the farmhouse with tables and chairs in the front garden. There are bacon rolls and a limited selection of groceries; they serve an extra pot of hot water when you order tea – always the sign of a good tea place – and they are a (limited) off-licence so you can buy cans of beer, lager or cider, or a bottle of wine (small selection) and drink in the garden.

Butt House (☎ 01748 886374, 🖥 butt housekeld.co.uk; 1S/1D/2D or T/1Tr, all en suite; 🛏; WI-FI; Ⓛ; Apr-end Sep) offers a warm welcome and highly praised food. It's a popular place and B&B costs £52.50-60pp (sgl from £70, sgl occ room rate) with an **evening meal** (à la carte menu – main course from around £13.50) served at 7pm, but guests need to call by 5pm on the day to place their menu choice. A laundry service costs from £8.50.

Keld Lodge (☎ 01748 886259, 🖥 keldlodge.com; 1S/3T/4D/1Tr all en suite, 1S/2D shared facilities; WI-FI; Ⓛ; 🐾; early Mar to mid Nov) is now a cosy country lodge with an above-average restaurant though it has been a YHA hostel. There is a drying room and most bedrooms have wonderful views, though some still have the feel of a pokey hostel dorm. Rates are from £45pp (sgl £45) in the two rooms which aren't en suite, from £57.50pp otherwise (sgl/sgl occ £57.50/75). The **bar-restaurant** (open for drinks Mon-Thur 2.30-9.30pm, Fri-Sun noon-9.30pm; food daily 5.30-7.30pm) is open to non-residents (booking recommended). Mains cost around £13 and they have Black Sheep ale on tap.

Just over a mile north of Keld on the Pennine Way, ***Frith Lodge*** (off Map 50; ☎ 01748 886489, 🖥 frithlodgekeld.co.uk; 3D/2T, all en suite; WI-FI; Ⓛ; May-end Sep) offers B&B from £58.50pp (sgl occ rate on request); evening meals (£17.95/21.95 for 2/3 courses) are also available and they have a licensed bar. It can also be accessed from the road just north of Keld Bunk Barn; continue north on the road for about 500m then take the bridleway/track on your right, signposted to Tan Hill. Frith Lodge can be seen from here on the opposite side of the dale on your right. After your stay you can rejoin the C2C Path via the Pennine Way.

Keld Green Café (☎ 01748 898778; **fb**; daily 9am-5pm) is a new (in 2022) venture that offers take-away food and hot drinks that can be eaten on outdoor picnic tables. The menu is currently limited to burgers, sausage baps, soup, sandwiches and cakes but they plan to expand to evening meals if there is demand.

For more accommodation options in Muker see p187 and in Gunnerside see p188.

THWAITE   off MAP 50, p175

About three-quarters of a mile down the road from Keld, on Angram Lane, is ***Greenlands B&B*** (☎ 01748 886532, 🖥 greenlandskeld.co.uk; 2D or T, both en suite; WI-FI; Ⓛ; Apr-end Oct) they charge from £52.50pp (sgl occ £95) and evening meals (see the website for details) are available. They also have a drying room and offer a laundry service (from £8.50).

Kearton Country Hotel (☎ 01748 886277, 🖥 keartoncountryhotel.co.uk; 1S/4D, all en suite; 🛏; WI-FI; Ⓛ; mid Feb-Dec) is about 1¼ miles further along the same road and is a good-looking place. However, they weren't providing B&B at the time of writing; check their website or give them a call for up-to-date information. Their *café* (Sat-Mon & Wed-Thur 10.30am-4pm, closes early if quiet) serves light lunches (noon-3.30pm), and there's a **bar** too.

Bus No 30 (Little White Bus) stops here, as does Arriva's No 831; see pp54-6 for details.

STAGE 8: KELD TO REETH   MAPS 50-56

Introduction

One might rightly assume the **original high-level route** is the way to go but many walkers who've done both find the **low-level (Swaledale Valley) route** (see pp184-9) just as agreeable – though don't be misled into thinking that it's that much easier!

The high-level walk as described in Wainwright's book begins at the foot of Keld village – a bit of a pain for those who've spent the night down in Thwaite from where following the valley alternative to Reeth makes sense. But if you wish to take the high-level route you could catch Little White Bus's No 30 service back up to Keld, though at the time of research the earliest one in the morning passes by Thwaite for Keld at a slightly too late 9.55am (see pp54-6 and check their website for details). Note that on this high-level route there's nowhere to buy any food or drink so come prepared.

The high-level route   Maps 51-56

The wildlife along this **11-mile (18km, 4½hr)** walk can be abundant, so try to set off as early as possible to increase your chances of encountering pheasants and deer. However, as with Stage 6 from Shap to Kirkby Stephen, this route is mainly about archaeology and the evidence of man's industrial enterprise in the far north of England. Today's walk takes you through a part of Yorkshire that has been forever scarred by the activities of lead mining. The first sign of this crops up at **Crackpot Hall** (Map 51), 30 minutes from Keld along a pretty trail high above the Swale. Though there's been a house here since the 16th century, the ruin you see actually dates from the 18th century and, while not directly connected to the mining industry, the farmhouse was once owned by one of the mine's managers. Quiet and ruined now, the location would be a nice spot for a wild camp were it allowed, as would be many of the mining ruins on this stage. 'Crackpot', by the way, means 'Deep hole or chasm that is the haunt of crows', and is not a comment on the value of the endeavours of the former residents.

The path bends north now from behind the Hall to pass an 'old barn' on the map and after a gate, traverses the narrow gorge of **Swinner Gill**. Make sure you head uphill to follow the correct trail or you'll eventually find yourself on a lower, parallel but precipitous sheep track barely two boots wide and clinging to the side of the gorge below the correct route – see Map 51.

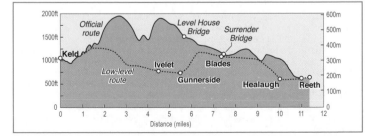

Whichever route you stumble on, before long you arrive at the eerie remains of **Swinner Gill smelting mill** with waterfalls alongside. Again, from here it's possible to follow a tricky path alongside the northern bank of **East Grain Beck** instead of the easier way a little higher up the valley side.

Once climbing east, after passing the last mill ruin on your left, look for a higher path after the first stream crossing about 250m on. Either way both paths deliver you with a sweaty brow onto the breezy expanse of **Gunnerside Moor**. There are grouse butts in the area; if people are out shooting you'll be relieved to know that they will stop to let you pass.

Initially climbing and passing **Moss Dam** to the south, on the ensuing descent you leave the track to curve north-east and descend steeply to more picturesque ruins at **Blakethwaite** (Map 52) in the valley of Gunnerside Beck. This is an ideal, if slightly premature, place for a picnic lunch out of the wind. While sitting on the grassy bank behind the large ruined peat store with its impressive arched windows (peat was used with coal to heat the smelting furnace), look for the flue coming down from the hill, finishing near the kiln on the western banks. From here the path zig-zags east back up onto **Melbecks**

ROUTE GUIDE AND MAPS

❑ LEAD MINING IN SWALEDALE

According to the best estimates, lead has been mined in Swaledale since at least Roman times, and very possibly there was some small-scale mining back in the Bronze Age. A couple of pigs (ingots) of lead, including one discovered in Swaledale with the Roman name 'Hadrian' marked upon it, have been found. A versatile metal which oxidises slowly, lead is used in plumbing (indeed the word 'plumbing' comes from the Latin for lead), shipbuilding and roofing as well as in the manufacture of glass, pottery and paint. During medieval times lead was much in demand by the great churches and castles that were being built at that time.

The onset of the Industrial Revolution caused mining in Swaledale to become more organised and developed from the end of the 17th century. The innovation of gunpowder blasting, too, led to a sizeable increase in production, and the Yorkshire sites were at the centre of the British lead-mining industry. Indeed, during the mid 19th century Britain was producing over half the world's lead.

But while some of the mine-owners grew fabulously wealthy on the proceeds, the workers themselves suffered appalling conditions, often staying for a week or more at the mine and spending every daylight hour inside it. Deaths were common as the mines were rarely built with safety in mind and as advances in technology drove the mines ever deeper, so conditions became ever more hazardous. Illnesses from the cramped, damp and insanitary conditions were rife. As if to rub salt into the wounds, many workers did not even own their own tools, but instead hired them from an agent. The industry continued to prosper throughout much of the 19th century until the opening of mines in South America led to an influx of cheaper imports sending many British mines into bankruptcy. Many workers drifted away, usually to the coal mines around Durham, or to London and North America, in search of better prospects. By the early 20th century many of the villages were struggling to survive. Indeed, in the words of one resident of Reeth, when the mines closed the village became a 'City of the Dead'. Thankfully, tourism today has gone some way to securing the future of these attractive mining villages, and with the establishment of Yorkshire Dales National Park the future looks a lot brighter for the villages of Swaledale.

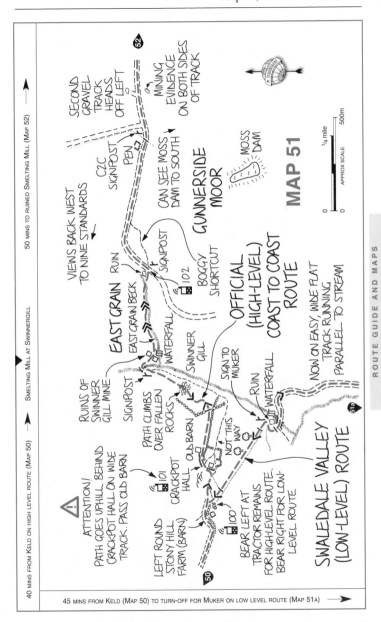

SECOND GRAVEL TRACK HEADS OFF LEFT

MINING EVIDENCE ON BOTH SIDES OF TRACK

C2C SIGNPOST
PEN

CAN SEE MOSS DAM TO SOUTH

MOSS DAM

GUNNERSIDE MOOR

MAP 51

¼ mile
APPROX SCALE
0   500m

VIEWS BACK WEST TO NINE STANDARDS

EAST GRAIN   RUIN

SIGNPOST

102

BOGGY SHORTCUT

EAST GRAIN BECK

WATERFALL

SWINNER GILL

OFFICIAL (HIGH-LEVEL) COAST TO COAST ROUTE

RUINS OF SWINNER GILL MINE

SIGNPOST

PATH CLIMBS OVER FALLEN ROCKS

101

OLD BARN

SIGN TO MUKER

RUIN

WATERFALL

NOW ON EASY, WIDE FLAT TRACK RUNNING PARALLEL TO STREAM

ATTENTION!
PATH GOES UPHILL BEHIND CRACKPOT HALL ON WIDE TRACK. PASS OLD BARN

CRACKPOT HALL

NOT THIS WAY

LEFT ROUND STONY HILL FARM (BARN)

BEAR LEFT AT TRACTOR REMAINS FOR HIGH-LEVEL ROUTE. BEAR RIGHT FOR LOW-LEVEL ROUTE

100

SWALEDALE VALLEY (LOW-LEVEL) ROUTE

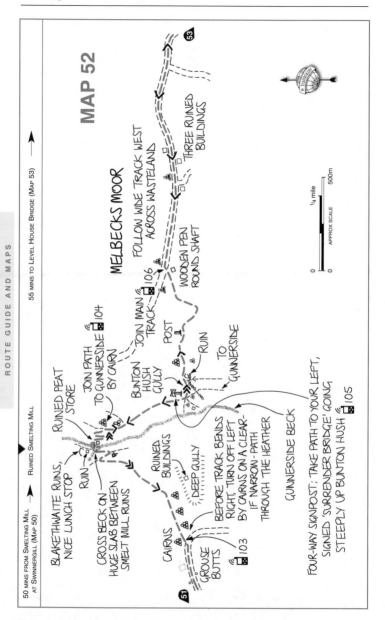

50 MINS FROM SMELTING MILL AT SWINNERGILL (MAP 50) → RUINED SMELTING MILL

55 MINS TO LEVEL HOUSE BRIDGE (MAP 53) →

MAP 52

MELBECKS MOOR

FOLLOW WIDE TRACK WEST ACROSS WASTELAND

THREE RUINED BUILDINGS

53

RUINED PEAT STORE

JOIN PATH TO GUNNERSIDE ☏104

BLAKETHWAITE RUINS, NICE LUNCH STOP

RUIN

CROSS BECK ON HUGE SLAB BETWEEN SMELT MILL RUINS

JOIN PATH TO GUNNERSIDE BY CAIRN

BUNTON HUSH GULLY

JOIN MAIN TRACK ☏106

POST

WOODEN PEN ROUND SHAFT

RUIN

TO GUNNERSIDE

RUINED BUILDINGS

DEEP GULLY

BEFORE TRACK BENDS RIGHT, TURN OFF LEFT BY CAIRNS ON A CLEAR-IF NARROW-PATH THROUGH THE HEATHER

GUNNERSIDE BECK

CAIRNS

☏103

GROUSE BUTTS

51

FOUR-WAY SIGNPOST; TAKE PATH TO YOUR LEFT, SIGNED 'SURRENDER BRIDGE' GOING STEEPLY UP BUNTON HUSH ☏105

0 —— ¼ mile
0 —— 500m
APPROX SCALE

☐ **IMPORTANT NOTE – WALKING TIMES**

All times in this book refer only to the time spent walking. You will need to add 20-30% to allow for rests, photography, checking the map, drinking water etc.

Moor. It's not uncommon to lose your way on the final climb onto the moor; we recommend that at the four-way **signpost for 'Surrender Bridge'** (Map 52, WPT 105), you either get stuck directly into Bunton Hush gully, or the ascent just to the south which is less of a landslip.

Once on the top, cairns or tracks lead to the wooden-penned shaft on the main track (WPT 106), a key point. Up here the landscape can be a bit of a shock. The mining relics encountered thus far have been rather quaint, but you are now faced by an eerie desolation stripped of topsoil by artificially channelled water to expose the minerals underneath. Such gullies, like the one you just clambered up, are known as a *hush*.

At the end of your 'moon walk' lies **Level House Bridge** (Map 53), where you cross **Hard Level Gill** before following it down to the **remains of Old Gang Smelting Mill**, the most extensive ruins yet where warning notices beseech you not to 'ruin the ruins'.

Soon you arrive at **Surrender Bridge** (Map 54) where you cross a minor road leading up to obscure Arkengarthdale and continue past another smelt-mill ruin, dropping down to bridge the finely named **Cringley Bottom** to continue with hopefully fine views of Swaledale's iridescent verdure and dry-stone walls (Map 55) as the track tumbles down to **Reeth**. *(main route text cont'd on p189)*

ROUTE GUIDE AND MAPS

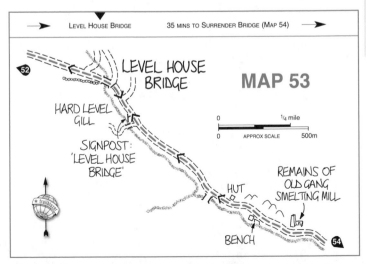

▼
→ LEVEL HOUSE BRIDGE   35 MINS TO SURRENDER BRIDGE (MAP 54) →

52

LEVEL HOUSE BRIDGE

MAP 53

HARD LEVEL GILL

SIGNPOST: 'LEVEL HOUSE BRIDGE'

0   ¼ mile
0   APPROX SCALE   500m

REMAINS OF OLD GANG SMELTING MILL

HUT

BENCH

54

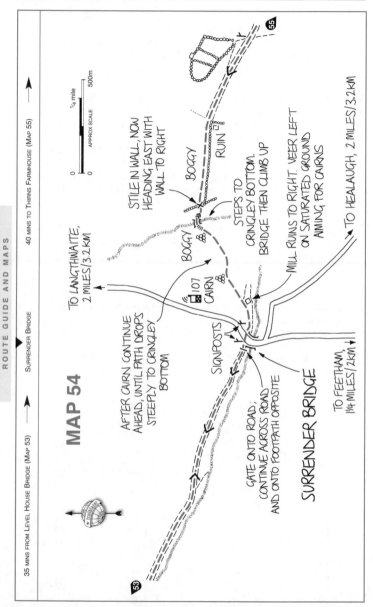

MAP 54

35 MINS FROM LEVEL HOUSE BRIDGE (MAP 53) — SURRENDER BRIDGE — 40 MINS TO THIRNS FARMHOUSE (MAP 55)

53

55

TO LANGTHWAITE, 2 MILES/3.2KM

STILE IN WALL, NOW HEADING EAST WITH WALL TO RIGHT

BOGGY

RUIN

STEPS TO CRINGLEY BOTTOM. BRIDGE THEN CLIMB UP

BOGGY

107 CAIRN

MILL RUINS TO RIGHT. VEER LEFT ON SATURATED GROUND AIMING FOR CAIRNS

TO HEALAUGH, 2 MILES/3.2KM

AFTER CAIRN CONTINUE AHEAD, UNTIL PATH DROPS STEEPLY TO CRINGLEY BOTTOM

SIGNPOSTS

GATE ONTO ROAD; CONTINUE ACROSS ROAD AND ONTO FOOTPATH OPPOSITE

SURRENDER BRIDGE

TO FEETHAM, 1¼ MILES/2KM

0 — 500m
0 — ¼ mile
APPROX SCALE

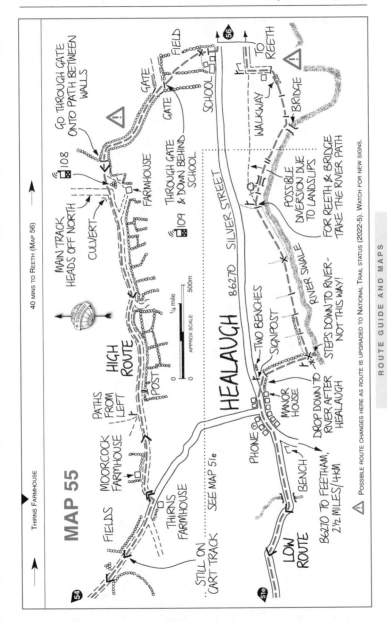

MAP 55

GO THROUGH GATE ONTO PATH BETWEEN WALLS

MAIN TRACK HEADS OFF NORTH

GATE

FIELD

TO REETH

56

⚠

108

FARMHOUSE

SCHOOL

GATE

CULVERT

THROUGH GATE & DOWN BEHIND SCHOOL

109

GATE

WALKWAY

BRIDGE

⚠

POSSIBLE DIVERSION DUE TO LANDSLIPS

FOR REETH & BRIDGE TAKE THE RIVER PATH

HIGH ROUTE

RIVER SWALE

B6270 SILVER STREET

POST

PATHS FROM LEFT

MOORCOCK FARMHOUSE

FIELDS

THIRNS FARMHOUSE   SEE MAP 51e

STILL ON .... CART TRACK

54

TWO BENCHES

SIGNPOST

STEPS DOWN TO RIVER – NOT THIS WAY!

HEALAUGH

DROP DOWN TO RIVER AFTER HEALAUGH

MANOR HOUSE

PHONE ☎

BENCH

B6270 TO FEETHAM, 2½ MILES/4KM

LOW ROUTE

51e

APPROX SCALE

0   500m

0   ¼ mile

⚠ POSSIBLE ROUTE CHANGES HERE AS ROUTE IS UPGRADED TO NATIONAL TRAIL STATUS (2022-5). WATCH FOR NEW SIGNS.

ROUTE GUIDE AND MAPS

Low-level Swaledale Valley alternative route
Map 51 p179, Map 51a, Map 51b, Maps 51d-e pp186-7, Map 56 p193

This option adds up to about 4½ **hours** (**11½ miles, 18.5km**) of *fairly* level walking and you may well end up in Reeth soon after lunch. Some Coasters are tempted to roll it in with the previous stage, making a hefty 23-mile day, but doing so you can expect to hobble into Reeth in a bit of a state. Others in a rush knock out Keld to Richmond in a day; about the same distance and probably with the same consequences.

Our advice? Take the first stage leisurely, stop frequently to admire the valley and commune with nature. Take the diversion to Muker. Then suppress the urge to press on with a pint or two of Old Peculier while overlooking Reeth's village green. It's a beautiful stroll, particularly in the early morning before the crowds gather. The path is so easy that for once you can fully appreciate your surroundings, looking for riparian wildlife such as herons, ducks and, so it is said, otters. The villages passed on the way are a joy, too.

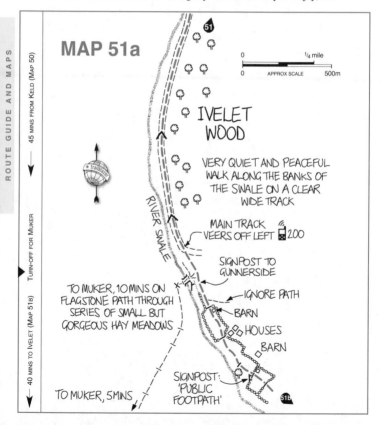

ROUTE GUIDE AND MAPS

45 MINS FROM KELD (MAP 50)

TURN-OFF FOR MUKER

40 MINS TO IVELET (MAP 51b)

MAP 51a

0   ¼ mile

0   APPROX SCALE   500m

IVELET WOOD

VERY QUIET AND PEACEFUL WALK ALONG THE BANKS OF THE SWALE ON A CLEAR WIDE TRACK

RIVER SWALE

MAIN TRACK VEERS OFF LEFT 📱 200

SIGNPOST TO GUNNERSIDE

IGNORE PATH

TO MUKER, 10 MINS ON FLAGSTONE PATH THROUGH SERIES OF SMALL BUT GORGEOUS HAY MEADOWS

BARN

HOUSES

BARN

SIGNPOST: 'PUBLIC FOOTPATH'

TO MUKER, 5 MINS

51b

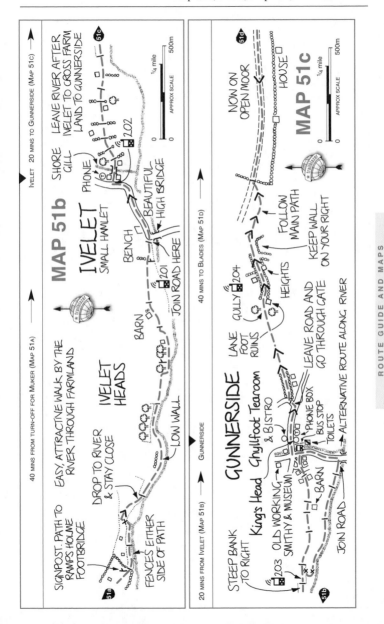

MAP 51b

40 MINS FROM TURN-OFF FOR MUKER (Map 51a) →

IVELET 20 MINS TO GUNNERSIDE (Map 51c) →

EASY, ATTRACTIVE WALK BY THE RIVER THROUGH FARMLAND

LEAVE RIVER AFTER IVELET TO CROSS FARM LAND TO GUNNERSIDE

SHORE GILL

PHONE

IVELET SMALL HAMLET

BENCH

BEAUTIFUL HIGH BRIDGE

JOIN ROAD HERE

202

201

BARN

IVELET HEADS

LOW WALL

SIGNPOST. PATH TO RAMPS HOLME FOOTBRIDGE

DROP TO RIVER & STAY CLOSE

FENCES EITHER SIDE OF PATH

APPROX SCALE

0   500m
0   ¼ mile

MAP 51c

20 MINS FROM IVELET (Map 51b) →

GUNNERSIDE →

40 MINS TO BLADES (Map 51d) →

NOW ON OPEN MOOR

HOUSE

FOLLOW MAIN PATH

KEEP WALL ON YOUR RIGHT

HEIGHTS

GULLY 204

LANE FOOT RUINS

LEAVE ROAD AND GO THROUGH GATE

ALTERNATIVE ROUTE ALONG RIVER

GUNNERSIDE

King's Head Ghyllfoot Tearoom & Bistro

PHONE BOX

BUS STOP

TOILETS

OLD WORKING SMITHY & MUSEUM

BARN

STEEP BANK TO RIGHT

203

JOIN ROAD

APPROX SCALE

0   500m
0   ¼ mile

ROUTE GUIDE AND MAPS

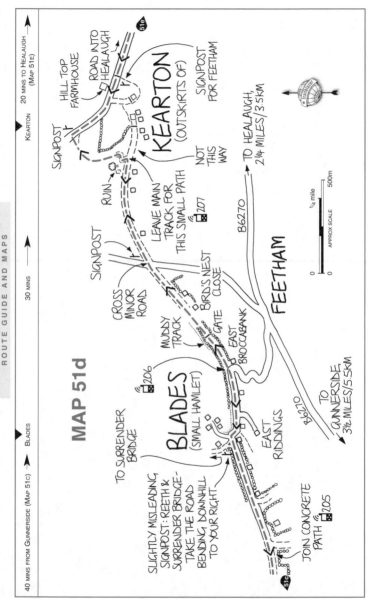

MAP 51d

TO SURRENDER BRIDGE

SLIGHTLY MISLEADING SIGNPOST: REETH & SURRENDER BRIDGE – TAKE THE ROAD BENDING DOWNHILL TO YOUR RIGHT

51c

JOIN CONCRETE PATH 📷 205

BLADES (SMALL HAMLET)

📷 206

EAST RIDDINGS

MUDDY TRACK

CROSS MINOR ROAD

SIGNPOST

GATE

EAST BROCCABANK

BIRD'S NEST CLOSE

FEETHAM

SIGNPOST

RUIN

LEAVE MAIN TRACK FOR THIS SMALL PATH

NOT THIS WAY

📷 207

SIGNPOST FOR FEETHAM

HILL TOP FARMHOUSE

ROAD INTO HEALAUGH

KEARTON (OUTSKIRTS OF)

51e

B6270

TO HEALAUGH, 2¼ MILES/3.5KM

TO GUNNERSIDE, 3½ MILES/5.5KM

B6270

APPROX SCALE
¼ mile
0 — 500m
0

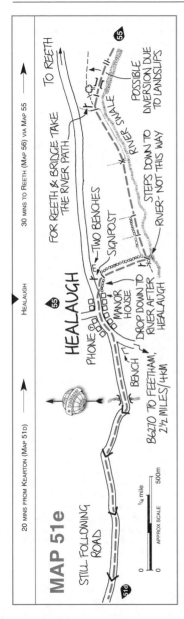

MAP 51e

STILL FOLLOWING ROAD

20 MINS FROM KEARTON (MAP 51D)

HEALAUGH

30 MINS TO REETH (MAP 56) VIA MAP 55

FOR REETH & BRIDGE TAKE THE RIVER PATH

TO REETH

POSSIBLE DIVERSION DUE TO LANDSLIPS

RIVER SWALE

STEPS DOWN TO RIVER - NOT THIS WAY

TWO BENCHES

SIGNPOST

HEALAUGH

PHONE

MANOR HOUSE

DROP DOWN TO RIVER AFTER HEALAUGH

BENCH

B6270 TO FEETHAM, 2½ MILES/4KM

¼ mile

500m

APPROX SCALE

Muker

Muker (off Map 51a and actually slightly off the route) is a very pleasant little place and one of James Herriot's (see Reeth p189) favourites. Pronounced 'Mewker', you'll find a **church** with the Ten Commandments written large upon the wall, and the lovely pub, ***The Farmers Arms*** (☎ 01748 886297, 🖳 farmersarmsmuker.co .uk; **fb**; **food** Apr-Sep Wed-Sun noon-2.45pm & 5.30-8.15pm, Oct-Mar Tue-Sun same but to 8pm; 🐾), which is a classic old country pub where muddy boots are welcome. They may close 3.30-5.30pm on wet weather days.

Muker has also been the home for over 30 years of **Swaledale Woollens** (🖳 swaledalewoollens .co.uk/muker-shop; Mar-Oct daily 10am-5pm, Nov & Dec to 4pm, Nov-Feb closed Tue & Thur), their raw material shorn from the hardy Swaledale sheep whose tough wool is considered ideal for carpets. The shop claims that it saved the village following the depression caused by the collapse of the mining industry. Following a meeting in the local pub, a decision was made to set up a local cottage industry producing knitwear, and today over 30 home workers are employed knitting the jumpers, hats and many other items available in the store, which is a couple of doors down from the pub.

The other side of the pub, and also on the main road that passes through the village, ***Muker Village Store and Teashop*** (☎ 01748 886409, 🖳 mukerteashop@btinter net.com; **fb**) comprises the **village store** (end Mar to end Oct Mon & Tue 10am-4pm, Thur-Sun 11am-4pm, Nov to Mar Thur-Sun 10am-noon), and a **tearoom** (end Mar to end Oct Mon & Tue 10am-4pm, Thur-Sun 11am-4pm; 🐾).

It's also worth checking out **The Old School Art Gallery and Café** (🖥 the oldschoolmuker.co.uk; Apr-Oct Thur-Tue 10am-5pm, Nov-Mar Thur-Sun 11am-4pm), a shop and art space showcasing local photography, sculpture and art. It also has a pleasant garden *café* out the back.

Little White Bus's No 30 **bus** stops here, as does DalesBus's No 830 and Arriva's No 831; see pp54-6 for details.

Gunnerside

Gunnerside (Map 51c; 🖥 gunnerside.info) has two options for food.

Kings Head (☎ 01748 883412, 🖥 kingsheadgunnerside.com; **fb**; summer bar Tue-Sun noon-10pm, food noon-2.30pm & 6-8.30pm, winter Wed-Sun but check in advance; WI-FI; 🐾) is a community-owned pub, which receives great reviews for its local ales and homemade food prepared with locally sourced produce as far as possible. Nearby is *Ghyllfoot Tearoom & Bistro* (☎ 01748

ROUTE GUIDE AND MAPS

❑ DRY-STONE WALLS

Along the Coast to Coast path you'll pass hundreds of dry-stone walls out of Britain's estimated 125,000 miles-worth. Beautiful and photogenic, particularly when covered in a layer of velvety green moss, they're probably the most ubiquitous feature of northern England's landscape. That said, few walkers give much thought to who built them, nor have any idea just how much skill and effort goes into making these walls.

Dry-stone walls, so called because they are built without mortar, have been around since Elizabethan times when, as now, they were used to demarcate the boundaries between one farmer's land and another. Many others were built during the Enclosure Acts between 1720 and 1840, when previously large fields shared between a number of farmers were divided into strips of land. A very few of these 18th-century walls are still standing: those nearest to a village tend to be the oldest, as it was this land that was divided and enclosed first. The fact that the walls have lasted so long is largely due to the care that goes into construction.

I am a Dry Stone Waller
All day I Dry Stone Wall
Of all appalling callings
Dry Stone Walling's worst of all
      Pam Ayres, 1978

The first step is to dig some deep, secure foundations. That done, the next step is to build the wall itself, or rather walls, for a typical dry-stone wall is actually made up of two thinner walls built back to back; a design that helps make the wall as sturdy as possible. Every metre or so a through or tie stone is built into the wall to bind the two halves together. It's estimated that one tonne of stone is required for one square yard of wall. Each stone is chosen carefully to fit exactly: a bad choice can upset the pressure loading, leading to an early collapse. Smaller chippings or pebbles are used to fill the gaps and a dry-stone waller we once met in the North Pennines reckoned he could erect just two metres of wall on a good day.

Dry-stone walling has had its heyday; it now faces competition from the wire fence which is a cheaper, simpler and just as effective a way of dividing land, and while the existing dry-stone walls have to be repaired occasionally, more often than not the farmer would rather do it himself than call in a professional. However, the art is certainly not dead; for further information visit the Dry Stone Walling Association's website (🖥 dswa.org.uk).

886239; **fb**; Mar-end Oct however, at the time of writing they weren't sure what days they would be open in 2023 so check in advance; WI-FI; 🐾 in a designated area).

Little White Bus's No 30 **bus** calls here as do Dalesbus's No 830 and Arriva's No 831; see pp54-6 for details.

From Gunnerside you have the option of dropping down to the river and following it all the way to Reeth. The official path, though, leaves the eastern edge of the village through a gate before crossing moor and farmland, and eventually dropping down to **Healaugh** (Map 51e). From here the path returns to the river to continue past the suspension bridge to **Reeth**, via Quaker Rd.

REETH (map p191)

Reeth, the 'capital' of Swaledale, is the archetypal Yorkshire dales village: flanked to north and south by mine-scarred valleys and ringed by dry-stone walls (see box opposite). At its heart lies a village green surrounded on all sides by several examples of those twin institutions of Yorkshire hospitality: the **tearoom** and the **pub**. As if to underline its Yorkshire credentials still further, it also has a renowned brass band. Hardly surprising, therefore, that the village was used as a location for many episodes of the quintessential 1980s Yorkshire TV saga *All Creatures Great and Small* based on the books of rural vet, James Herriot.

Mentioned in the Domesday survey nine centuries earlier, the village grew on the profits of the 19th-century mining boom, though unlike other nearby villages it could always claim a second string to its bow as the main market town for Swaledale (the market is still held on The Green on Fridays). After the mines closed, tourism gave Reeth a new lease of life and today the town hosts a number of B&Bs and hotels, as well as some **gift shops** and a small museum.

Swaledale Museum (🖳 swaledalemuseum.org; Mar/Apr-end Sep Mon-Thur 10am-5pm; £5) is housed in the old 19th-century Methodist school room. It holds some surprisingly intriguing exhibits and is well worth an hour of your time, particularly if you want to learn more about the local mining and farming industries. The museum also looks at the social history of the area in some detail, attempting to show how the locals used to live a hundred or more years ago.

Services

The **National Park visitor centre** (☎ 01748 884059, 🖳 yorkshiredales.org.uk; Apr-Sep daily 10am-4pm, Nov-end Mar Mon-Fri 10am-3.30pm, Sat & Sun 10am-1.30pm) is in Hudson House to the west of The Green.

On the other side of The Green the **general store** (Mon-Sat 8.30am-5.30pm-ish, Sun 10am-4.30pm-ish) has a **post office** (Mon-Fri 9am-5.30pm, Sat 9am-12.30pm).

If they have enough cash in the till and you spend about £10 The Black Bull will offer **cashback**.

Transport (see also pp54-6)

Little White Bus No 30 **bus** stops here as do Arriva's No 831 and Dalesbus's No 830 (seasonally on Sundays & Bank holidays).

For a **taxi**, try the companies in Kirkby Stephen (p163) or Richmond (p202).

Where to stay

There is no shortage of accommodation in Reeth, including two **hostels** on the outskirts of the village. The further of the two is *YHA Grinton Lodge* (off Map 56; ☎ 0345 371 9636, 🖳 yha.org.uk/hostel/yha-grinton-lodge; 5x2-, 1x3-, 9x4-, 4x6-bed rooms, some rooms en suite; ⓛ; WI-FI in public spaces; 🐾 on campsite only; mid Feb to mid Oct), an atmospheric old shooting lodge, but over a mile past Reeth, up a very steep hill. It is only half a mile from the path, however, and charges from £29 for a private room (sleeping up to two) though dorm beds (from £15pp) are available again. It offers meals, beer and wine, and a TV and a games room and there are drying facilities. Credit cards are accepted. They also allow **camping** (from £8pp), and have a variety of **camping pods** that sleep up to four people (from £39). Campers can use the hostel's facilities.

Just half a mile from Reeth and even closer to the path are the converted stone barns of *Dales Bike Centre* (Map 56; ☎ 01748 884908, 🖳 dalesbikecentre.co.uk; 2T/1Qd, all bunks, shared facilities; WI-FI; Ⓛ), a hostel in **Fremington** village that welcomes all outdoor enthusiasts, not just cyclists. There is laundry and drying facilities. Bunk and breakfast (cereals and a bacon sandwich) costs from £72/118/144-160 for 2-/3-/4-beds (sgl occ from £46). The Cakery Loft (4-bed) has a minimum two-night stay policy. **Food**-wise, there's a **café/lounge** (The Cakery; daily 9am-5pm); alternatively *Bridge Inn* (Map 56; ☎ 01748 884224; **fb**; WI-FI; 🐾; food daily noon-2pm & 6-8pm but to 8.30pm at the weekend) is just down the road for pub grub and a pint.

As well as the garden at the YHA, campers can also pitch up at *The Orchard Caravan & Camping Park* (Map 56; ☎ 01748 884475, 🖳 orchardcaravanpark .com; **fb**; 🐾 on lead; mid Mar-end Sep). The enthusiastic owners have transformed the place and, though dominated by caravans, it's still popular with C2Cers; walkers can **camp** here for £8/12.50 for one/two people (normal rate £17.50) and they have a **camping pod** (sleeps up to two, £40 per night for the pod). There are shower (20p) and toilet facilities. They prefer people to book in advance so they ensure they reserve enough camping space, especially in the peak season, but never turn down walkers. All arrival details will be emailed to walkers who book, drop-ins should follow the 'Enquiries' sign.

The Laurels Reeth (☎ 01748 880257, 🖳 thelaurelsreeth.com; 1D/2D or T, all en suite; WI-FI; 🐾) is a very comfortable B&B, in a restored Georgian house. B&B costs from £42.50pp (sgl occ £75) and there is a minimum stay of two nights at weekends in summer. It goes to great lengths to stress its dog-friendliness. However, they

were open for B&B on Friday and Saturday nights only at the time of research. *The Olde Temperance* (☎ 01748 884401, ☎ 07870 966295; 1S/2Tr, shared bathroom; 🐾; 🐾) is situated above a Christian bookshop and charges from £35pp (sgl/sgl occ £35), reduced for stays of two nights or more. The Christian bookshop is actually the dining room where breakfast is served.

Across The Green and above the tea-room (see Where to eat), the lovely *Ivy Cottage* (☎ 01748 884418, 🖳 ivycottage reeth.co.uk; 3D, all en suite; 🐾; WI-FI; Ⓛ) charges £42.50-50pp (sgl occ £75-90) for B&B. Note that check-in is from 4pm.

Enjoying the views from the top of the village, *Burgoyne Hotel* (☎ 01748 884292, 🖳 theburgoyne.co.uk; 6D/2D or T all en suite, 2D/1T private bathroom; 🐾; WI-FI; Ⓛ; 🐾) is the grandest place to stay here. B&B costs £55-125pp (sgl occ room rate). Dinner B&B rates are also available.

The Buck at Reeth (☎ 01748 884545, however, email contact is preferred, 🖳 the buckreeth.co.uk; 3D/1T/1Tr/1Qd all en suite; 🐾; WI-FI; 🐾; Ⓛ) describes itself as a pub and dining with rooms; one of the rooms has a four-poster bed with a roll-top bath. B&B costs £35-55pp (sgl occ room rate).

For **pubs with rooms** there are two options: *The Black Bull* (☎ 01748 884213, 🖳 theblackbullreeth.co.uk; 4D/2T/1D all en suite, one small D/one sleeps up to eight with private facilities; 🐾; WI-FI; Ⓛ; 🐾) which dates back to 1680 and has rooms (B&B costs from £40pp, sgl occ £60) overlooking The Green and down Swaledale. The en suite double room also has a bunk bed so can accommodate up to two children. At *The Kings Arms* (☎ 01748 884259, 🖳 thekingsarms.com, 🖳 kings armshotel@gmail.com; 6D/2T, all en suite; 🐾; WI-FI; Ⓛ; 🐾), next door, the rooms are bright and clean and come with a spacious bathroom. They charge £39-45pp (sgl occ from £60) for B&B.

Where to eat and drink
For an artisan bakery visit *Two Dales Bakery* (🖳 www.twodalesbakery.co.uk; **fb**; WI-FI; 🐾; Tue-Fri 9.30am-2.30pm, Sat to 3.30pm) at Reeth Dales Centre on Silver St;

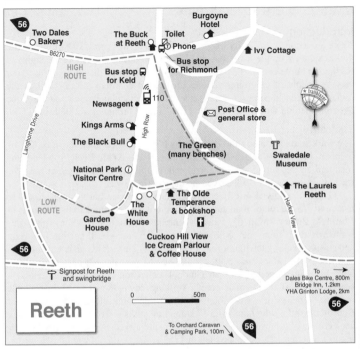

they serves toasties, bacon rolls, cakes and other baked delights.

The first eaterie you'll spy as you enter Reeth is *The White House* (☎ 01748 884569; Thur-Mon 11.30am-5pm, Fri to 8pm) where you'll find sandwiches (£4.50), cakes, ice-cream, and mezze (£6) on offer. There's a couple of benches outside, perfect for a rest, and a brew or a bite to celebrate your arrival. *Cuckoo Hill View Ice Cream Parlour & Coffee House* (☎ 01748 884929, 🖥 reethicecreamparlour.co.uk; Apr-Oct daily 11am-5pm, weekends only Nov-end Mar; WI-FI, 🐾), at the foot of The Green, tempts passing walkers with 12 flavours of ice-cream, including 'ginger', 'mochachino' and 'chocolate'. They also serve tea and coffee, and have wooden puzzles and games on each table.

Reeth has a couple of pubs which serve food as well as a good selection of cask ales. *The Kings Arms* (see Where to stay; Mon-Sat summer noon-2pm & 6-8pm, Sun same but to 7.30pm) is low-key, but serves decent pub grub, while the food at *The Black Bull* (see Where to stay; daily noon-2pm & 6-8pm) is another popular option; it's good for a pint with the locals, too. Note that opening hours in the winter months are variable for all the pubs.

The Buck at Reeth (see Where to stay) serves food all day with one menu from noon to 5pm and the evening menu 5-8pm. The menu is standard pub food with some vegan and gluten-free options.

1783 Restaurant & Bar (🖥 1783restaurant.co.uk) at **Burgoyne Hotel** (see Where to stay) offers fine dining and a bar menu (both daily 6-9pm). They are open to non residents but reservations are recommended for all.

STAGE 9: REETH TO RICHMOND   MAPS 56-61

Introduction

There are a couple of lovely tracts of woodland on this rural, **10½-mile (17km, 4½hr)** stage, a simple walk that should allow you time to explore the sights of Richmond at the end of the day if you set off early enough and don't lose your way. A couple of charming villages are passed en route too, as well as the remains of an old priory. Overall, it's not a spectacular day as you leave the Pennines behind but, if the weather's fine, a pleasant one nevertheless.

The route

The walk starts out along the B6270 which you've been tracking since Kirkby Stephen, but soon after leaving Reeth and crossing **Arkle Beck**, you leave the road and are led along a fence corridor through riverside pastures to meet the road again at Grinton Bridge over the meandering Swale.

Over the road you briefly continue along the Swale but then dart uphill to meet and cross a minor road and follow more walled pastures to the **remains of Marrick Priory** (Map 57), just 40 minutes from Reeth. (Sometimes this walled-pastures route may be blocked, in which case you'll need to turn right and stroll east along the minor road to the priory.) Though it's visible from a distance, casual visitors are no longer allowed to visit the adjacent ruins which have been incorporated into an Outdoor Education Centre. Nevertheless, it seems that staff don't mind people walking down the drive to inspect the remains. The priory was founded by local noble, Roger de Aske, for Benedictine nuns who numbered 17 at the time of its dissolution in 1540. There are a couple of tomb slabs in the grounds, including one by the entrance belonging to a Thomas Peacock who died in 1762 at the grand old age of 102.

Those disappointed at not being able to explore the ruins thoroughly will find some consolation in the walk to Marrick village, a pretty uphill amble through the first of this stage's woods, known as Steps Wood and notable as the first dense shade you may have experienced on the trail for several days. The path you're ascending is known as the **Nuns' Steps**, so-called because the nuns are said to have constructed the 375 steps as a walkway to the priory. At the top, after a couple of fields, lies the village that gave Marrick Priory its name.

From **Marrick** the trail begins a long north-easterly march to Marske through farmland punctuated by any number of tiny stiles and gates.

(cont'd on p196)

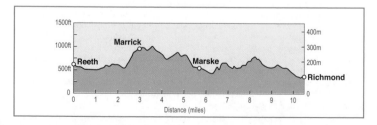

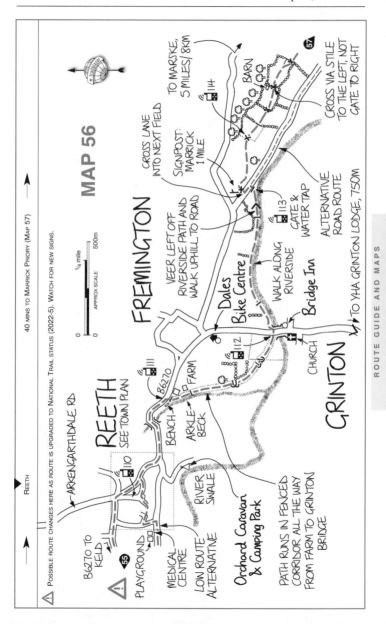

⚠ POSSIBLE ROUTE CHANGES HERE AS ROUTE IS UPGRADED TO NATIONAL TRAIL STATUS (2022-5). WATCH FOR NEW SIGNS.

MAP 56

ARKENGARTHDALE RD

B6270 TO KELD

PLAYGROUND

MEDICAL CENTRE

LOW ROUTE ALTERNATIVE

Orchard Caravan & Camping Park

PATH RUNS IN FENCED CORRIDOR ALL THE WAY FROM FARM TO GRINTON BRIDGE

RIVER SWALE

REETH
SEE TOWN PLAN

110

BENCH

ARKLE BECK

B6270

FARM

111

112

Dales Bike Centre

FREMINGTON

VEER LEFT OFF RIVERSIDE PATH AND WALK UPHILL TO ROAD

CROSS LANE INTO NEXT FIELD

SIGNPOST: MARRICK 1 MILE

TO MARSKE, 5 MILES/ 8KM

BARN

114

CROSS VIA STILE TO THE LEFT, NOT GATE TO RIGHT

57

113

GATE & WATER TAP

ALTERNATIVE ROAD ROUTE

WALK ALONG RIVERSIDE

Bridge Inn

CHURCH

GRINTON

TO YHA GRINTON LODGE, 750M

0   ¼ mile
0   500m
APPROX SCALE

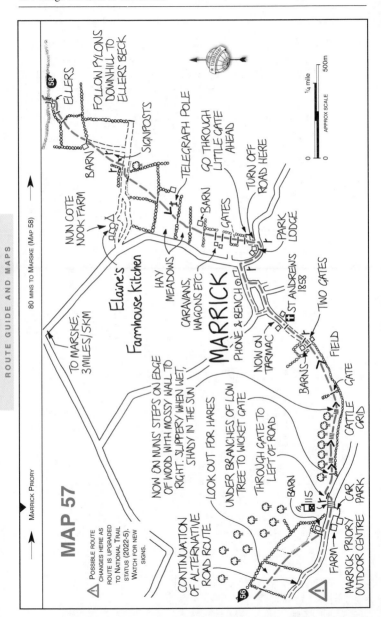

◄ MARRICK PRIORY

MAP 57

⚠ POSSIBLE ROUTE CHANGES HERE AS ROUTE IS UPGRADED TO NATIONAL TRAIL STATUS (2022-5). WATCH FOR NEW SIGNS.

CONTINUATION OF ALTERNATIVE ROAD ROUTE

MARRICK PRIORY OUTDOOR CENTRE

FARM

⚠

NOW ON NUNS' STEPS ON EDGE OF WOOD WITH MOSSY WALL TO RIGHT. SLIPPERY WHEN WET, SHADY IN THE SUN

LOOK OUT FOR HARES

UNDER BRANCHES OF LOW TREE TO WICKET GATE

THROUGH GATE TO LEFT OF ROAD

BARN

CAR PARK

CATTLE GRID

GATE

FIELD

TWO GATES

BARNS

NOW ON TARMAC

ST ANDREW'S 1858

PHONE & BENCH

MARRICK

HAY MEADOWS

CARAVANS, WAGONS ETC.

Elaine's Farmhouse Kitchen

TO MARSKE, 3 MILES/ 5KM

80 MINS TO MARSKE (MAP 58) →

NUN COTE NOOK FARM

SIGNPOSTS

TELEGRAPH POLE

BARN

GATES

GO THROUGH LITTLE GATE AHEAD

TURN OFF ROAD HERE

PARK LODGE

BARN

ELLERS

58

FOLLOW PYLONS DOWNHILL TO ELLERS BECK

¼ mile

APPROX SCALE

500m

0

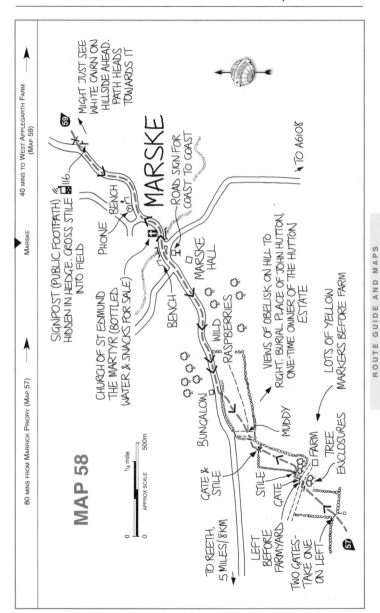

MAP 58

80 MINS FROM MARRICK PRIORY (MAP 57)

MARSKE

40 MINS TO WEST APPLEGARTH FARM (MAP 59)

APPROX SCALE

0 — 1/4 mile

0 — 500m

TO REETH, 5 MILES / 8 KM

LEFT BEFORE FARMYARD

GATE & STILE

TWO GATES—TAKE ONE ON LEFT

STILE

GATE

FARM

TREE ENCLOSURES

LOTS OF YELLOW MARKERS BEFORE FARM

MUDDY

VIEWS OF OBELISK ON HILL TO RIGHT. BURIAL PLACE OF JOHN HUTTON, ONE-TIME OWNER OF THE HUTTON ESTATE

BUNGALOW

WILD RASPBERRIES

BENCH

MARSKE HALL

ROAD SIGN FOR COAST TO COAST

CHURCH OF ST EDMUND THE MARTYR (BOTTLED WATER & SNACKS FOR SALE)

SIGNPOST (PUBLIC FOOTPATH) HIDDEN IN HEDGE. CROSS STILE INTO FIELD

PHONE

BENCH

MARSKE

TO A6108

MIGHT JUST SEE WHITE CAIRN ON HILLSIDE AHEAD. PATH HEADS TOWARDS IT

59

57

(cont'd from p192) On the way *Elaine's Farmhouse Kitchen* at *Nun Cote Nook Farm* (☎ 07711 337387, 🖳 nuncotenookcampsite.co.uk; 🐾) serves **snacks and drinks** (variable days/ hours) overlooking a quiet open field that gives farm camping a good name. They also offer a two-course **evening meal** (with the meat coming from their farm) from £12 and **breakfasts** from £8.50. **Camping** costs from £10pp inc shower. Even if you're not camping here, many Coasters agree Elaine's is well worth a detour for a brew, a snack (her home-made scones have won awards) and a chat about the price of wool.

Nun Cote Nook is just about the last hill farm so you bid farewell to the Pennines and tramp diagonally across pastures until you join the road to **Marske** and impressive Marske Hall (Map 58) on the right. Continuing up the hill, you pass the crenellated profile of **St Edmund the Martyr**, built on the site of an earlier church dating back to 1090 from which the north and south doors and hexagonal supporting pillars survive. St Edmund, incidentally, was a Saxon king put to death by the Danes in AD870. There are **snacks** and bottled water for sale in the church.

Half a mile out of the village the road is once again forsaken in favour of grassy pasture as the trail unfolds, bending east at the white cairn below **Applegarth Scar** (Map 59) to pick up the farm track to West Applegarth Farm.

The farms of Low, High and East Applegarth are passed before the trail continues into the sometimes muddy **Whitecliffe Wood** (Map 60), emerging 15 minutes later at **High Leases Farm** where the ensuing road walk can actually be paralleled on a footpath behind the fence on the right.

To aim for the village of **Hudswell** take the track on your right just after Hazelbeck Cottage and begin your trek south. Getting down to the footbridge over the River Swale is easy enough (as long as you follow Map 60 closely). Having crossed the bridge, follow the path ahead of you, climbing steps uphill to a gate. Go through the gate, then bear right and follow the path to the top of the steep hill where you pass through a wide gate. Walk halfway along the field then turn right to go through three small gates, before skirting the edge of the wood, and keeping left through one more gate from where you'll see Scar Close Caravan Park.

Join the road and walk along to *The George & Dragon* (Map 60; ☎ 01748 518373, **fb**; food Mon & Tue 2-8pm, Wed-Sat noon-2pm & 5-8pm Sun roast noon-4pm; WI-FI; 🐾). In 2016 it was voted **Britain's pub of the year** by real-ale society CAMRA and it's won a number of other awards since; quite an achievement considering the financially stricken pub had been forced to close just a few years earlier. Back then, in 2010, more than 200 villagers saved the business by each buying a share in their local boozer and turning it into a true heart of the community. It was taken over by new tenants in July 2022. These days, on Mondays and Tuesdays they serve paninis and toasties but for the rest of the week they offer standard pub meals including home-cooked pies (from £14.50) and numerous cask and keg ales as well as ciders and lagers. The pub also houses a small library and the village **shop** (Mon-Sat 9am-noon, Sun 10.30am-noon.

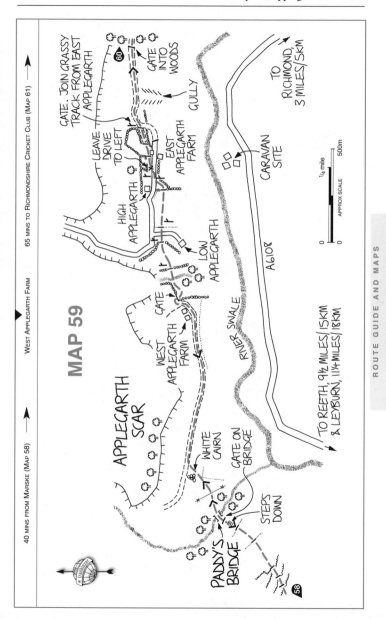

MAP 59

APPLEGARTH SCAR

WHITE CAIRN

GATE ON BRIDGE

PADDY'S BRIDGE

STEPS DOWN

WEST APPLEGARTH FARM

GATE

LOW APPLEGARTH

HIGH APPLEGARTH

EAST APPLEGARTH FARM

LEAVE DRIVE TO LEFT

GATE. JOIN GRASSY TRACK FROM EAST APPLEGARTH

GATE INTO WOODS

GULLY

CARAVAN SITE

RIVER SWALE

A6108

TO RICHMOND, 3 MILES/5KM

TO REETH, 9½ MILES/15KM & LEYBURN, 11¼ MILES/18KM

APPROX SCALE

0 — ¼ mile

0 — 500m

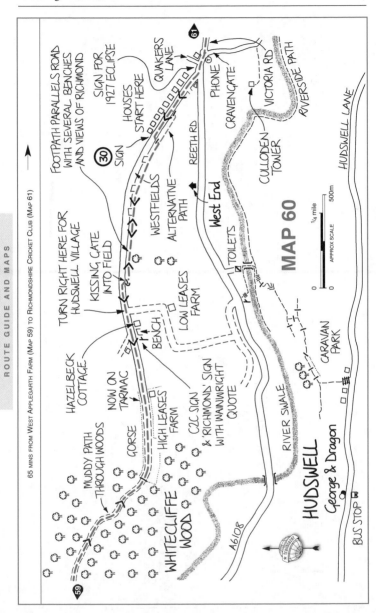

65 MINS FROM WEST APPLEGARTH FARM (MAP 59) TO RICHMONDSHIRE CRICKET CLUB (MAP 61)

FOOTPATH PARALLELS ROAD
WITH SEVERAL BENCHES
AND VIEWS OF RICHMOND

SIGN FOR
1927 ECLIPSE

QUAKERS
LANE

HOUSES
START HERE

61

30 SIGN

PHONE

REETH RD

CRAVENGATE

VICTORIA RD

CULLODEN
TOWER

RIVERSIDE PATH

HUDSWELL LANE

TURN RIGHT HERE FOR
HUDSWELL VILLAGE

KISSING GATE
INTO FIELD

WESTFIELDS

ALTERNATIVE
PATH

West End

TOILETS

MAP 60

0   500m
APPROX SCALE
0   ¼ mile

HAZELBECK
COTTAGE

NOW ON
TARMAC

BENCH

LOW LEASES
FARM

CARAVAN
PARK

MUDDY PATH
THROUGH WOODS

GORSE

HIGH LEASES
FARM

C2C SIGN
& RICHMOND SIGN
WITH WAINWRIGHT
QUOTE

RIVER SWALE

HUDSWELL
George & Dragon

BUS STOP

WHITECLIFFE
WOOD

59

A6108

Little White Bus's No 30 (see pp54-6) **bus** service stops outside the pub.

Back on the main trail (on the northern side of the river), fine views of **Richmond** soon emerge; terracotta and slate roofs backed by the distant Cleveland Hills until you enter the town's suburbs.

RICHMOND   MAP 61, p201

Up above a castle! Down below a stream!
Up above a ruin! Down below a dream!
Man made the castle, rude, forbidding, bare.
God made the river, swift, eternal, fair.

From the recollections of **Mr M Wise** as recorded in ***Richmond Yorkshire in 1830s*** (Wenham Publishers 1977).

This is the largest settlement on the Coast to Coast and feels it. Richmond is a busy market town that evolved around the **castle**, built by one Alan the Red in the 11th century.

As the castle fell into disrepair over time its stones were scavenged to build the surrounding houses, giving the entire town the same sombre hue. During the Georgian era, as the town's fortunes waned still further, Richmond discovered a new source of prosperity as a centre for fine cabinet-making. Many of the buildings leading off the main marketplace date back to this era (Richmondshire Museum, the town museum, is housed in a former cabinet-maker's workshop) and, following its restoration in 2003, the **Georgian theatre** is now said to be the finest in the land.

At the centre of the town is the large, cobbled square known as **Market Place** off which run numerous winding alleys, known as *wynds*. Most of the town's attractions can be found on or near this square, though a couple of the ruins nearby may also warrant further investigation.

Although it's a very pleasant place, the size and scale of Richmond – to say nothing of the noise, the bustle and the traffic – can come as something of a shock to fell-weathered Coasters used to more rural locales. As with so many provincial English towns, Richmond can get rowdy at weekends, but it does have its advantages in terms of the facilities it provides, as well as enough sights to amuse those who take the sensible decision to rest here for a day.

What to see and do

Richmond (🖳 richmond.org) is a great town to walk around, with plenty of twisting 'wynds' to explore and plaques installed here and there pointing out places of historical interest.

● **Richmond Castle** (☎ 01748 822493, 🖳 english-heritage.org.uk; Apr-Sep daily 10am-6pm, Oct daily to 5pm, Nov-Mar Sat & Sun only 10am-4pm; £7.80/7 adult/concs, EH members free) Without Richmond Castle it's arguable there would be no Richmond and while it ceased performing its castellan duties centuries ago, in the middle of the 1800s it found a new purpose as a tourist attraction and has been welcoming visitors ever since. Visitors are, however, advised not to rush headlong at the ruins like a troupe of marauding barbarians, but instead first acquaint themselves with the **exhibition** in the reception building; it gives a thought-provoking account of the history of the castle and the town as well as a display on how the castle was originally built. There's also an interesting section on WWI conscientious objectors (absolutists) who were held captive here. Their poignant graffiti still exists on the cell walls, though for protection these cells are today kept locked; copies of the graffiti can be seen in the exhibition. Now advancing to the ruins in an orderly and newly informed manner, you may be a little disappointed at first by the lack of surviving structures within the castle walls, though by reading the information boards dotted around, you should get a reasonable idea of how the castle once looked.

Scholars may be similarly entranced by the ruins of **Scolland Hall**, the finest ruins surviving from Alan the Red's time; most visitors, however, will find the views from the **keep** overlooking the town far more engrossing. A new museum opened within the castle in summer 2019.

ROUTE GUIDE AND MAPS

● **Georgian Theatre Royal** (☎ 01748 825252, 🖳 georgiantheatreroyal.co.uk) Built in 1788 by actor-manager Samuel Butler and now beautifully restored, this is the most complete Georgian theatre in the country as well as being the oldest working theatre in its original form. It's well worth a visit for a performance (check the website for schedules) or a fascinating backstage tour. From mid February (after the pantomime season) to early November small **guided tours** (£5) run on the hour from 10am until 4pm (Mon-Sat). You'll get to see the oldest surviving painted scenery in Britain as well as the theatre museum.

● **Richmondshire Museum** (☎ 01748 825611, 🖳 richmondshiremuseum.org.uk; Apr to end Oct daily 10am-4.30pm; £4) Another surprisingly absorbing local museum, similar in content to Reeth's Swaledale Museum (see p189), though bigger and with even more impressive exhibits. Highlights include **Cruck House**, a 15th-century building moved wholesale from Ravensworth in 1985, an exhibition tracing the history of transport (including an original penny farthing bicycle), and tellingly, most popular of all, the set of the vet's surgery from the TV series of *All Creatures Great and Small*.

● **Green Howards Museum** (☎ 01748 826561, 🖳 greenhowards.org.uk; Feb-mid Dec Mon-Sat 10am-4.30pm; £5) Richmond has a long military association and is the garrison town of Catterick, now many times larger than Richmond itself. The town's regiment, the Green Howards, have their own museum and headquarters in this former Holy Trinity Church. With a history spanning the Crimean and Boer wars, as well as military engagements on the North-West Frontier of India and more recent operations in neighbouring Afghanistan, the story of the regiment is a fascinating one. Highlights include the staggering 3750-strong medal collection awarded to members of the regiment.

● **Easby Abbey** Formerly and more properly known as **St Agatha's Monastery**, Easby Abbey (Map 62; 🖳 english-heritage .org.uk) lies about a mile to the east of Richmond Castle. You may get a distant view of it from across the Swale during the next stage of the walk, but if you've got the time we strongly advise you make a detour and pay a proper visit. Like those at Shap, the ruins at Easby were once part of a Premonstratensian Abbey, this one built in 1152, just 31 years after the founding of the order by St Norbert in Prémontré in Picardy, northern France. The monastery served the community for almost 400 years because, unlike many other orders who chose to cut themselves off from the outside world, the Premonstratensians saw it as their duty to minister to and serve the laity until Henry VIII brought about the dissolution. Unwilling to bow to Henry's demands, they joined the Pilgrimage of Grace in 1536, the most popular rebellion against Henry. Many monasteries were briefly restored by the rebels – St Agatha's at Easby among them. They were subsequently defeated and Henry set about exacting a chilling revenge on those who had dared to defy his orders, instructing his forces in the north to 'cause such dreadful execution upon a good number of inhabitants, hanging them on trees, quartering them and setting their heads and quarters in every town, as shall be a fearful warning'. While visiting, be sure to check out the **parish church** here at Easby, which has survived in remarkable condition and plays host to some wonderful 13th-century **wall paintings**. Look, too, for the 12th-century **panel of glass** depicting St John.

● **Other sights** There are two magnificent ruined towers in town. The first you'll come across is **Grey Friars Tower**, in the gardens off Queens Rd. This was once part of a Franciscan monastery, founded in 1258, though the tower itself wasn't built until sometime around 1500. The second, clearly visible to the west of town from Richmond Castle, is **Culloden Tower** (Map 60), a folly dating back to 1746. Amazingly, it's now a novelty holiday cottage (🖳 land marktrust.org.uk).

Services

Richmond Information Centre (☎ 01748 826468, 🖳 richmondinfo.net; daily 10am-4pm, end Oct to early Feb 10am-2pm) is in

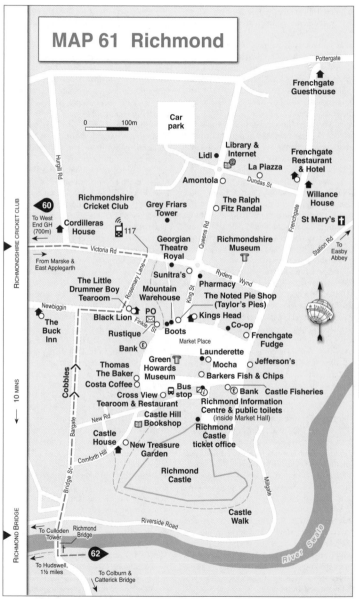

MAP 61 Richmond

0 ____ 100m

Car park

Pottergate

Frenchgate Guesthouse

Lidl ●

Library & Internet @

La Piazza

Frenchgate Restaurant & Hotel

Amontola ○

Dundas St

Willance House

Hurgill Rd

60
To West End GH (700m)

Richmondshire Cricket Club

Cordilleras House

Grey Friars Tower ●

📱 117

The Ralph ○ Fitz Randal

St Mary's ✛

Queens Rd

Frenchgate

Station Rd
To Easby Abbey

Victoria Rd

From Marske & East Applegarth

Georgian Theatre Royal

Richmondshire Museum 🏛

Sunitra's ○

Ryders Wynd

trailblazer

The Little Drummer Boy Tearoom

Mountain Warehouse

Rosemary Lane

King St

Pharmacy ○

The Noted Pie Shop (Taylor's Pies)

Newbiggin

Black Lion ○ ○

PO ✉

Finkle St

Kings Head ○

Co-op ○

Frenchgate Fudge ○

The Buck Inn

Rustique ○

Bank £

Boots

Market Place

Thomas The Baker ○

Green Howards 🏛 Museum

Launderette ●

Mocha ○

Jefferson's ○

Cobbles

Bargate

Costa Coffee ○

Cross View ○ Tearoom & Restaurant

Bus 🚌 stop

Barkers Fish & Chips ○

🛈 £ Bank Castle Fisheries

Richmond Information Centre & public toilets (inside Market Hall)

10 MINS

New Rd

Castle Hill 📖 Bookshop

Castle House

○ New Treasure Garden

Cornforth Hill

Richmond Castle ticket office

Richmond Castle

Milligate

Bridge St

Castle Walk

RICHMOND BRIDGE

Riverside Road

To Culloden Tower

Richmond Bridge

62
To Hudswell, 1½ miles

To Colburn & Catterick Bridge

River Swale

RICHMONDSHIRE CRICKET CLUB

ROUTE GUIDE AND MAPS

Market Hall in the middle of town. There are volunteers on hand to advise you as required. The website has an accommodation section, well worth a visit when planning your stay. The **library** (🖳 north yorks.gov.uk/richmond-community-library; Mon-Fri 10am-1pm & 2-5pm, Sat 10am-1pm) is a short walk from the centre at 10A Queens Rd, and has free WI-FI and offers **internet** access.

The **post office** (Mon-Fri 9am-4pm, Sat to 12.30pm) does foreign exchange and many major banks are represented on the main square and have those **ATMs** you've been longing for.

The **outdoors shop**, Mountain Warehouse (Mon-Sat 9am-5.30pm, Sun 10am-4pm) is on the northern side of the main square. Next door there's a **Boots** pharmacy (Mon-Sat 9am-5.30pm). A second **pharmacy**, Langhorn Pharmacy (Mon-Fri 9am-5.30pm, Sat 9am-1pm) is by the roundabout on King St.

For a **launderette** go to Johnsons the Cleaners (Mon-Sat 8.30am-5.30pm) on Market Place. Castle Hill **Bookshop** (🕿 01748 824243; Mon-Sat 10am-4pm), below the castle, has an excellent range of books and an interesting selection of local history.

For **food** shopping there's a Co-op (daily 7am-10pm) on Market Place and if you need a larger store there's a Lidl (Mon-Sat 8am-10pm, Sun 10am-4pm) on Queens Rd.

Transport (see also pp52 & pp54-6)

The nearest **railway station** is 12 miles away in Darlington (a stop on LNER's London–Edinburgh services), but there are plenty of **bus** services (Arriva's X26/X27 and Hodgson's No 29 & 34) going there from Market Place, and the journey only takes half an hour.

Little White Bus's No 30 runs up Swaledale to Keld. Dalesbus's No 830 and Arriva's 831 does a similar route on Sundays (mid May to mid Oct), while Hodgson's No 55 goes to Northallerton via Brompton-on-Swale. Northallerton is also a stop on LNER's rail service between London and Edinburgh.

For a **taxi**, try Amalgamated (🕿 01748 825112, 🖳 amalgamatedtaxis.co.uk).

Where to stay

The nearest **campsites** are convenient as they are right on the path but they are not in Richmond; *Hildyard Arms* (see p205), in Colburn, allows you to camp in the pub garden, and *St Giles Farm* (see p205) and *Thornborough Farm* (see p206) are slightly further on. There's also the excellent *Brompton Camping Barn* (see p208) two miles beyond Colburn. Unfortunately, there are no hostels in Richmond.

If you haven't pre-booked a **B&B**, go to the information centre to see if they can help. What follows is by no means exhaustive, but is our selection of the options based on readers' feedback and our own experiences.

Just west of the centre of town, *West End Guesthouse* (Map 60, p198; 🕿 01748 824783, 🖳 stayatwestend.co.uk; 1S/2D/1T, all en suite; WI-FI), at 45 Reeth Rd, is a comfortable place. B&B rates are around £40-46.50pp (sgl/sgl occ £75/70-83).

At 11 Hurgill Rd, near the cricket club, is *Cordilleras House* (🕿 01748 824628, 07587 150510; 1D/1D or T all en suite; ➼; WI-FI; Ⓛ) where B&B with a continental breakfast costs from £35pp (sgl occ room rate). Online booking is available through 🖳 www.airbnb.co.uk but book direct for the best rate.

Fellow Coasters recommend *Willance House* (🕿 01748 824467, 🖳 willancehouse .com; 1D/2D or T, all en suite; WI-FI; Ⓛ; Mar-Dec), at 24 Frenchgate, an oak-beamed house dating back to the 17th century; it's named after the first alderman (mayor) of Richmond. It has a guest lounge and B&B costs from £43pp (sgl occ £78; their breakfasts are recommended (they've even won awards for them). They also offer a laundry service (£7-10).

Almost opposite Willance House is the smart *Frenchgate Restaurant & Hotel* (🕿 01748 822087, 🖳 thefrenchgate.co.uk; 2S/1D/6D or T, all en suite; ➼; WI-FI; Ⓛ), 59-61 Frenchgate. With marble floors, limestone walls, freestanding bath tubs and showcasing local artists; one room also has a 1½-ton four-poster oak-framed bed. B&B costs from £74pp for a standard room (sgl/sgl occ from £98). It's worth checking the website for offers.

Further along Frenchgate, and at No 66, is *Frenchgate Guesthouse* (☎ 01748 823421, ⊒ 66frenchgate.com; 3D/5D or T/1Qd, all en suite; ✓; WI-FI; ⓛ); it has fine views down across the Swale. B&B costs from £65pp (sgl occ £98). This is another place that offers a laundry service.

On Market Place itself, there's *Kings Head* (☎ 01748 850220, ⊒ kingsheadrich mond.co.uk; 4S/11D/4D or T, all en suite; ✓; WI-FI; ⓛ; 🐾), probably the smartest hotel in town. B&B starts at £62.50pp (sgl/sgl occ £110-115/115). *Black Lion* (☎ 01748 518897, ⊒ www.blacklionhotelrich mond.co.uk; 1S/6D/4T/3Qd all en suite; ✓; WI-FI; ⓛ; 🐾), on Finkle St near Market Place, now offers B&B (£45-47.50pp, sgl/sgl occ from £80).

The Buck Inn (☎ 01748 517300, ⊒ thebuckrichmond.co.uk; 2D/2Tr/2Qd, all en suite; WI-FI; ⓛ; 🐾) on Newbiggin offers B&B from £32.50pp (sgl occ £65). Note, you may get a better rate by calling them direct when booking rather than through online vendors.

For a little luxury you could try *Castle House* (☎ 01748 823954, ⊒ castlehouse richmond.co.uk; 1S/6D/1Tr, all en suite; ✓; WI-FI; ⓛ), a boutique B&B on Castle Hill. Rooms start at £50pp (sgl/sgl occ £90) but if you really want to push the boat out, for £87.50pp (sgl occ £165) you could treat yourself to their Richmond Suite which has an open fire and a four-poster bed with free-standing bath and separate en suite with shower. The attention to detail here is evident with a complimentary drink on arrival and they are happy to dry wet clothes and do laundry (£10 a load).

Where to eat and drink
Disregarding fast-food outlets which you probably won't have walked halfway across the country to visit, there are lots of good places to eat in Richmond.

On Market Place, *Cross View Tearoom & Restaurant* (☎ 01748 825897, ⊒ crossviewtearooms.co.uk; Mon-Sat 9am-4.30pm, Sun 10am-4.30pm, if quiet they may close earlier; 🐾), which first opened its doors in 1988, still has a traditional tea room feel to it and is friendly and good value. Their pie of the day is £11.95.

For a more modern café experience, cross to the other side of Market Place to *Mocha* (☎ 01748 825655, ⊒ mocha chocolateshop.co.uk; **fb**; Mon-Sat 9am-5pm, Sun 10am-4.30pm; 🐾) is an award-winning café-cum-chocolate shop that sells beautifully crafted, delicate and rich real chocolates.

For early risers, the Market Place branch of *Costa Coffee* (Mon-Sat 7am-7pm, Sun 8.30am-6pm) opens at 7am most days. At 14 Finkle St, *The Little Drummer Boy Tearoom* (☎ 01748 850706, ⊒ thelittle drummerboytearoom.co.uk; **fb**; daily 9am-5pm; 🐾) is another popular spot for lunch or to watch the world go by. There's a full lunch menu (£6.95-9.95) as well as sandwiches, light bites, and afternoon teas to ponder over.

Richmond is well served by fish & chipperies with two, *Castle Fisheries* (daily noon-9.30pm, Sun to 9pm) and the much less impressive *Barkers Fish & Chips* (Mon-Thur 11am-9pm, Fri to 10pm, Sat to 9.30pm, Sun to 8.30pm) residing on Market Place. If you can't face the thought of another pub meal, a top-class British curry is a possibility so point yourself towards *Amontola* (☎ 01748 826070, ⊒ amontola.co.uk; daily 5-9.30pm) up on Queen's Rd. There's plenty of space and the service is great.

New Treasure Garden (☎ 01748 825827; **fb**; Wed-Mon 5.30-10.30pm, Sun to 10pm), at 7 Castle Hill, is a Cantonese restaurant.

Up on King St, *Sunitra's* (☎ 01748 829696; **fb**; Wed-Sat 5.30-8pm, takeaway 5.30-6.15pm), should have all your Thai food cravings covered.

For Italian fare, try *La Piazza* (☎ 01748 825008, ⊒ lapiazza-richmond.co .uk; daily noon-3pm & 5-10pm) which with its fountains and statuary is certainly doing its best to recreate the atmosphere of the Mediterranean on Richmond's Dundas St. Pizzas start at £8.95.

ROUTE GUIDE AND MAPS

The **restaurant** at *Kings Head* (see Where to stay) is very smart but pricey. They also do meals at the **bar** (both Mon-Sat noon-9pm, Sun to 8pm) which are less expensive, and 'artisan sandwiches' from 11am to 5pm. One of the best places to eat in Richmond is the French-run *Rustique* (☎ 01748 821565, ☐ rustiquerichmond.co.uk; daily noon-9pm, lunch to 4pm), on Finkle St. For the full Gallic experience have half a dozen snails if they are on the menu. It's all good value and you can get an excellent 2-/3-course set meal for £16.95/20.95 (Sun-Thur noon-9pm, Fri & Sat to 6.30pm).

Frenchgate Restaurant & Hotel (see Where to stay; daily 7-9pm) is another good, if expensive, choice for a relaxed evening's dining. Venison, turbot and your old friend, Swaledale lamb, often feature on the frequently changing menu. Their three-course set meal costs from £39; booking recommended. Some of the pubs lining Market Place can be extremely noisy with a couple catering largely to groups of local lads looking for a fight, especially at weekends.

A safer option is *The Buck Inn* (see Where to stay; food summer Thur & Fri 5.30-8pm, Sat & Sun noon-2.30pm), near Market Place on Newbiggin, which is a lot more friendly and relaxed, with great views across the river. The food is good value too (mains £7.95-9.95).

If you need something for your lunchbox, on Market Place try *The Noted Pie Shop* (Mon-Sat 7.30am-4.30pm) for their famous pies, or the early opening deli, *Jefferson's* (☎ 01748 821258; **fb**; Mon-Sat 8am-4pm; ✎), which also has a small café. Round it all off with a visit to *Frenchgate Fudge & Chocolate Makers* (Thur-Tue 10.30am-4.30pm), at 1 Frenchgate. Alternatively, you'll soon spot the queues outside the award-winning *Thomas the Baker* (☎ 01748 821157, ☐ thomasthebaker.co.uk; Mon-Sat 7.45am-4.15pm) at 27 Market Place.

For good **pub grub** in Richmond itself, try the *Black Lion* (see Where to stay; food daily noon-9pm; WI-FI; ✎). If you're on a tight budget *The Ralph Fitz Randal* (☎ 01748 828080, ☐ jdwetherspoon.com; food daily 8am-11pm; WI-FI), 6 Queens Rd, is the local branch of Wetherspoons. Another option is a visit to *The George & Dragon* (Map 60; see p196), 2km away in Hudswell.

STAGE 10: RICHMOND TO INGLEBY CROSS   MAPS 61-72

Introduction

This is the longest stage in this book but it's also the flattest so there's something to be said for Wainwright's suggestion of traversing the **Vale of Mowbray** in one fell day, rather than overnighting at Danby Wiske. It's a fairly uneventful walk by the standards of the Coast to Coast, much of it conducted on back roads, so the **22½ miles (36km, 8½hrs)** to Ingleby Cross are actually achievable. What you may want to also factor in is the pounding your trail-weary feet may get along the roads as well as on the following stage: a notably more gruelling 21-miler to Blakey Ridge.

There's also an **alternative route** between Bolton-on-Swale and Danby Wiske to consider following on this stage, which if opted for, will add a further

Elevation profile: Richmond — Colburn — Catterick Bridge — Bolton-on-Swale — Streetlam — Danby Wiske. 500ft. Distance (miles) 0 to 14.

mile (1.6km), and 20-30 minutes, to your itinerary. There's more on p212 to help make up your mind how you stage the next couple of days.

The fell-loving Wainwright lost little love on this tepid agricultural tract, not least the innocent hamlet of Danby Wiske, cruelly claiming it to be a low point in his project in more than just elevation. Things have obviously changed for the better (and were probably never that bad), and now there are B&Bs, and a pub to tempt you. So, in our opinion, there's a lot to be said for spending a morning ticking off a couple of sights in Richmond before setting out on the 13½ miles to Danby Wiske in the afternoon.

The route

Starting off from **Richmond Bridge** with a stroll along the Swale's southern bank, you leave the river for a terrace of houses and join the A6136, leaving it in turn along a lane to the left that passes a sewage works and subsequently a dark, occasionally muddy stretch of riverside woodland and fields. Be careful there may be one or more bulls in these fields and although we're assured they're friendly enough we wouldn't want to tempt fate by wearing red....

When you finally pop out of the trees – quite possibly to the sound of gunfire from the nearby garrison at Catterick (yep gunfire and bulls who knew a short stroll out of Richmond could be quite so exciting) – you traipse over or around more fields and farms to Catterick Bridge via **Colburn**.

COLBURN   **MAP 63, p207**

The village of Colburn has little to distract the eastbound hiker apart from the friendly *Hildyard Arms* (☎ 01748 832353, 💻 the hildyardarms.wordpress.com; **food** Apr-Sep daily noon-3pm & 6-9pm, Oct-Mar Fri-Sun 3-9pm; WI-FI; 🐾; Ⓛ). They have Richmond ales on tap. **Camping** is free but they prefer if you phone ahead. They also have two **shepherds' huts** (sleeping up to two inc bedding & towels; from £60).

Continental breakfast (£4-5) is available if requested in advance. There's a decent shower (50p) and they can usually do laundry for guests. All in all, a highly recommended pitstop on your walk.

There is a Premier **shop** (daily 7am-10pm) 10 minutes from the pub (and off route) if you're in desperate need of supplies. Arriva's X26 **bus** service calls in Colburn (see pp54-6).

From Colburn at one point the path skirts past the former site of St Giles Hospital that flourished alongside the river some 800 years ago, although if any trace of it remains today, it's best observed following a prolonged session at Hildyard Arms.

More conspicuous is *St Giles Farm* (☎ 01748 811372; 1T/1D/1Tr, all en suite; 🐾; WI-FI; Ⓛ); 🐾 in utility room) providing very comfortable **B&B** rooms (booking essential) from £55pp (sgl occ £65) and a pleasing **camping** spot in the well-tended garden. Camping (🐾) costs from £10pp including shower

Oaktree Hill — Ingleby Arncliffe — Ingleby Cross
200m / 100m / 0
15 16 17 18 19 20 21 22

and toilet facilities as well as the use of phone-charging points. Note that check-in is from 4pm.

The path continues above the river past ***Thornborough Farm*** (Map 64) where basic **camping** (£10pp inc toilet/washing facilities, no shower) is offered, and under the throbbing A1 trunk road to **Catterick Bridge**. Famed for its race-course and army camp, the name Catterick reaches back 2000 years when a strategic Roman garrison and town developed where Dere Street – today's A1(M) or Great North Road – bridged the Swale.

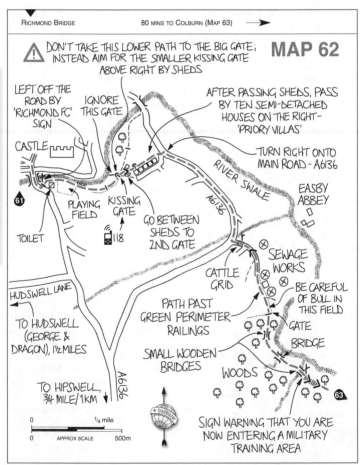

RICHMOND BRIDGE   80 MINS TO COLBURN (MAP 63) ──→

MAP 62

⚠ DON'T TAKE THIS LOWER PATH TO THE BIG GATE; INSTEAD AIM FOR THE SMALLER KISSING GATE ABOVE RIGHT BY SHEDS

LEFT OFF THE ROAD BY 'RICHMOND FC' SIGN

IGNORE THIS GATE

AFTER PASSING SHEDS, PASS BY TEN SEMI-DETACHED HOUSES ON THE RIGHT – 'PRIORY VILLAS'

CASTLE

TURN RIGHT ONTO MAIN ROAD – A6136

RIVER SWALE

EASBY ABBEY

61

PLAYING FIELD

KISSING GATE

📱118

GO BETWEEN SHEDS TO 2ND GATE

A6136

TOILET

SEWAGE WORKS

⊗ ⊗ ⊗ ⊗

CATTLE GRID

BE CAREFUL OF BULL IN THIS FIELD

HUDSWELL LANE

PATH PAST GREEN PERIMETER RAILINGS

GATE

BRIDGE

TO HUDSWELL (GEORGE & DRAGON), 1½ MILES

SMALL WOODEN BRIDGES

WOODS

63

TO HIPSWELL, ¾ MILE/1KM

A6136

0   ¼ mile

0   APPROX SCALE   500m

★ trailblazer

SIGN WARNING THAT YOU ARE NOW ENTERING A MILITARY TRAINING AREA

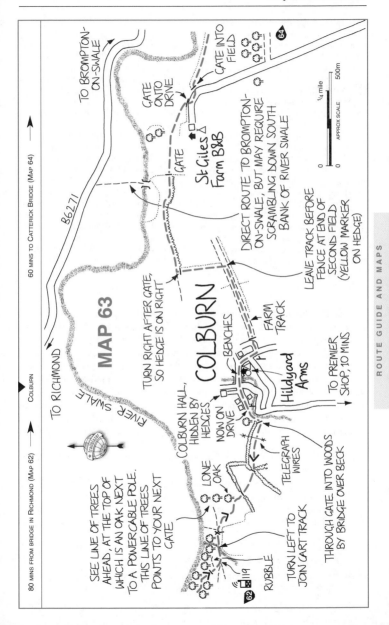

TO BROMPTON-ON-SWALE

TO RICHMOND

RIVER SWALE

B6271

MAP 63

COLBURN

GATE INTO FIELD

64

GATE ONTO DRIVE

GATE

St Giles Farm B&B

DIRECT ROUTE TO BROMPTON-ON-SWALE, BUT MAY REQUIRE SCRAMBLING DOWN SOUTH BANK OF RIVER SWALE

LEAVE TRACK BEFORE FENCE AT END OF SECOND FIELD (YELLOW MARKER ON HEDGE)

TURN RIGHT AFTER GATE, SO HEDGE IS ON RIGHT

NOW ON DRIVE

COLBURN HALL, HIDDEN BY HEDGES

BENCHES

FARM TRACK

Hildyard Arms

TO PREMIER SHOP, 10 MINS

TELEGRAPH WIRES

SEE LINE OF TREES AHEAD, AT THE TOP OF WHICH IS AN OAK NEXT TO A POWERCABLE POLE. THIS LINE OF TREES POINTS TO YOUR NEXT GATE

LONE OAK

TURN LEFT TO JOIN CART TRACK

THROUGH GATE INTO WOODS BY BRIDGE OVER BECK

RUBBLE

62

¼ mile

500m

0

0

APPROX SCALE

BROMPTON-ON-SWALE   MAP 64
Farmer's Arms (☎ 01748 818062, 🖳 the
bromptononswalefarmersarms.co.uk; 2D/
1T/1Qd, all en suite; WI-FI; ①; 🐾 bar only)
pub offers **B&B** from £42.50pp (sgl occ
£50) and also does **food** (Mon-Thur noon-
3pm & 5-8.30pm, Fri & Sat noon-4pm & 5-
8.30pm, Sun noon-4.30pm); note that the
food on Sunday is mostly a carvery though
there are a few other options.

The excellent-value and very welcoming *Brompton Camping Barn* (☎ 01748
818326, 🖳 chris01748@gmail.com; 🐾)
has three rooms (each sleeping up to four;
from £15pp) with bunk beds including
duvets and pillows, but no sheets (sleeping
sacks cost from £2 to rent). There's a fully
equipped kitchen, a large dining and lounge
area and a nice hot shower (10p; enough for
a very long shower). Plug sockets are
metered (£1 coins only). Booking for the
barn is recommended for groups. There's
also **camping** (from £7pp inc shower) for
half a dozen tents.

Right opposite the Barn there's a very
handy mini **supermarket** (Mon-Fri 7am-
7.30pm, Sat 8am-7.30pm, Sun 9am-6pm),
which also houses the local **post office**.

A few doors down is *The Crown* (☎
01748 811666; **fb**; 🐾); bar Mon-Thur 2-
11pm, Fri-Sun noon-11pm) pub, where
food is available (Sat & Sun noon-3pm,
Mon-Sat 5-7.30pm).

To get to the camping barn, continue
north once over the river, turn left down
Bridge Rd, pass under the A1(M) and join
West Richmond Rd; the barn is on the right,
a 15-minute walk from the bridge. If you're
coming from Richmond, though, you might
prefer to take a short cut by scrambling
down to the rarely used bridge over the
Swale River by Colburn Beck Woods (see
Map 63); you won't miss much.

Hodgson's No 34 & No 55 **bus** services stop on Bridge Rd; see pp54-6 for
details.

Having flirted with the river since leaving Richmond, you finally leave it
for good to march into the hamlet of **Bolton-on-Swale** (Map 65). There are no
refreshments here other than those possibly in the church, which is worth visiting, not least for its **memorial to Henry Jenkins**. He was a local man who lived
an unremarkable life except for its length; he claimed he was 169 when he died,
a fact which may explain the popularity of the village with retirees. The church
itself is even older, dating back to the 14th century, with Norman and Saxon
ancestors; you can see various bits of masonry from these earlier churches
inside, including part of an Anglo-Danish cross shaft in the vestry and part of a
pointed arch in the vestry roof. Hodgson's No 55 **bus** calls in Bolton-on-Swale;
see pp54-6.

More field-tramping ensues followed by a stretch of road-walking (Maps
65-67).

There is an **alternative route** that can be followed from Bolton-on-Swale
to Danby Wiske, although it's slightly (just under a mile) longer, no more interesting, features a stretch on the busy B6271, and is just as tough on the
ankles (Maps 65-68; p212).   *(cont'd on p212)*

❏ **IMPORTANT NOTE – WALKING TIMES**
All times in this book refer only to the time spent walking. You will need to add
20-30% to allow for rests, photography, checking the map, drinking water etc.

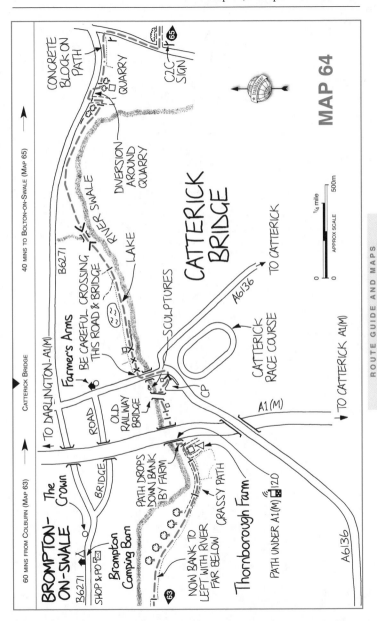

MAP 64

CATTERICK BRIDGE

BROMPTON-ON-SWALE

The Crown

B6271

SHOP & PO

Brompton Camping Barn

BRIDGE

ROAD

PATH DROPS DOWN BANK BY FARM

NOW BANK TO LEFT WITH RIVER FAR BELOW

GRASSY PATH

Thornborough Farm

PATH UNDER A1(M) 120

63

A6136

A1(M)

TO CATTERICK A1(M)

CATTERICK RACE COURSE

A6136

TO CATTERICK

CP

SCULPTURES

OLD RAILWAY BRIDGE

Farmer's Arms

TO DARLINGTON–A1(M)

BE CAREFUL CROSSING THIS ROAD & BRIDGE

LAKE

RIVER SWALE

B6271

DIVERSION AROUND QUARRY

CONCRETE BLOCK ON PATH

QUARRY

C2C SIGN

65

¼ mile

500m

APPROX SCALE

0   0

◀ BOLTON-ON-SWALE 40 MINS TO TURN-OFF TO WHITWELL (MAP 66) ▶

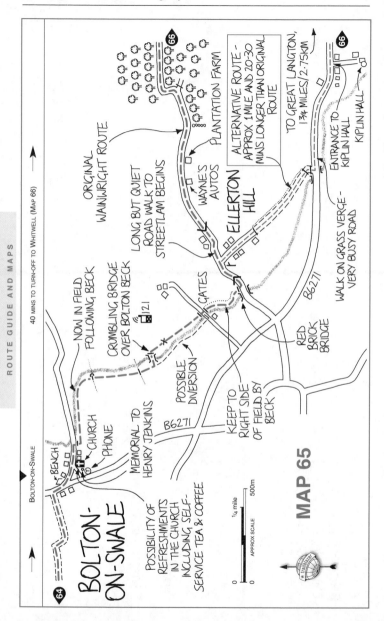

MAP 65

BOLTON-ON-SWALE

POSSIBILITY OF REFRESHMENTS IN THE CHURCH INCLUDING SELF-SERVICE TEA & COFFEE

BENCH
CHURCH
PHONE

MEMORIAL TO HENRY JENKINS

B6271

KEEP TO RIGHT SIDE OF FIELD BY BECK

POSSIBLE DIVERSION

CRUMBLING BRIDGE OVER BOLTON BECK

121

NOW IN FIELD FOLLOWING BECK

ORIGINAL WAINWRIGHT ROUTE

LONG BUT QUIET ROAD WALK TO STREETLAM BEGINS

WAYNE'S AUTOS

PLANTATION FARM

ALTERNATIVE ROUTE - APPROX 1 MILE AND 20-30 MINS LONGER THAN ORIGINAL ROUTE

GATES

ELLERTON HILL

RED BRICK BRIDGE

B6271

WALK ON GRASS VERGE - VERY BUSY ROAD

ENTRANCE TO KIPLIN HALL

KIPLIN HALL

TO GREAT LANGTON, 1¾ MILES/2·75KM

66

66

64

APPROX SCALE
0   ¼ mile
0   500m

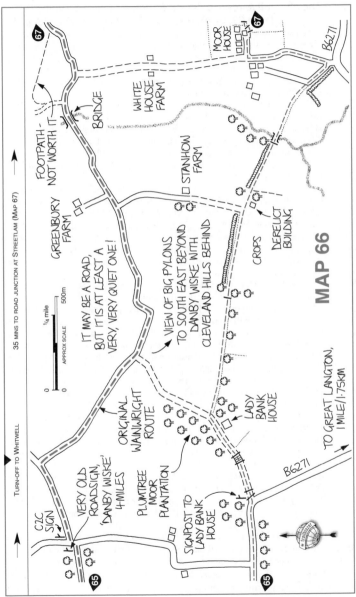

The alternative route between Bolton-on-Swale & Danby Wiske
(Map 65, p210; Map 66, p211; Map 67; Map 68, p215)

If you wish to minimise your time traipsing on tarmac this may be the route for you. Note that at the time of research there were no Coast to Coast path signs along this route so you will need to follow the maps in this book closely. Note, too, that much of it is spent on farmland, so it's no easier underfoot than the original route. **It's also just under one mile longer so will add an extra 20-30 minutes to your day**.

You start by following the path out of Bolton-on-Swale along Bolton Beck (Map 65). When you reach the road at the small cluster of houses at Ellerton Hill, head along the road to the south-east between some houses until you reach a gate and a farm track, which you follow until you reach the B6271, where you turn left. You would be well advised to walk as deep into the grass verge as you're able to here as cars and lorries hurtle along the B6271 like it's the M6 on a quiet day.

If you're ready for a break already, or your nerves are feeling a little shaky from your experience with the B6271's traffic, there's an option to stop for refreshments at **Kiplin Hall** (off Map 65; ☎ 01748 818178, 🖳 kiplinhall.co .uk; early Feb to early Nov Fri-Wed 10am-5pm; £10), where, if you wish to, you can use the *tearooms* (10am-3.30pm) without paying for a ticket for the hall and gardens. The hall was built (between 1622 & 1625) by George Calvert, Secretary of State to King James I and founder of the US state of Maryland.

You'll be glad to leave the B6271 at the point where the road bends south sharply (Map 66) and your walk will become far more satisfying, thankfully remaining so until you reach Danby Wiske. The path follows a clear track up to **Plumtree Moor Plantation** and Lady Bank House from where it carves its route through farmland; it's an easy trail to follow and you'll be glad that, when you reach the B6271 again, the path has the sense not to suffer any further dalliance with the road and turns immediately north towards Moor House. Here, the path again heads east. At **Moor House** it can be very muddy indeed and you have to navigate a number of gates and poorly maintained stiles. Essentially you are going around the farm and back into the fields; the route is easy to see although slightly harder to complete, thanks largely to conditions underfoot. You pass through more fields (Map 67) before arriving at the road at **Brockholme Farm** where you follow the road briefly south before taking the turning for High Brockholme Farm, which you pass through via a couple of gates. This stretch can be very damp underfoot if the weather has been poor but you'll struggle to get lost. Having walked alongside a series of hedges and fences you'll arrive at the road just to the south of the church at **Danby Wiske**. Follow the road towards and then past the church and you'll soon see the small green in the village's centre where you can greet your fellow walkers as they converge with you, having followed Wainwright's original route.

At **Streetlam** (Map 67) the path goes along an overgrown footpath towards more fields of pasture and livestock. One gets the feeling that some of the residents hereabouts aren't too happy with thousands of walkers trooping through their fields year after year. The path is unkempt, stiles are sometimes overturned and greetings are sometimes met with stony silence. Our advice: don't

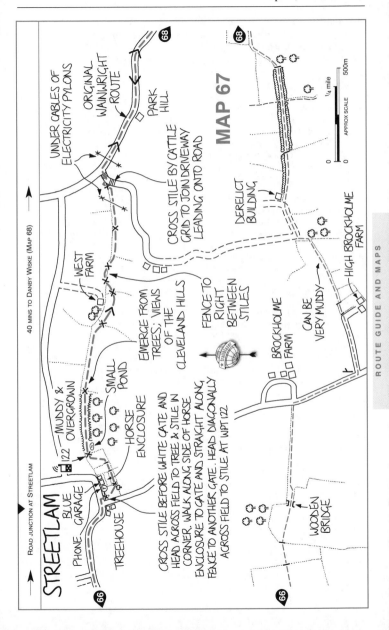

ROUTE GUIDE AND MAPS

MAP 67

APPROX SCALE

0 — 1/4 mile

0 — 500m

← ROAD JUNCTION AT STREETLAM

40 MINS TO DANBY WISKE (MAP 68) →

STREETLAM

PHONE

BLUE GARAGE

TREEHOUSE

122

MUDDY & OVERGROWN

SMALL POND

HORSE ENCLOSURE

CROSS STILE BEFORE WHITE GATE AND HEAD ACROSS FIELD TO TREE & STILE IN CORNER. WALK ALONG SIDE OF HORSE ENCLOSURE TO GATE AND STRAIGHT ALONG FENCE TO ANOTHER GATE. HEADS DIAGONALLY ACROSS FIELD TO STILE AT WPT 122

EMERGE FROM TREES; VIEWS OF THE CLEVELAND HILLS

WEST FARM

UNDER CABLES OF ELECTRICITY PYLONS

ORIGINAL WAINWRIGHT ROUTE

PARK HILL

CROSS STILE BY CATTLE GRID TO JOIN DRIVEWAY LEADING ONTO ROAD

FENCE TO RIGHT BETWEEN STILES

BROCKHOLME FARM

CAN BE VERY MUDDY

DERELICT BUILDING

HIGH BROCKHOLME FARM

WOODEN BRIDGE

antagonise them any more than we and our walking brethren already have: stick to the path, keep disturbances to their livestock to a minimum, take all your litter away with you – and if all that fails, should you meet one, just give them a cuddle. You'll shortly rejoin the road into **Danby Wiske**.

DANBY WISKE   MAP 68

Chances are you'd never heard of Danby Wiske before you set your sights on the Coast to Coast, but this tiny village with an 11th-century **Norman church** and a tidy village green is a renowned staging post on your trek. Having long outgrown the hurtful comments in Wainwright's guide, the proud villagers welcome trail-weary Coasters.

By the road that leads to the church you'll find *Honesty Tuck Shop*, a hut with an honesty box where chocolate bars, drinks, fruit and ice-creams can be purchased; sometimes (Apr-Oct) there's even home-made goodies such as cakes or a Bakewell tart. Walkers can make hot drinks in the camp kitchen and there are also toilet facilities. If you've no cash the relevant bank details are provided so that you can pay by bank transfer or PayPal.me.

Also next to the church and run by the same family, **camping** is available at *Church Holme Camping* (☎ 01609 600618, ⌨ danbywiskecamping.co.uk; no WI-FI but strong 4G; 🐾), a small family-run site with a mix of tents and caravans and a dedicated C2C paddock. They charge from £10 per tent plus £3pp; there are USB charging ports, self-service laundry facilities (just ask for detergent) and a toilet and shower block. There's a covered camp kitchen to cook in – with a table, kettle and a microwave – a washing up area, but also a small menu an evening meal (from £7) if preferred. Bacon baps, porridge and croissants (£2-4.50) are available for breakfast (with filter coffee or Yorkshire Gold tea).

The White Swan (☎ 01609 775131, ⌨ thewhiteswandanbywiske.co.uk), an award-winning real-ale pub, does **B&B** (3T/1Qd all en suite, 2T shared facilities; WI-FI; Ⓛ; 🐾 on lead on the floor in bar only) from £52.50pp (sgl occ £80). They also offer **camping** (£8pp) and breakfast (£10) is available for campers.

There are drying facilities here too and they are happy to do a service wash and dry (£8). **Food** (Apr-Oct daily noon-2pm) is generally available in the bar but call to check. For an evening meal (6.30-7pm) order by 5pm (a menu is available to choose from). Note that from November to March the pub is closed all day on Monday and Tuesday and during the week often only opens at 7pm but from noon at the weekends.

There are two other choices for B&B accommodation. *Ashfield House* (☎ 07790 557924 or ☎ 07817 745463, ⌨ ashfieldhouseC2C@gmail.com; 1D/2T both en suite showers; 🐾; WI-FI; Ⓛ; Apr-end Sep) where B&B costs £55pp (sgl occ £70). They are happy to book an evening meal at the White Swan for guests. *Inglenook B&B* (☎ 07957 836215, ⌨ inglenookbnb.co.uk; 1T private bathroom; WI-FI; Ⓛ; Apr-end Sep) charges from £45pp (sgl occ £60). There is a sitting room for guests with a TV and the proprietors will do a washing/drying load for £10. It's situated behind the White Swan.

As for the **church** – one of the very few in England that has no known dedication – only the solid oak door and the font are 11th-century originals, though much of the north aisle is only slightly younger. Look above the main door at the tympanum and you should be able to make out the outlines of three weathered figures. They've been interpreted as follows: the Angel of Judgement is weighing the soul of the figure on the right using the scales that he holds in his other hand, and though the evil deeds in one of the scales' pans outweigh the other, the third figure, the Angel of Mercy (Jesus Christ), has slipped his fingers under the pan containing the bad deeds, thus causing the good deeds to seem heavier.

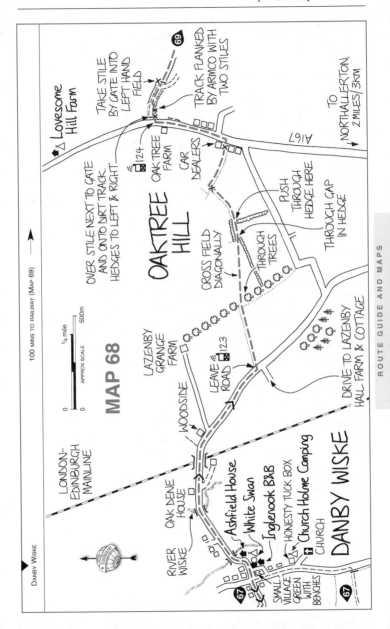

DANBY WISKE

100 MINS TO RAILWAY (MAP 69)

MAP 68

0   1/4 mile   500m
0   APPROX SCALE

LONDON-EDINBURGH MAINLINE

Lovesome Hill Farm

TAKE STILE BY GATE INTO LEFT HAND FIELD

TRACK FLANKED BY ARMCO WITH TWO STILES

69

OVER STILE NEXT TO GATE AND ONTO DIRT TRACK. HEDGES TO LEFT & RIGHT

124

OAK TREE FARM

CAR DEALERS

A167

TO NORTHALLERTON, 2 MILES/3KM

OAKTREE HILL

PUSH THROUGH HEDGE HERE

THROUGH GAP IN HEDGE

CROSS FIELD DIAGONALLY

THROUGH TREES

LAZENBY GRANGE FARM

WOODSIDE

LEAME ROAD

123

DRIVE TO LAZENBY HALL FARM & COTTAGE

OAK DENE HOUSE

Ashfield House

White Swan

Inglenook B&B

HONESTY TUCK BOX

Church Holme Camping

CHURCH

DANBY WISKE

RIVER WISKE

SMALL VILLAGE GREEN WITH BENCHES

67

67

From the bridge crossing the River Wiske outside the village, you can see the outline of the Cleveland Hills in the distance. Unfortunately, the other half of the Vale of Mowbray still lies before you (it's 8½ miles from Danby Wiske to Ingleby Cross), much of it as before on roads, but with a nifty back route sneaking up on **Oaktree Hill**.

OAKTREE HILL MAP 68, p215

This is not much more than a car dealership and a string of houses lining the A167 but less than half a mile north of the path is *Lovesome Hill Farm* (☎ 01609 772311, 🖳 lovesomehillfarm.co.uk; 1S/1D/1T/1Tr, all en suite; 🛏; WI-FI; ⒧), run by keen walkers who have done the C2C Path themselves. Despite the noise of the road, this place has been praised by walkers for the quality of its accommodation, the food and the opportunity to take a tour of the 165-acre farm. The double room has bunk beds so can be used by a family with children. **B&B** rates are from £50pp (sgl £60, sgl occ £75). Walkers with a dog can stay in their **bunk barn** (🐾; from £20pp inc shower, but bedding and breakfast extra) which has two rooms each sleeping up to four.

There is also space for **camping** (£12pp; 🐾) in their garden; campers can use the bunk barn showers and toilets. Both **evening meals** (from £20) and **breakfast** (£12) can be provided for campers (and bunkbarn) users if requested in advance; their homemade marmalade has won awards.

Here more tracks and quiet backroads link a series of busy farms as you cross both a railway line (Map 69) – before which there is the possibility of an honesty box tuck shop – and a beck or two to finally meet the busy **A19** (Map 71) at **Exelby Services**, where you'll find a small **shop** (open 24hrs) with a coffee machine, an **ATM** (£1.50 for withdrawals) and toilets. Campers should note that, unless you pop into Osmotherley, there are no village shops on the path until Glaisdale, over 30 miles away. However, the more pressing concern for all walkers will be crossing the four lanes of the A19 without being hit by a car and causing a pile-up. Be patient and take extreme care crossing. You'll probably have to do it in two parts by waiting halfway across by the lane barriers for the traffic to clear going in the other direction. A few years ago, a petition was started to try and get a bridge built but it seems that won't happen until someone actually does get killed. However, as part of the improvement works for the path to become a National Trail, Natural England is now hoping the Treasury will provide funding for this. Since Richmond is the constituency of Rishi Sunak (prime minister at the time of writing), keen to promote the National Trail and supporting villagers campaigning for a bridge it is possible something might actually happen.

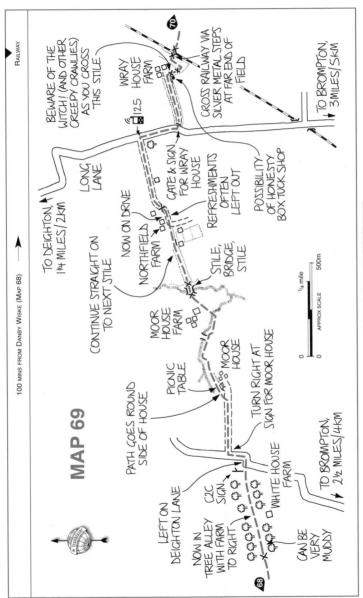

100 MINS FROM DANBY WISKE (MAP 68)

RAILWAY

MAP 69

TO DEIGHTON, 1¼ MILES / 2 KM

CONTINUE STRAIGHT ON TO NEXT STILE

NOW ON DRIVE

NORTHFIELD FARM

LONG LANE

BEWARE OF THE WITCH! (AND OTHER CREEPY CRAWLIES) AS YOU CROSS THIS STILE

WRAY HOUSE FARM

70

CROSS RAILWAY VIA SILVER METAL STEPS AT FAR END OF FIELD

TO BROMPTON, 3 MILES / 5 KM

12.5

GATE & SIGN FOR WRAY HOUSE

REFRESHMENTS OFTEN LEFT OUT

POSSIBILITY OF HONESTY BOX TUCK SHOP

MOOR HOUSE FARM

STILE, BRIDGE, STILE

PICNIC TABLE

MOOR HOUSE

PATH GOES ROUND SIDE OF HOUSE

TURN RIGHT AT SIGN FOR MOOR HOUSE

LEFT ON DEIGHTON LANE

C2C SIGN

NOW IN TREE ALLEY WITH FARM TO RIGHT

WHITE HOUSE FARM

CAN BE VERY MUDDY

TO BROMPTON, 2½ MILES / 4 KM

68

0   APPROX SCALE   500m
0   ¼ mile

ROUTE GUIDE AND MAPS

ROUTE GUIDE AND MAPS

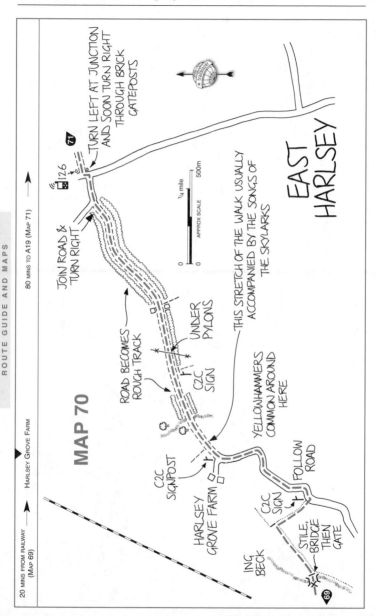

20 MINS FROM RAILWAY (Map 69) — HARLSEY GROVE FARM — 80 MINS TO A19 (Map 71)

MAP 70

TURN LEFT AT JUNCTION AND SOON TURN RIGHT THROUGH BRICK GATEPOSTS

71

126

JOIN ROAD & TURN RIGHT

ROAD BECOMES ROUGH TRACK

UNDER PYLONS

C2C SIGN

THIS STRETCH OF THE WALK USUALLY ACCOMPANIED BY THE SONGS OF THE SKYLARKS

EAST HARLSEY

¼ mile
APPROX SCALE
500m

C2C SIGNPOST

HARLSEY GROVE FARM

YELLOWHAMMERS COMMON AROUND HERE

FOLLOW ROAD

C2C SIGN

STILE, BRIDGE THEN GATE

ING BECK

69

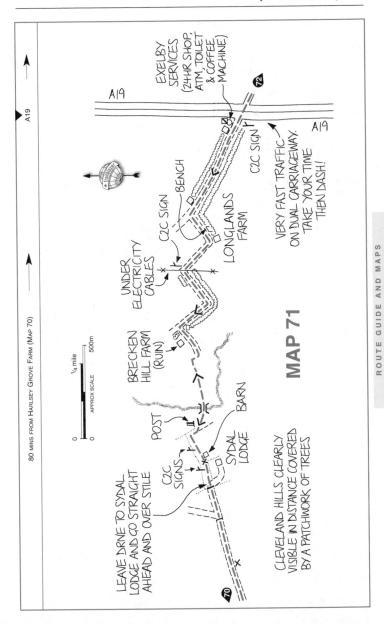

80 MINS FROM HARLSEY GROVE FARM (MAP 70)

A19

¼ mile
500m
APPROX SCALE

EXELBY SERVICES (24HR SHOP, ATM, TOILET & COFFEE MACHINE)

A19

A19

72

C2C SIGN

VERY FAST TRAFFIC ON DUAL CARRIAGEWAY. TAKE YOUR TIME THEN DASH!

BENCH

C2C SIGN

UNDER ELECTRICITY CABLES

LONGLANDS FARM

BRECKEN HILL FARM (RUIN)

MAP 71

POST

BARN

C2C SIGNS

SYDAL LODGE

LEAVE DRIVE TO SYDAL LODGE AND GO STRAIGHT AHEAD AND OVER STILE

CLEVELAND HILLS CLEARLY VISIBLE IN DISTANCE COVERED BY A PATCHWORK OF TREES

70

INGLEBY CROSS   MAP 72
& INGLEBY ARNCLIFFE

Sandwiched between two busy 'A' roads, Ingleby Cross and its twin Ingleby Arncliffe are surprisingly peaceful places if you're not camping.

Ingleby Cross is said to be named after its war memorial and in terms of services has nothing more than the **post office** (Mon 10am-noon), situated in the Blue Bell Inn.

Abbotts No 80 & No 89 **bus** services stop in Ingleby Cross as does Moorsbus's M5 (see pp54-6).

Where to stay and eat

In **Ingleby Arncliffe**, *Elstavale* (☎ 01609 882302, 🖳 elstavale.co.uk; 1D or T/1Tr, both en suite; WI-FI; (L)) offers **B&B** from £40pp (sgl occ £65). Note that the rooms are in a separate annexe and come with foot spas. There are great breakfasts (the owner is a former chef) and a most welcome cream tea on arrival – note that check-in is from 4pm unless arranged in advance.

Not far from the path is the very welcoming *Ingleby House Farm* (☎ 01609 882500, 🖳 inglebyhousefarm.co.uk; 1D/1D or T/1T, all en suite; WI-FI; (L); 🐾; Apr-end Oct), which has one room (double or twin) in the main house and a double and a twin in a separate converted cowbyre, as well as a delightful **shepherd's hut** (1D, en suite) in the flower-filled garden. B&B costs from £45pp (sgl occ £75). Run by friendly people, one of whom is a trained chef, you're welcomed with a cream tea on arrival and given an excellent breakfast the next day. A laundry service is also available

and the owners can offer pick-up and drop-off for those needing to stay an extra day.

The Blue Bell Inn (☎ 01609 882272, 🖳 thebluebellinninglebycross.co.uk; **fb**; 1S/2D/1T/1Qd, all en suite; WI-FI; (L); 🐾) in the centre of **Ingleby Cross** serves real ales and standard **pub meals** sometimes including the Middlesbrough staple, chicken parmesan (from £9.50), which is less Italian than it sounds. However, at the time of writing they weren't sure what days/hours they would serve food in 2023 so check in advance. You can also **camp** in the field out back for £10 per tent, including 24hr access to shower and toilets. Breakfast (from £7.50) is available if booked the night before. **B&B** costs from £40pp (sgl/sgl occ £60/70). Note, the pub may have more restricted opening hours in winter.

Opposite the pub is *The Joiner's Shop* (☎ 01609 882762; Tue-Sun 10am-4pm; WI-FI; 🐾), a lovely **café** serving speciality teas, Yorkshire-roasted Rounton Coffee as well as breakfasts and brunches. Their turmeric latte (£3.20) is especially good.

Just over a mile past the village, but right on the path, *Park House Country Guest House* (☎ 01609 882899, 🖳 park housecountryguesthouse.com; 2D/2T/2Tr, all en suite; WI-FI; (L); 🐾) is well worth the extra effort to get here. With a lovely lounge and grounds that hopefully you'll have the energy to appreciate. They no longer provide evening meals but are happy to book a table at the pub. However, they are licensed. B&B costs from £47.50pp (sgl occ £75).

OSMOTHERLEY
off MAP 72 & MAP 73, p225

Though a 20-minute walk off the Coast to Coast trail, Osmotherley is a delight and energetic walkers may want to visit, even if they're not staying here.

In the centre of the village stands a **market cross** and a **barter table**, believed to be the one from which John Wesley preached. Indeed, in Chapel Yard you can find what's believed to be Britain's oldest practising **Methodist chapel**, constructed in

1754. There's also the church, **St Peter's**, built on Saxon foundations.

The most distinctive things about Osmotherley, however, are its beautiful, **sand-coloured terraced cottages**, built for the workers who laboured at the flax mill that now houses the hostel. **Thompson's**, for years a time-warp shop that was once described as a 'mini Harrods', had been in the same family since 1786. It was sold by the late Grace Thompson in 2014 with a

71

INGLEBY ARNCLIFFE A172

TO SWAINBY, 2 MILES/3KM

Elstavale

Ingleby House Farm

INGLEBY CROSS

WATER TOWER

PHONE

WATER SOMETIMES LEFT OUTSIDE BY ROSE LEA COTTAGE

The Joiner's Shop (CAFÉ)

WAR MEMORIAL

Blue Bell Inn & PO

127

LEAVE ROAD HERE AND TURN LEFT ONTO STONY TRACK INTO ARNCLIFFE WOOD

INGLEBY CRICKET CLUB

CHURCH

FOLLOW SIGN FOR PARK HOUSE

DIANE'S FAMOUS FLAPJACKS FOR SALE

C2C SIGN

ARNCLIFFE WOOD

73

A172

NOT THIS WAY. IT'S NOT A SHORTCUT!

trailblazer

TO OSMOTHERLEY, 4 MILES/6.5KM

Park House Country Guest House

TELECOM TOWERS

PATHS OFF TO LEFT & RIGHT

CLEVELAND WAY

TRAIL FOLLOWS A LONG, WIDE AND WINDING TRACK THAT SNAKES ITS WAY THROUGH THE WOODS – CAN BE VERY MUDDY

SHORTCUTS FROM OSMOTHERLEY

0   ¼ mile
0   APPROX SCALE   500m

RELENTLESSLY UPHILL

SWAINSTYE FARM TRACK

MOUNT GRACE PRIORY

MAP 72

TO OSMOTHERLEY (FOLLOW CLEVELAND WAY SIGN), 20 MINS

CLEVELAND WAY SIGN

128

TO OSMOTHERLEY, 20 MINS

ROUTE GUIDE AND MAPS

restrictive covenant that it must continue to serve the community as a local shop. Despite the promise it hadn't reopened at the time of writing, but you can still view the small shop front, just beyond the two village pubs on the same side of the street as the Golden Lion.

To rejoin the trail, you needn't return to the junction with the Cleveland Way, but can take a short-cut up along Swainstye Farm track (on the left as you walk from the village towards Cote Ghyll caravan park), meeting up with the Cleveland Way and Coast to Coast paths at the Telecom Towers (see Map 72) or at Scarth Wood Moor (Map 73).

Services

There's a **post office** (Mon & Tue 9am-noon, Wed 1-4pm) in the village hall and a small **village store** (Mon-Sat 8.30am-5pm, Sun 9am-1pm), on the approach into the village centre, where they sell basic provisions and sandwiches.

Abbott's (AofL) No 80/89 **bus** services stop here (see pp54-6).

Where to stay

YHA Osmotherley is operated by the owners of Cote Ghyll Caravan Park as part of their franchise Enterprise scheme. It is called *Cote Ghyll Mill* (☎ 01609 883425, 🖳 coteghyll.com, 🖳 yha.org.uk/hostel/yha-osmotherley; 4x2-, 6x4-, 4x6-bed rooms, all en suite; WI-FI; (L)) on account of it being housed in an old flax mill. The rooms are very comfortable; each is en suite, with walk-in shower, toilet, wash basin and hair dryer, and the beds (which are all bunks) have their own reading lights and USB & phone-charger sockets. A private room costs approximately £63-76 for

two sharing. Meals (breakfast from £8.50; evening from £9) are generally available but there's a huge self-catering kitchen and the hostel is licensed. There is a TV room and a pool table and they accept debit but not credit cards. **Camping** is also available (£14-18.50pp). Coming from Arncliffe Wood, at the top end of the village turn left when you hit the road, rather than right down the hill into the village.

Just before the hostel, the excellent *Cote Ghyll Caravan Park* (contact details as for Cote Ghyll Mill; 🐾; WI-FI; book in advance in summer; Mar-Oct) has **camping** from £10.50pp inc toilet/shower facilities. Meals are usually available at Cote Ghyll Mill (unless it's booked out by a large group), but there's also a small on-site **shop**. Though the hostel is open all year, the campsite closes during the winter.

For **B&B** you need to walk down to the centre of the village. *Queen Catherine Hotel* (☎ 01609 883209, 🖳 queencatherine hotel.co.uk; 1S/1D/1T/1Tr, one up to five, two self-contained flats sleeping up to five/six, all en suite; WI-FI; (L); 🐾), at 7 West End, charges from £55pp (sgl/sgl occ from £75). The hotel is named after Henry VIII's wife, Catherine of Aragon, who is believed to have sheltered with monks at Mount Grace Priory. It is, surprisingly, the only hotel in England named after her.

Another pub with rooms, *The Golden Lion* (☎ 01609 883526, 🖳 goldenlion osmotherley.co.uk; 2D/5D or T, all en suite; WI-FI; (L); 🐾) is just opposite and charges £62.50-65pp (sgl occ from £100) for B&B.

The Three Tuns (☎ 01609 883301, 🖳 threetunsrestaurant.co.uk; 4D, all en suite; WI-FI; (L); 🐾), opposite The Green, is a popular restaurant (see Where to eat) that offers pleasant rooms to stay in too; B&B

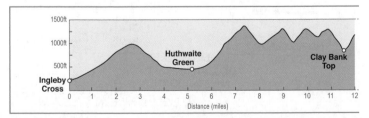

starts at £60pp (sgl occ £85). Back up the hill a little way is *Vane House* (☎ 01609 883406, 🖳 allan@vane house.co.uk; 3T/2D, all en suite; ☞; WI-FI; Ⓛ; 🐾), at 11A North End, with B&B for £70pp (sgl occ £120) and some of the best power-showers on the Path. They'll do laundry (£10 per load, £20 if includes a machine dry) and if arranged in advance (and for a small charge) offer pick-up and drop-off.

Where to eat and drink
The Three Tuns (see Where to stay; food daily noon-8pm) is a smart establishment with arguably the best food in town by some distance; nor is it overly expensive. For pub food, *The Golden Lion* (see Where to stay; food daily 5-8.30pm, Wed-Sun noon-2.30pm) is decent, although it is advisable to book in advance for an evening meal especially at the weekend. More down to earth, and much nicer for a pint with the locals, is *Queen Catherine Hotel* (see Where to stay; food daily noon-9pm) with some great homemade meals and plenty of real ales, including Wainwright's.

For something lighter try *The Coffee Shop Osmotherley* (☎ 07980 208034; Wed-Mon 9am-4.30pm; 🐾), a pleasant little café next to The Golden Lion; they serve coffee and tea and the menu includes (vegan) sandwiches as well as home-made scones and cakes. Note, the café doesn't have toilets, so customers have to use the nearby public ones.

For takeaway, head to *Osmotherley Fish and Chip Shop* (☎ 01609 883557; **fb**; Easter-Nov Wed-Thur 5-8.30pm, Fri & Sat noon-2pm, Fri 5-9pm, Sat 4-8.30pm, Nov-Easter Fri 5-8.30pm, Sat noon-2pm & 5-8pm), next to Queen Catherine Hotel, where a chip butty costs £1.70; regular fish & chips are £6.50.

STAGE 11: INGLEBY CROSS TO BLAKEY RIDGE MAPS 72-81

Introduction
At **21 miles (34km, 8hrs)**, this is another stage that many walkers consider splitting in two, particularly as there are five big climbs separating you from Blakey Ridge. Unfortunately, unless wild camping, it's less easily done than Stage 10 which is one reason you might want to spare yourself if coming from Richmond; you'll need to be in good shape to arrive at Blakey Ridge without looking like an extra from a George Romero zombie movie.

If you do divide the walk at **Clay Bank Top** and spend the night in one of the nearby villages, such as Great Broughton to the north or Chop Gate to the south, the next day (having returned to Clay Bank Top) is a relatively effortless 8½ miles (14km) to Blakey Ridge so you can easily add the 9½ downhill miles to Glaisdale and needn't lose much time. Providing you book in advance, the B&Bs at Great Broughton, Kirkby-in-Cleveland, and the other nearby villages are usually more than happy to collect you at Clay Bank Top and return you there the next morning.

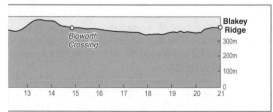

Weather and willpower depending, the all-in-one option has its plus points, however. For one thing, although the first half is a bit of a rollercoaster as the gradient profile reveals, once you've climbed one last time onto Urra Moor, some 12 miles (19.5km) from Ingleby Cross and following well over 1000 metres (nearly 3800ft) of accumulated ascent, the second half feels blessedly level and straightforward. Furthermore, many consider the Lion Inn at Blakey to be one of the more memorable pubs on the route, an isolated but busy tavern stranded atop a mist-bound moor with camping for Coast to Coasters only.

Thus our advice is as follows: if your feet are in good shape and there's room at the Inn (see p232, or elsewhere see p236), grab it and attempt the 21 miles in a day. If that doesn't suit your schedule, organise a B&B near Clay Bank Top and if necessary catch up by pushing on to Glaisdale – an 18-mile day.

One final thing: campers should note that there's **camping** at Lordstones (see p226 and they do also have some pods and roundhouses) and the Lion Inn.

As for the walk itself, this stage takes you into **North York Moors National Park** with, it is said, the world's largest expanse of heather. Depending on the weather, this could be a pleasant stage as you tramp merrily along, stopping only to admire the iridescent plumage of the clucking pheasant or savour the views south to the valleys of Farndale and north to the industrial glories of Teeside and your first view of the North Sea. Or it could be a miserable, claggy rain-soaked trudge with all views obscured by a bone-chilling mist while paramotors buzz menacingly overhead. Let's hope it's the former but either way, the waymarking is good so you're unlikely to get lost.

The route

From Ingleby Cross (Map 72) the walk begins with a climb up past the **church** (note the triple-decker pulpit and purple box pews) and on up into **Arncliffe Wood**, where the path takes a turn to the south. Having passed the turn-off for Park House Country Guest House (see p220) you climb steeply and at the southernmost point of the wood a hairpin bend sees Wainwright's climbing trail meet the Cleveland Way, established two years before Wainwright's original book was published and which you follow for almost the entire way to Blakey Moor. For Osmotherley, turn off south through the gate.

The route continues steeply up through Arncliffe Wood (get used to it, there's plenty more of it on this stage), with cleared forestry providing views back to the Vale of Mowbray as you pass some humming telecom towers to emerge onto the heather-clad **Scarth Wood Moor** (Map 73).

You soon leave the track and merge with the Lyke Wake Walk (see box p226) before going through **Clain Wood** and then joining the road briefly at pretty **Huthwaite Green** (Map 74). Here, haul yourself up a steep, wooded climb onto **Live Moor**, duly noting the first appearance of a number of stone boundary markers along the wayside. Note that the first of these cairns is much more than a mere navigational aid for lost hikers; it is in fact a Bronze Age burial mound that's more than 4000 years old!

The path now drops slightly and then ascends to **Carlton Moor** (Map 75), with its gliding club. At the far end of the moor is a **trig point** and another boundary marker, from where you may see the North Sea beyond the industrial

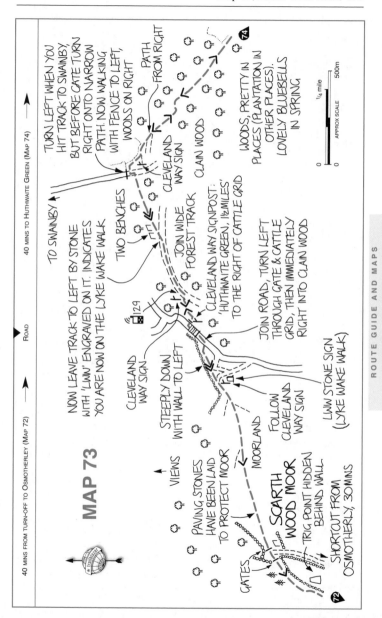

40 MINS FROM TURN-OFF TO OSMOTHERLEY (MAP 72) → ROAD → 40 MINS TO HUTHWAITE GREEN (MAP 74) →

MAP 73

TO SWAINBY

TURN LEFT WHEN YOU HIT TRACK TO SWAINBY, BUT BEFORE GATE TURN RIGHT ONTO NARROW PATH. NOW WALKING WITH FENCE TO LEFT, WOODS ON RIGHT

PATH FROM RIGHT

CLAIN WOOD

CLEVELAND WAY SIGN

NOW LEAVE TRACK TO LEFT BY STONE WITH 'LWW' ENGRAVED ON IT. INDICATES YOU ARE NOW ON THE LYKE WAKE WALK

TWO BENCHES

JOIN WIDE FOREST TRACK

129

CLEVELAND WAY SIGNPOST: 'HUTHWAITE GREEN, 1½MILES' TO THE RIGHT OF CATTLE GRID

CLEVELAND WAY SIGN

STEEPLY DOWN WITH WALL TO LEFT

JOIN ROAD, TURN LEFT THROUGH GATE & CATTLE GRID, THEN IMMEDIATELY RIGHT INTO CLAIN WOOD

FOLLOW CLEVELAND WAY SIGN

LWW STONE SIGN (LYKE WAKE WALK)

WOODS, PRETTY IN PLACES (PLANTATION IN OTHER PLACES). LOVELY BLUEBELLS IN SPRING

¼ mile

APPROX SCALE

500m

VIEWS

PAVING STONES HAVE BEEN LAID TO PROTECT MOOR

MOORLAND

SCARTH WOOD MOOR

TRIG POINT HIDDEN BEHIND WALL.

GATES

SHORTCUT FROM OSMOTHERLY, 30MINS

❑ THE LYKE WAKE WALK

The Lyke Wake Walk, which the Coast to Coast trail joins for part of the stretch across the moors, was the invention of one man. Local farmer and journalist Bill Cowley came up with the idea in 1955 when he claimed that, with the exception of one or two roads that run across the moors, one could walk the entire 40 miles over the North York Moors from east to west (or vice-versa) on **heather**.

Several walkers were keen to see if Mr Cowley was right, and it was agreed that the trail should start on Scarth Wood Moor, near Osmotherley, and finish in Ravenscar. To make the challenge tougher, the whole 40 miles had to be completed in 24 hours. The curious name comes from the Lyke Wake Dirge, possibly the oldest verse in the Yorkshire dialect and starts:

This yah neet, this yah neet,
Ivvery neet an' all,
Fire an' fleet an' cannle leet,
An' Christ tak up thy saul.

When thoo frae hence away art passed
Ivvery neet an' all,
Ti Whinny Moor thoo cums at last
An' Christ tak up thy saul.

'Lyke' was the local term for corpse and the song recounts the passage of the soul through the afterlife. Bill himself became the chief dirger and handed out black-edged cards to those who successfully completed the trail. There was also a Lyke Wake Club which he founded for those who completed the walk.

Unfortunately, the trail has suffered from hard times recently. Firstly, the popularity of the walk through the 1960s and 1970s, led to a fair amount of environmental damage. These days there are several different paths to choose from to limit the damage caused by the walkers. The death of Bill Cowley in 1994 dealt another blow to the trail and the demise of the original Lyke Wake Club in 2005 was a further setback. However, a New Lyke Wake Club (🖥 lykewake.org) has been set up to continue along much the same lines as the original organisation. See the website for details.

installations of Teeside, and where the path drops steeply around a quarry to a road. Crossing this and its adjacent stile, by a car park *Lordstones* (Map 76; ☎ 01642 778482, 🖥 lordstones.com; summer food daily 9am-3pm & Wed-Sat 5-7.45pm, winter subject to weather so check in advance; WI-FI) is well staged for a break. This is a busy hub serving both day- and dog-walkers who you'll meet and greet between here and Clay Bank Top. The **shop** is well stocked and includes a deli, and there's now a swanky **bar and restaurant** with outdoor seating, serving tea and coffee as well as food. There is a **utility block** with toilet and showers.

There are **camping** pitches (£25-40 per pitch but walkers can call to check; Apr-Oct; 🐾), as well as five furnished **glamping pods** (Mar-Dec; sleep up to 4; minimum 2-night stay in summer; from £85 per pod; 🐾) with a log burner and toilet & basin en suite. They also have bespoke timber-framed **roundhouses** (Mar-Dec; minimum 2-night stay in peak season; from £85 but no dogs and no running water) which sleep up to four people. Booking is recommended; contact Lordstones for further details.

ROUTE GUIDE AND MAPS

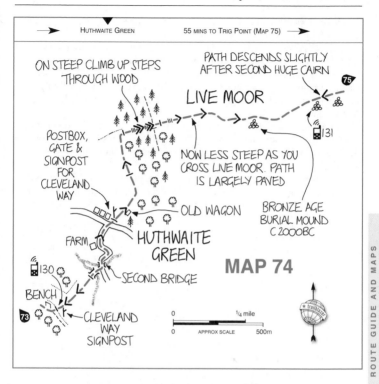

ROUTE GUIDE AND MAPS

Lordstones also offers two **drinking water taps** for passing hikers: one outside the utility block, the other on the near side of the shop.

From here, the cunning amongst you will have noticed that there is a **low-level path** that avoids all the steepness of the next few hours, all the way to Clay Bank Top. Take it if you must; the path is such that you can pretty much join it after every descent, allowing you to choose how many of the steep climbs to tackle, and circumnavigating any others.

But for those of you with an ounce of integrity (!) and who want to keep to Wainwright's path, another steep climb follows – this time up to **Cringle Moor**, with the superbly situated **Alec Falconer Memorial Seat** from where you can take in more views over the smokestacks of Teeside, the outlying cone of

---

❑ **IMPORTANT NOTE – WALKING TIMES**

All times in this book refer only to the time spent walking. You will need to add 20-30% to allow for rests, photography, checking the map, drinking water etc.

Roseberry Topping, and just ahead of it, an obelisk on Easby Moor commemorating locally born Captain James Cook.

Follow the bends south then east (towards and then away from the summit of Cringle Moor), skirt the cliffs of **Kirby Bank** and then tackle a steep descent. The rocky outcrop known as the **Wain Stones** (Map 77), and which resembles cake decorations, is clearly visible on top of the next moor, **Hasty Bank**. Note that it's safer to walk through, rather than around the stones (a favourite of Wainwright's).

If staying at Great Broughton or Beak Hills Farm (see p236) you may wish to divert from the path on the low-level signed trails (Maps 76 & 77) before the climb up to the stones as the road walk is said to be no fun at all. However, see box p230.

Otherwise, from the Wain Stones the path continues east to **Clay Bank Top** steeply dropping one more time to the B1257 and, for those staying in the nearby villages, a possible rendezvous with your hosts.

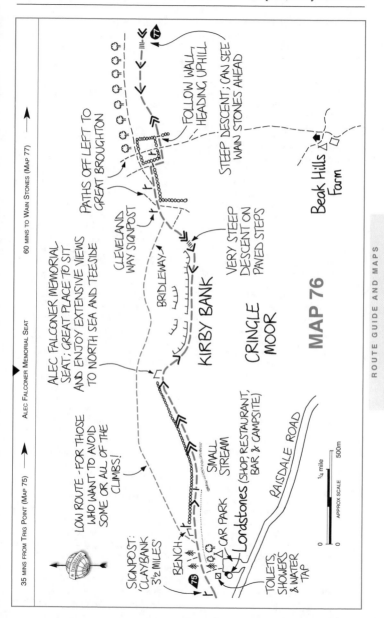

ALEC FALCONER MEMORIAL SEAT; GREAT PLACE TO SIT AND ENJOY EXTENSIVE VIEWS TO NORTH SEA AND TEESIDE

PATHS OFF LEFT TO GREAT BROUGHTON

FOLLOW WALL HEADING UPHILL

STEEP DESCENT; CAN SEE WAIN STONES AHEAD

CLEVELAND WAY SIGNPOST

BRIDLEWAY

KIRBY BANK

CRINGLE MOOR

VERY STEEP DESCENT ON PAVED STEPS

MAP 76

Beak Hills Farm

LOW ROUTE - FOR THOSE WHO WANT TO AVOID SOME OR ALL OF THE CLIMBS!

SIGNPOST: 'CLAYBANK 3½ MILES'

BENCH

CAR PARK

SMALL STREAM

Lordstones (SHOP RESTAURANT, BAR & CAMPSITE)

TOILETS, SHOWERS & WATER TAP

RAISDALE ROAD

¼ mile
APPROX SCALE
500m

NEAR CLAY BANK TOP   MAP 77
(Chop Gate, Great Broughton & Kirkby-in-Cleveland)

Half a mile from the trail if you leave it just after the descent from Kirby Bank and before the climb to Wain Stones (Maps 76 & 77), so cutting your day slightly short before reaching Clay Bank Top, you'll find Brian and Julie Cook at *Beak Hills Farm* (☎ 01642 778371, 💻 beakhillsfarm.co.uk; 1D or T/1Tr, shared facilities; WI-FI; ⓛ; 🐾). They also have a self-contained cottage (1T, shower facilities, basic kitchen), which they describe as a bothie, and which they use as an extra room. They offer **B&B** from £40pp (sgl occ £40) and an evening meal for £15. **Camping** is available for £5pp (inc toilet/shower facilities). If you're a solo-hiker you do not need to book to camp but it would be courteous to give them a call.

The nearest place to Clay Bank Top, where the B1257 bisects the Coast to Coast path, is **Urra** a mile to the south. However, at the time of research nowhere there was offering accommodation.

Chop Gate is three miles south of Clay Bank Top and not an enjoyable walk even if you can find the overgrown footpaths, but pick up is generally possible if you have booked. Moorsbus's seasonal M4 **bus** (May-Sep Sat, Sun & bank holiday Monday) calls at The Buck Inn; see pp54-6 for details.

The Buck Inn (☎ 01642 778334, 💻 the-buck-inn.co.uk; **fb**; 5D or T/1Tr, all en suite; WI-FI; ⓛ; 🐾) has rooms in the main building (B&B from £60pp, sgl occ £100) plus some **garden chalets** (B&B from £37.50pp, sgl occ room rate) with attached toilet and wash basin, and use of a separate shared shower block. **Camping** (up to two-man tents cost £15 per tent) is also available. Run by a German-British couple, we've had great reports from readers, about the beer and the **food** (summer daily 5-8pm, Sat & Sun 11am-3.30pm; winter Fri-Sat 10am-9pm, Sun to 8pm), both of which draw their influence from Germany and England. For B&B guests pick up from Clay Bank is complimentary but it costs £5 for campers.

Note that most accommodation options in Chop Gate, Great Broughton and Kirkby-in-Cleveland offer **free lifts** (for booked guests) from/to Clay Bank Top but these may only be during designated time periods so check when booking.

Great Broughton lies 2½ miles to the north of Clay Bank Top.

The Wainstones Hotel (☎ 01642 712268, 💻 wainstoneshotel.co.uk; 3S/14D/6T/1Tr, all en suite; ▾; WI-FI; ⓛ) offers **B&B** for £55-65pp (sgl/sgl occ from £89.50/99). **Food** is available in the Pembroke Bar (Mon-Sat noon-2pm & 5-8.30pm, Sun noon-8pm), which is open to non-residents. They also offer complimentary pick up and drop off to Clay Bank Top.

The walker-friendly *Bay Horse* (☎ 01642 712319, 💻 thebayhorse-great broughton.co.uk; **fb**; food Tue-Fri noon-2pm & 5.30-8.30pm, Sat noon-8.30pm, Sun noon-4.30pm; WI-FI), on the High St, serves very traditional north English **food**. Note that the pub is closed on Mondays.

Also, on High St is *The Jet Miners Inn* (☎ 01642 711377, 💻 thejetminers inn.co.uk; **fb**; food Wed-Sat noon-2pm & 5.30-9pm, Sun noon-2pm & 6-8.30pm; 🐾 on the outside terrace; WI-FI) where there's an array of hearty dishes to choose from. Booking ahead is advisable at both.

Abbotts (AofL) No 89 **bus** service stops here and also in Kirkby-in-Cleveland; see pp54-6. Just under a mile west of Great Broughton at **Kirkby-in-Cleveland** you could consider a night (or two) at *Meadowfields* (☎ 01642 712105, 💻 mead owfields.net; 1D private facilities; WI-FI; ⓛ; Hill Rd). **B&B** costs from £37.50pp (sgl occ room rate) and the owner can pick you up at any point between Osmotherley, Ingleby Arncliffe, and Clay Bank Top, meaning that, itinerary allowing, you could walk two stages of the path whilst spending two nights in the same accommodation. They will also book a table at a local pub for an evening meal and may be able to give you a lift to the nearest shop if

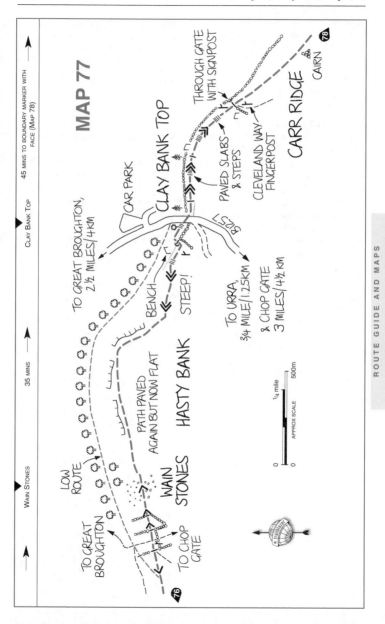

MAP 77

45 MINS TO BOUNDARY MARKER WITH FACE (MAP 78)

CLAY BANK TOP

35 MINS

WAIN STONES

CAR PARK

CLAY BANK TOP

THROUGH GATE WITH SIGNPOST

CARR RIDGE

CAIRN

PAVED SLABS & STEPS

CLEVELAND WAY FINGERPOST

TO GREAT BROUGHTON, 2½ MILES/4KM

B1257

BENCH

STEEP!

TO URRA, ¾ MILE/1.25KM & CHOP GATE 3 MILES/4½ KM

PATH PAVED AGAIN BUT NOW FLAT

HASTY BANK

LOW ROUTE

WAIN STONES

TO GREAT BROUGHTON

TO CHOP GATE

¼ mile

500m

APPROX SCALE

0

0

ROUTE GUIDE AND MAPS

required (a further two miles away in Stokesley). Note that there is another double room which can be let if there is a group of three or four people, but then the facilities are shared. The owner walked the Coast to Coast himself in 1974.

For a pub, 200 yards from the B&B, on Busby Lane, is *The Black Swan Inn* (☎ 01642 712512, 🖳 theblackswankirkby.co .uk; WI-FI; 🐾), which serves real ales and very reasonably priced standard pub **food** (Mon-Thur noon-2.30pm & 5-9pm, Fri & Sat noon-9pm, Sun noon-4pm), as well as a roast dinner on a Sunday.

From Clay Bank Top the Coast to Coast's penultimate climb is paved with steps and after 20 minutes the top of **Urra Moor** (Map 78) is reached where the gradient relents to what feels like nothing.

A wide track unrolls over the moor past a **trig point** near a **boundary marker with a hand carved on it** and after the **boundary marker with a face** carved onto it, you arrive at a junction of tracks (Map 79). It's here that the Cleveland Way breaks away to the north, while you continue on the wide track of the **former Rosedale Ironstone Railway** that used to serve the nearby iron mines over a century and a half ago. Passing above the head of pretty Farndale, renowned for its daffodils, the track curves round **High Blakey Moor** (Map 81) to your probable destination, the isolated Lion Inn (see below).

BLAKEY RIDGE   **MAP 81, p235**
For everybody, be they a walker or a motorist, Blakey Ridge *is Lion Inn* (☎ 01751 417320, 🖳 lionblakey.co.uk; 1T private bathroom, 8D/4Tr all en suite; 🛏;

WI-FI; Ⓛ; 🐾), the fourth highest inn in Britain (the highest, Tan Inn, lies near Keld) and one of the most charming on the route. The inn is nothing much to look at on the

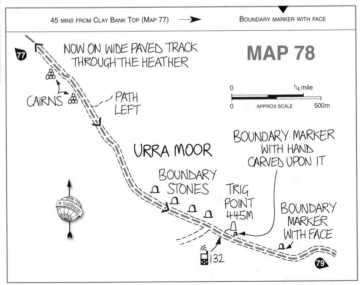

45 MINS FROM CLAY BANK TOP (MAP 77) ——→ BOUNDARY MARKER WITH FACE

MAP 78

NOW ON WIDE PAVED TRACK THROUGH THE HEATHER

CAIRNS PATH LEFT

0 ———— 1/4 mile
0 ———— APPROX SCALE ———— 500m

URRA MOOR

BOUNDARY MARKER WITH HAND CARVED UPON IT

BOUNDARY STONES

TRIG POINT 445M

BOUNDARY MARKER WITH FACE

132

77

79

trailblazer

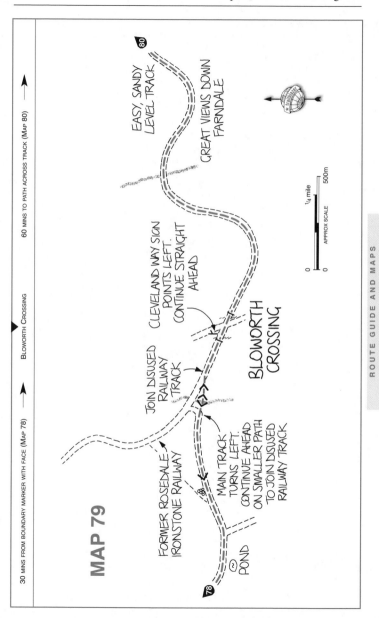

MAP 79

EASY, SANDY LEVEL TRACK

GREAT VIEWS DOWN FARNDALE

CLEVELAND WAY SIGN POINTS LEFT. CONTINUE STRAIGHT AHEAD

JOIN DISUSED RAILWAY TRACK

BLOWORTH CROSSING

MAIN TRACK TURNS LEFT. CONTINUE AHEAD ON SMALLER PATH TO JOIN DISUSED RAILWAY TRACK

FORMER ROSEDALE IRONSTONE RAILWAY

POND

APPROX SCALE

¼ mile

0   500m

80

78

ROUTE GUIDE AND MAPS

outside – largely thanks to the orange-coloured roof tiles – but inside, with its dark time-worn beams and open fires, it looks like the establishment it must have been nearly 500 years ago and is a great place to end the day. **B&B** rates are £27.50-62.50pp (sgl occ £30-110) depending in part on the size of the room – one of them

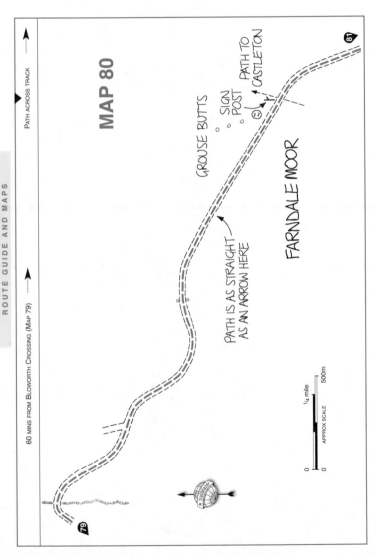

MAP 80

PATH ACROSS TRACK

60 MINS FROM BLOWORTH CROSSING (MAP 79)

79

PATH IS AS STRAIGHT AS AN ARROW HERE

GROUSE BUTTS

SIGN POST

PATH TO CASTLETON

80

FARNDALE MOOR

81

¼ mile

APPROX SCALE

0   500m

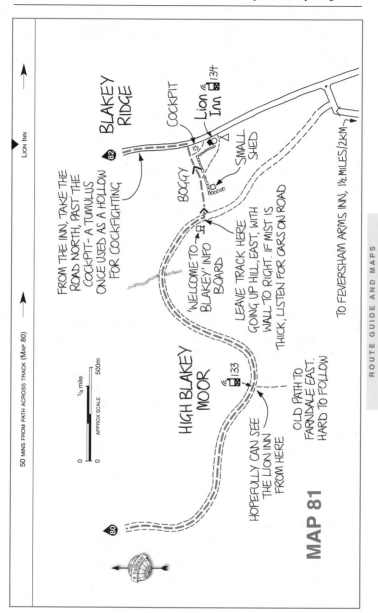

50 MINS FROM PATH ACROSS TRACK (MAP 80)

LION INN

FROM THE INN, TAKE THE ROAD NORTH, PAST THE COCKPIT - A TUMULUS ONCE USED AS A HOLLOW FOR COCKFIGHTING

BLAKEY RIDGE

COCKPIT

Lion Inn ⌂ ☐ 13+

82

BOGGY

SMALL SHED

"WELCOME TO BLAKEY INFO BOARD

LEAVE TRACK HERE GOING UP HILL, EAST, WITH WALL TO RIGHT. IF MIST IS THICK, LISTEN FOR CARS ON ROAD

HIGH BLAKEY MOOR

⌂ 133

¼ mile

500m

APPROX SCALE

0

0

HOPEFULLY CAN SEE THE LION INN FROM HERE

OLD PATH TO FARNDALE EAST. HARD TO FOLLOW

MAP 81

80

TO FEVERSHAM ARMS INN, 1½ MILES/2KM

is particularly tight for two sharing a twin; luckily, it's the twin with the private bathroom. The **food**, served at the bar and restaurant (daily noon-9pm; most mains £17.95), is tailor-made for walkers, being hearty, tasty, very traditional and warming on a cold night. And there's a fine selection of cask ales, as you'd expect from a remote Yorkshire pub. They now only let walkers **camp** (from £2.50pp) in the adjacent field and they prefer advance bookings. There is a bit of shelter offered by the dry-stone walls and showers/toilets are accessible when the pub's open. If requested the night before breakfast (£8.50) is available for campers too.

As Lion Inn is often booked up, readers have recommended an alternative. *Feversham Arms Inn* (☎ 01751 433206, 🖳 fevershamarmsinn.co.uk; **fb**; 1D/2D or T/ cottage for up to four, all en suite; 🛏; WI-FI;

(Ⓛ; 🍴) in **Church Houses**, down the hill in Farndale Valley, can be reached by heading south away from Lion Inn along the road, taking the first right (west) down Blakey Bank and Long Lane for about 1½ miles. B&B costs £40-47.50pp (sgl occ from £60); the cottage (self-catering, but the rate can include breakfast) costs from £85 to £105 for two sharing. The **food** (summer generally Mon-Sat noon-2pm & 6-9pm, Sun noon-7pm, winter days/hours vary so check in advance) is excellent and the owner will drive walkers back up the hill in the morning if convenient; or they can arrange a taxi.

Moorbus's seasonal and limited M3 **bus** service stops at The Lion Inn and the M6 at Ralph Cross (1½ miles from the Lion Inn but some of that is on the path); see pp54-6.

STAGE 12: BLAKEY RIDGE TO GROSMONT   MAPS 81-87

Introduction

For those who enjoy cosy English villages hidden amongst the gentlest, most bucolic scenery this fine country has to offer, the **13½-mile (22km, 5hr)** stroll down the **Esk Valley** to Glaisdale and on to Grosmont may be the best section of this walk. For charm, only the lakeland villages of Borrowdale and Grasmere come close to matching Egton Bridge and Grosmont, and it comes as no surprise that the nostalgic '60s village bobby TV show, *Heartbeat*, was filmed nearby. As a final destination on this stage, either Egton Bridge or Grosmont will do nicely. But first you have to get to the valley and that means getting down off the moors.

The route

The walk begins by following the tarmac north towards **Young Ralph Cross** (off Map 82), which just pokes its head over the horizon as you turn off right onto another road, this one signposted to Rosedale Abbey. *(cont'd on p241)*

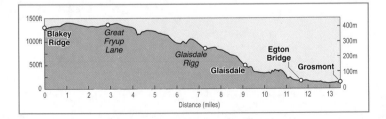

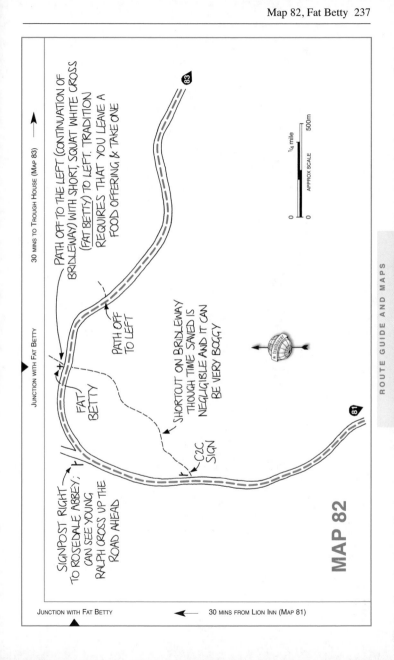

JUNCTION WITH FAT BETTY

30 MINS TO TROUGH HOUSE (Map 83) ➔

PATH OFF TO THE LEFT (CONTINUATION OF BRIDLEWAY) WITH SHORT, SQUAT WHITE CROSS (*FAT BETTY*) TO LEFT. TRADITION REQUIRES THAT YOU LEAVE A FOOD OFFERING, & TAKE ONE

PATH OFF TO LEFT

FAT BETTY

SHORTCUT ON BRIDLEWAY THOUGH TIME SAVED IS NEGLIGIBLE AND IT CAN BE VERY BOGGY

C2C SIGN

SIGNPOST RIGHT TO ROSEDALE ABBEY; CAN SEE YOUNG RALPH CROSS UP THE ROAD AHEAD

¼ mile

APPROX SCALE

500m

MAP 82

JUNCTION WITH FAT BETTY

30 MINS FROM LION INN (Map 81)

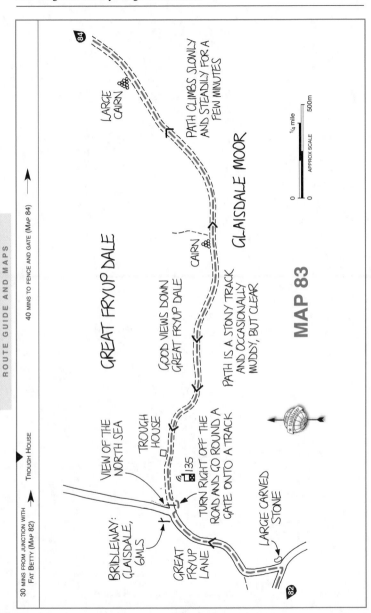

30 MINS FROM JUNCTION WITH FAT BETTY (MAP 82) ➤ TROUGH HOUSE ➤ 40 MINS TO FENCE AND GATE (MAP 84) ➤

MAP 83

GREAT FRYUP DALE

GLAISDALE MOOR

LARGE CAIRN

PATH CLIMBS SLOWLY AND STEADILY FOR A FEW MINUTES

CAIRN

GOOD VIEWS DOWN GREAT FRYUP DALE

PATH IS A STONY TRACK AND OCCASIONALLY MUDDY, BUT CLEAR

VIEW OF THE NORTH SEA

TROUGH HOUSE

135

TURN RIGHT OFF THE ROAD AND GO ROUND A GATE ONTO A TRACK

BRIDLEWAY: GLAISDALE, 6MLS

GREAT FRYUP LANE

LARGE CARVED STONE

0 ¼ mile
0 500m
APPROX SCALE

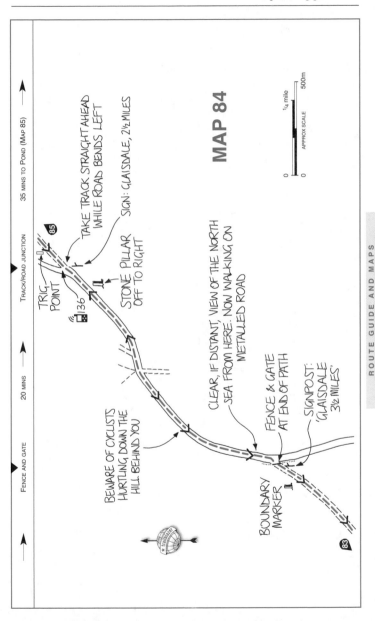

MAP 84

FENCE AND GATE

20 MINS

TRACK/ROAD JUNCTION

35 MINS TO POND (MAP 85)

TAKE TRACK STRAIGHT AHEAD WHILE ROAD BENDS LEFT

SIGN: GLAISDALE, 2½ MILES

TRIG POINT

136

STONE PILLAR OFF TO RIGHT

CLEAR, IF DISTANT, VIEW OF THE NORTH SEA FROM HERE. NOW WALKING ON METALLED ROAD

BEWARE OF CYCLISTS HURTLING DOWN THE HILL BEHIND YOU

FENCE & GATE AT END OF PATH

SIGNPOST: 'GLAISDALE 3½ MILES'

BOUNDARY MARKER

0   ¼ mile

0   500m

APPROX SCALE

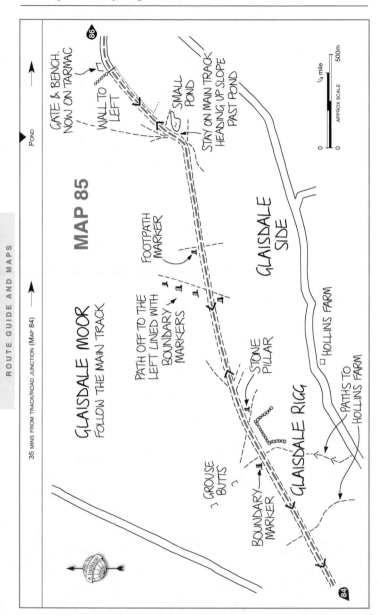

ROUTE GUIDE AND MAPS

35 MINS FROM TRACK/ROAD JUNCTION (MAP 84)

POND

MAP 85

GLAISDALE MOOR
FOLLOW THE MAIN TRACK

GATE & BENCH.
NOW ON TARMAC

WALL TO LEFT

SMALL POND

STAY ON MAIN TRACK
HEADING UP SLOPE
PAST POND

FOOTPATH MARKER

GLAISDALE SIDE

PATH OFF TO THE
LEFT LINED WITH
BOUNDARY
MARKERS

STONE PILLAR

HOLLINS FARM

GROUSE BUTTS

BOUNDARY MARKER

GLAISDALE RIGG

PATHS TO HOLLINS FARM

APPROX SCALE

0   ¼ mile

0   500m

(cont'd from p236) Soon you pass the stumpy white landmark known as **Fat Betty**, off the path to the left, where tradition requires you both take and leave a snack or a sweet (though some walkers have written to tell us that they found nothing when they arrived). Perhaps suitably revived, you then turn north-east into the wonderfully named **Great Fryup Lane** (Map 83, where one suspects Betty spent too much time) and leave the road to pass **Trough House**. The path can clearly be made out continuing eastwards round the southern side of **Great Fryup Dale** until the end of **Glaisdale Moor** where, on rejoining the road, the North Sea ought to be obvious at the far end of the valley, if you're not enveloped in moorland mist, that is.

After a mile of road walking, Coast-to-Coasters take to the track along **Glaisdale Rigg** (Map 85) past various standing stones, and a particularly well-hewn **boundary marker** to the left of the path. Continue on down to a junction near a small pond. Descend through farmland to the houses of **Glaisdale**.

GLAISDALE   MAP 86, p243

Ten miles (16km) from Blakey, the village of Glaisdale sprawls across its lofty perch above the Esk Valley.

The terraced houses that are a feature of the town were originally built for the workers in the ironstone mines of the late 19th century. Today **Robinson Institute** is a village hall that also acts as a small theatre. The late 18th-century **Church of St Thomas the Apostle**, near the upper end of Glaisdale, is notable for its 16th-century wooden font cover and communion table. (Don't be fooled by the '1585' date stone in the side of the steps leading to the tower, it's from an earlier chapel.) The church also contains a picture of Thomas Ferris, the beggar made famous in Glaisdale's other main sight, **Beggar's Bridge** at the other end of the village. In the 17th century, Ferris, a humble pauper, was courting the daughter of the wealthy local squire. In order to win her hand Ferris thought he needed to improve his standing in the community so with this in mind he struck upon a plan to set sail from Whitby and seek his fortune on the high seas. The night before he put this plan into action, Ferris went to visit his beloved who lived across the river. Unfortunately, the river was swollen by heavy rains and Ferris's dreams of a romantic farewell were dashed. The story, however, does have a happy ending: Thomas returned from his adventures on the sea a wealthy man and married his sweetheart,

and with part of his fortune built the Beggar's Bridge so that other young lovers from the neighbourhood would not suffer the same torment as he had that stormy night.

Housed in a private home on the road towards Beggar's Bridge is the quirky **Museum of Victorian Science** (☎ 01947 897440, 🖳 museumofvictorianscience.co .uk), which contains a geeky yet spellbinding collection of scientific instruments from a long-forgotten era. Visits are by guided tour only (Thur-Tue 1/day 10.30am or 2.30pm; approx 2hrs; £20pp inc tea break), and must be booked in advance by calling in the evening. Under 16s aren't allowed to visit.

Services

Glaisdale's village **shop** (Mon-Tue & Thur-Fri 8am-5.30pm, Wed & Sat 8am-12.30pm, Sun 9am-noon) is also home to the **post office** (Mon-Sat 8am-1.30pm, Sun 9am-noon).

Arriva's **bus** No 95 (Mon-Sat) travels up and down the Esk Valley from Lealholm to Whitby (see pp54-6).

Glaisdale is a stop on Esk Valley Railway; **train** services are operated by Northern (see box p52).

Where to stay and eat

Right by the path, *Greenhowe B&B* (☎ 01947 897217, 🖳 greenhowe.co.uk; 1S/1D

ROUTE GUIDE AND MAPS

shared facilities, 1Qd en suite; ☞; WI-FI; Ⓛ) charges from £48pp (inc for sgl/sgl occ) for B&B and offers two-course evening meals (£22) subject to 24hrs' notice.

Down near the railway station *Arncliffe Arms* (☎ 01947 897555, 🖳 arn cliffepubglaisdale.co.uk; 2S/2D/2T/1Tr, all en suite; WI-FI; Ⓛ; 🐾) charges from £50pp (sgl £70, sgl occ room rate). One of the doubles is in a self-contained annexe and has a bunk bed so can also sleep up to two children. They also lay on **food** (Apr-end Oct Mon-Fri 6-8pm, Sat & Sun noon-8.30pm, Nov-Mar Mon-Fri 6-8pm, Sat & Sun as for main season). They serve tea, coffee, sandwiches & cakes (summer noon-6pm), accept credit cards and have drying facilities. In winter during the week the pub is only open from 6pm onwards.

Half a mile from the village centre is the award-winning 17th-century *Red House Farm* (☎ 01947 897242, 🖳 red housefarm.com; 2D/1D or T, all en suite; ☞; WI-FI; Ⓛ if requested 24hrs in advance). Once a working farm and still the home of a few farm animals, it's been tastefully converted to retain many of the original features

to the point where it would be a shame to spend only one night here. B&B costs from £100pp for a single-night stay but £130pp for two nights (sgl occ room rate). For an extra £10pp you can use the indoor swimming pool, gym and steam room in the Red Farm Health Club. Note they don't offer evening meals.

At the very end of the village just across the tracks from the railway station is *Beggar's Bridge B&B* (☎ 01947 897409, 🖳 beggarsbridge.co.uk; 2D, both en suite; WI-FI; Ⓛ; Apr-end Sep), close to the lovelorn bridge. Rates are from £50pp (sgl occ £65).

Bev and Bob's Brew (☎ 01947 897842; **fb**; Easter-end Sep/early Oct Thur-Sat 10am-4pm, Sun till 3pm; WI-FI; 🐾), at Underhill Cottage, is an organic tea garden, aimed mostly for walkers. Most of the menu is home-made from bread to jams and pickles, soup, cakes and scones, and drinks. They have an honesty box (donations go to local organisations) for anyone who just wants to walk round the two-acre garden and they may allow people to have picnics there.

From Glaisdale you enter **East Arncliffe Wood**, walking along the river until the path winds up at a road where a left turn leads down the hill and into **Egton Bridge**.

EGTON BRIDGE   MAP 87, p245

A strong competitor for the accolade of prettiest village on the Coast to Coast, Egton Bridge is a delight; a hamlet of grand houses surrounding an uninhabited island on the

Esk. Everything about the place is charming, from the bridge itself – a 1990s' copy of the original 18th-century structure washed away in a flood in 1930 – to the

---

❏ ST HEDDA

The 7th-century British saint, Hedda, crops up a few times on the Coast to Coast walk, even though he is these days more closely associated with Winchester, Hampshire. He began his episcopal career at Whitby Abbey (whose striking remains you may have spied from Glaisdale Moor), where he was educated and rose to become abbot.

His big break came in AD676 when he was consecrated as the Bishop of Wessex by St Theodore of Tarsus, at that time the Archbishop of Canterbury. He ruled over the diocese for 30 years, during which time he moved the see (the area of ecclesiastical jurisdiction) from Dorchester to Winchester and became chief advisor to King Ina. Described by the Venerable Bede as 'a good and just man, who in carrying out his duties was guided rather by an inborn love of virtue than by what he had read in books', he died in AD705 and is buried at Winchester Cathedral.

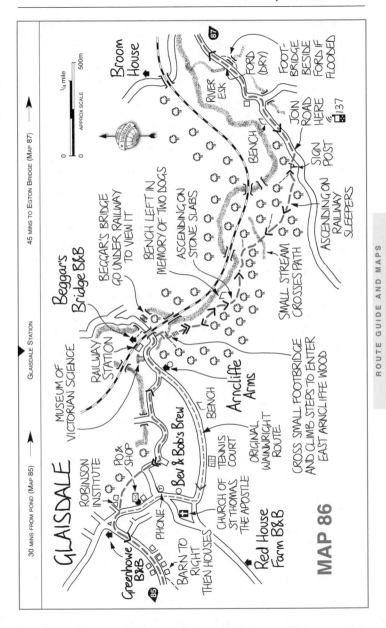

GLAISDALE

Beggar's Bridge B&B

Broom House

MUSEUM OF VICTORIAN SCIENCE

ROBINSON INSTITUTE

PO & SHOP

Bev & Bob's Brew

RAILWAY STATION

Arncliffe Arms

Greenhowe B&B

PHONE

BARN TO RIGHT THEN HOUSES

TENNIS COURT

CHURCH OF ST THOMAS THE APOSTLE

Red House Farm B&B

BENCH

ORIGINAL WAINWRIGHT ROUTE

CROSS SMALL FOOTBRIDGE AND CLIMB STEPS TO ENTER EAST ARNCLIFFE WOOD

MAP 86

BEGGAR'S BRIDGE GO UNDER RAILWAY TO VIEW IT

BENCH LEFT IN MEMORY OF TWO DOGS

ASCENDING ON STONE SLABS

SMALL STREAM CROSSES PATH

ASCENDING ON RAILWAY SLEEPERS

BENCH

SIGN POST

JOIN ROAD HERE

RIVER ESK

FORD (DRY)

FOOT-BRIDGE BESIDE FORD IF FLOODED

¼ mile

500m

0

APPROX SCALE

ROUTE GUIDE AND MAPS

stepping stones that lead across to the island and the mature trees that fringe the settlement. The Catholic **St Hedda's Church**, too, is incredibly grand given the tiny size of Egton Bridge. On the exterior are a series of friezes while inside, behind glass to the right of the altar, are the relics of Nicholas Postgate, a local Catholic priest and martyr hung, drawn and quartered for continuing to practise his faith in 1679. See the box on p242 for details about St Hedda himself.

Services

There are public **toilets** and a public **telephone** in the centre of Egton Bridge.

Egton Bridge is a stop on the Esk Valley Railway; **train** services are operated by Northern (see box p52). Arriva's **bus** No 95 also travels up and down the Esk Valley (see pp54-6).

Where to stay and eat

It would be a surprise indeed if somewhere like Egton Bridge didn't have decent accommodation, and the village doesn't disappoint. *The Horseshoe Hotel* (☎ 01947 895245, ☐ thehorseshoehotel.co.uk; 4D/2T, all en suite; ✆; WI-FI; ①; ♣), right on the walk at the start of the village, fulfils every expectation of a country inn, with an expansive beer garden, a lavish array of local ales and a snug interior. **B&B** costs £40-60pp (sgl occ approx £85). **Food** (generally

Mon-Sat noon-3pm & 6-8.30pm, Sun noon-8.30pm) is served; main courses cost £15-25, and there's also a **farm shop** (daily 10am-4pm) selling light snacks.

A little way to the west of the village, *Broom House* (Map 86; ☎ 01947 895279, ☐ broom-house.co.uk; 1T/3D, 3D in suites, all en suite; ✆; WI-FI; ①; Mar-Nov) is a 19th-century farmhouse described by one reader as more of a country house hotel with a touch of class; the suites have sitting areas and there is a guest lounge with an honesty bar. They charge £57.50-75pp (sgl occ room rate) for B&B but there is a two-night minimum stay policy.

Postgate Inn (☎ 01947 895241, ☐ postgateinn.com; 3D, all en suite; ✆; WI-FI; ①; ♣), aka 'The Black Dog' in the British television series *Heartbeat*, is another top choice with **food** served daily (light lunches noon-2.30pm, meals 6.30-8.30pm; booking advised), and **B&B** costing from £47.50pp (sgl occ room rate). They don't accept advance bookings for a single-night stay in the peak season or at the weekend year-round but it is always worth contacting them to check availability.

On Broom House Lane by the banks of the Esk, and next to the village's famous stepping stones, is *The Old Mill* (☎ 01947 895351, ☐ theoldmillegtonbridge.com; 1D/1T/1Tr all en suite, 1T with private bathroom; ✆; WI-FI; ①; Apr-late Oct). B&B costs £40-65pp (sgl occ £70-120).

The next mile or so from Egton Bridge to Grosmont takes you past the elegant **Egton Manor** along an old toll road (the original toll charges are still written on a board hanging from **Toll Cottage**, halfway along).

It's an easy walk now, taking you under the railway and along the River Esk and into **Grosmont**.

GROSMONT   MAP 87

After the quaint, picture-perfect settlements of the preceding few miles, Grosmont emerges as a grittier and more distinctive sibling. Indeed literally so as from the rail crossing in the village centre, a row of soot-stained terraces claw their way up the hill, caked by the acrid fumes that once belched from three ironstone smelting furnaces 150 years ago.

These days this less glamorous heritage is all but forgotten as tourists and steam rail enthusiasts alike flock to ride the locomotives of **North York Moors Railway** (☎ 01751 472508, ☐ nymr.co.uk). Featured as the 'Hogwarts Express' in the original *Harry Potter* movie, it's definitely worth hanging about to see at least one loco in motion before leaving Grosmont.

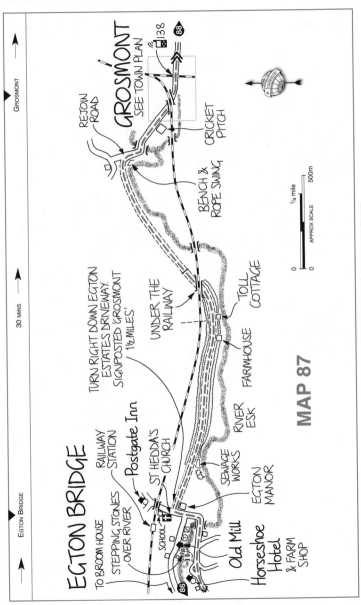

EGTON BRIDGE

← EGTON BRIDGE   30 MINS →   ► GROSMONT

TO BROOM HOUSE

STEPPING STONES OVER RIVER

RAILWAY STATION

Postgate Inn

St HEDDA'S CHURCH

SCHOOL

Old Mill

Horseshoe Hotel & FARM SHOP

86

SEWAGE WORKS

ECTON MANOR

RIVER ESK

FARMHOUSE

TOLL COTTAGE

UNDER THE RAILWAY

TURN RIGHT DOWN EGTON ESTATES DRIVEWAY. SIGNPOSTED GROSMONT 1½ MILES'

BENCH & ROPE SWING

CRICKET PITCH

REJOIN ROAD

GROSMONT
SEE TOWN PLAN

138
88

MAP 87

¼ mile
0   500m
0   APPROX SCALE

Better still, why not try timing your arrival so that you can take a return ride to Pickering or Whitby? By now you deserve to take the weight off your feet. Trains to Pickering (70-75 mins), or Whitby (25-30 mins) leave Grosmont 4-8 times a day; some are drawn by a diesel rather than a steam engine, so if you want that authentic chuff-chuff sound check the timetable (see the website for full details).

While you're waiting, follow the alleyway leading through a long train tunnel to the **sidings and loco sheds** to gain an insight into what it takes to keep these engines on track. The tunnel is thought to be the oldest passenger train tunnel in the world, hewn out around 1829 to serve a horse-drawn railway designed by none other than George Stephenson. Regarded as the 'Father of Railways', it was Stephenson who foresaw a future in a network of interlinked rail lines along which engines powered by steam would go on to span and help consolidate the riches of the British Empire. During the tunnel excavations viable quantities of iron ore were unearthed, leading to the ironstone-mining boom along the Esk Valley.

There's a **church**, too, with a boulder of Shap granite outside the west door, deposited here by a glacier which lost its way back in the Ice Age.

The settlement, originally known as 'Tunnel', went on to gain the name Grosmont and is today a one-street village where both modern and heritage railway lines intersect, and which has all the essentials a weary trekker needs.

Services
Grosmont Co-operative Society (🖳 grosmontcoop.co.uk; **fb**; Mon-Fri 7.30am-5.30pm, Sat 8am-5.30pm, Sun & bank holidays 9am-5pm) claims to be the oldest independent Co-op in the country having been in business here for over 150 years! The modestly stocked **shop** is also home to the **post office** (Mon-Fri 9am-noon) where you can **withdraw cash** with most UK bank cards.

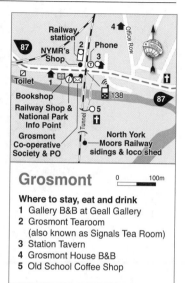

Grosmont

0   100m

Where to stay, eat and drink
1 Gallery B&B at Geall Gallery
2 Grosmont Tearoom
   (also known as Signals Tea Room)
3 Station Tavern
4 Grosmont House B&B
5 Old School Coffee Shop

Transport
Grosmont is a stop on Northern Rail's Esk Valley Railway line; **trains** go to Whitby (20-25 mins) and to Middlesbrough (70 mins); see box p52 for more details. See also North York Moors Railway (p244).

Arriva's **bus** No 95 also travels up and down the Esk Valley; Whitby is 30 minutes from here (see pp54-6).

Where to stay and eat
In high season if there's some sort of railway event happening, accommodation in Grosmont can be scarce. One option is to catch the train to Whitby and stay there.

B&B is on offer at *Gallery B&B* (☎ 01947 895007, 🖳 chrisgeall.com/gallery-b-b; 1D/3D or T, all en suite, 1D private bathroom; ☞; WI-FI; Ⓛ), part of **Geall Gallery**, on Front St, the village's main drag. The comfortable rooms (from £57.50pp, sgl occ £95) are decorated with atmospheric artwork from the gallery downstairs.

Station Tavern (☎ 01947 895060; **fb**; 2D/1T, all en suite; ☞, WI-FI; 🐾) does

B&B for £50-60pp (sgl occ room rate) and serves **pub grub** (summer Mon-Sat noon-3pm & 5-8pm, Sun noon-6.45pm, winter Wed-Sat & Sun only); if guests are staying on Monday or Tuesday in the winter they will do a meal for them. As it's pretty much the only place in Grosmont where you can eat in the evening, you'll almost certainly meet your fellow Coast to Coasters here.

Further on, *Grosmont House* (☎ 01947 895699, 🖥 grosmonthouse.co.uk; 1S/3D/2T, all en suite; WI-FI; late Mar/early Apr-end Oct) is a delightful old place and the gardens have wonderful views down over the railway. Rates are £47.50-62.50pp (sgl occ room rate), but they often require a two-night minimum stay at weekends. They also have a self-contained flat (1D; ☛; from £125 per night, sgl occ room rate) with self-

catering facilities; breakfast (£13pp) may be available but it is essential to request in advance. Note that the flat is generally only let out for a minimum of three nights.

Grosmont boasts two excellent **tearooms**. The lovely *Old School Coffee Shop* (☎ 01947 895758, 🖥 grosmontcoffee shop.co.uk; call or check online for up-to-date opening times; 🐾) was formerly the village primary school and has a great view of the steam railway. They welcome walkers, don't mind muddy boots and offer a flask-filling service for a small donation to the RNLI. In July and August they serve pizzas on a Friday and Monday evening.

There's also *Grosmont Tea room* (also known as *Signals Tea Room* (early Apr-end Oct daily 9am-4.30pm; 🐾 garden area only) on the railway platform.

STAGE 13: GROSMONT TO ROBIN HOOD'S BAY   MAPS 87-95

Introduction
Time to saddle up for the last stage, but don't be fooled into thinking this is a mere formality – as the savage climb out of Grosmont will soon demonstrate. It's a long stretch totalling **15½ miles (25km, 6hrs)** with enough ups and downs, and boot-squelching bogs, to ensure that you arrive in Robin Hood's Bay suitably dishevelled. The scenery is largely similar to what's gone before: desolate moorland punctuated with short road stages and, in a superior echo of the first leg, a grand finale along the sea cliffs prior to the final descent to the Bay. The most pleasant surprise, especially on a hot day, is the transit of Little Beck Wood, a narrow belt of the most heavenly woodland in North Yorkshire.

The route
First, there's that calf-popping 700ft (230m) climb up to **Sleights Moor** (Map 88), part of the intriguingly named Eskdaleside Cum Ugglebarnby, which is how you may feel if you missed breakfast. Be careful as finding the route out of Grosmont can be confusing. With views north-east to the well-ventilated ruins of Whitby Abbey or back down into misty Eskdale, you pass the **High Bride Stones** – five ancient standing monoliths – to the right of the road.

(cont'd on p250)

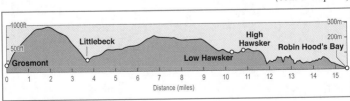

ROUTE GUIDE AND MAPS

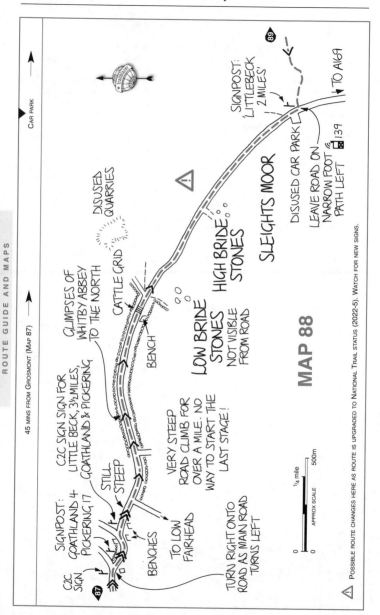

45 MINS FROM GROSMONT (MAP 87) ➤

CAR PARK ▶

C2C SIGN

SIGNPOST: GOATHLAND 4 PICKERING 17

BENCHES

TURN RIGHT ONTO MAIN ROAD AS MAIN ROAD TURNS LEFT

TO LOW FAIRHEAD

STILL STEEP

C2C SIGN SIGN FOR LITTLE BECK, 3½ MILES, GOATHLAND & PICKERING

VERY STEEP ROAD CLIMB FOR OVER A MILE. NO WAY TO START THE LAST STAGE!

GLIMPSES OF WHITBY ABBEY TO THE NORTH

BENCH

CATTLE GRID

DISUSED QUARRIES

LOW BRIDE STONES NOT VISIBLE FROM ROAD

HIGH BRIDE STONES

SLEIGHTS MOOR

MAP 88

DISUSED CAR PARK

LEAVE ROAD ON NARROW FOOT PATH LEFT 🏠 139

SIGNPOST: 'LITTLEBECK 2 MILES'

TO A169

89

0   ¼ mile
0   500m
APPROX SCALE

⚠ POSSIBLE ROUTE CHANGES HERE AS ROUTE IS UPGRADED TO NATIONAL TRAIL STATUS (2022-5). WATCH FOR NEW SIGNS.

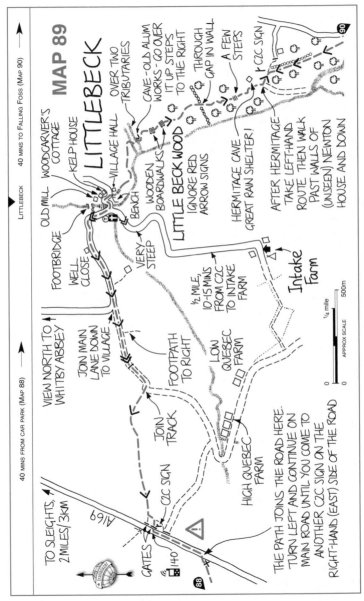

40 MINS FROM CAR PARK (MAP 88) ——— LITTLEBECK ——— 40 MINS TO FALLING FOSS (MAP 90)

MAP 89

LITTLEBECK

VIEW NORTH TO WHITBY ABBEY

WOODCARVER'S COTTAGE

KELP HOUSE

VILLAGE HALL

OVER TWO TRIBUTARIES

CAVE—OLD ALUM WORKS—GO OVER IT UP STEPS TO THE RIGHT

THROUGH GAP IN WALL

A FEW STEPS

C2C SIGN

90

OLD MILL

FOOTBRIDGE

WELL CLOSE

JOIN MAIN LANE DOWN TO VILLAGE

BENCH

WOODEN BOARDWALKS

VERY STEEP

LITTLE BECK WOOD

IGNORE RED ARROW SIGNS

HERMITAGE CAVE GREAT RAIN SHELTER!

AFTER HERMITAGE TAKE LEFT-HAND ROUTE PAST WALLS OF (UNSEEN) NEWTON HOUSE AND DOWN

FOOTPATH TO RIGHT

½ MILE, 10-15 MINS FROM C2C TO INTAKE FARM

Intake Farm

JOIN TRACK

LOW QUEBEC FARM

¼ mile

0   500m

APPROX SCALE

0

HIGH QUEBEC FARM

C2C SIGN

TO SLEIGHTS, 2 MILES/ 3KM

A169

GATES

1:40

88

THE PATH JOINS THE ROAD HERE. TURN LEFT AND CONTINUE ON MAIN ROAD UNTIL YOU COME TO ANOTHER C2C SIGN ON THE RIGHT-HAND (EAST) SIDE OF THE ROAD *(cont'd from p247)* (Incidentally, the confusing jumble of the Low Bride Stones stands just below them on a terrace, to your right as you pass over the cattle grid.) Opposite a disused car park turn left onto a path (WPT 139) and cut a corner down to the A169 where you turn left again along the road (Map 89) for a few hundred metres until a Coast to Coast sign heralds the path dropping down through more heather to **Littlebeck**.

LITTLEBECK   MAP 89, p249

Littlebeck is another tiny village with a lengthy past; it's hard to imagine today's picturesque rural idyll was actually once a centre of alum mining in the 17th to 19th centuries. Alum, by the way, is used in dyeing as well as tanning leather. A hundred tons of shale would be produced in order to extract just one ton of alum, so it seems remarkable the surrounding land appears so unscarred.

Littlebeck has one other minor claim to fame as the home of master woodcarver Thomas Whittaker who died in 1991. His house, now called **Woodcarver's Cottage**, is on the bend above the **Old Mill**, though it can't be visited. Whittaker exclusively used English oak and would 'sign' every piece of his furniture with a gnome; in German folklore the oak tree's guardian. Above the cottage is **Kelp House**, where kelp, used in the processing of alum, would have been stored.

Fifteen minutes south of the village and half a mile from the path, is the wonderfully welcoming *Intake Farm* (☎ 01947 810273, 🖳 intakefarm.com; 1D en suite, 1D/1T/1Tr private facilities; ✒; WI-FI; Ⓛ; 🐾), an ideal place to stay for those who want to spin out the last day into an easy 12-miler. **B&B** costs from £45pp (sgl occ £60), and it costs from £8pp (inc shower) to **camp**. It's some distance to the nearest pub but they'll happily lay on an excellent homecooked evening meal (£18), for campers as well, if booked in advance. Breakfast for campers costs £8. We consider it one of the better B&Bs along the trail. Whilst you can reach the farm from the centre of the village, it's quicker to join the track to the right (south) of the Coast to Coast path heading off the A169 via both High Quebec Farm and Low Quebec Farm, though the last section through the farmland can be boggy.

Pretty as Littlebeck is, it's nothing when compared to the beauty that awaits in **Little Beck Wood**. This really is a stunning 65 acres of woodland, filled with oak trees, deer, badgers, foxes and birdlife galore. There are also a couple of man-made features to see on the way including the mysterious **Hermitage** (Map 89), a boulder hollowed out to form a small cave; ideal for an emergency bivvy shelter. Above the entrance is etched the year '1790'.

More delights await as the path from the Hermitage leads you down to **Falling Foss** (Map 90), a 20m-high waterfall alongside the remains of Midge Hall, a former gamekeeper's cottage now enterprisingly converted into *Falling Foss Tea Garden* (☎ 07723 477929, 🖳 fallingfossteagarden.co.uk; Easter-end Sep daily 10am-4pm; 🐾). It's a great place for a coffee and cake, an ice-cream or a light lunch before you leave the woods for the final hike to the sea.

Suitably refreshed, head along **May Beck** to the car park at the southern extremity of the wood. Here you turn back north and walk along the road, looking back over the valley you've just walked through and the moors beyond. A traverse of two other moors, **Sneaton Low Moor** and the innocuously named Graystone Hills, follows. The former is now fairly easy to negotiate, the diversion

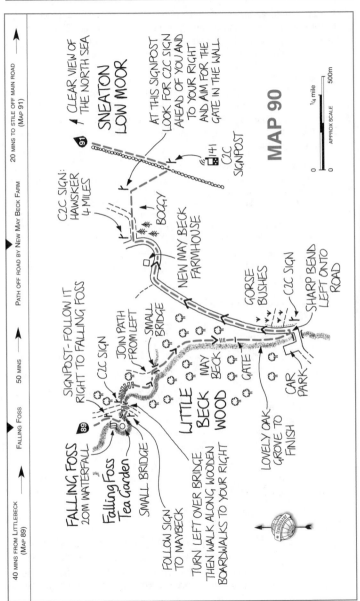

CLEAR VIEW OF THE NORTH SEA

SNEATON LOW MOOR

AT THIS SIGNPOST LOOK FOR C2C SIGN AHEAD OF YOU AND TO YOUR RIGHT AND AIM FOR THE GATE IN THE WALL

C2C SIGNPOST

MAP 90

¼ mile

APPROX SCALE

C2C SIGN: HAWSKER 4 MILES

BOGGY

NEW MAY BECK FARMHOUSE

SIGNPOST - FOLLOW IT RIGHT TO FALLING FOSS

C2C SIGN

JOIN PATH FROM LEFT

SMALL BRIDGE

GORSE BUSHES

C2C SIGN

SHARP BEND LEFT ONTO ROAD

FALLING FOSS 20M WATERFALL

Falling Foss Tea Garden

SMALL BRIDGE

LITTLE BECK WOOD

MAY BECK

GATE

CAR PARK

FOLLOW SIGN TO MAYBECK

TURN LEFT OVER BRIDGE THEN WALK ALONG WOODEN BOARDWALKS TO YOUR RIGHT

LOVELY OAK GROVE TO FINISH

ROUTE GUIDE AND MAPS

that's been introduced for once helping rather than hindering navigation, though the rather lean waymarks and confusing paths across **Graystone Hills** (Map 91) to **Normanby Hill Top** (Map 92; west of the A171) can require a good sense of direction or some luck, even in bright sunshine; see box p92. Both moors are extremely boggy in places.

All being well, you'll eventually emerge on a road and should turn left here. Continue down the road where before long you will no doubt be thrilled to spot the first road sign to Robin Hood's Bay indicating it's only '3½ miles' by road. But for you, my friend, the walk is not over; turn right to follow Back Lane past York House Caravan Park (Map 93) and into the village of **High Hawsker** on the A171 Whitby road.

HIGH HAWSKER　　　MAP 93, p254

In the village the *Hare & Hounds* (☎ 01947 880453, 🖳 hareandhoundshaws ker.co.uk; **fb**; **food** Mon-Thur noon-2.30pm & 5-9pm, Fri-Sat noon-9pm, Sun noon-5pm; WI-FI; 🐕) serves hot meals as well as sandwiches. Note, the pub closes

between 3pm and 5pm Monday to Thursday.

There's **camping** nearby at *York House Caravan Park* (☎ 01947 880354, 🖳 york housecaravanpark.co.uk; 🐕 campsite only not pods; WI-FI free in bar but otherwise

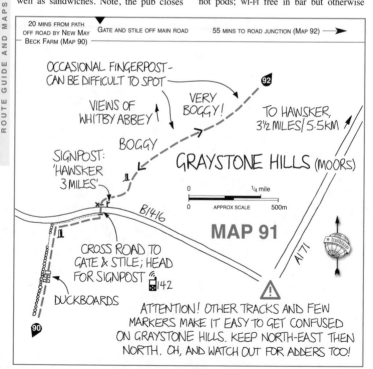

20 MINS FROM PATH OFF ROAD BY NEW MAY BECK FARM (MAP 90)　　GATE AND STILE OFF MAIN ROAD　　55 MINS TO ROAD JUNCTION (MAP 92) →

OCCASIONAL FINGERPOST - CAN BE DIFFICULT TO SPOT

VIEWS OF WHITBY ABBEY ↑

VERY BOGGY!

TO HAWSKER, 3½ MILES/5.5KM ↗

92

BOGGY

SIGNPOST: 'HAWSKER 3 MILES'

GRAYSTONE HILLS (MOORS)

B1416

0 ──── ¼ mile
0 ──── 500m
APPROX SCALE

MAP 91

CROSS ROAD TO GATE & STILE; HEAD FOR SIGNPOST 📱142

DUCKBOARDS

90

A171

ATTENTION! OTHER TRACKS AND FEW MARKERS MAKE IT EASY TO GET CONFUSED ON GRAYSTONE HILLS. KEEP NORTH-EAST THEN NORTH. OH, AND WATCH OUT FOR ADDERS TOO!

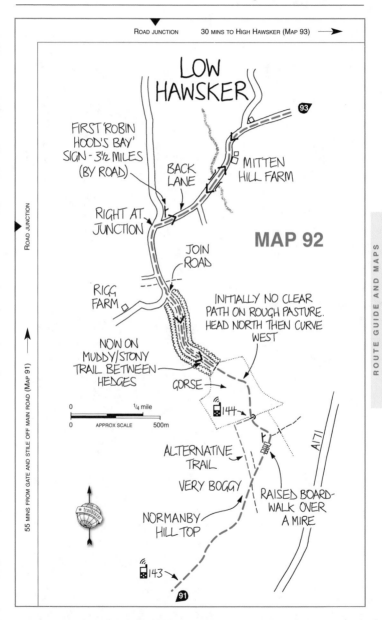

ROAD JUNCTION   30 MINS TO HIGH HAWSKER (MAP 93) →

LOW HAWSKER

93

FIRST 'ROBIN HOOD'S BAY' SIGN - 3½ MILES (BY ROAD)

BACK LANE

MITTEN HILL FARM

RIGHT AT JUNCTION

MAP 92

JOIN ROAD

RIGG FARM

INITIALLY NO CLEAR PATH ON ROUGH PASTURE. HEAD NORTH THEN CURVE WEST

NOW ON MUDDY/STONY TRAIL BETWEEN HEDGES

GORSE

144

A171

ALTERNATIVE TRAIL

VERY BOGGY

RAISED BOARD-WALK OVER A MIRE

NORMANBY HILL TOP

143

91

0   ¼ mile
0   APPROX SCALE   500m

ROUTE GUIDE AND MAPS

ROAD JUNCTION

55 MINS FROM GATE AND STILE OFF MAIN ROAD (MAP 91) →

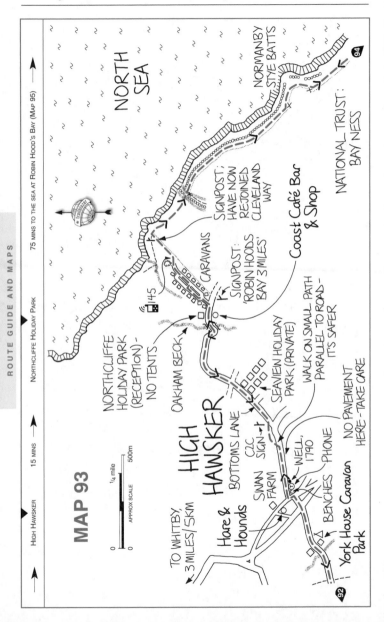

ROUTE GUIDE AND MAPS

High Hawker ← 15 MINS → Northcliffe Holiday Park 75 MINS TO THE SEA AT ROBIN HOOD'S BAY (MAP 95) →

MAP 93

¼ mile
APPROX SCALE
0 — 500m

NORTH SEA

NORMANBY STYE BATTS

SIGNPOST; HAVE NOW REJOINED CLEVELAND WAY

NATIONAL TRUST: BAY NESS

94

CARAVANS

SIGNPOST: 'ROBIN HOODS BAY 3 MILES'

Coast Café Bar & Shop

NORTHCLIFFE HOLIDAY PARK (RECEPTION) – NO TENTS

OAKHAM BECK

145

WALK ON SMALL PATH PARALLEL TO ROAD – IT'S SAFER

HIGH HAWSKER

BOTTOMS LANE

SEAVIEW HOLIDAY PARK (PRIVATE)

CtC SIGN↑

SWAN FARM

WELL, 1740

NO PAVEMENT HERE – TAKE CARE

TO WHITBY, 3 MILES/5KM

Hare & Hounds

BENCHES PHONE

York House Caravan Park

92

chargeable; early Feb-early Jan), which has shower and toilet facilities as well as a shop which stocks a few essentials. Prices for two adults and a **tent** cost £15-30 depending on the season and the type of pitch you opt for, and they have eight unfurnished, but carpeted and heated camping **pods** (£30-50 for up to two people) some of which sleep up to four adults or a family.

Arriva's **bus** X93 stops by the Hare & Hounds; see pp54-6.

From High Hawsker, the remains of your eastward marathon takes you down past sprawling caravan parks and *Coast Café Bar* (Map 93; ☎ 01947 881044, 🖳 coast-cafebar.com; **fb**; Mar-Nov Tue-Sun 10am-4pm, Fri & Sat 5.30-8pm; WI-FI; 🐾 back part of café only), where you can get a last-minute snack for the final stretch, unless you pass by on a Monday or a Tuesday, when it's closed. They have vegan and gluten-free options and are licensed.

And so you arrive at the **North Sea** to rejoin the Cleveland Way and England Coast Path and stride weary but unbeaten along the blustery clifftops towards Robin Hood's Bay. Though the tiny beach at Robin Hood's Bay appears half an hour before you actually set foot on it, the village itself, tucked away by the headland, is concealed until the very last moment. But eventually, having passed a coastguard station and **Rocket Post Field** (Map 94) from which coastguards used to practise aiming their rescue rockets, you join Mount Pleasant North at the top end of Robin Hood's Bay. Take a left at the end of the

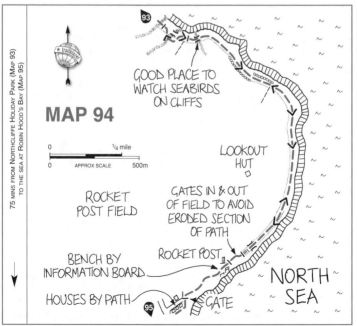

MAP 94

75 MINS FROM NORTHCLIFFE HOLIDAY PARK (MAP 93)
TO THE SEA AT ROBIN HOOD'S BAY (MAP 95)

GOOD PLACE TO
WATCH SEABIRDS
ON CLIFFS

0   ¼ mile
0   APPROX SCALE   500m

LOOKOUT
HUT

ROCKET
POST FIELD

GATES IN & OUT
OF FIELD TO AVOID
ERODED SECTION
OF PATH

ROCKET POST

BENCH BY
INFORMATION BOARD

NORTH
SEA

HOUSES BY PATH

95   GATE

ROUTE GUIDE AND MAPS

road and follow Station Rd to a roundabout from which you follow the steep street down, down, down to the bay. You arrive at the slipway, or Dock as it's known, and all that remains is to liberate that pebble you've carried from St Bees beach, dip your toes in the sea and then toast your fine achievement in Wainwright's Bar at Bay Hotel (see pp259), not forgetting to sign their book.

And that's it. Your Coast to Coast walk is over. Congratulations: you've walked the width of England, and quite probably more than 200 miles, which is certainly something to be pleased about. But not quite as satisfying as knowing there's no more walking on the agenda*.

ROBIN HOOD'S BAY   MAP 95

Robin Hood's Bay is the perfect place to finish: a quaint, cosy little fishing village that in high summer becomes a busy seaside resort that is entirely in keeping with the picturesque theme of the walk. It's well worth more than just one night's stay if you've got time. Though fishing has declined since its heyday in the 19th century, there's been a revival thanks to its crab grounds, reputedly the best in the north.

The old town huddles around the Dock, row after row of terraced, stone cottages arranged haphazardly uphill with numerous twisting interconnecting alleyways and paths to explore. Within them are several pubs and tearooms where you can celebrate. There are also gift, souvenir and antique shops aplenty, as well as certificates (see Bay Hotel, p259) for newly ennobled Coast to Coasters.

The **Old Coastguard Station National Trust Visitor Centre** (☎ 01947 885900, 🖳 www.nationaltrust.org.uk; Feb-end Nov daily 10am-5pm, other school hols daily to 4pm, other times weekends only 10am-4pm) sits right by the end of the trail and has some great displays including a mini wind machine and an aquarium of marine life.

There's also a small **museum** (🖳 museum.rhbay.co.uk; free entry, donations welcome) which relies on volunteers so the opening days/hours vary though are typically noon-4pm or 1-3pm (check the website).

If you're staying in one of the B&Bs at the top of the village, pick up your key on the way down in case you get delayed celebrating down at the Bay Hotel.

Services

The official tourist information **website** (🖳 robin-hoods-bay.co.uk) has plenty of useful information, including a comprehensive list of **accommodation**.

The **post office** (Mon-Sat 9am-5.30pm, Sun 9am-5pm) is housed inside a **general store** (Mon-Sat 8am-5.30pm, Sun 8am-5pm) that offers **cashback** on UK-only bank cards. There is **no ATM in town** though most UK bank-card holders can get money out at the post office.

If you've any aches and pains after the walk a visit to **Treat Therapy** (🖳 treatther apy.co.uk; **fb**) could be just the ticket. But note, you will need to have booked your appointment a few days in advance.

Transport   (see also p52 & pp54-6)

Arriva's X93/X94 **bus** runs north to Whitby (20 mins) and on to Middlesbrough (90 mins) for trains to Darlington – or south to Scarborough (40 mins), the nearest place for a train to York. The bus stop is on Thorpe Lane, just north of the main car park. For a **taxi**, call Bay Taxis (☎ 01947 880603, 🖳 bay-taxis.co.uk).

Where to stay

Robin Hood's Bay is divided into Upper Bay, the development dating from the Victorian era at the top of the hill, and the quainter and more congested 17th-century Lower Bay or 'Old Town' down by the sea, where there are fewer accommodation options and rooms are less spacious. Not since Grasmere have you paused to stay in such a busy tourist 'honeypot', so it's worth remembering that rooms at weekends and in

---

* However, it would be possible to walk on to Scarborough (about 12 miles; 4-5hrs) on the Cleveland Way and get a train from there.

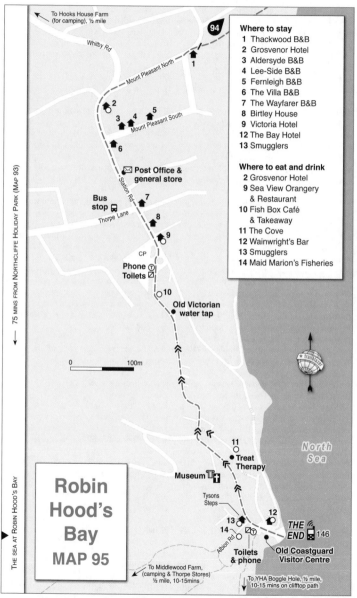

Where to stay
1 Thackwood B&B
2 Grosvenor Hotel
3 Aldersyde B&B
4 Lee-Side B&B
5 Fernleigh B&B
6 The Villa B&B
7 The Wayfarer B&B
8 Birtley House
9 Victoria Hotel
12 The Bay Hotel
13 Smugglers

Where to eat and drink
2 Grosvenor Hotel
9 Sea View Orangery
  & Restaurant
10 Fish Box Café
   & Takeaway
11 The Cove
12 Wainwright's Bar
13 Smugglers
14 Maid Marion's Fisheries

To Hooks House Farm
(for camping), ½ mile

Whitby Rd

Mount Pleasant North

94

1

2

3

Mount Pleasant South

4 5

6

Post Office &
general store

Station Rd

Bus
stop

7

Thorpe Lane

8

9

CP

Phone
Toilets

10

Old Victorian
water tap

0   100m

11
Treat
Therapy

North
Sea

Museum

Tysons
Steps

Robin
Hood's
Bay
MAP 95

13

14

Albion Rd

12

THE
END   146

Toilets
& phone

Old Coastguard
Visitor Centre

To Middlewood Farm,
(camping & Thorpe Stores)
½ mile, 10-15mins

To YHA Boggle Hole, ½ mile,
10-15 mins on clifftop path

75 MINS FROM NORTHCLIFFE HOLIDAY PARK (MAP 93)

THE SEA AT ROBIN HOOD'S BAY

ROUTE GUIDE AND MAPS

holiday periods may be hard to come by and some places may even insist on a **minimum stay of two nights** for advance bookings.

Both of the **campsites** can be pretty crowded in summer with families, dogs and caravans. The first, *Middlewood Farm Holiday Park* (☎ 01947 880414, 🖳 middle woodfarm.com; 🚾; WI-FI but not free; 🐾) is a smart and efficient operation with a laundry room and the finest ablutions block in North Yorkshire. Camping (Easter-Oct) costs from £10pp for hikers including showers (and toilets) but for £1 you can take a bath. They are very 'pro' Coast to Coasters and will always try to accommodate campers arriving on foot even at busy times, but prefer 24 hours' warning of your arrival if possible. They also offer wool-insulated wooden glamping **pods** (all year) that sleep up to four adults and come with plug sockets, a kettle, fridge and microwave as well as mattresses but no bedding. A pod costs £57-80 for up to two people for one night. However, they may request a two- or three-night minimum stay over busy periods. They also have washing and drying facilities (£4-5). It is a 10- to 15-minute walk from the end of the route, by Bay Hotel; head up Albion Rd and go past Maid Marion's chippy. For provisions (or to catch a bus) you do not need to return downhill to Robin Hood's Bay; a 10-minute walk along Middlewood Lane will take you to *Thorpe Stores* (**fb**; daily 8am-7pm) and the nearest bus stops (on Thorpe Lane in **Fylingthorpe** for the X93) for both Scarborough and Whitby.

High on a hill above the town, you may want to check into the more modest but no less popular *Hooks House Farm* (☎ 01947 880283, 🖳 hookshousefarm.co.uk; 🐾 on a lead; Mar-Oct) before walking the last mile or two down to the sea as the walk back can be quite an effort. **Camping** here costs from £11pp including showers and use of a kitchen.

YHA Boggle Hole (☎ 0345 371 9504, 🖳 yha.org.uk/hostel/boggle-hole; 1 x single, 1x2-, 6x3-, 5x4-, 6x5-, 2x6-, 1x9-bed rooms; WI-FI in communal areas; (Ⓛ) has two main buildings. The first is a former corn mill with 42 beds and the usual facilities plus a sandpit, mermaid, old boat and pirates. The second, the Crow's Nest, is an

environmentally friendly building with 44 beds (en suite rooms available) up some steep steps. Both are located in a ravine about a mile south of the village and reachable either along the shore or the inland road past Middlewood Farm Holiday Park. Private rooms cost from £50 for one person (2 people from £79). Hopefully, dorm beds will also be available by the time you are here. There is 24hr access, a drying room and credit cards are accepted. The hostel is also popular with non-residents thanks to its *Quarterdeck Café* (breakfast for guests 7-9.30am, food daily 11am-8.30pm; WI-FI; 🐾) where a cuppa and a cake will set you back no more than £3.95; it is also licensed.

In town there are plenty of hotels, guesthouses and B&Bs to choose from; the official town website (see Services) has a list. Accommodation is most prolific in Upper Bay, where *Thackwood* (☎ 01947 880858, 🖳 thackwood.com; 2D/1T, all en suite; 🚾; WI-FI) is the first **B&B** you spot as the trail comes into town. B&B costs £55-60pp (sgl occ room rate); they don't accept advance bookings for single-night stays at the weekends but may do nearer the time. The double rooms have a sea view and the twin a moor view.

On Mount Pleasant South there's more of the same with the pick of the bunch being *Lee-Side* (☎ 01947 881143, 🖳 lee-side.co.uk; 1D/1T/1D or T all en suite, 1D private bathroom; 🚾; WI-FI) with B&B for £45-52.50pp (sgl occ from £65). Also on Mount Pleasant South is *Aldersyde B & B* (☎ 01947 880689, 🖳 aldersyde-robin hoodsbay.co.uk; 1D/1D or T both en suite, 1D or T private facilities; 🚾; WI-FI), which has been recommended by some readers; they charge from £55pp (sgl occ £100). And finally *Fernleigh B&B* (☎ 01947 880523, 🖳 fernleigh-robin-hoods-bay.co .uk; 3D/1D or T, all en suite; WI-FI) which charges £50-75pp (sgl occ £90-140).

On Station Rd is *The Grosvenor Hotel* (☎ 01947 880320, 🖳 thegrosvenor .info; 7D/2Tr/1Qd, all en suite; 🚾; WI-FI; (Ⓛ) with B&B from £35pp (sgl occ room rate), while still on Station Rd, *The Villa* (☎ 01947 881043, 🖳 thevillarhb.co.uk; 2D/1D or T, all en suite; WI-FI; (Ⓛ) is another Victorian property. They have retained period features such as the cast-iron fireplaces and the servant bells. B&B rates are from £62.50pp (sgl occ £110). All dietary requirements, coeliac in particular, are catered for by these friendly people.

A further string of B&Bs on Station Rd leads down towards the old town. They're all pretty similar. Readers have recommended the rooms – and the food – at ***The Wayfarer*** (☎ 01947 880240, 🖳 wayfarer-robinhoodsbay.co.uk; 4D/1D or T, all en suite; WI-FI; Ⓛ; Feb-Dec). B&B costs from £49.50pp (sgl occ £85). Nearby is ***Birtley House*** (☎ 01947 880566; 5D, all en suite; ▾; WI-FI) charges £42.50-65pp (sgl occ from £76.50) but you'll need to book a two-night stay.

Alongside these ***The Victoria Hotel*** (☎ 01947 880205, 🖳 victoriarhb.com; 10D/4D or T/2Qd, all en suite; ▾; WI-FI; Ⓛ) charges £50-85pp (sgl occ room rate). The alleyway next to The Victoria leads onto a road with great views down to the old town.

In the **old town**, most options are long-stay self-catering holiday apartments and many of the places that do offer B&B-style accommodation request a two-night minimum stay. If you can't stay that long, try ***Smugglers Bistro, Bar & Lodgings*** (☎ 01947 880099, 🖳 smugglersrhb.co.uk; **fb**; 3D, all en suite; WI-FI), which has self-catering apartments available for single-night stays (B&B from £45pp, sgl occ room rate).

As close to the walk's end as the tides will allow, ***Bay Hotel*** (☎ 01947 880278, 🖳 bayhotel.info; 2D both en suite, 1D private bathroom; ▾; WI-FI; 🐕) has B&B for £50-60pp (sgl occ usually room rate).

Where to eat and drink

It has to be said that Robin Hood's Bay is not the easiest place to celebrate your monumental achievement with fine dining. The cuisine here seems strictly seaside traditional: pubs, takeaways and bucket 'n' spade snackeries, but there are a few notable exceptions.

There are one or two good **tea rooms** to relax in should you arrive early and need to wind down. ***The Cove*** (☎ 01947 880180, 🖳 thecoverhb.com; **fb**; summer daily 9.30am-4pm, winter hours variable; WI-FI; 🐕), in the heart of the old-town alleyways, is the smartest place, and has a lovely seaview terrace out back. The building was formerly a Wesleyan chapel. Note that weddings are sometimes held here so it may be closed. During summer, there's pizza on offer in the evenings (5.30-9pm).

Further back, up near the top of the hill, the no-frills ***Fish Box Café & Takeaway*** (☎ 01947 880595, 🖳 fishbox whitby.co.uk; Apr-Oct Mon-Sat 11am-7pm, Sun to 6pm, Nov-Feb weekends only) is a **fish & chip** restaurant really, but also does coffee and cakes and has great sea views, both from the tables inside and from its outdoor terrace. You can also get fish & chips at the takeaway-only ***Maid Marion's Fisheries*** (Sun-Thur noon-6pm, Fri & Sat noon-8pm) up an alleyway by Smugglers.

Also down at the Dock, beside the official end to the path, a visit to ***Bay Hotel*** (see Where to stay; food daily noon-9pm) is almost obligatory. The main **bar** is upstairs, and has a seaview terrace, but in peak periods they also open the so-called **Wainwright's Bar** downstairs. The pub sells mementos of the walk, including certificates; don't forget to sign their book to record your success (the log book will be in the upstairs bar if Wainwright's Bar is closed).

Arguably the best place to eat is ***Smugglers*** (see Where to stay; bar Wed & Fri-Sun noon-11pm, Thur from 3pm), a wine bar and bistro (food Wed-Sun 6pm-late; booking advised) down by the Dock with seafood dishes and stone-baked pizzas. When researching this edition, it was first salivated over by fellow walkers as far back as Keld.

The best place to eat in the higher part of town, **Victoria Hotel**'s (see Where to stay; food daily 8am-8.30pm) ***Sea View Orangery & Restaurant*** is popular (booking is recommended for evening meals), as is ***The Grosvenor Hotel*** (see Where to stay, food Apr-Oct daily noon-2.30pm & 5-8.30pm, Sat & Sun noon-8.30pm) which serves a varied menu of traditional favourites for £9.95-12.95 alongside seasonal specials.

APPENDIX A: TAKING A DOG

Many are the rewards that await those prepared to make the extra effort required to bring their best friend along the trail. You shouldn't underestimate the amount of work involved, though. Indeed, just about every decision you make will be influenced by the fact that you've got a dog. If you're also sure your dog can cope with (and will enjoy) walking 12 miles or (significantly) more a day for several days in a row, you need to start preparing accordingly. You also need to be sure that your dog will be able to negotiate the many stiles on the path – or that you'll be able to lift them over if they can't! Extra thought also needs to go into your itinerary. Study the village facilities table on pp34-5 (and the advice on p31).

Looking after your dog

To begin with, you need to make sure that your own dog is fully **inoculated** against the usual doggy illnesses, and also up to date with regard to **worm pills** (eg Drontal) and **flea preventatives** such as Frontline. **Pet insurance** is also a very good idea; if you've already got insurance, do check that it will cover a trip such as this. Perhaps the most important implement you can take with you is the **plastic tick remover**. While fiddly to use, these do help you to remove the tick safely (ie without leaving its head behind buried under the dog's skin).

Being in unfamiliar territory makes it more likely that you and your dog could become separated. All dogs in the UK must, by law, be microchipped, but you should also make sure your dog has a **tag with your contact details on it** (your mobile phone number is best).

When to keep your dog on a lead

● **On mountain tops** Sadly, every year, a few dogs die falling off steep slopes.

● **When crossing farmland** with any livestock in, but particularly in the lambing season (Feb-end May) when your dog can scare the sheep, causing them to lose their young. Farmers are allowed by law to shoot at and kill any dogs that they consider are worrying their sheep. During lambing, most farmers would prefer it if you didn't bring your dog at all. The exception to the dogs on leads rule is if your dog is being attacked by cows. The advice in this instance is to let go of the lead, head speedily to a position of safety (usually the other side of a gate or stile) and call your dog to you.

● **Around ground-nesting birds** It's important to keep your dog under control when crossing an area where certain species of birds nest on the ground; on parts of the trail (particularly east of Shap near Oddendale and around Sunbiggin Tarn, as well as on the North York Moors) there are notices ordering owners to keep their dogs on a lead to protect endangered ground-nesting birds between March and July; dogs can cause them to desert their nests.

Most dogs love foraging around in the woods but make sure you have permission as some are used as 'nurseries' for game birds and dogs must be on a lead.

What to pack

● **Food/water bowl** Foldable cloth bowls are popular with walkers   ● **Medication**
● **Lead and collar** An extendable one is probably preferable for this sort of trip
● **Bedding** A simple blanket may suffice   ● **Raingear & old towel**   ● **Hygiene wipes**
● **Collapsible dog crate** If using a baggage-transfer service this may be a useful addition
● **Poo bags** Essential   ● **A favourite toy** Helps prevent your dog from pining
● **Food/water** Bring treats as well as regular food to keep up your mutt's morale
● **Corkscrew stake** Available from camping or pet shops, this will help you to keep your dog secure in one place while you set up camp or doze   ● **Tick remover** See above

In towns, villages and fields where animals graze or which will be cut for silage, hay etc, you need to pick up and bag dog excrement. I always leave an exterior pocket of my rucksack empty so I can put used poo bags in there (for deposit at the first bin we come to).

I keep all the dog's kit together and separate from the other luggage (usually inside a plastic bag inside my rucksack). Some dogs sport their own 'doggy rucksack', so they can carry their own food, water, poo etc. **Henry Stedman**

APPENDIX B: WHAT3WORDS REFS ON MAPS

These what3words refs correspond to waypoints on maps and may be useful in an emergency; see p81

001 surreal.thrashing.bongo	052 brimmed.completed.condiment	103 hillside.broadcast.appointed
002 cheese.skewing.renewals	053 rationed.frail.workforce	104 twinge.personal.deleting
003 unfounded.graphic.deeper	054 bucked.bids.saddens	105 deranged.shield.tilt
004 chuck.lamps.explain	055 customers.critic.starters	106 bypassed.beauty.lemmings
005 bulletins.originate.submit	056 adverbs.early.organisms	107 toothpick.rally.stops
006 evolution.dialects.warmers	057 trophy.describes.think	108 tips.timing.decorated
007 sobbed.stealthier.eats	058 unpacked.verifying.slower	109 hiker.outbound.twitchy
008 luck.shatters.taped	059 minder.squeaking.articulated	110 coiling.providing.disprove
009 scorecard.magically.likes	060 paused.televise.costumed	111 float.detective.siesta
010 work.tricycle.inserted	061 unopposed.drawn.unloading	112 ticket.scratches.minerals
011 mull.sharpness.protest	062 expressed.gymnasium.appear	113 marker.sleeps.amplifier
012 automatic.petty.anyway	063 ecologist.deflation.germinate	114 equality.apply.nuzzling
013 gossip.gave.simulator	064 leaflet.motivations.unloads	115 images.trickles.animate
014 annoys.enchanted.guarded	065 depths.saved.gathering	116 proofread.debt.somebody
015 edge.gown.botanists	066 enforced.onlookers.anode	117 sunblock.envelope.stands
016 chum.drifter.seaside	067 foods.trailers.pesky	118 fitter.hacking.backswing
017 costly.marbles.ambient	068 revolting.youth.slope	119 frostbite.united.lordship
018 cakes.ballparks.nicknames	069 stereos.woods.decanter	120 glaze.allies.majors
019 clapper.could.premature	070 buckling.uproot.shortens	121 sampled.maybe.ombudsman
020 panics.potential.acted	071 eradicate.restriction.newer	122 squeaks.variety.commenced
021 empires.skylights.dubbing	072 perfectly.treetop.reissued	123 swaps.obscuring.zaps
022 invest.feast.generated	073 miracle.amicably.stalemate	124 letters.magnetic.comply
023 cheer.uttering.half	074 rebirth.garages.knowledge	125 closed.lamenting.myself
024 follow.thinnest.bookings	075 freedom.smooth.influence	126 snips.etchings.dozen
025 hindering.curtains.fur	076 deriving.jets.library	127 windmill.hamper.cocktail
026 worked.elbow.dwarf	077 rescue.scans.relatives	128 fewer.putty.selects
027 runner.annotated.canoe	078 wing.amphibian.dorm	129 parts.generally.smarter
028 fronted.loved.unfocused	079 budgeted.rock.hopefully	130 kickbacks.fights.logged
029 refrained.tunes.sling	080 grips.stacks.norms	131 recur.riverbank.gross
030 stability.spared.hairspray	081 sweetener.spot.unusually	132 digit.jazz.flinches
031 crackling.snippets.rebounded	082 applauded.poets.snoozing	133 landings.badminton.hungry
032 reds.toothpick.wiggly	083 pocketed.send.upon	134 waged.fists.revives
033 sheets.unwound.tests	084 consonant.hero.scream	135 collision.choice.pointer
034 tango.forgot.watching	085 sage.ourselves.frost	136 glows.flow.prestige
035 risen.rebounds.claw	086 hails.clouding.funds	137 ahead.cookie.wrong
036 last.assemble.craziest	087 signature.armrest.treating	138 assist.outnumber.spurned
037 unfilled.pushy.dairies	088 intrigued.slurred.homeward	139 drama.paddle.subtitle
038 shaped.mammoths.shirt	089 riots.gained.dynasties	140 dreading.kicks.mush
039 evenings.reminds.golden	090 rejoined.deals.harvest	141 helped.remaking.vest
040 tenses.registers.merchant	091 decoder.handsets.frog	142 traders.handy.acquaint
041 lifetimes.ruins.seatbelt	092 grips.stacks.norms	143 array.wiping.squish
042 portfolio.argue.factored	093 sage.ourselves.frost	145 slurping.purist.functions
043 groups.dull.pocketed	094 purse.offstage.scouted	146 overt.glosses.horizons
044 hike.following.rabble	095 bleat.fractions.petrified	200 verdict.recline.hawks
045 distorts.boardroom.slick	096 dormant.partly.martini	201 huddled.unions.reefs
046 inefficient.inquest.dove	097 facing.overpaid.text	202 avocado.stated.outwit
047 tiger.pebbles.ferried	098 princes.explain.ironclad	203 declines.overdone.loss
048 teaches.compacts.jigging	099 budgeted.rock.hopefully	204 fight.dorms.handyman
049 wool.flickers.lawns	100 lottery.colleague.blown	205 gasping.newlywed.sweeping
050 vintages.balanced.flap	101 irony.woes.slimming	206 baguette.risks.again
051 climbing.challenge.verges	102 superbly.wiped.hamster	207 brick.fetches.alternate

APPENDIX C: GPS WAYPOINTS ON MAPS

Each GPS waypoint below was taken on the route at the reference number marked on the map as below. See p261 for the list of what3words refs that correspond to these waypoints. Gpx files for waypoints can be downloaded from 💻 trailblazer-guides.com.

MAP NO	WAY-POINT	OS GRID REF	DESCRIPTION See p261 for what3words refs
Stage 1: St Bees to Ennerdale Bridge			
1	001	NX 96042 11791	Mile Zero; Coast to Coast sign on St Bees beach
3	002	NX 97898 14269	Take gate on right, then go downhill to railway tunnel
3	003	NX 98500 14189	Footbridge with gate
4	004	NX 98932 14175	Head N-E keeping forest and fence on your right
4	005	NX 99608 14346	Cross A595 and pass C2C statue; E into Moor Row
4	006	NY 00768 13923	Turn off road E into field
5	007	NY 01558 13494	Turn right into Kiln Brow (opposite Cleator Stores)
5	008	NY 02295 13356	Blackhow Farm; turn right after farm buildings to road
5	009	NY 03055 13338	Stile in fence; follow wall ESE towards summit
5	010	NY 03743 13052	Cairn along walls; not the summit
5	011	NY 04148 12893	Dent Hill summit (353m), small cairn
5	012	NY 04352 12765	Gate in fence, continue SE
6	013	NY 04535 12668	Junction, follow track going ENE to tall stile
6	014	NY 05532 12979	Gate by wall
6	015	NY 05744 13873	Cross Nannycatch Beck; gorse hillside opposite
7	016	NY 06942 15811	Ennerdale Bridge over River Eden
Stage 2: Ennerdale Bridge to Borrowdale (Rosthwaite) low route			
9	017	NY 12493 13874	Bridge at eastern end of Ennerdale Water
10	018	NY 14564 14122	Turn off north for high-level route via Red Pike
10	019	NY 17713 13216	A path leads E up to Scarth Gap Pass (Hay Stacks)
11	020	NY 19118 12508	Gate at junction of paths
12	021	NY 20278 12033	Cross Loft Beck by two cairns and ascend
12	022	NY 20548 12383	Top of Loft Beck at boggy saddle; turn E by cairn
12	023	NY 20802 12417	Gate in Brandreth Fence
12	024	NY 21135 12465	Cairns; now head NE
13	025	NY 21366 12632	Join wide, clear path with bigger cairns
13	026	NY 21593 13455	Turn east at the ruin of the Drum House
14	027	NY 25825 14939	Turn off by bus stop in Rosthwaite and cross bridge
Stage 3: Borrowdale to Grasmere			
16	028	NY 28313 11202	Top of Lining Crag; bogs & cairns to Greenup Edge
16	029	NY 28602 10526	Twin cairns just after fence post; Greenup Edge
17	030	NY 29558 10287	Fenceposts at top of Easedale; two routes diverge
17	031	NY 30160 10411	Top of Calf Crag (538m)
18	032	NY 32744 09202	Helm Crag
18	033	NY 32712 08536	Gate on left for Poet's Walk route
18	034	NY 33260 08458	Join road just E of Thorney How
Stage 4: Grasmere to Patterdale			
19	035	NY 33952 09817	Two Tongue paths separate
20	036	NY 34908 11680	Grisedale Hause (Pass)
21	037	NY 36932 13393	Summit of The Cape (841m); head N briefly to cairn
21	038	NY 36975 13678	Cairn; descent NE from St Sunday Crag begins
24	039	NY 37927 14728	Wall joins from E
24	040	NY 38680 15699	Turn right (SE) at oak tree

MAP NO	WAY-POINT	OS GRID REF	DESCRIPTION See p261 for what3words refs

Stage 5: Patterdale to Shap

MAP NO	WAY-POINT	OS GRID REF	DESCRIPTION
25	041	NY 40053 16146	Pass a house on the left then take the right-hand path
25	042	NY 40793 15619	Boredale Hause; flat grassy area with drain covers
25	043	NY 41104 14953	Paths diverge but soon join up
26	044	NY 42550 13650	Wall turns south and fence starts; continue E on path
26	045	NY 42761 13574	By wall, turn SE
26	046	NY 43106 13121	Cross stream and pass through remains of wall
27	047	NY 43629 12849	Walls meet; path becomes track and curves to the S
27	048	NY 43924 12259	Turn sharp left (NE) at cairn for track to Kidsty Pike
27	049	NY 44735 12583	Kidsty Pike summit (784m)
28	050	NY 45900 12588	Minor path to N; continue E to start of steep descent
28	051	NY 46839 11894	Bridge at end of descent at Haweswater reservoir
30	052	NY 50559 16134	Go through gate E of dam
30	053	NY 51132 16000	Ladder stile in wall near stream
30	054	NY 52026 16221	Turn right up side of field by gully
31	055	NY 53372 16466	After bog, turn right, SE, just before Rosgill Bridge
32	056	NY 53868 15625	Head E here across fields to Shap Abbey
33	057	NY 56210 15555	The Hermitage, Shap

Stage 6: Shap to Kirkby Stephen

MAP NO	WAY-POINT	OS GRID REF	DESCRIPTION
34	058	NY 57700 13950	After passing through wall head diagonally left
34	059	NY 57916 13829	Gate through wall by farm; head E across farm drive
35	060	NY 58568 13573	Steps down to quarry access road then up again
36	061	NY 59961 11826	Junction of paths at S corner of plantation. Head ESE
36	062	NY 60406 11733	Limestone pavement by the twin trees; track curves to S
36	063	NY 60836 10784	E at wall corner then NE past gully near Robin Hood's Grave
39	064	NY 67383 07661	Bridleway sign and access info; join road
40	065	NY 67138 07336	Signboard and waymark for the Dales Highway
40	066	NY 67101 06984	Faint, unmarked junction; turn E across Ravenstonedale Moor
40	067	NY 67621 06930	Wooden bridge over mud by enclosure
40	068	NY 69342 06501	Drain by the road with a hilltop reservoir to the E
41	069	NY 72068 05957	Smardale Bridge over Scandal Beck
42	070	NY 74695 07269	Through gate to road
42	071	NY 75630 07479	Aim diagonally for field corner and gully
43	072	NY 77423 08375	Kirkby Stephen Market Square
45	073	NY 81047 06732	Signpost for Nine Standards; Red and Blue routes go E, Green route goes S

Stage 7: Kirkby to Keld
● Green route (Dec-Apr)

MAP NO	WAY-POINT	OS GRID REF	DESCRIPTION
45	074	NY 81305 05950	Stone pens by wall
45	075	NY 81278 05146	Head of Rigg Beck
45	076	NY 80800 04633	Path joins from NW; continue S to road
45	077	NY 80810 04467	Four paths meet, head S then SSE to B6270
48	078	NY 83106 02787	Leave road at signpost, or soon take easier track left
48	079/099	NY 83542 02774	Red route joins track by Red route sign

● Blue route (Aug-Nov)

MAP NO	WAY-POINT	OS GRID REF	DESCRIPTION
46	082	NY 82495 06561	Nine Standards
46	083	NY 82544 06111	Trig point 662m

MAP NO	WAY- POINT	OS GRID REF	DESCRIPTION See p261 for what3words refs

● Blue route (Aug-Nov) *(cont'd)*

47	084	NY 82689 05836	First signpost; mire around
47	085/093	NY 82736 05728	Key junction signpost in a boot-eroded mire; Blue and Red routes diverge
47	086	NY 83608 05632	Waypoint on Blue route
47	087	NY 84157 05563	Waypoint on Blue route
47	088	NY 84635 05204	C2C signpost at descent to Whitsundale Beck
48	089	NY 84873 03745	Fold and old shelter
48	090	NY 85250 03380	Vicinity of blue post by fence
49	091	NY 85536 03263	Turn S between signpost and wall

● Red route (May-July)

46	082	NY 82495 06561	Nine Standards
46	083	NY 82544 06111	Trig point 662m
47	084	NY 82689 05836	First signpost; mire around
47	093/085	NY 82736 05728	Key junction signpost in a boot-eroded mire; Red and Blue routes diverge
47	094	NY 82830 04950	White stick nearby
47	095	NY 82823 04381	Cairn. Can see pillar cairn S of here
48	096	NY 83098 03785	Tall pillar, built from mill stones; head SE here
48	097	NY 83280 03636	Footbridge; ignore 'no access' sign to E and head for next waypoint
48	098	NY 83352 03582	White-topped pole; descend to Green route track
48	099/079	NY 83542 02774	Point where Red route joins Green; continue E

● All routes

| 49 | 080/092 | NY 85583 03012 | Signpost; all routes converge by beck and wall |
| 50 | 081 | NY 87689 01633 | Leave track for indistinct scar-top path (or descend to road) |

Stage 8: Keld to Reeth

| 51 | 100 | NY 90464 00863 | Bear left at tractor remains for high-level route, right for low-level route |

● High route

51	101	NY 90594 00864	Crackpot Hall; path goes uphill behind the hall
51	102	NY 91865 01300	Climb out of East Grain ends and path joins track
52	103	NY 93189 01309	Leave track to NE; descent to Gunnerside Beck
52	104	NY 93782 01747	Join path to Gunnerside by cairn
52	105	NY 93988 01332	Four-way signpost for Surrender Bridge; turn E up Bunton Hush (gully)
52	106	NY 94709 01420	Join main track near wooden pen around mine shaft
54	107	NY 99363 00007	Cairn after Surrender Bridge
55	108	SE 02712 99739	Cairn; head ENE for wall corner
55	109	SE 03321 99494	Through gate & down behind school
56	110	SE 03813 99295	Reeth village green

● Low route

51a	200	SD 91014 98674	Main track veers off left, take path to right
51b	201	SD 93295 97817	Join road
51b	202	SD 93600 97989	Leave road in Ivelet, cross Shore Gill, head E
51c	203	SD 94488 98054	If direct route to Gunnerside unclear, take river path
51c	204	SD 96355 98286	Gully

MAP NO	WAY-POINT	OS GRID REF	DESCRIPTION See p261 for what3words refs
51d	205	SD 97385 98160	Join concrete path
51d	206	SD 98420 98436	Leave road, follow muddy track
51d	207	SD 99535 98999	Leave main track for small path
56	110	SE 03813 99295	Reeth village green

Stage 9: Reeth to Richmond

56	111	SE 04272 99087	Leave main road to right, take path along river behind farm
56	112	SE 04647 98581	Cross road by bridge and continue along the northern side of Swale
56	113	SE 05412 98630	Gate and water tap; cross road and enter field to N
56	114	SE 05708 98625	Head for stile in fence
57	115	SE 06622 97883	Cattle grid near Marrick Priory Outdoor Centre
58	116	NZ 10897 00916	Signpost (public footpath) hidden in hedge. Cross stile into field
61	117	NZ 17033 01012	Turn right into Rosemary Lane, Richmond

Stage 10: Richmond to Ingleby Cross

62	118	NZ 17494 00656	Kissing gate on right leads to sheds and path to houses
63	119	SE 18611 99429	Path junction
64	120	SE 22732 99420	Path under A1(M
65	121	SE 26050 98454	Crumbling bridge over beck
67	122	SE 31230 98932	Join muddy, overgrown path at stile
68	123	SE 34873 98550	Leave the road and head ENE along edge of field
68	124	SE 36146 99166	Turn E off the A167
69	125	SE 38890 99773	No obvious sign but turn S here onto road
70	126	NZ 41763 01057	Brick gateposts
72	127	NZ 44962 00629	Crossroads opposite Blue Bell Inn

Stage 11: Ingleby Cross to Blakey Ridge

72	128	SE 45403 98603	Cleveland Way sign
73	129	NZ 44760 00404	Join track, leave woods, head ENE
74	130	NZ 48952 00288	Leave track through gate; turn NE down across field
74	131	NZ 50499 01301	First cairn
78	132	NZ 59411 01512	Near trig point (445m)
81	133	SE 66677 99442	A path leads S to Farndale East; not easy to follow
81	134	SE 67914 99725	Lion Inn pub, Blakey

Stage 12: Blakey Ridge to Grosmont

83	135	NZ 69990 01919	Turn right (E) off road and go round gate onto a track
84	136	NZ 73998 04022	Junction near trig point
86	137	NZ 79303 04644	Path emerges from Arncliffe Wood; turn left onto road
87	138	NZ 82819 05246	Grosmont level crossing

Stage 13: Grosmont to Robin Hood's Bay

88	139	NZ 85514 04255	Leave moorland road by Littlebeck signpost
89	140	NZ 86174 04720	Turn E off A169 for descent to Littlebeck
90	141	NZ 89912 03519	C2C signpost
91	142	NZ 90712 03993	Cross road (B1416) to gate and stile
92	143	NZ 91778 04649	Open moor
92	144	NZ 92088 05505	Kissing gate in fence
93	145	NZ 94062 08147	NE end of caravan park, just before sea cliffs
95	146	NZ 95325 04849	The end! Slipway by Bay Hotel in Robin Hood's Bay.

INDEX

Page references in red type refer to maps

❑ OLD NORSE NAMES

We have the Vikings to thank for many names in the north of England. Unless otherwise stated the following are derived from Old Norse words.

Place names		Landscape features	
Borrowdale	Valley of the fort	Beck	Stream
Ennerdale	Valley of the River Ehen	Dale	Valley
Glaisdale	Valley of the River Glas	Fell	Mountain
Grasmere	Grass lake (Old English)	Force / Foss	Waterfall
Grosmont	Big hill (Old French)	Garth	Enclosure
Grisedale	(Gris dalr) Valley of pigs	Ghyll / Gill	Ravine
Keld	Spring (of water)	Hause	Narrow neck of land
Kirkby	Village with church	Mere	Lake / pond (Old English)
Marrick	Horse ridge	Ness	Headland
Marske	Marsh	Pike	Peak
Patterdale	Patrick's Valley	Rigg	Ridge
Richmond	Strong hill	Scar	Bare rocky cliff or crag
	(Old French: Riche monte)	Tarn	Lake
River Rothay	Trout river	Thwaite	Clearing or meadow
St Sunday Crag	St Dominic's Crag (Celtic)		
Ullswater	Water with a bend		

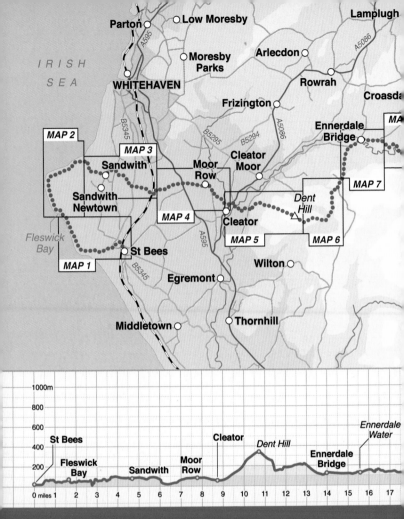

Maps 1-7 – St Bees to Ennerdale Bridge

14 miles/22.5km – 6¼ hrs

Maps 7-14 – Ennerdale Bridge to Rosthwaite (Borrowdale)

15 miles/24km – 6½ hrs (low route)

NOTE: Add 20-30% to these times to allow for stops

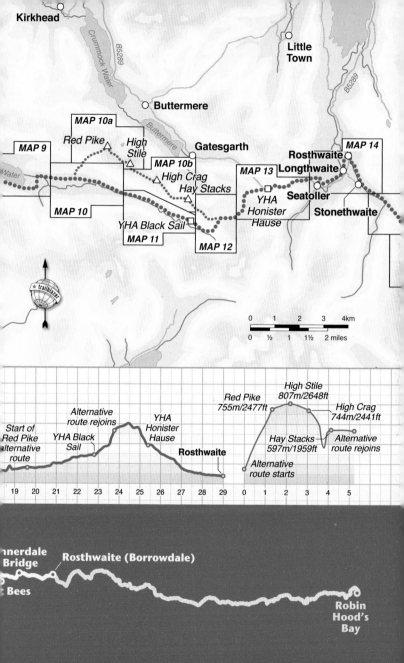

Kirkhead

Little Town

Crummock Water

B5289

B5289

Buttermere

Buttermere Water

MAP 10a

Red Pike

High Stile

MAP 9

MAP 10b

Gatesgarth

MAP 14

Rosthwaite

Water

High Crag

Hay Stacks

MAP 13

Longthwaite

MAP 10

YHA Black Sail

YHA Honister Hause

Seatoller

MAP 11

MAP 12

Stonethwaite

trailblazer

| 0 | 1 | 2 | 3 | 4km |

| 0 | ½ | 1 | 1½ | 2 miles |

Start of Red Pike alternative route

Alternative route rejoins

YHA Black Sail

YHA Honister Hause

Red Pike 755m/2477ft

High Stile 807m/2648ft

High Crag 744m/2441ft

Hay Stacks 597m/1959ft

Alternative route rejoins

Rosthwaite

Alternative route starts

19 20 21 22 23 24 25 26 27 28 29 0 1 2 3 4 5

nnerdale Bridge

Rosthwaite (Borrowdale)

t Bees

Robin Hood's Bay

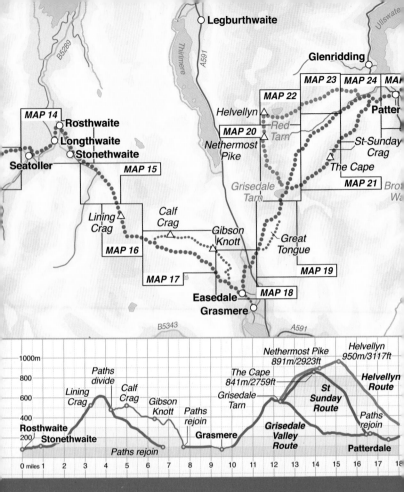

Maps 14-18 – Rosthwaite to Grasmere

9 miles/14.5km – 4-5½hrs (low route)

Maps 18-25 – Grasmere to Patterdale

8½ miles/13.5km – 3-4hrs (via Grisedale Pass)

Maps 25-34 – Patterdale to Shap

15½ miles/25km – 6½hrs
NOTE: Add 20-30% to these times to allow for stops

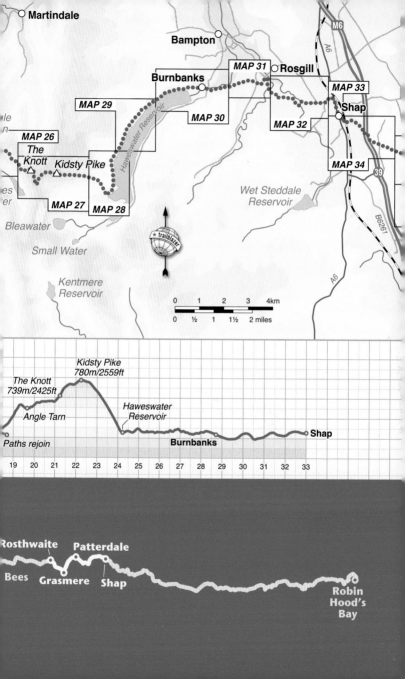

Martindale

Bampton

MAP 31

Burnbanks

Rosgill

MAP 33

MAP 29

Shap

MAP 26

The
Knott

Kidsty Pike

MAP 30

MAP 32

MAP 34

MAP 27

MAP 28

Bleawater

Small Water

Wet Steddale
Reservoir

Kentmere
Reservoir

★ trailblazer

0   1   2   3   4km
0   ½   1   1½   2 miles

Kidsty Pike
780m/2559ft

The Knott
739m/2425ft

Angle Tarn

Haweswater
Reservoir

Shap

Paths rejoin

Burnbanks

19 20 21 22 23 24 25 26 27 28 29 30 31 32 33

Rosthwaite

Patterdale

Bees   Grasmere   Shap

Robin
Hood's
Bay

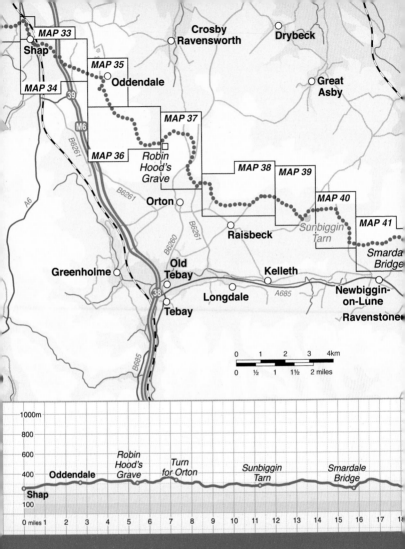

Maps 34-43 – Shap to Kirkby Stephen
20½ miles/33km – 7hrs

Maps 43-50 – Kirkby Stephen to Keld
13 miles/21km – 5-6hrs (via high routes)
NOTE: Add 20-30% to these times to allow for stops

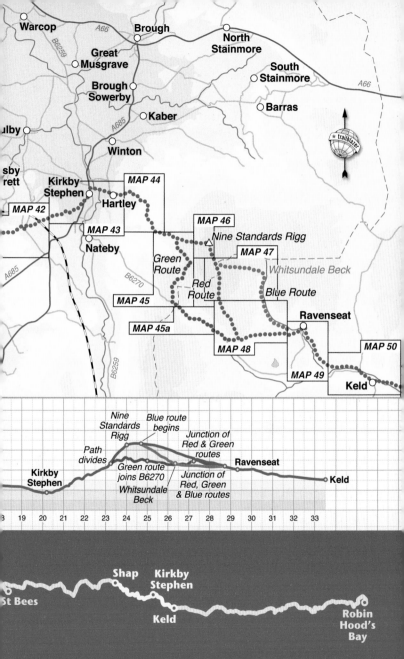

MAP 44

MAP 42

MAP 43

MAP 46

Nine Standards Rigg

MAP 47

Whitsundale Beck

Green
Route

Blue Route

Red
Route

MAP 45

MAP 45a

Ravenseat

MAP 50

MAP 48

MAP 49

Keld

Warcop

Brough

North
Stainmore

Great
Musgrave

South
Stainmore

Brough
Sowerby

Barras

Kaber

ulby

Winton

sby
rett

Kirkby
Stephen

Hartley

Nateby

A66

B6259

A66

A685

A685

A66

B6270

B6259

★ trailblazer

Nine
Standards
Rigg

Blue route
begins

Junction of
Red & Green
routes

Path
divides

Green route
joins B6270

Junction of
Red, Green
& Blue routes

Ravenseat

Kirkby
Stephen

Whitsundale
Beck

Keld

8   19   20   21   22   23   24   25   26   27   28   29   30   31   32   33

Shap   Kirkby
       Stephen

St Bees

Keld

Robin
Hood's
Bay

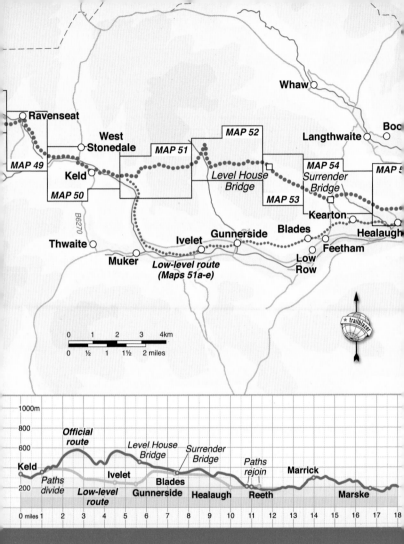

Maps 50-56 — Keld to Reeth

11 miles/18km — 4½hrs

Maps 56-61 — Reeth to Richmond

10½ miles/17km — 4½hrs

NOTE: Add 20-30% to these times to allow for stops

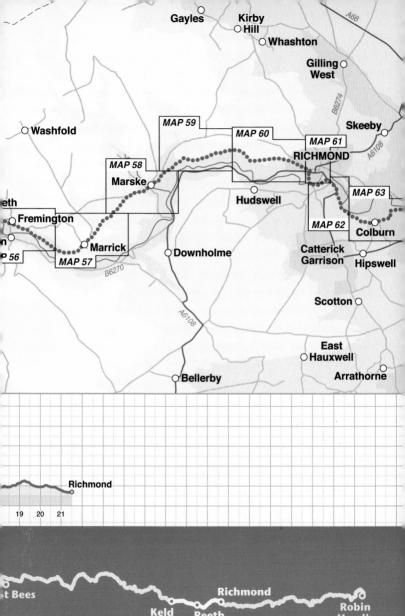

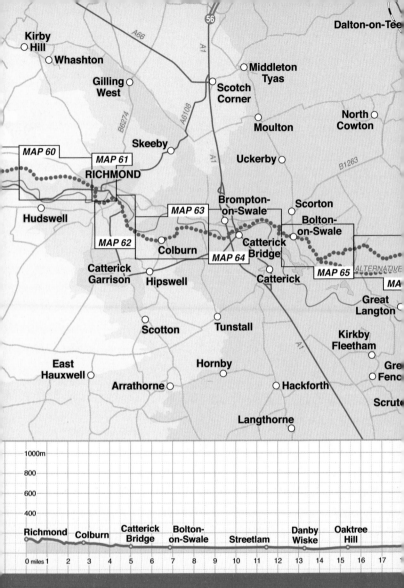

MAP 60

MAP 61

RICHMOND

MAP 62

MAP 63

MAP 64

MAP 65

Kirby Hill

Whashton

Gilling West

Skeeby

Hudswell

Colburn

Catterick Garrison

Hipswell

Scotton

East Hauxwell

Arrathorne

Middleton Tyas

Scotch Corner

Moulton

North Cowton

Uckerby

Brompton-on-Swale

Scorton

Bolton-on-Swale

Catterick Bridge

Catterick

Great Langton

Tunstall

Kirkby Fleetham

Hornby

Hackforth

Langthorne

Dalton-on-Tee

ALTERNATIVE

MA

Gre Fenc

Scrut

1000m							
800							
600							
400							

Richmond   Colburn   Catterick Bridge   Bolton-on-Swale   Streetlam   Danby Wiske   Oaktree Hill

0 miles 1   2   3   4   5   6   7   8   9   10   11   12   13   14   15   16   17

Maps 61-72 — Richmond to Ingleby Cro

22½ miles/36km – 8½hrs
NOTE: Add 20-30% to these times to allow for stops

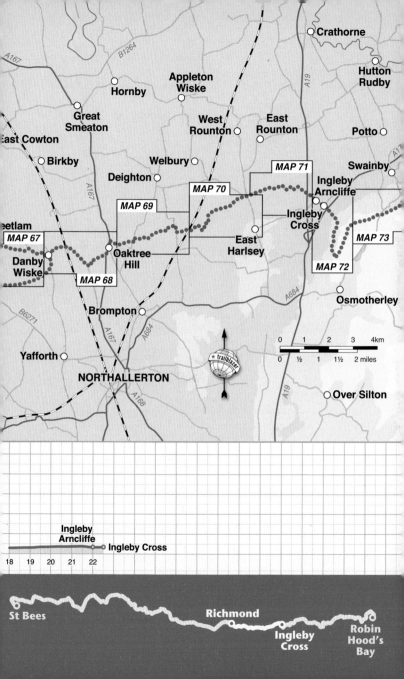

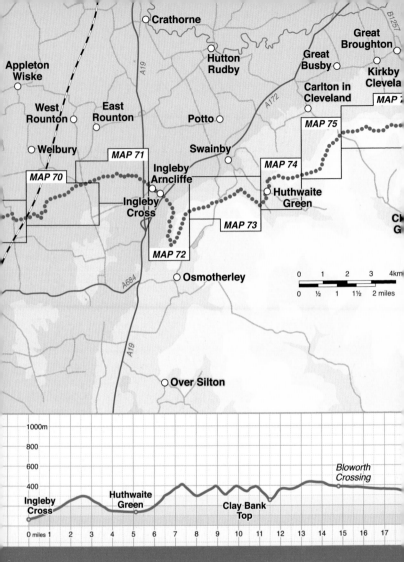

Crathorne

Great
Broughton

B1257

Great
Busby

Hutton
Rudby

Appleton
Wiske

A19

Kirkby
Cleveland

Carlton in
Cleveland

MAP

A172

West
Rounton

East
Rounton

Potto

MAP 75

Welbury

MAP 71

Swainby

Ingleby
Arncliffe

MAP 70

MAP 74

Ingleby
Cross

Huthwaite
Green

C
G

MAP 73

MAP 72

| 0 | 1 | 2 | 3 | 4km |

| 0 | ½ | 1 | 1½ | 2 miles |

A684

Osmotherley

A19

Over Silton

1000m

800

600

Bloworth
Crossing

400

Huthwaite
Green

Ingleby
Cross

Clay Bank
Top

0 miles 1 2 3 4 5 6 7 8 9 10 11 12 13 14 15 16 17

Maps 72-81 — Ingleby Cross to
Blakey Ridge

21 miles/34km – 8hrs
NOTE: Add 20-30% to these times to allow for stops

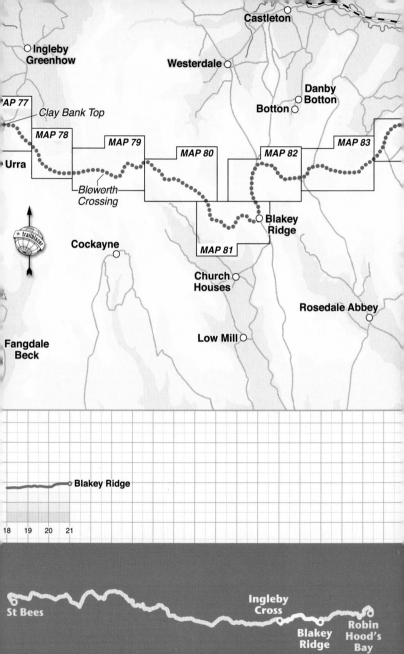

Castleton

Ingleby
Greenhow

Westerdale

Danby
Botton

Botton

AP 77

Clay Bank Top

MAP 78

MAP 79

MAP 80

MAP 82

MAP 83

Urra

*Bloworth
Crossing*

Blakey
Ridge

Cockayne

MAP 81

Church
Houses

Rosedale Abbey

Fangdale
Beck

Low Mill

★ trailblazer

Blakey Ridge

18   19   20   21

St Bees

Ingleby
Cross

Blakey
Ridge

Robin
Hood's
Bay

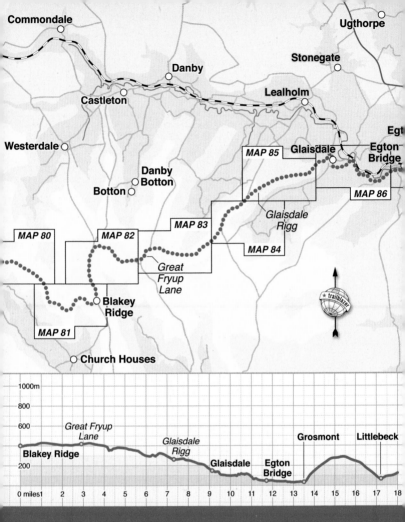

Commondale

Ugthorpe

Stonegate

Danby

Lealholm

Castleton

Egt

Westerdale

MAP 85   Glaisdale

Egton
Bridge

Danby
Botton

MAP 86

Botton

Glaisdale
Rigg

MAP 80

MAP 82

MAP 83

MAP 84

Great
Fryup
Lane

Blakey
Ridge

MAP 81

Church Houses

1000m

800

600   Great Fryup
Lane

Glaisdale
Rigg   Grosmont   Littlebeck

Blakey Ridge   Glaisdale   Egton
200   Bridge

0 miles1   2   3   4   5   6   7   8   9   10   11   12   13   14   15   16   17   18

Maps 81-87 — Blakey Ridge to Grosmon

13½ miles/22km — 5hrs

Maps 87-95 — Grosmont to
Robin Hood's Bay

15½ miles/25km — 6hrs
NOTE: Add 20-30% to these times to allow for stops

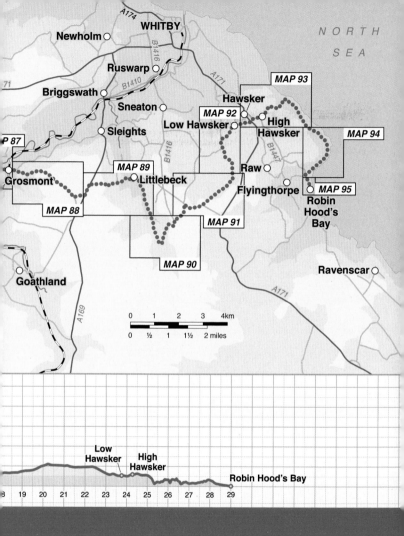

MAP 93
MAP 92
MAP 94
MAP 87
MAP 89
MAP 88
MAP 95
MAP 91
MAP 90

NORTH
SEA

WHITBY
Newholm
Ruswarp
Briggswath
Sneaton
Hawsker
Low Hawsker
High
Hawsker
Sleights
Raw
Grosmont
Littlebeck
Flyingthorpe
Robin
Hood's
Bay
Goathland
Ravenscar

Low
Hawsker
High
Hawsker
Robin Hood's Bay

18 19 20 21 22 23 24 25 26 27 28 29

St Bees
Grosmont
Blakey
Ridge
Robin
Hood's
Bay

	St Bees	Sandwith	Moor Row	Cleator	Ennerdale Bridge	Ennerdale YH	Black Sail YH	Honister Hause	Seatoller	Rosthwaite	Easedale	Grisedale Tarn	Patterdale	Burnbanks	Shap	Broadfell Farm	Ravenstonedale
St Bees	0																
Sandwith	5	0															
Moor Row	8	3	0														
Cleator	9	4	1	0													
Ennerdale Bridge	14	9	6	5	0												
Ennerdale YH	19	14	11	10	5	0											
Black Sail YH	23	18	15	14	9	4	0										
Honister Hause	26	21	18	17	12	7	3	0									
Seatoller	30	25	22	21	16	11	7	4	0								
Rosthwaite	32	27	24	23	18	13	9	6	2	0							
Easedale	42	37	34	33	28	23	19	16	12	10	0						
Grisedale Tarn	46	41	38	37	32	27	23	20	16	14	4	0					
Patterdale	53	48	45	44	39	34	30	27	23	21	11	7	0				
Burnbanks	64	59	56	55	50	45	41	38	34	32	22	18	11	0			
Shap	69	64	61	60	55	50	46	43	39	37	27	23	16	5	0		
Broadfell Farm	77	72	69	68	63	58	54	51	47	45	35	31	24	13	8	0	
Ravenstonedale	84	79	76	75	70	65	61	58	54	52	42	38	31	20	15	7	0
Kirkby Stephen	89	84	81	80	75	70	66	63	59	57	47	43	36	25	20	12	5
Ravenseat	99	94	91	90	85	80	76	73	69	67	57	53	46	35	30	22	15
Keld	102	97	94	93	88	83	79	76	72	70	60	56	49	38	33	25	18
Reeth	113	108	105	104	99	94	90	87	83	81	71	67	60	49	44	36	29
Marrick	118	113	110	109	104	99	95	92	88	86	76	72	65	54	49	41	34
Richmond	124	119	116	115	110	105	101	98	94	92	82	78	71	60	55	47	40
Colburn	127	122	119	118	113	108	104	101	97	95	85	81	74	63	58	50	43
Catterick Bridge	129	124	121	120	115	110	106	103	99	97	87	83	76	65	60	52	45
Bolton on Swale	130	125	122	121	116	111	107	104	100	98	88	84	77	66	61	53	46
Danby Wiske	138	133	130	129	124	119	115	112	108	106	96	92	85	74	69	61	54
Oaktree Hill	140	135	132	131	126	121	117	114	110	108	98	94	87	76	71	63	56
Ingleby Cross	147	142	139	138	133	128	124	121	117	115	105	101	94	83	78	70	63
Arncliffe Wood	148	143	140	139	134	129	125	122	118	116	106	102	95	84	79	71	64
Carlton Bank	155	150	147	146	141	136	132	129	125	123	113	109	102	91	86	78	71
Clay Bank Top	159	154	151	150	145	140	136	133	129	127	117	113	106	95	90	82	75
Blakey Ridge	168	163	160	159	154	149	145	142	138	136	126	122	115	104	99	91	84
Glaisdale	178	173	170	169	164	159	155	152	148	146	136	132	125	114	109	101	94
Egton Bridge	180	175	172	171	166	161	157	154	150	148	138	134	127	116	111	103	96
Grosmont	181	176	173	173	167	162	158	155	151	149	139	135	128	117	112	104	97
Littlebeck	185	180	177	176	171	166	162	159	155	153	143	139	132	121	116	108	101
High Hawsker	192	187	184	183	178	173	169	166	162	160	150	146	139	128	123	115	108
Robin Hood's Bay	198	193	190	189	184	179	175	172	168	166	156	152	145	134	129	121	114

Coast to Coast Path
DISTANCE CHART

miles (approx)

	Kirkby Stephen	Ravenseat	Keld	Reeth	Marrick	Richmond	Colburn	Catterick	Bolton on Swale	Danby Wiske	Oaktree Hill	Ingleby Cross	Arncliffe Wood	Carlton Bank	Clay Bank Top	Blakey Ridge	Glaisdale	Egton Bridge	Grosmont	Littlebeck	High Hawsker	Robin Hood's Bay
Kirkby Stephen	0																					
Ravenseat	10	0																				
Keld	13	3	0																			
Reeth	24	14	11	0																		
Marrick	29	19	16	5	0																	
Richmond	35	25	22	11	6	0																
Colburn	38	28	25	14	9	3	0															
Catterick	40	30	27	16	11	5	2	0														
Bolton on Swale	41	31	28	17	12	6	3	1	0													
Danby Wiske	49	39	36	25	20	14	11	9	8	0												
Oaktree Hill	51	41	38	27	22	16	13	11	10	2	0											
Ingleby Cross	58	48	45	34	29	23	20	18	17	9	7	0										
Arncliffe Wood	59	49	46	35	30	24	21	19	18	10	8	1	0									
Carlton Bank	66	56	53	42	37	31	28	26	25	17	15	8	7	0								
Clay Bank Top	70	60	57	46	41	35	32	30	29	21	19	12	11	4	0							
Blakey Ridge	79	69	66	55	50	44	41	39	38	30	28	21	20	13	9	0						
Glaisdale	89	79	76	65	60	54	51	49	48	40	38	31	32	23	19	10	0					
Egton Bridge	91	81	78	67	62	56	53	51	50	42	40	33	32	25	21	12	2	0				
Grosmont	92	82	79	68	63	57	54	52	51	43	41	34	33	26	22	13	3	1	0			
Littlebeck	96	86	83	72	67	61	58	56	55	47	45	38	37	30	26	17	7	5	4	0		
High Hawsker	103	93	90	79	74	68	65	63	62	54	52	45	44	37	33	24	14	12	11	7	0	
Robin Hood's Bay	109	99	96	85	80	74	71	69	68	60	58	51	50	43	39	30	20	18	17	13	6	0

TRAILBLAZER TITLE LIST

For more information about Trailblazer and our
expanding range of guides, for guidebook updates or
for credit card mail order sales visit our website:

trailblazer-guides.com

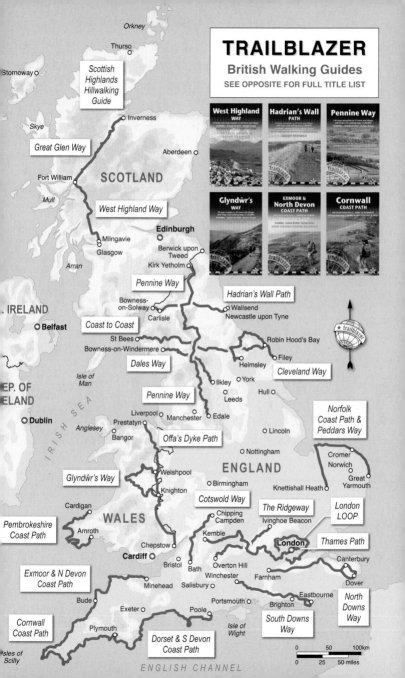

TRAILBLAZER

British Walking Guides

SEE OPPOSITE FOR FULL TITLE LIST

West Highland WAY

Hadrian's Wall PATH

Pennine Way

Glyndŵr's WAY

EXMOOR & North Devon COAST PATH

Cornwall COAST PATH

Orkney

Thurso

Stornoway

Scottish Highlands Hillwalking Guide

Inverness

Skye

Great Glen Way

Aberdeen

Fort William

SCOTLAND

Mull

West Highland Way

Edinburgh

Milngavie

Glasgow

Arran

Berwick upon Tweed

Kirk Yetholm

Pennine Way

Bowness-on-Solway

Hadrian's Wall Path

Wallsend

Newcastle upon Tyne

N. IRELAND

Belfast

Coast to Coast

Carlisle

St Bees

Bowness-on-Windermere

Robin Hood's Bay

Filey

Dales Way

Helmsley

Cleveland Way

Isle of Man

Ilkley

York

Pennine Way

Leeds

Hull

REP. OF IRELAND

Dublin

IRISH SEA

Liverpool

Manchester

Edale

Lincoln

Anglesey

Prestatyn

Bangor

Offa's Dyke Path

Nottingham

ENGLAND

Glyndŵr's Way

Welshpool

Knighton

Birmingham

Norfolk Coast Path & Peddars Way

Cromer

Norwich

Great Yarmouth

Cardigan

WALES

Knettishall Heath

Pembrokeshire Coast Path

Amroth

Cotswold Way

Chipping Campden

The Ridgeway

London LOOP

Chepstow

Kemble

Ivinghoe Beacon

Cardiff

Bristol

Bath

Overton Hill

London

Thames Path

Exmoor & N Devon Coast Path

Minehead

Winchester

Salisbury

Farnham

Canterbury

Dover

Bude

Exeter

Portsmouth

Poole

Brighton

Eastbourne

North Downs Way

Cornwall Coast Path

Plymouth

Isle of Wight

South Downs Way

Dorset & S Devon Coast Path

Isles of Scilly

ENGLISH CHANNEL

| 0 | 50 | 100km |
| 0 | 25 | 50 miles |

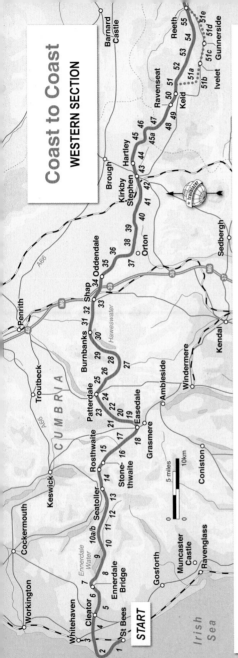

Coast to Coast
WESTERN SECTION

START

Irish Sea